Forecasting and Managing Risk in the Health and Safety Sectors

Luisa Dall'Acqua
Scientific Lyceum TCO, Italy & University of Bologna, Italy

A volume in the Advances in Human Services and Public Health (AHSPH) Book Series

IGI Global
DISSEMINATOR OF KNOWLEDGE

Published in the United States of America by
IGI Global
Medical Information Science Reference (an imprint of IGI Global)
701 E. Chocolate Avenue
Hershey PA, USA 17033
Tel: 717-533-8845
Fax: 717-533-8661
E-mail: cust@igi-global.com
Web site: http://www.igi-global.com

Library of Congress Cataloging-in-Publication Data

Names: Dall'Acqua, Luisa, 1962- editor.
Title: Forecasting and managing risk in the health and safety sectors / Luisa Dall'Acqua, editor.
Description: Hershey PA : Medical Information Science Reference, [2019] | Includes bibliographical references.
Identifiers: LCCN 2018037642| ISBN 9781522579038 (hardcover) | ISBN 9781522579045 (ebook)
Subjects: | MESH: Risk Management | Health Care Sector | Safety Management | Decision Making | Forecasting--methods | Models, Theoretical
Classification: LCC RA427.3 | NLM W 74.1 | DDC 362.1028/9--dc23 LC record available at https://lccn.loc.gov/2018037642

This book is published in the IGI Global book series Advances in Human Services and Public Health (AHSPH) (ISSN: 2475-6571; eISSN: 2475-658X)

British Cataloguing in Publication Data
A Cataloguing in Publication record for this book is available from the British Library.

All work contributed to this book is new, previously-unpublished material.
The views expressed in this book are those of the authors, but not necessarily of the publisher.

For electronic access to this publication, please contact: eresources@igi-global.com.

Advances in Human Services and Public Health (AHSPH) Book Series

ISSN:2475-6571
EISSN:2475-658X

Editor-in-Chief: Jennifer Martin, RMIT University, Australia

MISSION

The well-being of the general public should be a primary concern for any modern civilization. Ongoing research in the field of human services and public healthcare is necessary to evaluate, manage, and respond to the health and social needs of the global population.

The **Advances in Human Services and Public Health (AHSPH)** book series aims to publish high-quality reference publications focused on the latest methodologies, tools, issues, and strategies for managing the health and social welfare of the public. The AHSPH book series will be especially relevant for healthcare professionals, policy makers, government officials, and students seeking the latest research in this field.

COVERAGE

- Public Funding
- Healthcare Reform
- Assistance Programs
- Social Welfare Policy
- Social Work
- Public Welfare
- Domestic Violence
- Health policy
- Youth Development
- Poverty

IGI Global is currently accepting manuscripts for publication within this series. To submit a proposal for a volume in this series, please contact our Acquisition Editors at Acquisitions@igi-global.com or visit: http://www.igi-global.com/publish/.

The Advances in Human Services and Public Health (AHSPH) Book Series (ISSN 2475-6571) is published by IGI Global, 701 E. Chocolate Avenue, Hershey, PA 17033-1240, USA, www.igi-global.com. This series is composed of titles available for purchase individually; each title is edited to be contextually exclusive from any other title within the series. For pricing and ordering information please visit http://www.igi-global.com/book-series/advances-human-services-public-health/102256. Postmaster: Send all address changes to above address.

Titles in this Series

For a list of additional titles in this series, please visit:
https://www.igi-global.com/book-series/advances-human-services-public-health/102256

Mental Health Policy, Practice, and Service Accessibility in ContemporarySociety
Jennifer M. Martin (Swinburne University, Australia)
Medical Information Science Reference • ©2019 • 323pp • H/C (ISBN: 9781522574026) • US $245.00

Socio-Cultural Influences on Teenage Pregnancy and Contemporary Prevention easures
Devi Akella (Albany State University, USA)
Information Science Reference • ©2019 • 349pp • H/C (ISBN: 9781522561088) • US $195.00

Nutraceutical and Functional Foods in Disease Prevention
Raj K. Keservani (Chhatrapati Shahu Ji Maharaj Group of Institutions, India) Anil K. Sharma (Delhi Institute of Pharmaceutical Sciences and Research, India) and Rajesh K. Kesharwani (Nims University Rajasthan, India)
Medical Information Science Reference • ©2019 • 569pp • H/C (ISBN: 9781522532675) • US $215.00

Ethical Issues in Social Work Practice
Antonio Sandu (Ştefan cel Mare University of Suceava, Romania) and Ana Frunza (LUMEN Research Center in Social and Humanistic Sciences, Romania)
Information Science Reference • ©2018 • 328pp • H/C (ISBN: 9781522530909) • US $195.00

Global Perspectives on Human Migration, Asylum, and Security
Christina M. Akrivopoulou (Hellenic Open University, Greece)
Information Science Reference • ©2018 • 268pp • H/C (ISBN: 9781522528173) • US $185.00

Nutraceuticals and Innovative Food Products for Healthy Living and Preventive Care
Amit Verma (SDAU, India) Kajal Srivastava (GBPUAT, India) Shivom Singh (ITM University, India) and Hukum Singh (Forest Research Institute, India)
Medical Information Science Reference • ©2018 • 462pp • H/C (ISBN: 9781522529705) • US $245.00

For an entire list of titles in this series, please visit:
https://www.igi-global.com/book-series/advances-human-services-public-health/102256

IGI Global
DISSEMINATOR OF KNOWLEDGE

701 East Chocolate Avenue, Hershey, PA 17033, USA
Tel: 717-533-8845 x100 • Fax: 717-533-8661
E-Mail: cust@igi-global.com • www.igi-global.com

Editorial Advisory Board

Table of Contents

Detailed Table of Contents

It has been well-known that the chance of successfully delivering a software project within an allocated time and budget is very low. Most of the researches in this area have concluded that "user's requirements" of the systems is one of the most difficult risks to deal with in this case. Interestingly, until today, regardless of amount of effort put into this area, the possibility of project failure is still very high. The issue with requirement can be significantly increased when developing an artificial intelligence (AI) system, where one would like the systems to autonomously behave. This is because we are not only dealing with user's requirements, but we must also be able to deal with "system's behavior" that, in many cases, do not even exist during software development. This chapter discusses a preliminary work on a framework for risk management for AI systems development projects. The goal of this framework is to help project management in minimizing risk that can lead AI software projects to fail due to the inability to finish the projects on time and within budget.

Because of the huge amount of data and information in the decision-making and strategic choices processes, basing decisions on information directly collected from the sources is not conceivable. A decision-making analyst becomes a fundamental pillar in both the corporate field and the institutional world. This role is becoming increasingly complex and specialized, critical within the cycle of the intelligence analysis, for the relationships that bind it to the other stakeholders, and for the methodological and technological tools that support it. The purpose of this chapter is to explore the milestones of the intelligence analysis deriving from a close collaboration between social sciences, cognitive science, computer engineering, and ICT in order to respond to the different needs in the field of risk management, safety, investigations, and applied intelligence.

Although the future of society is hazy, a workable vision of the future can be developed from existing computer modeling of key parameters like population and sea level. This vision is referred to in this chapter as the driven future. The future of humans and artificial intelligence (AI) is then reconsidered from within the context of this driven future. Specific examples of how AIs might be utilized to address real human problems in this future are developed. The modifications to the way humans and AIs interact to facilitate addressing major problems is then discussed, including the human/machine symbiosis and the application of corporate persons directly to AIs.

The system dynamics approach was developed by Jay Forrester from MIT during 1950s to analyze the complex behavior in administration with computer simulation in social sciences. System dynamics is a form of the systems approach as a methodology to understand the dynamic behavior of complex systems. The basis of system dynamics is to understand how system structures cause system behavior and system events. This chapter aims to develop a system dynamic model. System dynamics approach was adopted to build a bed capacity management model using a software package, Vensim.

Modern technologies have presented the world with a plethora of new opportunities, from the mundane (reduced input rigor) through to new outcomes that eluded our collective wisdom and knowledge. These changes have confronted organizations with

Environmental education is a new discipline, which has been gaining increasing importance in recent decades. It is a fundamental tool to sensitize citizens and communities to greater responsibility and attention to environmental issues and good governance of the territory. The educational component allows us to transform scientific languages into simple languages that can be appropriated and understood by the different social groups, and the environmental component that tries to reconstruct. These relationships are created by man with nature, but through cultural parameters. The growing concern for environmental devastation has its roots in the decade of the 1970s. Countless efforts have been made to draw the attention of populations to this topic. Among these attempts come out different approaches such as sustainable development that uses environmental education and local sustainability as tools to prevent damages. This chapter describes the key theoretical and government references that support environmental education, focusing on their relationship and the rising of a new sector of work.

Preface

TIMING

The United Nations Intergovernmental Panel on Climate Change's (IPCC) Special Report 1.5, "Global Warming of 1.5°C," was released (8 October 2018) near the end of the preparation of this book. It describes significant risks to society from climate change. The report was not published until after most of this book had already been written. However, this book is timely in that it is about forecasting and handling risks, and the IPCC SR1.5 report defines grave risks to all the peoples of Earth.

IPCC SR1.5

The UN document on climate change, "Global Warming of 1.5 C," Special Report 1.5, Technical Summary (IPCC SR1.5), dated 8 October 2018, begins with the following statement list:

Framing and Context

Human-induced warming reached approximately 1°C (±0.2°C likely range) above pre-industrial levels in 2017, increasing at 0.2°C (±0.1°C) per decade (high confidence)…

Warming greater than the global average has already been experienced in many regions and seasons, with average warming over land higher than over the ocean (high confidence)…

Past emissions alone are unlikely to raise global-mean temperature to 1.5°C above pre-industrial levels but past emissions do commit to other changes, such as further sea level rise (high confidence)…

1.5°C-consistent emission pathways are defined as those that, given current knowledge of the climate response, provide a one-in-two to two-in-three chance of warming either remaining below 1.5°C, or returning to 1.5°C by around 2100 following an overshoot...

This report assesses projected impacts at a global average warming of 1.5°C and higher levels of warming...

Ethical considerations, and the principle of equity in particular, are central to this report, recognising that many of the impacts of warming up to and beyond 1.5°C, and some potential impacts of mitigation actions required to limit warming to 1.5°C, fall disproportionately on the poor and vulnerable (high confidence)...

Climate adaptation refers to the actions taken to manage impacts of climate change by reducing vulnerability and exposure to its harmful effects and exploiting any potential benefits...

Ambitious mitigation actions are indispensable to limit warming to 1.5°C while achieving sustainable development and poverty eradication (high confidence)...

Multiple forms of knowledge, including scientific evidence, narrative scenarios and prospective pathways, inform the understanding of 1.5°C...

There is no single answer to the question of whether it is feasible to limit warming to 1.5°C and adapt to the consequences...

The document then goes on to provide detailed technical discussions of how these conclusions were reached, including results of the latest computer modeling efforts. A large number of technical specialists worldwide have reviewed this work.

The most striking change from earlier IPCC documents is the assertion that 1.5°C is now understood to be the cutoff between a world temperature rise that society can adapt to and a world temperature rise that would be unacceptably disruptive to society. This is not to say that limiting the rise to 1.5°C will be easy or that this work can be done in the background while most people continue with their present lifestyles. What it does say is that meeting this goal is critical to the continuance of society as people currently know it and that most people will have to make many adjustments.

Such a change in temperature will have enormous repercussions. The problems discussed in this document and the need to avoid surpassing the 1.5°C limit represent substantial risk management problems in the health and safety sectors for both developed and developing countries. These problems will be intensified and prolonged if the 1.5°C limit is exceeded; the social and infrastructure damage may then be irreparable.

History

The earlier IPCC Fifth Assessment Report (AR5, 2014) was used as the basis for the Paris Agreement (22 April 2016) on climate change. It used 2.0°C as the highest acceptable figure for world temperature rise and 3.0°C as likely to be unacceptable. At the time, the world's political leaders believed that it would be very difficult to reach these figures without unacceptable disruptions to the world economy and political structures.

The current world temperature rise since the start of the Industrial Revolution (200 years ago) was assessed in this report at 0.87°C. This is about halfway to the 1.5°C limit. Unfortunately, the rate of global temperature rise is exponential. Society will not have as much time before the 1.5°C limit is reached.

The decrease of the transition mark from 2.0°C to 1.5°C may not sound like a lot, but it massively increases the amount society needs to change to stay under the new limit. In addition, the new limit reduces the time available for corrective action by decades.

Expectation

The IPCC SR1.5 paints two very different pictures of the future of the human population of Earth:

- **Below 1.5°C:** If society as a whole can organize a massive response to the problems of climate change and maintain that effort over several decades, then society can expect that current political and economic institutions will survive if they successfully adjust to the new situation. There will be major dislocations of low-income populations and all major seaside cities will require new, and very expensive, flood and storm protection infrastructure. Seaside retirement homes will be a thing of the past.
- **Above 2.0°C:** If society fails to take major action, then sea level rise will continue unabated and areas of the tropics may become uninhabitable by humans. A great many people will suffer, and it is not currently knowable which economic and political institutions will survive under these conditions.

No Silver Bullet

It is very unlikely that there is just one solution to all the global problems presented in IPCC SR1.5 -- expect **no** silver bullet. More likely, the resolution will involve millions of people, assisted by their machines, doing everything they can think of that even seems helpful. Most efforts will do relatively little, but a few could achieve spectacular results. Based on our current state, it is impossible to know which efforts will work well and which efforts will generate even more problems. Society simply will not know the result until many possible remedies have been tried.

Below is a chapter-by-chapter discussion of many of the ideas in this book that might be useful in addressing some of the problems highlighted in IPCC SR1.5:

CHAPTER BY CHAPTER

Chapter 1: A Framework for Risk Management in AI System Development Projects

Chapter 1 discusses the risks involved in developing an artificial intelligence (AI) project for industrial applications. It makes the point that AI is not a panacea and that there are widely understood risks that will have to be managed. Then a framework for managing those risks is proposed.

Addressing the historic problems associated with global warming described in the IPCC SR1.5 will clearly require the application of all the innovative technical tools that can be developed in time. AI is widely seen as one of these key technologies.

There are many risks in developing AI. For example, a critical step in the development of an AI is its training on a known data set. Typically, a moderate-sized data set for which the correct answers for each entry are known is divided into two parts. The first part is for training and the second is for testing. If, for example, the desired result is to distinguish important emails from spam, a database of some thousands of emails that have already been reliably identified is used. The AI then reads the training emails and learns to make the required distinction. The AI then sorts the emails in the test group and is rated on how well it performs the task.

Often, a number of iterations are needed to develop an algorithm that is highly effective. Training sessions that are deemed successful must then be scaled up to address real-world problems.

One important risk is that biases that are built into the development and training databases will be taught to the AI. Training an AI with a racist database has been shown to produce a racist AI.

Global warming of any amount will flood out large numbers of lowland farmers, particularly in places like Bangladesh. If society can limit the average global temperature rise to 1.5°C as discussed in the IPCC Special Report, then existing emergency relief programs may be able to cope. The more likely result, however, will be that millions of people will be driven from their homes and forced into camps.

A custom AI should be able to function as a critical member of teams taking on the problems of these camps. The individual task may include (1) identifying health and sanitation issues; (2) reuniting separated family members; and (3) developing resettlement plans for hundreds of thousands of families.

Historically, racial and religious biases in placement have been a real problem that has stranded people in such camps for years. There is a real risk that data developed from past camp experiences, intended to both train and then test the AI algorithms, will contain these biases. An AI so trained could then perpetuate the biases.

Great technical skill will be needed to develop the dozen or so separate AI algorithms needed to address the problems of the refugee camps, but great social skill will also be needed to eliminate biases while matching families to communities that can and will accept them. Developing teams with members who have the necessary expertise in both areas will pose a difficult management problem, even more so with AIs as important team members.

It is therefore necessary to recognize the risks involved and to develop a proper framework to address them.

Chapter 2: Scientific Intelligence, Decision Making, and Cyber Security

Chapter 2 deals with cyber security. It provides a discussion of the state-of-the-art security at the national, human, societal, and world levels. It then continues with topics like intelligence collection with:

1. HUMINT (HUMan INTelligence)
2. TECHINT (TECHnical INTelligence)
3. OSINT (Open Source INTelligence)

Any effort to address the problems of global warming as discussed in IPCC SR1.5 must assign significant resources, both financial and managerial, to the problems of cyber security. The participants in such an effort must assume that many of the people they must deal with are not acting in good faith and are only there to gain personal advantages. Their reasons for detractive efforts will include:

1. Denial of global warming

2. Anger at being forced to change personally
3. Religious conservatism
4. Personal gain

Many good people are going to be very upset by the consequences of global warming and thus may fall under the influence of bad actors. For example, as the sea level rises, many seaside lots will have to be removed from the property market. Some will be subject to repeated rising water during storms so often that there will be no justification for rebuilding on the property after each storm. Others might lose access to their homes due to high tides destroying roads or bridges. Others will lose services such as power, water, and sewage. Often, but not always and not always fairly, these conditions lead to a government buyout of distressed properties.

People need to know that the buyout process is open and aboveboard, that it is not influenced by behind-the-scenes political considerations or just plain corruption. The decision process therefore must be both open and guarded against corrupt manipulation. In cyberspace, these two concepts often contradict each other.

In other cases, new tools may come under attack. Artificial intelligences (AI) are expected to provide many critical services. Many of these systems use a learning process called deep learning. Late in the development process, an AI will be trained with a large data set and then tested with another. By just looking at the internal parameters of an AI, it is often hard to tell exactly what the training covered and which concepts stuck. The functionality of an AI is only as good as its training.

If the initial training and testing blocks have biases, even obscure ones, an AI will retain those biases. Care must also be taken to ensure that external actors do not obtain the power to retrain an AI for subversive purposes.

On the one hand, society cannot take on the problems outlined in IPCC SR1.5 without the latest tools. On the other, users must not be naive about possible misuse of those tools.

Chapter 3: The Coming Human/Machine Symbiosis, Effects on Society, and Business Planning

Chapter 3 provides a model of world population and sea level rise in the near future. It then uses artificial intelligence (AI) as an example of how modern technologies could be used to address the societal problems that can be expected given this model.

From the standpoint of IPCC SR1.5, both of these modeled concepts are critical. Special Report 1.5 describes how a world temperature rise below 1.5°C is probably manageable, but anything above that level poses a major risk to society as a whole. This chapter models how this temperature rise will result in substantial sea level rise that will cause major population displacements and destruction of shoreline infrastructure. IPCC SR1.5 details the necessity of stopping worldwide temperature rise before it reaches the 1.5°C level, so society will have a chance of stopping sea level rise at a sustainable level.

The second element of the modeling used in this chapter is world population. While this element is not discussed prominently in IPCC SR1.5, it is critical to any effort to address the social problems caused by global warming. After an exponential rise started during the Industrial Revolution, the human population of Earth is on track to peak after 2050 at about 10 billion people. The end of this historic exponential rise is not caused by "moral restraint, vice, and misery" as predicted by Thomas Malthus. Instead, the peak is being caused by a change in the reproductive model used by most women. In earlier times, women had little choice but to bear many children, only to see many of them die. Under the new model, women now have the power to have only a few children who are all likely to survive into adulthood.

A number of possible ways individuals may respond to the upcoming social problems, predicted by both this model and IPCC SR1.5, are then discussed. The most important of these possible responses is buy-in, which is a human mental structure that allows a person to hear an idea, envision themselves succeeding at the idea, get into action, and then stay in action. This approach has influenced a long list of successful large technical projects.

This chapter then lists technical advances that society should expect under this combined model and advances that it should **not** expect, which leads to a more detailed discussion of how AIs may be used and developed to take on problems like those discussed in IPCC SR1.5. The assertion here is that AI that are independent operators are not needed. What is needed are AIs that team up with humans at all levels.

In conclusion, society is now aware that major problems are coming. It already has a powerful set of tools and working plans that are available to address the problems discussed in IPCC SR1.5, and the possibility of developing even more powerful tools is real.

Chapter 4: System Dynamics Modeling for Public Health Bed Capacity Planning

Chapter 4 provides a discussion of system dynamics as a major management tool and provides an example of public health bed capacity planning. System dynamics is another of the powerful computer-based tools that can be directly applied to address the problems of global warming described in IPCC SR1.5. Following the example here, planning public health bed capacity can be scaled up to the regional level of hospital access.

The ideas in this chapter could be applied to the rise of the sea level that has already started to disrupt civic activities in places like Dorchester County, Maryland, USA (Horton, 2018). If society can limit global warming to the 1.5°C level described as safe in IPCC SR1.5, then this type of encroachment will grow until about 2100 and then level off. If society is not successful in staying under the limit, then the sea level will continue to rise for an indeterminate period and by an indeterminate amount.

The effect in a locality often starts slowly with monthly high tides, covering low points in roads to a depth of an inch or two. The number of days each month these flood tides occur then slowly grows. Brackish water covering a road, even to an inch or two, can render the road unsafe for vehicles such as school buses and ambulances. The brackish water (1) makes it difficult for the driver to see if the road is still intact; (2) affects the vehicle's brakes; and (3) reduces the life of the vehicle due to rust raising maintenance costs.

The creeping effect is often punctuated by major storms that damage homes and infrastructure, most critically bridges. If a house is repeatedly damaged by rising water, then the cost of flood insurance for that property often becomes so high that the property cannot be sold and may be abandoned. People with established interests who own and sell such seafront properties working to maintain the local property market may exacerbate this problem. The overall effect is to reduce the number of people living in the area in a patchy manner and to delay planning.

The system dynamics example in this chapter covers planning for the number of hospital and other health care beds needed in a specific hospital. Such beds are expensive to construct and maintain, but a shortage of beds in an emergency can result in excessive deaths.

An effective response to IPCC SR1.5 will require extensive planning to address the rising tides over decades. Regional planning will need to include defining which properties will need to be abandoned due to blocking of access as well as storm damage. That planning must be detailed enough to include the number of hospital beds accessible over time as well as beds for the elderly. Dynamic systems analysis needs to be scaled up to the task and extended in time. Fortunately, this type of analysis can be and is, after all, dynamic.

Chapter 5: Future of Jobs and Humans in a Tech-Centric World

Chapter 5 provides a discussion of human jobs and automation. It discusses the likelihood of machines taking over even more human jobs, what the consequences of this may be, and what could be done to ease the expected social disruption. A government-guaranteed universal basic income (UBI) is discussed as one possible approach.

The global warming problems discussed in IPCC SR1.5 put most of these arguments on hold until after the more threatening problems are addressed. Society simply needs to have an enormous number of people, assisted by machines, hard at work on demanding problems. The situation demands all hands to the pumps.

Artificial intelligence (AI) designers can incorporate very basic concepts into their designs that will both help address our current problems and set up a safe and productive future for humans afterwards. These concepts might include:

1. **Human/Machine Symbiosis**: Major AIs should be designed to work on teams with humans. All work on AIs indistinguishable from humans should be defunded.
2. **Corporate Persons**: Major AIs should be incorporated, making them corporate persons. They will then be subject to control by a board of directors, be functional economic entities, and pay taxes.
3. **Small Teams**: Medium-sized AIs could be designed to team with one person. These AIs could function as data analyzers, cyberspace bodyguards, health watchers, and much more. What the relationship cannot be is master/slave, since who is on top can too easily be switched.

After the crisis of the 21st century has passed, with its considerable societal disruptions but also with the stabilizing of the human populations of the world, then society will have to revisit the question of jobs for humans. The level of disruption of society is expected to be great enough to render all current arguments that do not consider these problems moot.

The current state of society will simply be history, and society will have to take a new look at itself.

Chapter 6: Orientism Management Strategy for Training Policy Makers in Emergency Decision Making

Chapter 6 discusses key topics in political science and includes a detailed discussion of Orientism Management (OM). It provides details on the skills that a leader in politics or high-level business management needs. The process of policymaking is discussed in detail, especially with respect to handling risks at all levels. The chapter then ends with a more detailed discussion of the specific elements of the Orientism Framework and mindset.

This analysis provides a clear example of the type of powerful and well-thought-out procedures that could be brought to bear on the climate change problems discussed in IPCC SR1.5.

IPCC SR1.5 makes a distinction between 1.5°C and 2.0°C. At the lower figure, powerful tools, like OM, should be able to provide structure for action even in a somewhat disrupted world. At the higher figure, the disruption may be too high to allow society's best tools to work. This is the major risk that is now expected to materialize somewhere between these two global temperature levels.

Political leaders may not be sufficiently well versed in the level of political science theory shown in Orientism, but they can certainly select cabinet and shadow cabinet people who are highly competent. Good people are out there. Good processes are out there.

The problems of global warming are now being addressed in many places, but the work is currently piecemeal. The longer society waits before taking on these problems in a unified manner, the more likely the economic and social changes that occur are to be unworkably disruptive.

Currently, the major problem is lack of leadership. Fortunately, political leaders show a marked skill at finding a political movement headed in some direction and then jumping out in front of it. This suggests that a grassroots movement may be needed to initiate a large, unified effort on global warming.

The global warming problems laid out in IPCC SR1.5 are daunting. Fortunately, society has powerful tools like OM that will enable society to make a massive number of relatively small local efforts while keeping the overall thrust focused and effective at the whole Earth level.

Chapter 7: Talent Management – Retaining Distinctive Human Capital Sustainably

Chapter 7 discusses human resources management and development in a major company. A detailed study of talent sourcing and retention as a competitive advantage at Toyota South Africa Motors (TSAM) is discussed with the conclusion that "highly skilled human capital is critical for organizational sustainability, achieving business objectives, and gaining competitive advantage."

Managerial talent is discussed as a key factor in the success of any large organization, but it takes time and resources to make a program effective in the long term.

Developing human resources talent then is a good example of the type of valuable management process that can be expected to remain available under the IPCC SR1.5 effort if the world average temperature rise can be kept below 1.5°C. If the world average temperature cannot be held to this limit, then there may not be time and resources for valuable long-term efforts like building the talent of the managers who must take on all the resulting breakdowns.

Efforts to address the problems put forth in IPCC SR1.5 are currently limited by the talent and vision of high-level management. Critical skills like generating buy-in for effective environmental action are simply not being taught. The longer corrective action is delayed, the less time society will have for important efforts like the development of managerial talent. These managers are the very people society will need to take on the problems that too often will then appear as unrelenting and beyond management's skills and experience.

Chapter 8: Risks and Benefits of Effective Techniques and Technologies in Education – A Historical Overview

Chapter 8 provides a history of educational technology starting with a description of early efforts and then a detailed look at current concepts:

1. Digital resources and tools for the digital society
2. Cognitive tutoring
3. Educational robotics
4. Computational thinking and serious games
5. Simulation, virtual, augmented, or mixed reality

The chapter then ends with a discussion of effective improvement, the challenges being faced, and the opportunities those challenges bring forward.

IPCC Special Report 1.5 makes clear the critical part education in general and education on the use of technology in particular will have to play in addressing the great problems of climate change. Four areas are particularly critical:

1. **Teaching Leaders:** The primary reason for society's slow start on addressing climate change is simply weak leadership. The effort will not truly start until a cadre of leaders have been trained in both the necessity for action and the opportunities for effective action.
2. **Training Workers:** Then the real work can start. This will require the training of massive numbers of people in clearly defined tasks with potential to address the real problems.
3. **Training AIs:** One of the key technologies that will be needed to address these problems will be artificial intelligence (AI). These devices need a lot of training too. Their value as tools is completely dependent on the quality of their training. Eliminating biases from the training is particularly difficult.
4. **Learning From Earth:** Earth itself has much to teach people about the climate and where society is being taken by climate change. Earth is not at risk. It has been so hot at times that there were no ice caps at the poles, dinosaurs lived

above the Arctic Circle, and a great shallow sea reached from Hudson Bay to the Gulf of Mexico. It is not Earth itself that is in danger; it is human society on Earth that is.

Teaching is key to starting a worldwide effort to address climate change. Learning is key to getting enormous numbers of people to take effective action. Society cannot start this effort without teaching; society cannot succeed in this effort without learning.

Chapter 9: Bioethics of Innovation – Innovative Practices, Global Health Delivery, and Environmental Safeguards

Chapter 9 provides a cautionary tale about overdependence on information and computer technology (ICT) to solve business and social problems. It provides historic examples of problems that were created when such applications werc handled poorly. The examples are from the experience of the Olivetti Corporation in developing early business computers for Europe. This warning is well taken when planning efforts to address the major problems of global warming described in IPCC SR1.5.

Many groups are developing powerful computer-based tools with excellent prospects for addressing these problems. Early on, however, it may be very difficult to predict which problems a specific tool will be good for addressing and which problems other approaches would handle better. This specifically applies to new applications like artificial intelligence (AI).

This problem may be compounded by early developers' need to raise funds and interest in their new approach. Over-the-top claims may appear to them to be the best way to get from raw idea to commercial product.

That said, society will not be able to address these problems without applying the latest technological innovations. The approach this chapter suggests is that everyone take a deep breath and then look carefully at new technologies and how they can be best applied.

This will require teams that contain both people knowledgeable in the new computer technology under testing and people knowledgeable in the specific field in which the new technology is to be applied. Once a new technology has been demonstrated to be effective and unlikely to lead to other serious problems, new specialty teams can be trained more widely to apply the specific technology.

In this process, AIs may be important team members and support the team in many ways, but they are unlikely to be team leaders or liaisons between the team and the human customer. The well-thought-out efforts of a great many real people will be needed to develop the new technologies needed to address these great problems. AIs might, however, provide critical data reduction and other technical support.

Chapter 10: Ecology, Sustainability, and Scientific Education – The Evolution of an Environmental Pedagogy

Chapter 10 supports society's efforts to address the problems in IPCC SR1.5 in the field of environmental education (EE). It summarizes the history of EE, particularly in Europe, with detailed discussion of this movement in Italy. This chapter provides a number of important lists related to environmental education:

1. Key challenges
2. Main problems
3. Historic organizations in Europe
4. The main steps of the origin of EE in Europe
5. The origin of Italian EE
6. The critical ecological areas for EE
7. EE goals
8. EE objectives
9. The basic principles of deep ecology

One key concept used in this chapter is sustainable development. Since the Industrial Revolution, a world economy based on markets has produced enormous wealth that has raised millions of people out of abject poverty. Critics point out that that wealth has not been distributed fairly, but clearly there exists enough wealth to take on the problems in IPCC SR1.5.

That long period of economic prosperity was based critically on growth. That growth, in turn, has contributed to the degradation of the natural environment, which is critical to the support of human life. The question then becomes, can society modify its economic and business models so that prosperity for an enormous number of people can coexist with a sustainable Earth?

The Paris Agreement of 2016 set the limit of the rise in average global warming at 2.0°C, the highest temperature compatible with current economic and political structures, but that number was more political than scientific. IPCC SR1.5 reduces that level to 1.5°C based on a much more comprehensive technical study. The 1.5°C limit now defines sustainable growth.

This new limit requires more corrective action sooner. This chapter details the field of environmental education as a key part of what is needed to support this increased level of action among the populace. People will take action to address these problems only if there is adequate education available for them to both understand the problem and to see that their actions can make a positive contribution.

If environmental education did not already have a long history, society would have to invent it now.

CONCLUSION

We can do this. Society has the resources. Society has enough information to make a start and the means to generate more information as needed. Society has an entire industry devoted to producing the latest technological innovations.

What is needed now is an enormous number of competent, dedicated people in sustained, and at times heroic, action. Society can expect just such people to come forward given effective leadership. It is that leadership that society now most needs to find.

Tom Riley
The Big Moon Dig, USA
December 2018

REFERENCES

Horton, T. (2018). *High Tide in Dorchester*. Bay Journal Film. Retrieved from http://hightidedorchester.org/

IPCC SR1. 5. (2018). *Global Warming of 1.5 C Technical Summary*. Retrieved October 2018 from http://ipcc.ch/report/SR15/

Acknowledgment

I would like to acknowledge the help of all the people involved in this project. Without their support, this book would not have become a reality.

A special thank is for Eng. John Tom Riley (The Big Moon Dig, USA) regarding his in-depth and fine-tuning analysis of reviewed chapters, and for writing the scientific preface to this book.

I wish to acknowledge the very valuable help and encouragement I received from my Colleagues and friends, especially Ms. Irene Maria Gironacci (LIST Center, Luxembourg), Dr. Amitabh Anand (Skema Business School, France) and Dr. Giulia Pulcini (University of Camerino, Italy). Most of the authors also served as referees; I highly appreciate their double task.

I wish to place on record our deep appreciation and thanks to Ms. Jordan Tepper, Book Development Editor (IGI Global) for her support, cooperation and attention to details to bring out the publication of this book in time.

Lastly, I wish to thank my family for the understanding and support in providing me with all the necessary facilities to enable me to complete my work and above all, I am immensely thankful to the Almighty.

Luisa dall'Acqua
Scientific Lyceum TCO, Italy & University of Bologna, Italy

Chapter 1
A Framework for Risk Management in AI System Development Projects

Kitti Photikitti
Assumption University of Thailand, Thailand

Kitikorn Dowpiset
Assumption University of Thailand, Thailand

Jirapun Daengdej
Assumption University of Thailand, Thailand

ABSTRACT

It has been well-known that the chance of successfully delivering a software project within an allocated time and budget is very low. Most of the researches in this area have concluded that "user's requirements" of the systems is one of the most difficult risks to deal with in this case. Interestingly, until today, regardless of amount of effort put into this area, the possibility of project failure is still very high. The issue with requirement can be significantly increased when developing an artificial intelligence (AI) system, where one would like the systems to autonomously behave. This is because we are not only dealing with user's requirements, but we must also be able to deal with "system's behavior" that, in many cases, do not even exist during software development. This chapter discusses a preliminary work on a framework for risk management for AI systems development projects. The goal of this framework is to help project management in minimizing risk that can lead AI software projects to fail due to the inability to finish the projects on time and within budget.

DOI: 10.4018/978-1-5225-7903-8.ch001

INTRODUCTION

In the past few years, there is no concept that catch attentions from businesses and even leaders of countries around the world like the use and advancement of Artificial Intelligence (AI). In 2016, the White House released a report on future directions and considerations for AI called "Preparing for the Future of Artificial Intelligence" (Felten & Lyons, 2016). A "National Artificial Intelligence Research and Development Strategic Plan", which lays out a strategic plan for Federally-funded research and development in AI, is also released, accordingly. In fact, in 2016, President Obama said during his interview with MIT's Joi Ito and WIRED's Scott Dadich that:

We've been seeing specialized AI in every aspect of our lives, from medicine and transportation to how electricity is distributed, and it promises to create a vastly more productive and efficient economy. If properly harnessed, it can generate enormous prosperity and opportunity.

For Russia, President Putin states that the nation that leads in AI 'will be the ruler of the world' (Vincent, 2017). In addition, for China, President Xi Jinping targets that China will become the global leader in AI by 2030 (Chandler, 2018).

On the other hand, in commercial world, Pichai, CEO of Google, stated at the company's annual event called Google I/O 2017 that Google's vision has been changed from "Mobile First World to an AI First World" (Zerega, 2017). Microsoft has been investing heavily in AI for more than 25 years. Amazon has a dedicated AI unit that spread and provide support on applied researches in AI to the company's projects (Levy, 2018).

Regardless of its popularity in both public and private sectors, unfortunately, a large number of AI system development projects around the world are considered to be failed. In addition to the news around the world that report on failure of autonomous cars in various incidents, in 2016, TechRepublic reported "Top 10 AI Failures of 2016", which led to results such as:

- AI built to predict future crime was racist
- Non-player characters in a video game crafted weapons beyond creator's plans
- Insurance company uses Facebook data to issue rates, shows bias
- Robot injured a child, and
- AI-judged beauty contest is racist

Especially with the incidents related to life and threat of people, an article by MIT Technology Review is dedicated to a certain kind of failure of the AI system, self-driving cars (Emerging Technology, 2018). In addition, according to an article published in Harvard Business Review, April, 2017, most of the AI projects in organizations tend to fail unless an appropriate approach in implementation of the system is adopted (Hosanagar & Saxena, 2017). This followed by an article in Harvard Business Review by Satell who suggests a number of important points that should be considered by organizations in order to increase the chance of success in AI system development projects (Satell, 2018).

Regardless of what AI is, AI system is simply a software that has to be written. Even though some of the AI systems can develop itself, but, to start, the system has to be properly design and code (Simonite, 2017). Then, depending on the applied concept, some of the systems may be able to further develop themselves when certain conditions are met. This means that regardless of how the AI system is developed, knowledge and experience in software project management still play an important role in the success of the projects.

As far as software project management is concerned, it has long been evidenced that one of the most important issues that in many cases lead to project failure is "user requirements" (Verner, Sampson, & Cerpa, 2008; Pratt, 2017). Unfortunately, the issue of requirements can easily be magnified in some AI system. This is because the aim of most of the AI systems is to allow the software to independently adjust its reasoning process according to various input entered and automatically perceived by the systems. This kind of systems that may act autonomously according to the input, which sometimes not foreseen even by the human designers (European Commission, 2018). As a result, it is clear that issues related to "user requirements" are considered as "potential risks" for project management when building the AI systems.

The aim of this research is to develop a risk management framework that can be used during project management of AI systems development. Note that, as an ongoing research, the aim of this preliminary work is only to focus on "risk identification" of risk management framework. The main contribution of the work is in proposing a set of "risks" novel to the traditional software development project, which are introduced by requirements of AI system development.

This chapter is organized as follow. The following section provides background of all concepts concerned in this research starting from software development projects, followed by AI systems, and finally overview of risk management framework. Then, the discussion continued with sections on Literature Reviews, A Proposed Framework for Risk Management, Future Research Directions, and Conclusion, respectively.

BACKGROUND

In order to provide readers with necessary background information on various terms and concepts used in this chapter, this section is dedicated to giving overview pictures of relevant technologies and concepts include:

- Software development project
- AI systems
- AI system development project
- Risk management framework

Software Development Project

In general, there are a number of approaches in developing a software. Each of the approaches involves different number of steps in their processes. The following figure depicts three popular approaches in software development.

Regardless of the approach applied in software development projects, in most cases, there are five main steps in software development process (Sommerville, 2015), which include:

- Requirements
- Design
- Implementation
- Verification
- Maintenance

Unfortunately, despite a large number of researches on finding approaches to software development, large portion of the projects still fail due to unable to cope with issues related to "requirements" (Gulla, 2012; Pratt, 2017). Various researches have been conducted in order to understand characteristics of the requirements (Christel & Kang, 1992; Bano & Ikram, 2010). Problems with requirements can be classified into two main issues, which are:

- Requirement creep (or scope creep) which refers to uncontrollable growth of requirements
- Unclear requirements which considered to be the most important issue in software development projects

Figure 1. Approaches in software development by Omar El Gabry

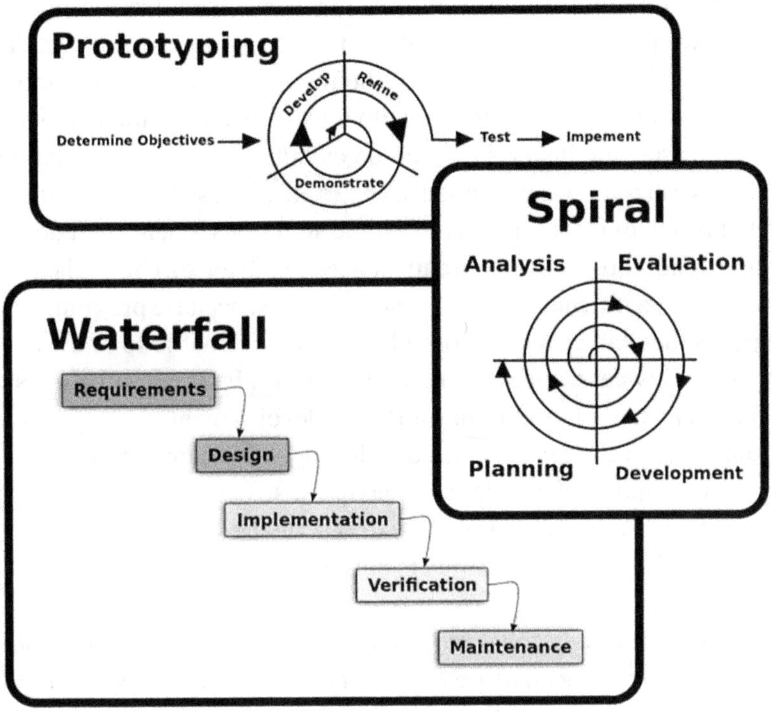

AI Systems

Intelligent system should ideally perform "like a human" in a limited sense. Intelligent system should to some extent be able to learn to perform given tasks and make decisions. (Pratihar & Jain, 2010)

A famous definition of "intelligence" is defined by Albus (Albus, 1991), which states that:

...intelligence is defined as an ability of a system to act appropriately in an uncertain environment, where appropriate action is that which increases the probability of success, and success is the achievement of behavioral sub-goals that supports the system's ultimate goal.

In general, a computer software can only perform according to codes that have been written by programmers. In other words, programmers have to imagine every move what software they are coding should do in response to a given input. According to the definition of "intelligence", one of the major issues when developing an AI software is the system must be able deal with *uncertain* environment or *uncertainty*. In most of the cases, the uncertainty can be calculated in advance, that means all possible actions can be preprogrammed to cope with all possible input to the systems. However, the problem is that there can also be situations where even developers of the software cannot foresee some circumstances in advance. This is the reason why accidents occurred with a number of autonomous cars, because programmers cannot write programs that can cover all possible situations. Unable to know all possible situations or, in this case, input to the software in advance can be considered as "*unclear requirements*" in traditional software development.

Unfortunately, the challenges when developing AI systems are not just unable to know all possible input to the system, but people also expect the systems to "learn". According to one of the most referenced textbook on the subject by Tom M. Mitchell (Mitchell, 1997), "Machine Learning" is defined as:

A computer program is said to learn from experience E with respect to some class of tasks T and performance measure P, if its performance at tasks in T, as measured by P, improves with experience E.

According to the definition, AI systems that can learn will improve its performance according to its new experience. In general, we as a human can only run faster than our previous run, if something in our body has been enhanced, or we run with different movement from last time. For the AI system, this means that software itself behave differently when compared with previous run.

From the two important characteristics of the AI systems discussed above, as far as AI system development is concerned, this means the system must be able to deal with both unexpected *input* and *behavior*.

With regard to increasing the chance of success in AI system development projects, Satell suggests 4 important issues that have to be considered for the projects (Satell, 2018), which are:

1. You need to make your purpose clear.
2. Choose the tasks you automate wisely.
3. Choose your data wisely.
4. Shift humans to higher-value social tasks.

Risk Management Framework

Risk is unavoidable and every organization needs to take action to manage it in a way that it can justify to a level that is acceptable. The appropriate range of responses to a risk will depend on the nature, size and complexity of the risk. Paul Hopkin. (Hopkin, 2018)

Recall the fact that uncertainties existed in AI projects. These uncertainties are considered as "risks" in AI system project management. Being able to effectively and efficiently deal with the risk is one of the most important issues for businesses, as a result, large number of studies have been dedicated to risk management in organizations. Consequently, a number of definitions have been so far given to the term "risk". The followings are some examples of the definitions.

According to David Hillson, one of the leaders in risk management, risk is defined as:

A subset of uncertainty, it is an uncertainty that is matter, what matter that can affect our objective.

For a well-known institute in project management, in their Project Management Body of Knowledge (PMBOK) (Project Management Institute, 2017), project risk is defined as:

An uncertain event or condition that, if it occurs, has a positive or negative effect on one or more project objectives such as scope, schedule, cost, or quality.

In addition, The Association for Project Management (APM) defines risk as:

An uncertain event or set of circumstances that, should it occur, will have an effect on achievement of one or more objectives.

According to ISO 31000, risk is defined as:

The effect of uncertainty on objectives.

Regardless of the definitions currently existed in literatures, one of the most important activities in managing a project is being able to manage project's risks. The following is the overview of risk management from Priti Sikdar (Sikdar, 2017):

Risk management is all about planning risk identification, analyzing risks using qualitative and quantitative methods, and then planning mitigation strategies.

With regard to risk management, in general, ISO 31000 particularly emphasis on context and states, especially internal, external, and risk management context when undertaking risk management activities.

According to the overall picture of risk management discussed above, from risk identification to planning mitigation strategies, these activities are linked together and formed a core element of the management, a risk management process. According to Paul Hopkin (Hopkin, 2018), Risk Management Process consists of 7 related activities which are:

1. Recognition of Risks
2. Ranking of Risks
3. Responding to Significant Risks
4. Resourcing Controls
5. Reaction (and Event) Planning
6. Reporting of Risk Performance
7. Reviewing the Risk Management System

Figure 2 shows risk management process and its seven activities.

In comparison, according to the Standards Australia (2009), a Risk Management Process has also been defined as a separated set of activities. Figure 3 shows the process.

According to the Figure 3 shown above, there are six key elements of the process, which are:

1. Establish the context
2. Risk identification
3. Risk analysis
4. Risk treatment
5. Communication and consultation
6. Monitoring and review

Figure 2. Risk management process
(Adapted from Hopkin, 2018)

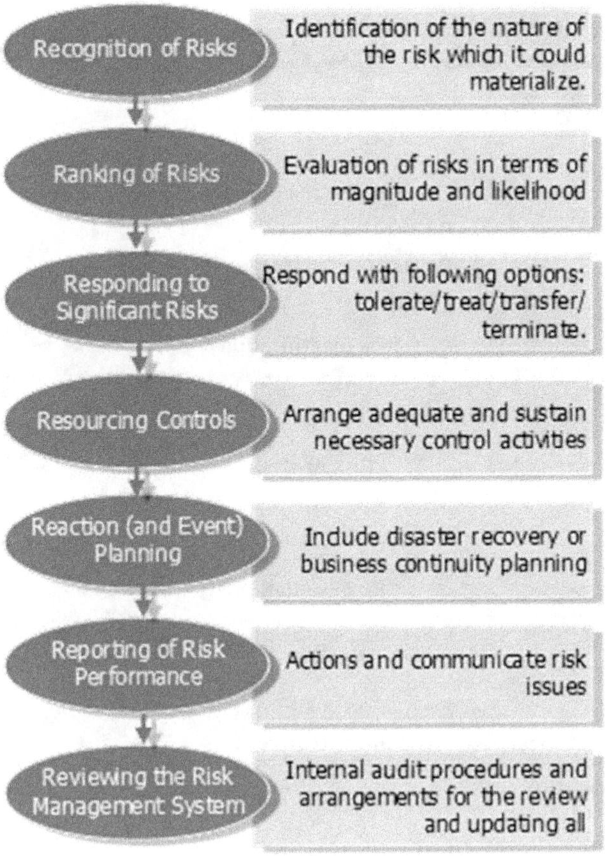

Regardless of the number of steps or activities existed in the risk management process, as far as risk management framework is concerned, the risk management process is generally supported by 3 main elements, which are:

1. Risk Architecture,
2. Risk Strategy, and
3. Risk Protocols

Figure 4 shows elements of Risk Management Framework (Hopkin, 2018).

Figure 3. Australian/New Zealand risk management standard: AS/NZS ISO 31000: 2009

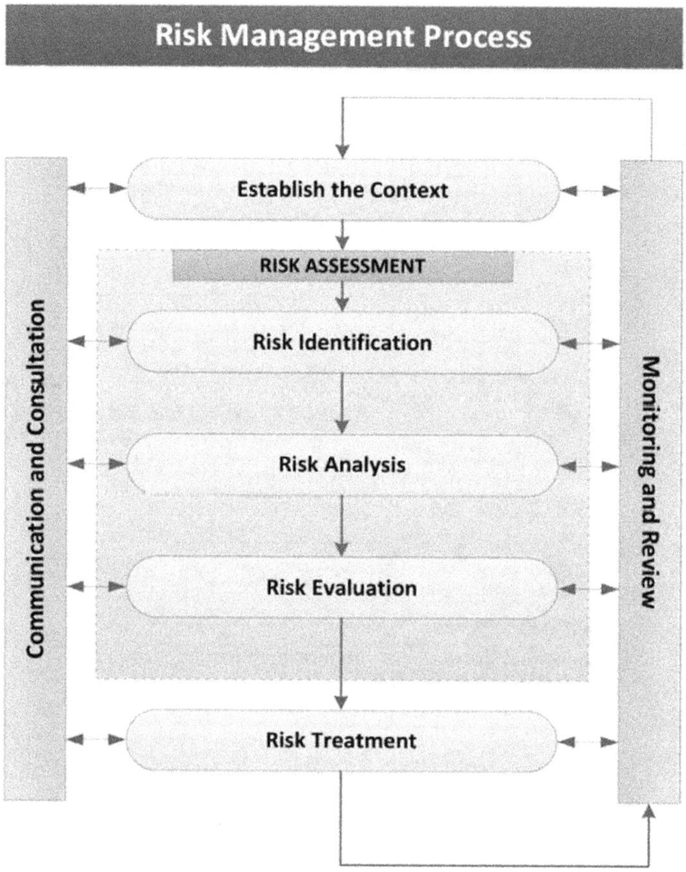

Figure 4. Risk management framework
(Adapted from Hopkin, 2018)

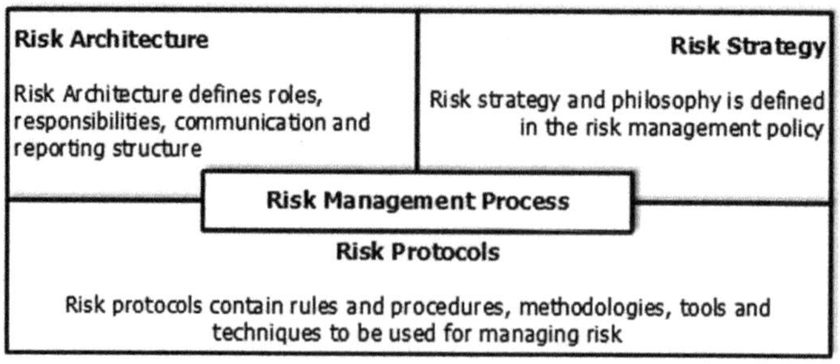

However, since the process is considered to be the core of risk management, there are a number of researches that focuses only on the process. In such cases, the process itself is considered to be the entire framework for risk management. As a result, the above three elements are considered as parts of the process.

LITERATURE REVIEWS

Recall issues raised from developing AI systems are about uncommon types of risks that the AI projects normally introduce. The reviews conducted in this research cover both general framework for risk management and a specific topic related to issues introduced in AI systems, which is "risk identification".

As far as the framework is concerned, according to ISO31000, a risk management framework is a set of components that supports risk management in organization. Currently, there are two types of components, which are:

1. Foundations which include:
    a. Risk management policy,
    b. Objectives,
    c. Mandate, and
    d. Commitment
2. Organizational arrangements which include:
    a. Plans,
    b. Relationships,
    c. Accountabilities,
    d. Resources,
    e. Processes, and
    f. Activities involved in managing organizational risk.

In Standards Australia (2009), Risk Management Framework consists of five key elements, which are:

1. **Mandate and Commitment**: A strong and sustained commitment from management is required to ensure the ongoing risk management in organization.
2. **Design of Framework for Managing Risk**: A systematic approach is required in designing a risk management framework.

3. **Implementing Risk Management**: A risk management process has to be applied through a risk management plan at all relevant levels and functions within the organization.
4. **Monitoring and Review of the Framework**: Organization should continually ensure that risk management supports organizational performance.
5. **Continual Improvement of the Framework**: By using results of monitoring and reviews, the risk management framework, policy and plan can be improved.

As for the risk identification, Kaplan, R. S. and Mikes, A. proposed a risk management framework, which deals with uncertainty in business. They have identified a number of sources of external risks (Kaplan & Mikes, 2012), which are:

- Natural and economic disasters with immediate impact. This includes natural and economic disasters.
- Geopolitical and environmental changes with long-term impact. This also includes situations such as coups and wars; and global warming which lead to long-term environmental impacts.
- Competitive risks with medium-term impact. This includes radical strategic policies of competitors and emergence of disruptive technologies.

In addition, Crispin Piney proposes that the risk identification step should be separated into two steps which are: Basic Identification and Detailed Identification (Piney, 2003). The following shows possible approaches that can be used within the two proposed steps.

- Basic Identification
  - SWOT Analysis
  - Analogy
- Detailed Identification
  - Interviewing
  - Assumptions Analysis
  - Document Reviews
  - Delphi Technique
  - Brainstorming

Another interesting work on risk identification is done by a team at MITRE Corporation (Rebovich, 2014). In addition to arguing the risk identification can be done based on historical information from similar projects or programs, the team also emphasize that risk identification is an iterative process that evolved overtime. New risks are identified as the project progresses.

From all the literatures considered in this research, to our knowledge, it is clear that listing of all risks in most of the works in risk management assume either historical data existed, or human experts can foresee what can occur with organization, or both. Unfortunately, this is not the case for development of AI system projects.

A PROPOSED FRAMEWORK FOR RISK MANAGEMENT

No one really knows how the most advanced algorithms do what they do. That could be a problem. Will Knight (Knight, 2017)

Recall all constraints occurred within the AI system development projects, especially the fact that AI systems are expected to:

- Autonomously perform itself tasks without supervision, and
- Learn to survive in the situations where even developers of the system cannot foresee the situation.

According to the fact that, in general, risk identification process is normally done based on either using comprehensive database of the events on the past projects, or brainstorming sessions by the project teams (National Research Council, 2005). The challenge is that one of the key components of human creative thinking is the ability to apply knowledge learnt from one context and use it with another (Baraniuk, 2018). This means that all knowledge learnt could be used by the system when encountering with unseen situations/environments.

Overall Framework

As mentioned earlier, in this preliminary work, instead of proposing an entirely new framework, the framework suggested by Robert S. Kaplan and Anette Mikes (Kaplan and Mikes, 2012) is used as our starting point. With the characteristics

Figure 5. Matrix of knowledge
(Meredith, 2014)

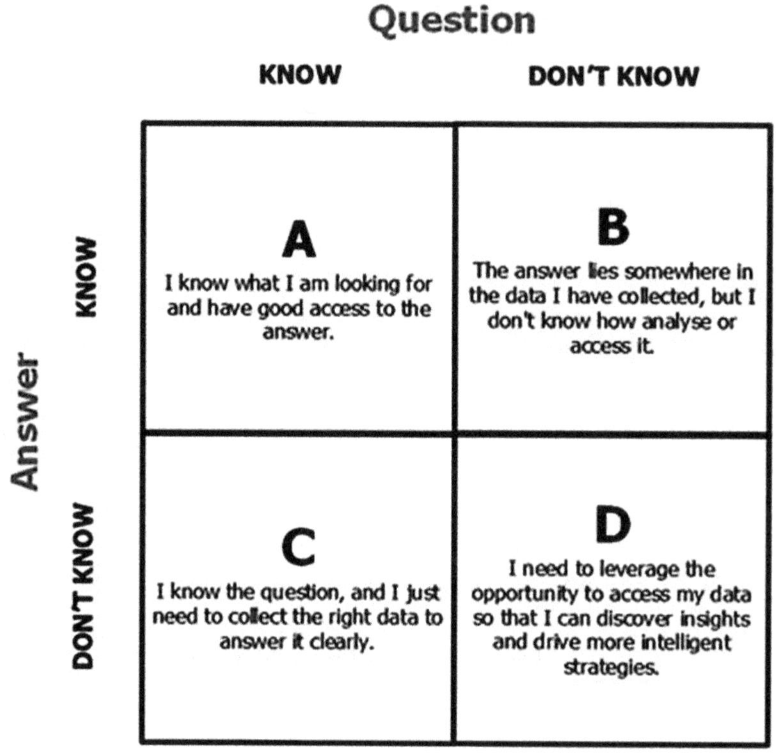

of AI system development projects discussed above, we only focus on proposing solutions for issue of risk identification at this stage.

As far as overall picture of the framework is concerned, the framework by Robert S. Kaplan and Anette Mikes focuses on the three types of risks organizations have to deal with. These types of risks are:

1. **Preventable Risks:** They are internal risks, which usually are:
    a. Result from within the organization
    b. Controllable by the organization, and
    c. Should be eliminated or avoided.
2. **Strategy Risks:** Unlike other preventable risks, strategy risks usually also relate to returns expected by company. In general, if the high returns expected,

then the company has to accept more risks. In other words, it is high risk high return, although the profit is high, the risks will also high.

3. **External Risks:** External risks such as natural and political issues are uncontrollable. Unfortunately, the risks still have to be identified and mitigated as much as possible.

Classifying Risks Using Matrix of Knowledge

In order to deal with unforeseen requirements that can turn out to risks for AI projects, a systematic approach is needed. In this case, the matrix of knowledge by Maycottes Meredith is used as an approach to classify different types of knowledge the AI system have to deal with (Meredith, 2014). Figure 5 depicts details of the matrix.

According to the matrix, as far as the risk is concerned in this research, the "Question" in this matrix can be considered as the risk. The followings explain how the 4 groups of Question-and-Answer can be used to describe our risk and its solution:

- Risk Type "A" is referred to the situation where company know both risks and solution (or answer) for the risks.
- Risk Type "B" occurs when the required solution for the risk are already existed inside the historical data, the company only need to find domain experts who can help them to analyze and/or retrieve the answers for them.
- Risk Type "C" happens with the company when they know the risks, but do not know how to deal with them. In this case, they have to spend extra effort in finding solutions to the risks that they know or identify. In this case, solution to the risk may or may not be resided within the company.
- Risk Type "D" arises when the company encounter do not know both the possible risks and their solutions due to the fact that the AI system may behave in unexpected way in order to response to unforeseen situations.

Risk Identification for Risk Type "D"

This type of risk is a special risk that lead to this research. The AI system can behave unexpectedly in order to deal with situations which is unforeseen even by its developers. There are two approaches to the issue of risk identification for this type of risk, which are:

1. **Data-Driven Approach:** Similar to what have been discussed in other works in this field, risks can be identified by analyzing historical records of operations occurred in the company. However, in this particular case, we have to invest a large amount of efforts in trying to ensure that the historical data to be used does actually cover all possible events or problems that may occur with the company. This can help minimize the chance that the AI system will encounter an unknown situation that can lead it to behave expectedly. For example, bank can use credit card transactions of customers as input into an AI system in order to allow the system to learn how to improve itself with credit card application processing task. By using such input, the system can learn all possible risks that can occur as far as the given data is concerned. In addition, AI for insurance underwriting task, which is usually responsible for evaluating risks of customers, can learn potential risks from a set of previous claims of cutomers.
2. **Duplicating How the Reasoning Process of the AI Systems Being Developed:** In case that the historical data is not available, or available but the company knows that the data that they have does not cover all possible situations that may happen to the company, different approach to risk identification has to be applied.

Most of the AI system has an engine called "Reasoning Process" (Cox & Raja, 2011). In case of Risk Type D, the AI system's reasoning process has to be understood by the development team. In other words, the AI system development team have to ensure that all reasoning process of the AI system are well known by the team. This because, since historical data is unreliable, the risk identification process need to trace and understand the AI system's reasoning process in order to identify the risks as many as possible.

FUTURE RESEARCH DIRECTIONS

Since this is only a preliminary work in the research on risk management framework for AI system development projects, there are still a number of issues and topics that require continuing efforts. According to the risk management framework, example of these topics are:

1. At the overall framework level:
    a. Risk Architecture,
    b. Risk Strategy, and

   c. Risk Protocols
2. At the risk management process level, the topics are:
   a. Risk analysis
   b. Risk treatment
   c. Communication and consultation
   d. Monitoring and review

Note that regardless of the topics to be covered in further researches, the main issue that has to be all the time considered is the fact that the AI systems are "autonomous" and the systems can "learn" according to their new input or environment.

CONCLUSION

This chapter presents a framework for risk management in AI system development projects. At the current stage, the main contribution of this research focus mainly on solutions to issues related of risk identification. The main challenge of the risk identification in this case is the fact that the AI system can behave in unexpected way, given an unforeseen situation. The solutions are proposed based on two well-known concepts called Matrix of Knowledge of management community, and Meta-reasoning of AI community.

Regardless of what have been discussed in this chapter, there are still a large number of remaining issues, if ones want to minimize the risk of running autonomous systems that can behave unexpectedly according to their input. As a result, in order to deal with the remaining issues, researches in this area can be incrementally conducted. For example, starting from the systems that behave in expected way, then proceed by adding uncertainty into the system. Increasing of the uncertainty can be done until reaching the goal, which is the system can deal with totally unexpected input.

REFERENCES

Albus, J. S. (1991). Outline for a Theory of Intelligence. *IEEE Transactions on Systems, Man, and Cybernetics*, *21*(3), 473–509. doi:10.1109/21.97471

Standards Australia. (2009). *Australian/New Zealand Risk Management Standard: AS/NZS ISO 31000: 2009*. Author.

Bano, M., & Ikram, N. (2010). Issues and Challenges of Requirement Engineering in Service Oriented Software Development. In *Proceedings of the Fifth International Conference on Software Engineering Advances*. IEEE Xplore.

Baraniuk, C. (2018, January 25). For AI to Get Creative, It Must Learn the Rules—Then How to Break 'Em. *Scientific American*.

Chandler, C. (2018). *Why China Has An Edge In the A.I. Arms Race*. Retrieved July 2018, from http://fortune.com/2018/06/25/artificial-intelligence-in-china/

Christel, M. G., & Kang, K. C. (1992). *Issues in Requirements Elicitation*. Technical Report. CMU/SEI-92-TR-12. ESC-TR-92-012. Software Engineering Institute. Carnegie Mellon University.

Cox, M. T., & Raja, A. (2011). *Metareasoning: Thinking about Thinking*. MIT Press. doi:10.7551/mitpress/9780262014809.001.0001

Emerging Technology from the arXiv. (2018, March). When an AI finally kills someone, who will be responsible? Legal scholars are furiously debating which laws should apply to AI crime. *MIT Technology Review*.

European Commission. (2018). *Statement on Artificial Intelligence, Robotics and 'Autonomous' Systems*. European Group on Ethics in Science and New Technologies. Publications Office of the European Union, 2018.

Felten, E., & Lyons, T. (2016). *The Administration's Report on the Future of Artificial Intelligence*. Retrieved July 2018, from https://obamawhitehouse.archives.gov/blog/2016/10/12/administrations-report-future-artificial-intelligence

Gulla, J. (2012). *Seven Reasons IT Projects Fail. IBM Systems Magazine*.

Hopkin, P. (2018). *Fundamentals of Risk Management: Understanding, Evaluating and Implementing Effective Risk Management*. Kogan Page.

Hosanagar, K., & Saxena, A. (2017, April). The First Wave of Corporate AI Is Doomed to Fail. *Harvard Business Review*.

Kaplan, R. S., & Mikes, A. (2012, June). Managing Risks: A New Framework. *Harvard Business Review*.

Knight, W. (2017, April 11). The Dark Secret at the Heart of AI. *MIT Technology Review*.

Levy, S. (2018). *Inside Amazon's Artificial Intelligence Flywheel: How deep learning came to power Alexa, Amazon Web Services, and nearly every other division of the company*. Retrieved July 2018, from https://www.wired.com/story/amazon-artificial-intelligence-flywheel/

Meredith, M. (2014). *The Value of Knowing What You Don't Know You Don't Know*. Retrieved July 2018, from https://www.umbel.com/blog/services/know-what-you-dont-know/

Mitchell, T. M. (1997). *Machine Learning*. McGraw-Hill Science/Engineering/Math.

National Research Council. (2005). *The Owner's Role in Project Risk Management*. The National Academies Press.

Piney, C. (2003). *Risk Identification: Combining the Tools to Deliver the Goods*. Paper presented at PMI® Global Congress 2003—EMEA, The Hague, South Holland, The Netherlands.

Pratihar, D. K., & Jain, L. C. (2010). Toward Intelligent Autonomous Systems. In D. K. Pratihar & L. C. Jain (Eds.), *Intelligent Autonomous Systems: Foundations and Applications* (p. 1). Springer-Verlag Berlin Heideberg. doi:10.1007/978-3-642-11676-6_1

Pratt, M. K. (2017). *Why IT Projects Still Fail.* Retrieved July 2018, from https://www.cio.com.au/article/625522/why-it-projects-still-fail/

Project Management Institute. (2017). *A Guide to the Project Management Body of Knowledge (PMBOK® Guide)*. Project Management Institute.

Rebovich, G. Jr. (2014). *Systems Engineering Guide*. The MITRE Corporation.

Reese, H. (2016). *Top 10 AI failures of 2016*. Retrieved July 2018, from https://www.techrepublic.com/article/top-10-ai-failures-of-2016/

Satell, G. (2018). How to Make an AI Project More Likely to Succeed. *Harvard Business Review*, (July): 2018.

Sikdar, P. (2017). *Practitioner's Guide to Business Impact Analysis*. Auerbach Publications. doi:10.1201/9781315187884

Simonite, T. (2017, January). AI Software Learns to Make AI Software: Google and Others Think Software that Learns to Learn Could Take Over Some Work Done by AI Experts. *MIT Technology Review*.

Sommerville, I. (2015). *Software Engineering*. Pearson.

Verner, J., Sampson, J., & Cerpa, N. (2008). What Factors Lead to Software Project Failure? In *Proceedings of Second International Conference on Research Challenges in Information Science* (pp. 71-80). IEEE Xplore. 10.1109/RCIS.2008.4632095

Vincent, J. (2017). *Putin Says the Nation that Leads in AI 'Will be the Ruler of the World'*. Retrieved July 2018, from https://www.theverge.com/2017/9/4/16251226/russia-ai-putin-rule-the-world

Zerega, B. (2017). *AI Weekly: Google Shifts from Mobile-First to AI-First World.* Retrieved July 2018, from https://venturebeat.com/2017/05/18/ai-weekly-google-shifts-from-mobile-first-to-ai-first-world/

KEY TERMS AND DEFINITIONS

Artificial Intelligence (AI): A field of study that focuses on mimicking human thought and learning process by using computerized systems.

Autonomous System: A system that has ability to acquire input, analyze it, reason the result, and act automatically without human intervention.

Risk: An uncertainty that an interested event/activity will not meet expected outcome.

Risk Management: Process of identifying and assessing risks in order to develop strategies to manage risks.

Chapter 2
Scientific Intelligence, Decision Making, and Cyber-Security

Luisa Dall'Acqua
Scientific Lyceum TCO, Italy & University of Bologna, Italy

ABSTRACT

Because of the huge amount of data and information in the decision-making and strategic choices processes, basing decisions on information directly collected from the sources is not conceivable. A decision-making analyst becomes a fundamental pillar in both the corporate field and the institutional world. This role is becoming increasingly complex and specialized, critical within the cycle of the intelligence analysis, for the relationships that bind it to the other stakeholders, and for the methodological and technological tools that support it. The purpose of this chapter is to explore the milestones of the intelligence analysis deriving from a close collaboration between social sciences, cognitive science, computer engineering, and ICT in order to respond to the different needs in the field of risk management, safety, investigations, and applied intelligence.

DOI: 10.4018/978-1-5225-7903-8.ch002

INTRODUCTION

The Context

Governments as well as business organizations constantly make decisions under conditions of uncertainty. In the realm of security and foreign policy this poses a strong challenge. In order to increase the efficiency of policy-making, governments usually create dedicated entities for these tasks. These could be in-house research departments, automatic data collection systems or traditional intelligence agencies.

The States with advanced Intelligence organizations can be assumed to be more influential than states that lack this resource. Sometimes conflicts throughout history have been fuelled or even instigated by misconceptions and faulty evidence. That shows how much this resource can be crucial to guarantee a global sureness and stability (Fägersten, 2015).

In the actual globalized world, the safety finds its place in the natural/engineering sciences and medicine. The similar concept, security, is a key concept for social scientists (see figure 1): it refers to the prevention of intentional threats that may harm human beings, their possessions or 'acquired values'.

Most of the States of the world have placed the need to adapt the instruments for the protection of their global security, both internally and internationally, using ever more consistently, given the nature of the threat, incisive information research modality, necessary to guide choices and prevent risks.

Security efforts are targeted at different levels (Berg & Boss, 2014):

- *National security* at the level of states
- *Human security* at a sub-state level of individuals (Hampson, 2008)
- *Societal security* at a sub-state level of groups (Buzan et a. (1998)
- *World security* at the supra-state level of regions or even the entire globe (Booth, 2007)

The meaning of the national security concept varies according to the individual states and the changing of historical contexts.

This concept maintains its stability over time in countries of consolidated democratic tradition, with strong social cohesion, characterized by an intense sense of belonging of citizens to the institutions, to draw characteristics and boundaries. On the opposite, there are those situations in which conflicts emerge between legitimate powers, vulnerability, as well as historical conditions of separation between citizens and the political establishment.

Their likelihood of success depends on the ability to ensure continuous innovation, to adapt flexibly to the scenarios and to approach the result, in terms of security, so as the national community expects from the investment of its resources.

The choices concerning intelligence require wide sharing and concrete actions, first of all by the political decision-makers who are, for the functions that are competing, the policymakers and the first users of the product.

A public policy is based also on the decision-making analysis, a study of problematic situations characterized by complexity. Often by uncertainty comes from the difficulty to probabilistically establish the consequences of an action.

The analysis of decisions should consider all the elements of the process and all their possible complex combinations (Dente, 2014), so as A. Einstein meant stating "Make everything as simple as possible. But not simpler".

Today, big data can make the identification of unexpected, extrapolating and mutant events more difficult.

To date we have three heuristic strategies:

- **Paradigmatic (in the Sense of Kuhn):** It aims at identifying crisis situations: the greater the number of crises the more likely a "black swan" could be present. A black swan is an event or occurrence that deviates beyond what is normally expected of a situation and is extremely difficult to predict.
- **Legislation:** It refers to what should logically happen
- **Morphological***:* It refers to what could (possibly and not presumably) occur

The theory of games, cryptography, distributed networks: different concepts come together to give life to a series of rules that takes the name of "block-chain", a revolutionary technology that imposes a change of perspective in the basic logic that govern the military world, the finance, property, value, agreements, security, and many other aspects of our society. Applied to the Intelligence, it stands as a scientific and operational discipline (Calligiuri, 2016). destined to stabilize and harmonize political power.

A DEFINITION OF INTELLIGENCE

Several definitions of Intelligence were provided in different application contexts.

Technically, the term Intelligence means:

- The end product of an analytical process that: evaluates information gathered from different sources, integrates the relevant information into a

Figure 1. Security
(Freely retrieved from Berg, 2014)

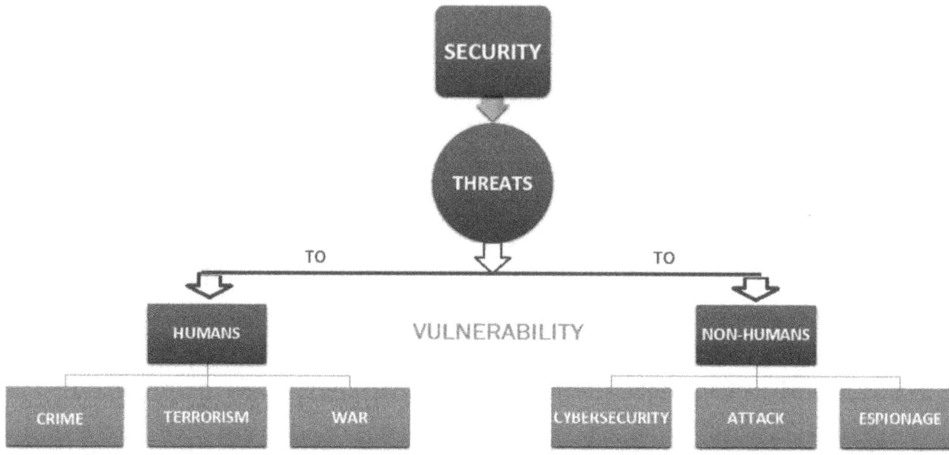

logical package, estimates and predicts actions, produces a conclusion of a phenomenon, using the scientific approach to problem solving (analysis)

- The value-added product resulting from the collection, evaluation, analysis, integration, and interpretation of all available information regarding one or more aspects of a decision-making need, and which is immediately or potentially significant for a decision-maker (Fleisher & Bensoussan, 2003)
- Analysis for a possible forecasting knowledge to let decision-makers choose and adopt the better strategy and, consequently to decide in a timely, convenient and effective manner. In this prospective vision, Intelligence facilitates and directs the choice of strategy and the decision-maker should be confident in it, adopting decisions consistent with the scenarios developed by the Intelligence Analyst (AA.VV, 2014)

According to the context:

- The search of secret information. This feature is less and less true with the advent of the new era of information where many of the secret information until some time ago are commercially available or even available on the Internet (Malfanti, 2005)
- The organization that works to produce and defend crucial knowledge for a State and all the activities carried out secretly by that organization (Malfanti, 2005)

- The information security activity, divided into several phases that take the name of the intelligence cycle
- Information for decision-makers, from business people to sports coaches to policymakers. As secret state activity, it's designed to understand or influence foreign entities (Treverton et al.,2006)
- the competitive intelligence applied to the business intelligence, investigative intelligence, political intelligence or applied to the fight against crime
- search and processing of news (on threats, dangers and opportunities) useful to support the political authority on the protection of the interests of the country
- a complex of activities carried out in relation to States, organizational structures and / or individuals, considered hostile, rival, competitive or otherwise of interest for the achievement of specific objectives, aimed at collecting, processing and disseminating information aimed at meeting the fundamental needs of knowledge (AA.VV, 2014)
- central and peripheral institutions and structures responsible for the development and conduct of informational activities (AA.VV, 2014)
- the institutional Intelligence, of the State, in which the information dealt with regards military matters or international politics

With the aim of protecting national security. the word intelligence has a double meaning:

- *Subjective*, which refers to the complex of structures and activities aimed at collecting useful information for the purposes of the protection of national security
- *Objective*, which refers to the product of this activity (the information) functional to support the decisions regarding the protection of the interests of a country. This is therefore an important activity aimed at protecting: the independence, integrity, and sovereignty of a State, the democratic institutions posed by the founding constitution, the international profile of the State, the fundamental freedoms and the rights of the citizens (constitutionally guaranteed), as well as all the international political, military, economic, scientific and industrial sectors (Malfanti, 2005)

Some possible explanatory variables are:

- Political bureaucracy (i.e. Inter-agency relationships)
- Organization theory: risk management, routinized procedures, promotion of specific types of analysis
- Psychological factors (cognitive dissonance and other biases)
- Historical contingency
- Technological change
- Demands from politicians and policymakers
- Threat perceptions, internal vs. external threats, changes in the international system

THE INTELLIGENCE ANALYST

The analyst is the figure who takes care of transforming raw data, collected through the various information channels. The product is a material suitable for being understood and used by the management level, that is, those figures that, within an organization, dealing with defining strategies or making choices.

The abundance of data dramatically increases the methodological and technological notions that the analyst must have available in order to carry out his work in a profitable way. In this context, the institutional world has matured the conscious need for a "new central figure of the analyst (which is clearly distinguished from the traditional investigative agent in terms of the skills possessed, as well as the location and assigned organizational tasks)" (Pollari, 2001).

The analysis is a process that uses scientific and non-scientific methods, mixing intuition and experience, mathematical models and computer simulations, common sense and formal methodology.

In synthesis, the analyst is who transforms information into Intelligence, deals with organizing, verifying and making information easily comprehensible (Malfanti, 2005).

The product of the Intelligence, elaborated by the analyst, is oriented to different areas of interpretation, which deals with Competitive Intelligence, are (Herring, 1996).:

- Preventing surprises to the membership organization by providing early warnings services
- Supporting decision making
- Identifying and keeping competitors in check

- Helping develop strategies
- Playing a key role in gathering and reporting information

In the institutional world, other aspects are (Shulsky & Schmitt, 2002):

- *Indication and Warnings*, to identify the precursors and signals precursors of dangers and threats
- *Current Intelligence*, representation of the state of the Intelligence updated on time
- *Basic Intelligence,* representation of knowledge concerning the most disparate topics that may affect the organization of belonging
- *Periodic Reports,* state-of-the-art regarding antagonistic organizations (or nations)
- *Intelligence Estimates,* the forecast intelligence able to design future developments allowing the development of strategic plans

The process of analysis must develop according to three distinct moments: description, explanation and prediction (Bontempi, 2003). These three phases, the same as those of the scientific method, make it possible to explain the assumptions, to identify laws and correlations and finally to formulate theories.

The fundamental difference between the work of scientific research and that of Intelligence analysis lies in the approach, generalist in the first case and analytic of the particular in the second.

The role of the analyst is an integral part of the so-called Cycle of Intelligence.

INTELLIGENCE CYCLE

The purpose of a theoretical model of the intelligence cycle is to aid understanding of the logic of the process and introduce the varied activities that contribute to intelligence production.

The intelligence process is cyclic in nature, since intelligence requires constant review and updating if it is to remain current and relevant to the decision-maker's needs. It is a cycle because there is no solution of continuity between the response to needs and the new request for information deriving from the previous elaboration. It consists of planning, collection, processing, analysis, and dissemination stages.

Starting for simplicity from the request phase, decision makers, politicians or companies, determine a demand based on their strategic needs

After a planning phase in which information acquisition strategies are decided, a more or less secret and more or less risky collection phase follows, depending on whether we are talking about military plans or marketing plans, information same. Once the necessary information has been obtained, we continue with the analysis and production phase of the real intelligence, which will be distributed at this point, first of all to the applicants but also to all the other structures that are supposed to can take advantage of it (Malfanti, 2005).

Cycle of Intelligence describes the complex of the phases in which the information security activity is articulated, from the indications of the Government Authorities to the dissemination of intelligence products to institutional users, passing through information planning, information research and processing (AA.VV, 2012).

The intelligence cycle drives the day-to-day activities of the intelligence community (IC). It starts with the needs intelligence 'consumers' – that is, policymakers, military officials, and other decision makers who need intelligence information in conducting their duties and responsibilities. These needs – also referred to as intelligence requirements – are sorted and prioritized within the IC and drive the collection activities of the members of the IC. Once information has been collected, it is processed, initially evaluated, and reported to both consumers and 'all-source' intelligence analysts at agencies like the CIA, DIA, and State Department Bureau of Intelligence and Research. All-source analysts are responsible for performing a more thorough evaluation and assessment of the collected information by integrating the data obtained from a variety of collection agencies and sources, both classified and unclassified (Goldman, 2011).

The general steps of tasking are: planning, collecting, processing, analyzing, and disseminating intelligence (see Figure 2). The Intelligence Analyst participates in the cycle at various points, not only in the obvious phase of analysis and reporting, but also in the planning phase, determining the type of analysis required and in the data collection phase determining the type of information necessary for that specific problem.

Planning and Direction

When we are tasked with a specific job, we begin planning what we'll do and how. We move in a specific direction to get the job done, listing what we know about the issue and what we need to find out. We discuss ways to gather the necessary intelligence.

Once the objectives set out, how to get the information is planned, a planning and organizational resources to obtain accurate occurs. The strategic areas are set by identifying and ranking in priority levels of the policy areas of service and what information is desired, so set by the heads of the intelligence service and political bodies and, where appropriate, military they serve. The type and content of information that is available and the availability and reliability of sources and channels of communication is studied. At this stage in the same way the participation of commanders and intelligence chiefs required and follow the guidelines of the security policy and military of the Force, Agency and Nation. It is required to be aligned with the national strategy (Escuela de las Américas. Inteligencia de Combate, n.d.).

Collection

Collection management is the process that aligns intelligence needs with information collection and processing capabilities and assets within the various intelligence collection disciplines.

Decision-maker collects information overtly (openly) and covertly (secretly). Reading foreign newspapers and magazine articles, listening to foreign radio, and watching overseas television broadcasts are examples of "overt" (or open) sources

Figure 2. The intelligence cycle

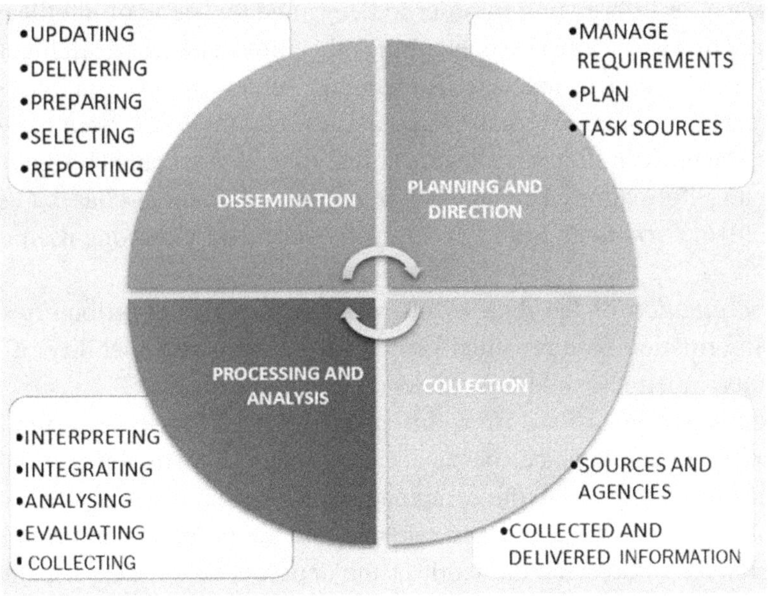

for us. Other information sources can be "covert" (or secret). such as information collected with listening devices and hidden cameras. We can even use space-age technology like satellite photography. For instance, some analysts could actually view how many airplanes are present at a foreign military base by looking at a picture taken from a satellite in space (The Intelligence Cycle, n.d.).

The collection management process answers the needs of intelligence consumers while making the most economical and effective use of intelligence collection resources. As such, collection management has two distinct functions:

- Collection Resource Management;
- Collection Operations Management.

Collection resource management aligns intelligence needs and priorities with available resources while considering budgetary constraints. On the other hand, collection operations management assigns specific collection tasks to a specific intelligence discipline or a specific system in order to make the most economic and effective use of the collection assets available.

Analysis and Processing

It is the step by which intelligence is produced from data information. It consists of three steps: (1) recording of information for comparison with other items by hand; (2) assessment of information in order to determine the value of intelligence; and (3) interpretation of information concerning other information and intelligence hand in order to reach a conclusion as to its meaning. All this involves an assessment of all resources: decisions, external events, issues, geographical, political, cultural, economic, scientific, military, strategic or biographical, that cannot be ignored when dealing with information. The analysis is performed in three phases (Velanquez Hurtado, 2016; *Escuela de las Américas. Inteligencia de Combate*, n.d.):

- The *evaluation* of the data is to discriminate which contribute to meeting the information requirements formulated in terms of reliability of sources, validity, timeliness, relevance, relevance and usefulness.
- The *integration* of data from different sources is based on a fundamental principle of intelligence: never accept a single information authority. It is getting a synergy where the combination of information from different means of obtaining a whole is most relevant and scope of the information each separately. To describe the work of the departments of analysis. Integration can be a daunting and complex task when data from numerous sources have

varied, so it is necessary to provide that much data and documents submitted to the lower levels of protection are spread horizontally among other analysts and departments.

- The *interpretation* of the data, with the dual aim of determining what is accurate and what is relevant to meet the political needs, which are usually alike, explanation and understanding of the phenomenon analyzed as a forecast about its consequences and predictable evolution. The interpretation is the task of experts in the field of analysis (politics, economics, technology, military, and terrorism) possesses both knowledge and sufficient capacity for imagination and creativity to relate data, predicts events, and get into the mind of enemy.

Dissemination

The next phase of the intelligence cycle is diffusion or dissemination and use of intelligence, which is the result of all intelligence activities. To be useful, it must be reported properly and in time the commander, his older and to those who need state (*Escuela de las Américas. Inteligencia de Combate*, n.d.).

After reading the final analysis and learning the answer to the original question, the policymaker may come back with more questions. Then the whole process starts over again.

The "Analytic Thinking and Presentation for Intelligence Producers" Guideline draws a detail of the requisites needed to prepare a presentation that correctly summarizes the activity carried out. from the analyst in the previous phases of work (Analytic thinking and presentation for intelligence producers, , n.d.). The presentation according to the manual can be enriched by rewarding moments if it becomes an instrument for the analyst to assert his abilities in public.

The fundamental concepts highlighted in the manual are directly linked to the needs of the decision-making level to which the presentation will be exposed. Depending on these needs, the following conditions emerge: to be able to read the presentation in a format already known to avoid distracting attention from the content; having very little time available and inversely proportional to the importance of the content.

Nothing should be left to chance but every single element will be evaluated and defined; the right importance must be given to the graphic image through the use of multimedia tools that support and summarize the textual content and the exhaustiveness of the texts that represent the concise verbalization of the analysis phases performed by the analyst. On the other hand, a different attitude must be taken when the analyst's work proves to be useful not only for the decision maker who requested it, but also for other branches of the company or institution.

Some Debates

There are debates about the problems of substance and form that in any case lead to faults and failures of intelligence, to misuse and misunderstanding of the phases that make up the intelligence cycle. It brings to light the weaknesses and problems that exist within the intelligence cycle to date, showing and evidencing the lack of knowledge and awareness, as well as obsolescence of existing operational environment in the 21st century (Velanquez Hurtado, 2016). Here, some examples.

In his text "Sherman Kent and the profession of intelligence analysis", Davis contextualizes a historical concept, about intelligence, in the document the author allows to have a deeper and updated vision of the work done by Kent, and his contributions to intelligence and analyzing information to get to turn it into intelligence (Davis, 2002). Kent developed the process of the intelligence cycle, and deeply ideas about analyzing the information. Moreover, the author talk about Kent's during his work in intelligence and different works done in the intelligence structures, owing to which nowadays Sherman Kent is called the father of intelligence. The text provides a thorough analysis of the main problems that the cycle has, since the world and intelligence are evolved in the digital age.

Hulnick, a former agent of the CIA and analyst in the US air force, describes drawbacks, problems, weaknesses and vices that are typical of the intelligence and the current cycle of intelligence, talks about the problems that are typical of planning, collection and analysis information, the barriers that exist in the cycle and intelligence, also plays with the themes of counterintelligence, and covert operations arguing not to be parts of the cycle and the process (Hulnick, 2006).

Duyvesteyn et al studied the future of intelligence and the end of the current intelligence cycle, weaknesses and problems presented for decision making, analysis and production of intelligence. They explain major issues such as the importance of technology with the intelligence, this is presented as one of the threats in this new age of technological knowledge and the same time the advantages to produce intelligence with the use of technology and information systems alongside the cyberspace and the web, that are weapons and tools to strengthen the processes and the intelligence cycle, serving as tools to be used as an opportunity to face the different threats that has the intelligence and will confront in the future (Duyvesteyn et al, 2014)

Evans, a renowned British researcher of military studies and defence, provides the evidence of the weaknesses that exist within the intelligence cycle and the relationship between commanders and their staffs, with the stages of the intelligence cycle, providing comparison between failure and success of intelligence operations related to the use of the intelligence cycle which has been observed. Likewise, errors that are committed in planning and the relationship between the appreciations of the commanders as well as the results of the analyses delivered by the members of staffs are described; also, the author of the book speaks about changes in the operational environment within the context of the new information age (Evans, 2009).

Phythian analyzes the concept of the intelligence cycle shows its nature and different characteristics possessed by the intelligence and the process of the intelligence cycle, showing the importance of the cycle in the evolution of intelligence for many years. Then describes different types of intelligence that currently exist and how they are related to the process of collection and analysis of information that is used in intelligence, demonstrating a better way to use computer networks and the cyberspace in the current intelligence. On the other hand, he also makes a comparison between private, business and military sectors, describing their characteristics, advantages, and disadvantages and uses. The author together with other experts prove that the intelligence needs to evaluate the use of intelligence technology systems to take advantage in this age and puts the idea in the context of the death of the intelligence cycle (Phythian, 2013).

Keen focuses on the use of analysis systems of information and its importance in helping to understand and analyze the data that analysts receive in all fields of intelligence. Here the complex processes that possess the collection of information are described for its subsequent analysis where the information is surpassing the mental capacities of analysts and operators that are facing the problem of analyzing the amount of information that exists since the time when technological knowledge has opened the spectrum of the flow of information through computer networks. The paradox of man vs. machine is exposed, where a human being is limited by multiple characteristics of human nature, and the machine serves as an aid to support the understanding of the vast multitude of existing information. The needs that require intelligence and the cycle to lean on technology, using information analysis systems and other developments, are shown. Is studied, the complexity of the cycle is studied, to support the intelligence activity in the management of intelligence to decision-making (Keen, 1977) .

Puong Fei Yeh states that the increase in the use of technologies and systems for data collection, data analysis and mining information, which allows to process, filter, and disseminate the intelligence information, leave the evidence of the need to merge the capacities of computer systems, such as autonomous systems, robots, software analysis and other applications, with the knowledge and rationing of analysts or agents who work on intelligence.The internet of things is something that proves that everything is situated connected to a network or signal, which is controlled or analyzed by a system of technological information, where it is known that there are threats and vulnerabilities that may affect our organizations (Puong Fei Yeh, 2015).

AN OVERVIEW OF THE INTELLIGENCE COLLECTION

In the world of intelligence, the term "source" indicates any source of information, meaning that the human informant or the company database, as well as satellite photography or telephone interception, are indicated with the same generic term. For historical reasons, on the other hand, the source was above all the informant or the infiltrator in the enemy camp, when this was the only way to obtain information from the opposing camp.

In a wide range of sources, intelligence information is usually categorized in terms of various "INTs" around the world. They can be the main types:

- **HUMINT (HUMan INTelligence):** The historical figure of the informant is more institutionally
- **TECHINT (TECHnical INTelligence):** A wide variety of these sources, the intelligence collected through technological means
- **OSINT (Open Source INTelligence):** Another fundamental constituent source, the analysis of open sources, which takes into account all the information available on the network, in the press, on databases and which is available anyway of anyone.

Human Intelligence (HUMINT)

Human intelligence (HUMINT) is derived from human sources. It can refer to the clandestine acquisition of photography, documents, and other materials, by personnel in diplomatic and consular posts; debriefing of foreign nationals and citizens who travel abroad; and official contacts with foreign governments.

Figure 3. Intelligence collection sources

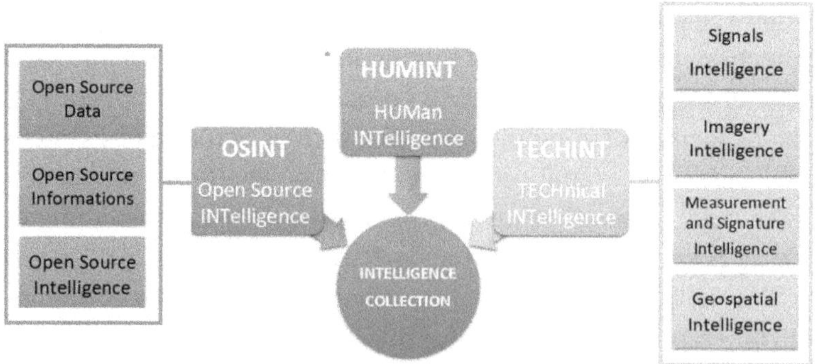

Historically HUMINT was the only source of all the Intelligence collected, from historical times up to the forties of the last century. It still remained the main source until the eighties.

All espionage, first among the allies and the Nazi bloc and then between the two blocks of the Cold War, was based on the figure of the informant, the defector, and the infiltrator.

In the new fight between the Western bloc and the world of Islamic religious fanaticism or international terrorism, it is no longer possible to think of easily infiltrating a terrorist group often based on family or tribal ties or to convince people who are deeply motivated by religious convictions.

In the case of industrial espionage, however, HUMINT remains one of the cornerstones of information gathering, both through direct contact with the employee from the "enemy" company and through the work of people who, despite being unrelated to the company, have easy access to data, such as cleaning staff or IT consultants.

Many studies have been carried out, both social and psychological, to identify and classify the salient characteristics that make the human nature more or less prone to "betrayal". Undoubtedly, a very detailed picture of the potential agent is necessary in order to identify potentialities and gaps (Malfanti, 2005)..

From this point of view, L. Longo defined a method, called I.B.A., through which all the information necessary to frame the operator is formalized. In particular, the physical and aesthetic characteristics, the state of health, the personal and family history, character and temperament, ideological assumptions, social behavior and habits, work and the social environment are analyzed. For each of these characteristics, a detailed list of the information to be acquired is presented, giving a complete picture of the "spy" profile (Longo, 2003).

Technical Collection Methods and Technologies (TECHINT)

The gathering of information through technological tools began during the First World War with the first aerial photographs of the enemy camp and continued its run up to the present day, becoming the first source of supply. The progress of technology then opened up other avenues for information gathering, and the simultaneous transfer of communication over electronic or digital media did the rest.

Nowadays, any human communication is virtually interceptable and can be acquired by anyone. The problem is how to deal with the huge amount of data collected and how to identify important information.

The only means of contrast with the interception of communications is the use of encryption mechanisms, which at least can make the acquisition of information more difficult. The new mechanisms of quantum encryption would also allow highlighting the successful interception of the message, thus making the interception itself useless.

In the last thirty years, especially by the great US intelligence agencies, there has been a huge increase in the importance attributed to TECHINT, with the conviction of being able to discover and predict everything with the analysis of photos and communications.

Unfortunately, neither the aerial photos nor the telephone tapping and other communications has succeeded in giving indications on Iraqi mass destruction weapons or on the 9/11 attack (Malfanti, 2005)..

Techint includes (Phythian, 2013):

- **Signals Intelligence (SIGINT):** The Intelligence of the interception of the signal (and therefore of the communications). It comprises:
    - Communications intelligence (COMINT)
    - Electronic intelligence (ELINT)
    - Foreign instrumentation signals intelligence (FISINT)"

One of the limitations of SIGINT is to be now drowned by an enormous amount of signal and information that can need a further strong investment on the technologies of classification and cataloging of the information thus obtained, as well as on the human resources required to translate and understand the ultimate meaning of what is intercepted.

- **Imagery Intelligence (IMINT):** It includes representations of objects reproduced electronically or by optical means on film, electronic display devices, or other media. Imagery can be derived from visual photography, radar sensors, infrared sensors, lasers, and electro-optics.
- **Measurement and Signature Intelligence (MASINT):** It is intelligence data technically derived from different images than SIGINT. It employs a broad group of disciplines including nuclear, optical, radio frequency, acoustics, seismic, and materials sciences.
- **Geospatial Intelligence (GEOINT):** It is the analysis and visual representation of security-related activities on Earth. It is produced through an integration of imagery, imagery intelligence, and geospatial information.

The management systems, storage, analysis, data transmission and protection of digital and computer information are in constant development; they are moving exponentially and delivering even greater benefits to intelligence.

The huge amounts of existing data that must be handled by intelligence agencies have opened a world of possibilities in terms of resources, sources and solutions that enable better analysis and better communication channels.

There are a number of tools, both methodological and technological, that facilitate the analyst's work, especially in situations where the data collected are insufficient or overabundant. Obviously, the methodologies and the technological tools only support to the activity of the analyst, who must, however, base his own choices and decisions on his own critical capacity.

Undoubtedly, any methodology cannot improve the quality of the information in use, but can instead help to identify errors or gaps in the information itself.

Analytical methodologies are systematic criteria established and refined over time to manage and organize information in order to develop knowledge and make decisions. These are methodologies that range from a simple classification of events to the use of computer programs for the development of scenarios.

Criteria

According to a modern school of thought (Fleisher & Bensoussan, 2003). the different methodologies can be classified according to six fundamental characteristics:

- **Orientation to the Future:** History does not help to predict the future and an analysis based on the experience of the past can be absolutely meaningless. A good methodology must open new perspectives, looking deeply into the future.
- **Accuracy:** The analyst must produce an Intelligence that is as accurate as possible. The level of accuracy derives in particular from the quality of the data and information obtained during the previous phases of the Intelligence production process.
- **Efficient Exploitation of Resources:** Data collection must be carried out in such a way that the costs relating to this criterion are considered to be less than the benefits that may derive from it. For example, the timing that data collection needs can be not comparable with the urgent needs expressed by decision makers.

- **Objectivity:** Often the analysis activity is influenced by preconditions related to the environment and to the organization in which the analyst moves. The analyst should nullify these influences.
- **Utility:** By definition, the analyst's work should respond to the needs expressed by the decision-making level, in a particular context. A useful methodological aid should help the analyst produce outputs related to "things necessary to know" compared to "useful things to know".
- **Currency:** It concerns the production of outcome in time for the application of the resultants.

Within the sphere of institutional intelligence, the simplest methodologies to reduce complexity to easily manageable dimensions are those of ordered classification, chronologically, or by source or by an event in order to allow an easy comprehension of the relations of cause and effect.

Techniques

Numerous analytical methods have been developed in the economic intelligence field, most of which are based on macro and microeconomic data that can be grouped into five broad categories (Malfanti, 2005) (see Figure 4):

- **Strategic Analytical Techniques:** It is the analysis of the capabilities of an organization, the aims of the organization itself and the characteristics

Figure 4. Criteria and techniques

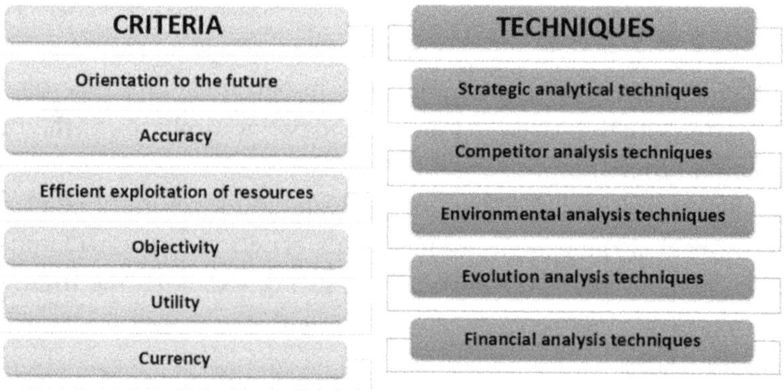

of the environment in which the organization moves in order to determine its strategic planning. An example is the "SWOT analysis" which takes into account Strengths (strengths) and Weaknesses (weaknesses) of an organization comparing them with Opportunities (opportunities) and Threats (threats) offered by the surrounding environment.

- **Competitor Analysis Techniques:** These methodologies concern the value chain in terms of supply and necessity, trying to identify inconsistencies or gaps to be exploited strategically by the organization conducting the analysis.
- **Environmental Analysis Techniques:** This analysis is carried out observing external elements, considering how these elements can play an active role in the evolution of a situation and elaborating strategies that can take into account the presence of external constraints taking advantage of them.
- **Evolution Analysis Techniques:** Through these techniques the rules that describe the life of events, products or technologies apply to predict possible scenarios in which context potential can be highlighted.
- **Financial Analysis Techniques:** They concern the financial status of the organizations are used to indicate which strategic investments may be, separating them from operational management in order to determine the optimal management of funds according to the expected growth.

The technological tools available to the analyst are basically of two types:

- those necessary *for understanding* data and information (such as software for decryption or for the acquisition of images and texts).
- those used for the active search *for useful information* within large amounts of data such as data warehouse, data mining or text mining tools (Knowledge Discovery tools). They allow highlighting relationships or behaviors within large amounts of data.

Open Source Intelligence (OSINT)

According to a definition widely accepted in doctrine, the term OSINT is intended to describe the information available and open to public access, which has undergone a process of research, selection, sorting and reporting to a specific recipient in order to meet a defined need information.

The analyst at this stage of data collection, and therefore of interaction with sources in the broad sense, takes on a dual role. First it has the task of determining the type of data necessary and the way of collecting the data itself, then, once the information has been collected, the actual analysis work begins, ie the transformation of the information into Intelligence, or information validated, interpreted and ready to be passed to the political level or company guidance.

Obviously, at this stage, the analyst's work is assisted by specialized personnel and by tools or methodologies that allow him to carry out his / her task in the best possible way (Malfanti, 2005).. In the case of information from open sources, the problems are related to the overabundance of data, which often makes it difficult, if not impossible, to retrieve the desired information. However, several tools have been implemented to help the analyst in his task, from the tools of DataWareHouse to Data Mining and Text Mining.

Open sources, obviously, do not allow access to secret information, which is the real purpose of Intelligence, but often allow to determine scenarios or have indirect confirmations.

Among the open sources it is necessary to make a precise distinction between the types and processes available (Massa, 2015):

- Open Source Data, a complex area of primary reference sources, such as photographs, images, documents, audio and video recordings, satellite images, oral debriefing, etc.
- Open Source Informations, secondary raw data emerged and appropriately filtered by the analysis of OSD data. They are generally composed of raw data that can be agglomerated, generally with an editing process.
- Open Source Intelligence, information derived from a voluntary process of analysis, filtering, distillation and dissemination to a specific selected category, suitable to meet particular information needs, using its own Intelligence processes.

In the OSINT process, in other words, proven intelligence techniques apply to the wide variety of open sources of information. For example a meaningful article in an online newspaper (OSI) is used to support a military operation. A photo accompanying the article may be useful for identifying the location of the insurgents geographically and could be used to support a tailor-made operation to attack the rebels.

Specifically, a Validate Open Source Intelligence (OSINT-V) is information that has been given a high degree of certainty. It can only be produced by an Intelligence All Source analyst with access to even classified sources working for a government or coalition of nations. This information is considered validated when there is no official confirmation of non-truthfulness coming from classified sources.

CYBER-INTELLIGENCE AND SECURITY

The information is a fundamental pillar in intelligence work. It flows and moves in the cyberspace, so the management needs be framed within a process that fully involves the use of computer systems that operate into cyberspace.

The cyberspace has delivered a new operational environment to intelligence agencies, since, through its enormous capacity for global information flow, it has placed the intelligence into uncharted territory but with great potential for the use and application of intelligence in the 21century.

The cyberspace requires that the intelligence adapt this environment, and, therefore, the intelligence process must change and project itself as a technological intelligence process, leading to the integration of man and machine in function to obtaining the results that will lead to success, both operational and strategic. The new intelligence process is clearly explained and tuned to existing technological capabilities, where the systems of collection, analysis, projection and dissemination of the intelligence information would be integrated in an agile, confident and secure way in all fields and with all types of intelligence (Ciluffo & Cardash, 2013).

The Cyber Intelligence increases its importance in this new age of technological development since its proper use allows obtaining strategic results without the use of large resources, achieving savings of resources and efforts to the defense. It permits treatment of the intelligence available more clear, precise, fast and potentially successful for the fulfillment of the objective. In cyber intelligence, two opposite but indispensable logics coexist: on the one hand the intelligence of events, a purely human talent, on the other the technologies, which are part of our way of life, conditioning and perceiving reality.

Caligiuri correctly sees a close relationship between Intelligence, as a preventive activity, and prediction, but it is with cyber-Intelligence that the forecasting activity acquires an empirical basis made possible by big data. They contain volumes of news that can be calculated in exabytes (up to 10 at the 18th power and further expandable). It is no longer necessary to know the causes for practical and forecasting purposes, but only "what". Forecasting activity tends to become a-causal (Caligiuri, 2016).

But Cyberspace also expands exponentially the risk and latent threats to information and intelligence agencies. Information systems, infrastructures, information are interconnected and vulnerable to attacks of all kinds.

That is why any country or institution must have a cyber defense strategy; responsible for stipulating and address the protection of cyberspace (Eom et al, 2012).

In the strategy of cyber defense, the counterintelligence as part of intelligence is responsible for protecting and developing all kinds of protection activities. It must be oriented with the cybersecurity, to vanify the most of existing vulnerabilities and clearly identify the latent risks, as each of the threats, potential and existing, which the intelligence and information have.

Cybersecurity and counterintelligence, strengthened and technologically advanced, further shielding the intelligence process where information becomes the main asset of value, so should join the whole process of intelligence (Velanquez Hurtado, 2016).

In the last decades, companies, civil, governmental and military organizations all over the world are fighting cyber-conflicts daily within Cyberspace. The dynamism and ambiguity of cyber-attacks, constantly evolving, impose the adoption of new techniques, methodologies and skills analized to the contrast of the threats present on the Internet. They are defensive / offensive tools that can not disregard the search and continuous acquisition of online information regarding the peculiarities of the opponents.

In this scenario, cybernetic espionage and counter-espionage play a fundamental role in protecting the integrity of information assets.

Every day cyber-attacks are reported from different sources. What we know is that cyberspace is an ideal place for criminal activities and that you can not reach a total level of Cyber-Security. The cyber-criminals have in fact time and resources to plan a targeted attack, and very often manage to infiltrate the network exploiting a minimum vulnerability, remaining hidden for a long time to identify the opportunities for attack, are invisible in the network for many months. Their actions are hidden in the enormity of the data that cross the company's IT infrastructure.

Cyber-Crimes

The so-called cyber-criminals include a phenomenology that is much diversified.

The more common figure is a hacker, referred to subjects with special technical skills so high as to be able to break into computer systems, able to commit any type of crime.

The identification of the author of these crimes is particularly difficult because it is indeed possible to erase the traces of his action, use any computer and maintain anonymity using pseudonyms or false information.

The authors of the computer crimes are distinguished in Berg and Keymolen (2017):

- **Insider:** They exploit the knowledge of the computer systems of the institution or company in which they work to commit a crime (the most frequent are computer fraud, the damage of computer equipment, the theft of information).
- **Outsiders:** They use the technique of social engineering, pretending to someone else, through elephone or modem, in order to receive information, or spoofing, which consists in pretending to be a person authorized to operate within the institution or company in order to request password and username to the system administrator.

The types of computer crime most frequently committed by these subjects are industrial espionage, sabotage, computer terrorism and credit card scams and ATM. The techniques used range from interception of data through sniffer or vampires to the diversion of the data in favor of another account.

This crime is very dangerous because it is characterized by premeditation and a distorted perception of the seriousness of the crime.

Depending on objectives and methods of execution, it is possible to identify three types of hackers:

- **Hackers:** Those who show their skill in introducing into hardly penetrable systems
- **Crackers:** Those whose sole objective is destruction or serious damage computer systems or sites through the introduction of viruses
- **Hackers of Different Connotations:** Such as lucrative hackers, techno vandals, the cyber-terrorists and the lammers (those who use programs made by real hackers).

Hacker profiling deals with the analysis and constitution of the personal, socio-demographic profiles, character and psychological characteristics of the organizers of a cyber attack. In a time like the one we live in, where everything is technological, new pathologies have been born linked precisely to the use of technology, such as for example, technostress and technophobia, ie disorders in which the difficulty of cohabiting with the technological means leads to a control of the impulses.

On the basis of the psychological aspects and the motivations that drive them to act, it is possible to distinguish hackers in 5 categories:

- **Casual Hackers:** They tend to be motivated by curiosity and gratification of an attack
- **Political Hackers:** They militate in favor of a cause and their attacks, as well as their knowledge and experience, they are motivated by the adherence to an ideal.
- **Organized Crime:** Consists of professional experts who therefore hardly leave traces of their work and whose motivations have essentially an economic nature
- **Squatters:** They are characterized by the impersonality of their attacks as their goals they are often independent of the recipient and the identity of the attacked system owner, the motivations that drive the IT attack, in fact, tend to be games, with not necessarily criminal purposes.

In general, computer forensics indicates the technical-investigative activity aimed at identifying, acquiring, preserving, managing, analyzing and interpreting of digital traces, found within computers or electronic devices, as well as their own correlation to the facts, to the circumstances, to the hypotheses and to the traces of any nature, discovered or however, afferent to the fact investigated (Tonellotto, 2014).

It is therefore indisputable that the purpose of information technology forensic is also the interpretation of the data present on computers, without however being limited to one simple systematic engineering analysis, but taking into account all the context investigated, the acquired clues, the elements, and hypotheses formulated in the course of the investigations.

Correlating then the various elements it is possible to contextualize the information data, making it a source of evidence that can be used in an intelligence investigation.

Traces detected on a computer do not always make it possible to base an accusation about the commission of an IT crime by virtue of the possibility of remaining in the typical anonymity of Internet; however, at the same time, the Internet presents the second side of the coin almost total impossibility of completely erasing the traces of his conduct.

The objective of the digital forensic investigator is precisely to identify, acquire, analyze and correlate the IT data with all the elements, both tangible and intangible, collected during the surveys, therefore the IT skills need to be combined high investigative skills.

The technical skills will then be used in the analysis of the main features of the information technology, highlighting, for example, operating systems, programs, dates of use by the various users, dates of last access and last shutdown, the presence of systems conditional access, updates downloaded to the system and the presence of antivirus and so Street.

The first actions of the European legislator aimed at providing a regulatory framework for the fight of computer crimes dating back to almost thirty years ago. In particular, the first provision in computer crime is issued in 1989 by *The European Committee on Crime Problems* (CDPC) in the form of Recommendation No. 9 on the crime.

This Recommendation, despite being a non-binding act for the Member States containing the simple invitation to comply with it, however, is a starting point for the legislation on the matter as it has elaborated a dual type of cybercrime, on the basis of which, for example, Italy issued Law 547/93.

The second Recommendation in 1995, No. 133, concerned the procedures to be followed at various levels in cases of crimes committed within the Information Technology. It expresses the relative concern, on the one hand, to the risk that electronic systems information can be used to commit crimes and, from the other to the lack of forecast, within the legal systems of the Member States, such appropriate powers to gather evidence during the investigations.

The Recommendation affirms the importance of adopting a regulatory framework which allows the investigating authorities to make use of all the technical measures necessary for allowing the collection of data traffic in the investigation of serious confidentiality offenses, integrity and security of IT communications.

Cyberterrorism

Scholars that are interested in understanding terrorism, study the reasons why people become terrorists. Why or how they radicalize for instance, and which factors play a role in their choice to conduct terrorist attacks.

Terrorism is a form of intentional harm that is generated willfully, and consciously by individuals against others. Here too the risk is generated, actively initiated by human actors.

Terrorist organizations have evolved exploiting the computerization of the most technologically advanced countries. In the academic field, according to international institutional sources, it is possible to find two main orientations regarding the problem of a definition of cyber-terrorism.

- **Target-Oriented Cyberterrorism:** The network is intended as a target and as a weapon, it consists in attacks or threats of attacks against computers, networks and information stored therein, in order to intimidate or force a government or its population to behave in order to achieve political effects or social, or in acts that block or destroy computerized nodes of critical infrastructures such as the Internet, telecommunications, electricity networks, the banking system, etc.
- **Tool-Oriented Cyberterrorism:** The network is intended primarily as a tool and as a support. It, therefore, consists of operations conducted on the Web and politically motivated with the aim of causing serious consequences, such as loss of life or substantial economic damage, or terror. The network, therefore, represents a support allowing to carry out all the activities related to the management and survival of the terrorist organization, such as propaganda, fundraising, communication, organization, and recruitment.

The phenomenon of Cyberterrorism is becoming increasingly dangerous: It is anonymous, can be conducted at a distance, has an impressive amount of objectives available, makes recruitment and fundraising easy, it can strike, even if not always in a lethal way, an extremely large number of objectives and, finally, is able to generate a much greater coverage by the media

Chulki J and Sungjin A. describe a variety of serious security incidents occur and appropriate educational environment to develop the information security management system. They apply a learning environment model to enhance the level of data protection and information security management and direction of efforts to find ways to improve the model for improvement to propose (Chulki & Sungjin, 2014) .

CONCLUSION

This work wanted to describe the milestone of an Intelligence Analysis, to better profile the involved professional as well as the field of applications.

Intelligence supports national security planning, diplomacy, homeland security, and enforcement of our laws (George & Rishikoc, 2011).

In addressing national security decision making, of which intelligence is a significant component, what former national security advisor, Lt. Gen. Brent Scowcroft, wrote after the collapse of the Soviet Union, still applies today: "Today the problem is much harder than it was during the Cold War. Then, we faced a single overriding challenger, a reality that shaped the world and our policies. Globalization is eroding borders and individual states' abilities to manage transnational challenges such as financial crises, environmental damage, networked terrorists, and international crime, to name a few" (George&Rishikoc, 2011).

Over time, scholars in the field of security studies started to broaden the scope of their field of study in two ways. Originally, the field focused almost exclusively on the role of nation-states in generating and dealing with security risks. Nowadays, it also studies the role of other levels of government, and it studies the ways in which large corporations, or even groups of citizens, or individuals can shape security risks.

Besides the traditional tracking of foreign military capabilities and scrutiny of foreign government intentions, intelligence is used for the new problem sets of the twenty-first century (nuclear proliferation, terrorism, failing states, cyber threats, global warming, and the international economic reshuffle).

Usually, the fruits of intelligence collection and analysis remain unknown to the public at large. Intelligence analysts work for a variety of organizations, most notably federal government agencies in all the world.

The tasks involved in this line of work entail extensive research into and collection of information from many sources. Intelligence analysts then sort, target, and identify relevant data, which is reported to key officials. In many cases, military experience is either required or highly desired. But engineering and scientific backgrounds, mathematics, hard sciences, information technology and languages are especially important; as well people with skills in languages; chemical, biological and nuclear information technology, skills in cybersecurity and law enforcement. For many agencies, a background in political science, criminal justice, psychology, or regional studies can be useful.

REFERENCES

AA.VV. (2012). *Glossario Intelligence: il linguaggio degli organismi informativi*. Retrieved from: http://silendo.org/2012/07/05/glossario-intelligence-il-linguaggio-degli-organismi-informativi/

AA.VV. (2014). *Lezioni sull'Intelligence, Sistema di informazione per la Sicurezza della Repubblica*. Retreived from: https://www.sicurezzanazionale.gov.it/sisr.nsf/wp-content/uploads/2014/05/lezione-intelligence.pdf

Analytic thinking and presentation for intelligence producers. (n.d.). Retrieved from: https://ia800201.us.archive.org/23/items/CIA_Analytic_Thinking_and_Presentation_for_Intelligence_Analysis_Training_Handbo/CIA_Analytic_Thinking_and_Presentation_for_Intelligence_Analysis_Training_Handbook.pdf

Bontempi, M. (2003). Introduzione all'Intelligence e alla Controintelligence istituzionale. In Dispense per il Master in Intelligence and Security (2nd ed.). dell'Università di Malta.

Booth, K. (2007). *Theory of world security*. Cambridge University Press. doi:10.1017/CBO9780511840210

Buzan et a. (1998). *Security: A new framework for analysis*. Boulder, CO: Lynne Rienner Publishers, Inc.

Caligari, M. (2016). *Cyber Intelligence. Tra libertà e sicurezza*. Donzelli Editore.

Chulki, J., & Sungjin, A. (2014). A Study on the Improvements of Information Security Management System for Environment Education Institutes. International Journal of Security and its Applications, 8(4), 247-252.

Cilluffo, F. J., & Cardash, S. L. (2013). Cyber Domain Conflict in the 21st Century. *Seton Hall J. Dipl. & Int'l Rel.*, *14*, 41.

Davis, J. (2002). Sherman Kent and the Profession of Intelligence Analysis. *Occasional Papers*, *1*(5).

Dente, B. (2014). *Understanding Policy Decision*. Springer. doi:10.1007/978-3-319-02520-9

Duyvesteyn. (2014). *The Future of Intelligence: Challenges in the 21st Century*. Routledge. doi:10.4324/9780203071472

Eom, J. H. (2012). Cyber military strategy for cyberspace superiority in cyber warfare. In *Cyber Security, Cyber Warfare and Digital Forensic (CyberSec). 2012 International Conference* (pp. 295-299). Academic Press. 10.1109/CyberSec.2012.6246114

Escuela de las Américas. Inteligencia de Combate. (n.d.). Retrieved from: http://www.derechos.org/nizkor/la/libros/soaIC/cap3.html

Evans, G. (2009). Rethinking Military Intelligence Failure. Putting the Wheels Back on the Intelligence Cycle. *Defence Studies*, *9*(1), 22–46. doi:10.1080/14702430701811987

Fägersten, B. 2015). Intelligence and decision-making within the Common Foreign and Security Policy. In European Policy Analysis. Swedish Institute of European Security Studies.

Fleisher, C. S., & Bensoussan, B. E. (2003). *Strategic and Competitive Analysis: Methods And Techniques for Analyzing Business Competition*. Upper Saddle River, NJ: Prentice Hall.

Goldman, J. (2011). *Words of Intelligence: An Intelligence Professional's Lexicon for Domestic and Foreign Threats, Security and Professional Intelligence Education Series*. Scarecrow Press.

Hampson, F. O. (2008). Human security. In P. D. Williams (Ed.), *Security studies: An introduction* (pp. 229–244). London: Routledge.

Herman, H. (2001). *Intelligence services in the information age*. London, UK: Frank Cass Publishers.

Herring, J. (1996). Creating the intelligence system that produces analytical intelligence. In B. Gilad & J. Herring (Eds.), *The art and science of business intelligence* (pp. 53–81). Greenwich, CT: JAI Press.

Hulnick, A. (2006). What's wrong with the Intelligence Cycle. *Intelligence and National Security*, *21*(6), 959–979. doi:10.1080/02684520601046291

Keen, G. (1977). The intelligence cycle: a differentiated perspective on information processing. In *Proceedings of the June 13-16, 1977, National Computer Conference* (pp. 317-320). ACM. 10.1145/1499402.1499458

Longo, L. M. (2003). Il fattore umano nel controspionaggio industriale. In Dispense per il Master in Intelligence and Security (2nd ed.). dell'Università di Malta.

Malfanti, F. (2005). Il ruolo dell'analista di Intelligence. *Intelligrate*. Available in: https://intelligrate.it/downloads/IntelligenceAnalyst.pdf

Massa, A. (2015). OSINT e Cyber intelligence: tecniche di investigazione nella rete. *Sicurezza e Giustizia, 3*. Available in: https://www.sicurezzaegiustizia.com/numero-iii-del-mmxv/

Phythian, M. (2013). *Understanding the intelligence cycle*. Routledge. doi:10.4324/9780203558478

Pollari, N. (2001). Ipotesi di lavoro per l'intelligence economica: strutture organizzative e moduli operativi. *Sisde*. Available in: http://www.sisde.it

Puong, F. Y. (2015). The Case for Using Robots in Intelligence Analysis. *Studies in Intelligence, 59*(4). Available in: https://www.cia.gov/library/center-for-the-study-of-intelligence/csi-publications/csi-studies/studies/vol-59-no-4/pdfs/Yeh-Automated-Analysis.pdf

Shulsky, A. N., & Schmitt, G. J. (2002). *Silent Warfare: understanding the world of intelligence* (3rd ed.). Dulles, VA: Brassey's Inc.

The Intelligence Cycle. (n.d.). Retrieved from https://www.cia.gov/kids-page/6-12th-grade/who-we-are-what-we-do/the-intelligence-cycle.html

Tonellotto, M. (2014). Evidenza informatica, computer forensics and best practices. Rivista di Criminologia, Vittimologia e Sicurezza, 8(2).

Treverton, G. F., Jones, S. G., Boraz, S., & Lipscy, P. (2006). *Toward a Theory of Intelligence Workshop Report*. National Security Research Division, U.S. Department of Defense. Available in: https://www.rand.org/content/dam/rand/pubs/conf_proceedings/2006/RAND_CF219.pdf

van den Berg, B., & de Bos, T. (2014). *On (the emergence of) cyber security science and its challenges for cyber security education*. Tallin: NATO.

van den Berg, B., & Keymolen, E. L. O. (2017). Regulating security on the Internet: Control versus trust. *International Review of Law Computers & Technology, 31*(2), 188–205. doi:10.1080/13600869.2017.1298504

Velásquez Hurtado, L. A. (2016). *Colombia and the intelligence cycle in the 21st century, the digital age* (Master's Thesis). Institute of Computer Science, University of Tartu. Available in: https://comserv.cs.ut.ee/home/files/Velasquez+Hurtado+CyberSecurity+2016.pdf?study=ATILoputoo&reference=0F5176FB1F90355934306790E8C049BBCD9E422E

KEY TERMS AND DEFINITIONS

Black Swan: An event or occurrence that deviates beyond what is normally expected of a situation and is extremely difficult to predict.

Block-Chain: The possibility that many people can write entries into a record of information, and a community of users can control how the record of information is amended and updated.

Cyber-Intelligence: A complex of activities planned and applied to identify, monitor, measure, and monitor information on digital threats, as well as data on intentions and activities of opposing entities.

Cyber-Security: A set of technologies, programs, processes, and techniques designed and implemented to protect computers and computer networks.

Intelligence: The analytical process for specific needs of anticipated knowledge, to allow decision makers to choose and adopt the strategy to be pursued and, consequently, to decide in a timely, convenient, and effective manner; the competitive intelligence regarding the business intelligence, or investigative intelligence applied to the fight against crime.

Intelligence Analyst: Who takes care of transforming raw data, collected through the various information channels, into material suitable for being understood and used by the management level.

Chapter 3
The Coming Human/Machine Symbiosis, Effects on Society, and Business Planning

John Thomas Riley
The Big Moon Dig, USA

ABSTRACT

Although the future of society is hazy, a workable vision of the future can be developed from existing computer modeling of key parameters like population and sea level. This vision is referred to in this chapter as the driven future. The future of humans and artificial intelligence (AI) is then reconsidered from within the context of this driven future. Specific examples of how AIs might be utilized to address real human problems in this future are developed. The modifications to the way humans and AIs interact to facilitate addressing major problems is then discussed, including the human/machine symbiosis and the application of corporate persons directly to AIs.

DOI: 10.4018/978-1-5225-7903-8.ch003

INTRODUCTION

To understand the future relationship between humans and machines, society must generate a reasonable understanding of the other great forces that are currently driving its future. Society must then picture humans and machines intermixed within that vision of its Driven Future.

The future of society cannot be precisely predicted; there is simply too much chaos. Yet the value of such predictions is so high to any organization, and to society as a whole, that a thoughtful attempt is warranted. The approach used in this chapter is to first summarize the best available computer models of two key parameters [demographic transition and sea level rise] and then to apply these models' major results to building a vision of the future driven by these models.

If this work is not done, then an implicit assumption is made that society's future in the 21st century will be very like the present except for the one or two parameters, like AI, under specific discussion. This invalid assumption tends to validate the choice of useless projects for development, such as games, instead of directly taking on real, identifiable human needs that could sensibly become markets.

Based on this Driven Future, the effects of rapid technology advancement can be fruitfully discussed. A few examples of today's latest social and technological developments are considered to distinguish breakthroughs that would clearly be disruptive [a ten-times-better battery] and those that are popular but so improbable that their continued reference constitutes an obstacle to understanding [flying cars]. Artificial intelligence (AI) -- with its supporting big data, robotics, and virtual realities -- is then developed more fully as the main example.

THE FORESEEABLE FUTURE

How much of the future can a manager envision to support practical planning?

Building a Model of the Future

It is often difficult for an organization to reach an internal agreement on its vision of the future. Positive trends are easily accepted, but a vision including major problems for society [global warming, etc.] can be very contentious. Failing to share a vision can cause major problems in the future for any organization, but the process of developing a consistent vision can be a positively disruptive process.

The best available approach to building the needed vision of the future is currently to exploit the most well advanced computer models. Specifically two well-advanced models are available to build a working vision of the Driven Future: (1) Demographic Transition and (2) Sea Level Rise.

World Population Models

The human population of the Earth was one of the very first parameters modeled on computers, with the first examples as early as the 1960s. Today's population models benefit from this early start, from far better current demographic data and mathematics (Gleick, 1987), and from generations of better machines (Meadows, 2004; Demographic Transition, 2017; Kurzgesagt, 2016).

Very few people are even aware that the population of the Earth is approaching a historic peak.

Figure 1. United Nations world population model

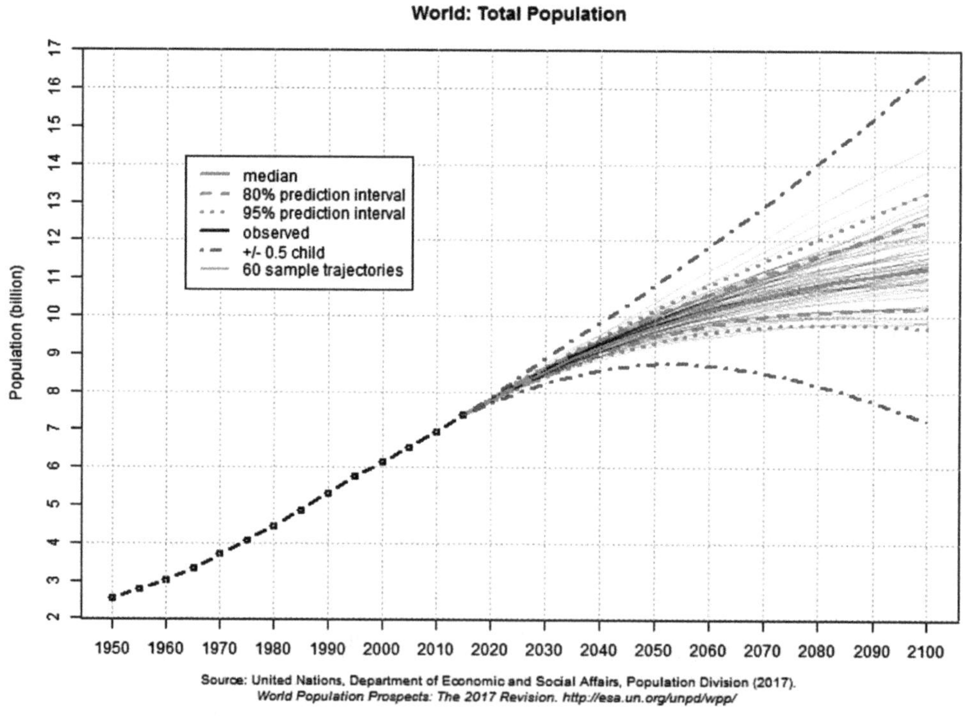

Some institutions, such as the United Nations (Population Division, 2018), do publically present this idea by running a number of models with slight variations of parameters and then taking the mean as a conservative estimate. (See Figure 1)

This typically produces a gradual peak between 2050 and 2150 that is slightly over 10 billion people but provides very little other detail. The time past the peak simply is not covered in this diagram.

The output of previously published models can be assembled into a graph covering a much wider time period. Such an assembly is shown in Figure 2 under the name the Driven Future. This assembly cannot be used for precise prediction but it can provide general insights.

The Driven Future for world human population is graphed in Figure 2. Only estimates are available for world population before 1950, so a modest error bar that is wider in the past is shown. From 1950 to 2016, the estimates are much better and constitute reliable data. This is by far the best available data set used here.

Figure 2. World Human Population Driven Future Assembly

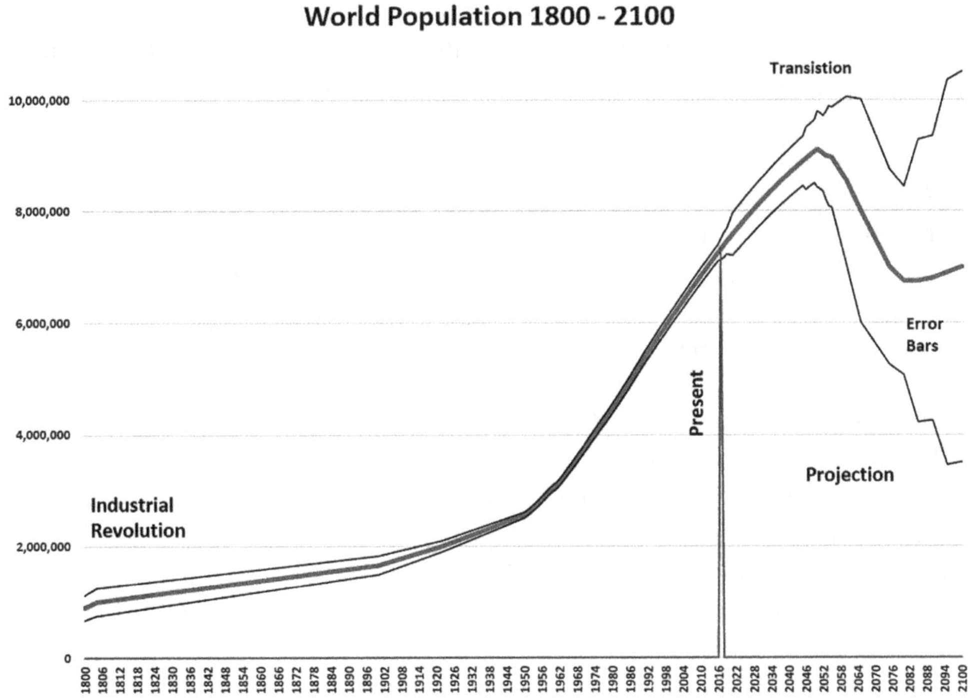

After 2016, the values become projections generated by computer models and the error bars start to open up again. From the peak around 2050 onward, the models become chaotic and the error bars expand wildly. Even though simulated, these error bars are a critical planning element and may be generated in computer models by use of Monte Carlo methods, by varying internal parameters and making an enormous number of runs. This wide expansion is related to the uncertainty in our knowledge of how much damage people will be doing to the Earth's sustaining environment during the peaking transition.

In some ways, this chaos is good. Formal chaos is very sensitive to initial conditions [called the Butterfly Effect] as is the case here. The unpredictability of the distant population estimates mean that they are sensitive to minor changes in the driving parameters that could be affected today. Today's actions affecting our future is therefore a real possibility.

From a naturalistic standpoint, the Butterfly Effect means that if thousands of butterflies flap their wings thousands of times, then it is possible that one of those wing flaps, by chance, could grow into a distant weather system. However, it is impossible to tell which flap of the wings had the effect among the thousands that did not.

From a management standpoint, the Butterfly Effect means that if thousands of people and organizations take millions of actions to address great problems, there is a real possibility of substantive progress. The catch is that it will always be impossible to say which action actually did the job.

Sometime after 2100, the model shows a settling to a steady state population for Earth, but the value for that period is simply not predictable at present. Society is on track for a sustainable Earth; it is just not clear how many people will be living on it.

Trusting the Models

Modern computer models not only lead to better predictions but also to a better understanding of the conditions under which these predictions can be trusted. A vision of the future can now be chosen whose major properties are good enough to warrant it being used as a basis for planned action, even if the year-by-year predictions still show large error bars.

The key elements of the Driven Future taken from this model summary are:

- **The Rise:** The world population curve has been on an exponential rise since the Industrial Revolution.

- **Wars:** The combination of WWI, the flu epidemic of 1918, and WWII only slowed the rise slightly, and this setback was quickly made up over the following two decades.
- **Growth Is *Not* Forever:** Population growth cannot continue exponentially forever; the ecology of the Earth will simply not sustain runaway growth indefinitely.
- **The Peak:** The human population of the Earth will peak at around 10 billion near 2050; the exact number and year is not critical, but that there will be a peak is.
- **Eventual Sustainable Earth:** The human population of Earth will then settle to some value that the Earth can sustain for the long run.
- **Too Chaotic to Predict:** The exact population levels after the peak are too chaotic to predict with any utility, even when exploiting modern computer power.

None of these elements is particularly disastrous, but most of these elements do cause major problems that must be planned for and then addressed.

No matter what predictions are used about the future of society for planning purposes, the predictions must at least be consistent with these general precepts of the population curve. The Driven Future meets this requirement.

Demographic Transition

Technically the population peak is described as the third demographic transition, with the four key transitions being *(Demographic Transition, 2017):*

1. **First Transition:** The change from nomadic hunting and gathering to farming and cities [long before the Common Era]
2. **Second Transition:** The Industrial Revolution [about 1800]
3. **Third Transition:** The world population peak [2050 – 2100]
4. **Fourth Transition:** Stabilizing to a sustainable Earth [after 2100]

The peak [the day with the most human beings who will ever be alive at one time] is currently estimated to be about 33 years in the future; people alive today will be alive when this peak occurs. Major sociological changes are inevitable -- think of the changes that came with the Industrial Revolution -- but going through this transition will be a critical, and now unavoidable, step to moving to a sustainable Earth.

It is clearly a mistake to use a later date for the peak in planning simply as an excuse to take no action today.

Malthus Was Wrong

Thomas Robert Malthus [1766 – 1834] (Malthus, 2018) was an English cleric and scholar who is best known today for one pamphlet, "An Essay on the Principle of Population" [1826]. Few pamphlets have had such a powerful and lasting effect on human history. In his pamphlet, Malthus made the case that:

1. Human population grows exponentially.
2. Means of human subsistence grow only linearly.
3. Population growth is stopped only by moral restraint, vice, and misery.

This pamphlet forecasted peaking of human population and then a precipitous drop. This population catastrophe has been approached historically several times but then delayed each time by technology. For example, at the beginning of the 20th century, the peak was delayed by the Haber process [1909] for fixing nitrogen from the air to make synthetic fertilizer. It is theoretically possible that the next transition could be delayed again by major technological advancements; say a practical and safe fusion reactor. However, there are only about 33 years remaining to the peak, so a world-changing breakthrough of this level, even if developed, is unlikely to be implementable in this short time period.

In the 1960s, Malthus's idea experienced a popular resurgence, resulting in it being picked up again in the early days of computer modeling. The argument proved politically divisive and was soon dropped from the public discourse without the argument ever conclusively being addressed one way or the other.

By 2000, it became clear that human reproductive rates were in fact falling. The effect was first identified in the developed countries, but a decade or two later it showed up in developing countries too (World Population, 2018).

The driving factor here is biology. Most animal populations show a drop-off in fertility as their populations saturate the available living environment. This process usually starts long before death by privation sets in disastrously, as in Malthus's vision.

For humans, the specific driver is the reduction in the number of children born to each woman (Rosling, 2018). In the USA, this number has fallen drastically since the Great Depression from around eight to now less than two. Reductions in child mortality and improvements in the education and health care available to women have empowered them to move from having a large number of children and only a few surviving to having only a few children but looking after them very well.

Malthus missed this mother and child effect completely, yet it is much more powerful than even war and pestilence combined. There will be a population peak but that peak does **not** then predict a collapse.

Climate Change Models

The second major area where computer modeling can provide a workable basis for a vision of the future is in climate change. Critical results of climate change in the present to 2100, the time period defining the Driven Future, include:

- **Sea Level Rise:** The sea levels will rise enough to force displacement of large numbers of people and the reconstruction of major amounts of infrastructure.
- **Uncertainty of the Weather:** The weather will simply be different from what people have historically experienced.

Knowing the kinds of problems that are coming allows some basic planning even though the exact date or severity of any specific event cannot be predicted accurately.

Figure 3. Sea Level since the Industrial Revolution

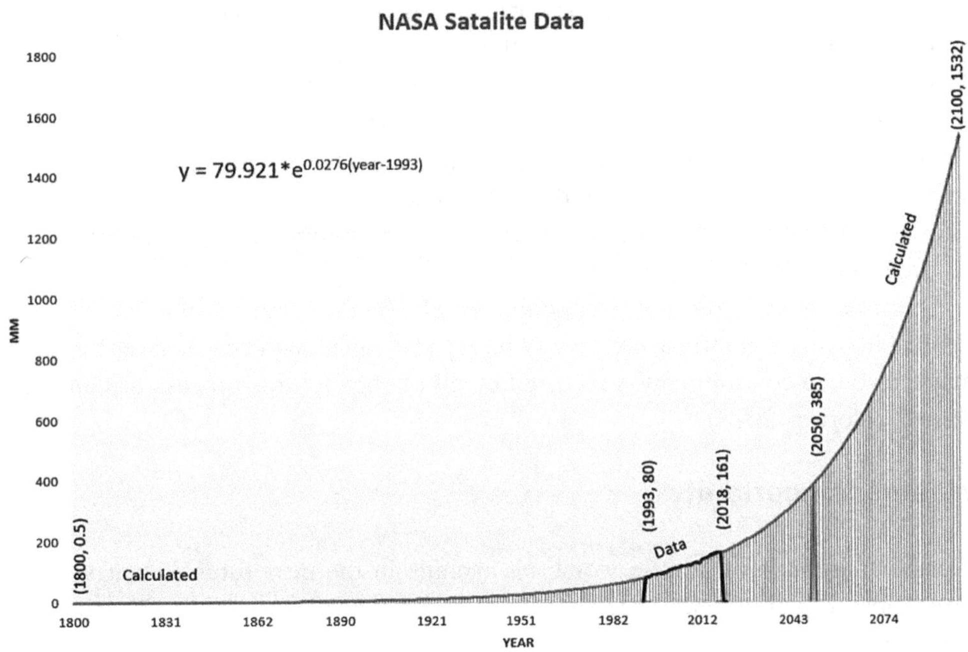

Sea Level Rise

The exact amount of sea level rise predicted varies somewhat from place to place but this rise is clearly an exponential over time. (Frances, 2018) (Gregory, 2013) (JPL, 2017)

Figure 3 Sea Level since the Industrial Revolution displays a block of 25 years of NASA Multi-Mission Ocean Altimeter Data. (NASA, 2018) This work assembles data from a number of Earth observation satellite missions over a 25-year period.

The year 1800, which marks the beginning of the Industrial Revolution, is assigned the value of almost zero for the calculations. An exponential formula [equation in the figure] was fitted to the NASA data and then that equation was used to calculate the extended range both past and future.

This figure shows the sea level rise from the start of the Industrial Revolution in 1800 to 2018 to have been about 161 mm [6.3 inches] and the figure farther projects it to rise to 385 mm [15.2 inches] by 2050. Figure 3 then estimates a 2100 level of 1532 mm [60.3 inches].

These estimates are conservative in the since that an enormous amount of glacial ice currently exists on land and a significant amount of it is in danger of melting. Should that melting continue well into the next century, there would then be liquid water enough for the oceans to rise eventually by many meters.

The sea level rise to date provides a strong warning against business-as-usual. Early planning at this time using the currently available calculations could be of immense value; even more so should the more challenging levels eventually happen. Therefor planning is critical and the vision of the future used for that planning becomes a key factor.

In summary, the seas will rise; people will be on the move, both rich and poor. Critical housing and infrastructure will have to be abandoned and then replaced. A major resource commitment is required by all of society; this process has already started. (Horton, 2018)

Weather Uncertainty

Weather may be only a little worse on average in the near future but it will be impossible to plan for catastrophic events. This change is critical for anyone who works outside, for example:

1. **Farmers:** They work outside and when they can do critical tasks [like plowing] is dependent on the temperature and moisture content of the soil.
2. **Fishermen:** They work outside, are subject to physical danger in foul weather, and their equipment is subject to loss. In addition, their historical catch may disappear or migrate to a new location.
3. **Construction Workers:** Keep in mind the immense amount of rebuilding of infrastructure that will be driven by sea level rise.

Farming is a particularly critical example as not only does weather uncertainty make it difficult to plant and raise to maturity the right crops for an area, but also the same uncertainty raises the chance of unexpected pests and diseases (Parshley, 2018). Flooding is also a historic problem for farmers, and it is expected to become more common.

Sometimes weather uncertainty can affect entire nations. Around 2009 there was a major drought in Syria's farming regions that lasted several years. This drought drove much of the population of the region into the larger cities. Social unrest then resulted, which developed into a war. The current war in Syria, with its major population displacements, can therefore be discussed in terms of a water war.

Population Displacement, Poor

Large numbers of poor people will be displaced by both rising sea levels and uncertain weather. This problem is particularly critical in nations like Bangladesh, where very large populations of poor people have historically farmed low-lying land. Furthermore, several island countries may simply vanish beneath the waves.

Current mass migrations from Syria and the African Sahel have been caused by drought. These migrations, in turn, have caused major political and social problems for Europe. These migrations can serve as examples of what is to be expected. There is no shortage of problems that will only become more persistent. There are many current examples which could be used for leadership development and training right now.

Population Displacement, Rich

Many people in developed countries will be displaced also. Seafront property was once at a premium, but as sea level rises and nuisance tides now encroach on once valuable property, the cost of flood insurance can make such property simply unsellable. This can bring financial ruin to individual families, retired people, and whole communities. This problem is already well established in Maryland's historic tidal counties (Horton, 2018).

Major military installations near water will also have to be rebuilt. This process has already started at installations like the Naval Station Norfolk, Virginia. In addition to the massive work on the base itself, new housing for tens of thousands of workers will have to be constructed.

Standing on Solid Ground

The outlook is not completely bleak. The Industrial Revolution has left human society in surprisingly good shape, much better than most people give it credit for (Rosling, 2018; Pinker, 2011, 2018). Great strides have been made in raising an enormous number of people out of abject poverty, even if these advances have not been complete, uniform, or even widely appreciated.

Technological development is also moving forward at unprecedented rates. Although many advances do not have obvious applications to real human problems, many do enhance society's ability to provide exactly what is needed.

There is no reason that society cannot apply enormous resources to taking on the great problems it now faces. This may not solve them for everybody, but the effort can certainly reduce a massive amount of human misery. This needed effort stands on a sound foundation of accomplishment through decades of economic and technological development, but these great needs demand great leadership if society is to proceed to answers in a timely manner.

WORKING UNDER THIS DRIVEN FUTURE

Working with this Driven Future, what problems and opportunities can be seen?

Publicly Facing the Great Problems

Human beings may show any of seven major reactions to the great problems of the 21st century:

1. **Active Denial:** This mental state is marked by a longing for the past and a willingness to fight over priorities and resources. They ask, "How could humans possibly effect something as big as the Earth?"

2. **Muddling Through:** These people face the problems day-by-day, but developing a full vision of the future is just too upsetting. Famously this approach is credited with winning WWII.
3. **Boil the Frog:** People may simply ignore a slowly growing problem, like sea level rise, until the problem is only belatedly recognized as a great problem and then it may be too late for a comprehensive solution.
4. **Yes, But Not Yet:** These are major problems but there is time and we do not need to be in action quite yet.
5. **Scared Into Action:** People will get into action if frightened by their leaders, but they do not tend to stay in action for the long haul if driven only by fear.
6. **Buy in to Action:** Some people take on the problems head-on even if the available actions at first appear nearly hopeless. They buy-in through envisioning themselves succeeding with an idea provided by their leadership. They then get a great emotional relief in simply being in action and they stay in action, often for decades.
7. **Trust the Singularity:** These people say, "Technological advances will soon overwhelm all the problems." They expect a small number of specialist to save all of society. They say, "Personally I do not have to, and am not qualified to take action". *(SingularityHub,* 2017)

The large number and variety of these reactions makes the job of a project manager trying to address any major problem particularly difficult.

Managing Public Response

As future predictions are, at best, a view through a glass darkly, it is not possible to say that any of these approaches are completely right or that any of them are completely wrong. Some, however, lead to planning to address major problems and to take advantage of new opportunities while others do **not**. Most are simply stalls to justify no actions at this time.

Scared into action has been used extensively by the ecology movement but the results have been unsatisfactory. This approach does get people into action but they often burn out and their interactions with other people can become confrontational.

If an organization does not develop a shared vision of the future, then it is making Muddling Through its default operational choice. In a century of rapid change like the 21st, this is a very weak position. Such organizations will be subject to being blindsided by problems they did not see but could have seen, and they will miss many opportunities presented by new developments.

The best of these reactions by far for a manager is buy-in. It requires the use of language to invite a target audience to envision themselves succeeding with an idea. If successfully initiated, buy-in can keep a person in focused action for decades. Using buy-in successfully, however, takes knowledge, talent, and experience.

The public reaction that is most dominant at any given time is likely to shift, often suddenly, affected by both time and circumstance. These shifts for society as a whole do not come smoothly but rather jump from one path to another (Winston, 2014). Such jumps are consistent with the chaos in the underlying process (Gleick, 1987).

From a management stand point it is question of timing. Waiting too long when a major change is coming can be costly and even lead to the end of the company. Taking action too early can often lead to major expense while organizations that waited just the right amount of time avoid much of the expense of early action. This is why the second organization to enter a field often beats the first. Still the planning itself is valuable. The company plan may become useless with fast change hits but the research and analysis done in making the plan can save the day.

The Gay Pride movement is a good example of such a sudden shift. In the Bronze Age, this social norm was common. However, it offended social norms during the exponential population growth phase and was strongly repressed. Today, it has suddenly become an accepted social norm again as the population approaches a peak that marks a major transition.

Critical Advances

There are a number of promising technological developments with a real chance of happening soon. If they come into full commercial production, they will certainly change the world:

1. **Better Batteries:** If new battery technologies are at least four times better than the current lithium-ion batteries, then the electric car will become the car for all and will support the development of wind and solar as the primary powers for civilization. Two candidates have already been developed to the point that their wide introduction in this time period is quite possible: titanium/barium (*EEStor,* 2017) and graphene.
2. **AI Specialty Chips:** Deep learning chips are coming on the market soon (Hsu, 2016; Gent, 2018). These will greatly reduce the size and power requirements of AIs. This should do for AI what the graphics card did for graphic-based games. These chips will both make the big AI systems, as in data clouds, much

bigger, better learners and also facilitate much more learning in small personal appliances like cell phones.

3. **Better Computers:** Although the leading technology may change, continued advances in computational cost and speed can be relied upon.
4. **Bigger Internet:** The internet and related social media in some form are going to become even more important to people's lives. This will require complex security and personal privacy improvements.

Specifically, these developments will reduce the cost of AI and therefore make their use explode (Agrawal, 2018a). These developments will be world changers that will require major planning if they are to be useful for real problems; this planning is best initiated before the products actually disrupt the current markets.

A Waste of Time

There are also several concepts that are **not** critical to the Driven Future simply because their exact values do not now matter very much:

- The exact date of the peak [2050 – 2100].
- The exact maximum number of people on Earth at the peak [9.5 billion to 11 billion].
- The final sustainable value for population on Earth for the long run [11 billion to 1 billion].
- How much of these problems are caused by humans and how much would happen if people were not here. A fix is needed either way.

Discussion of these topics is now simply a waste of time and energy; such discussions rarely affect a person's mental state nor change society.

Not Going to Happen

Several popular technology ideas about the future are also excluded from the Driven Future:

- **Flying Cars:** General aviation will continue to exist; heavy personal traffic in the sky will **not**. Flying machines need high-grade fuel and use it inefficiently. The terrorist problem alone could stop this idea.

- **Apollo to the Moon-Type Mars Program:** Talk is cheap. The political will for a publicly financed trip back to the Moon or to Mars is simply not available, and the resources are sorely needed for other major problems here on Earth. Still, a very different grassroots space effort may be possible (dall'Acqua, 2018a).
- **Room-Temperature Superconductors:** There is no current science to support room-temperature superconductors. In contrast, successful large industrial production of liquid-nitrogen temperature superconductors is a real possibility.

Though very popular, particularly in science fiction literature, these ideas have little or no chance of coming to fruition in the next 50 years and are now a major distraction to effective planning.

The Driven Future Summarized

The Driven Future for society can then be summarized as follows:

- The human population of the Earth will rise to a peak in about 33 years and then move toward a sustainable level some decades later.
- The oceans of the world will rise enough to cause massive relocation of human populations and require the reconstruction of an enormous amount of infrastructure.
- The weather cannot be counted on to be what has occurred historically, thus disrupting many normal planning processes.
- Society is fundamentally very strong, and enormous resources can be applied to these problems given appropriate leadership.
- New technologies will continue to be developed and can be applied directly to real human problems, but society cannot count on finding silver bullets for every major problem.

Management can either take this Driven Future as a summation of disasters or as a listing of human challenges and opportunities. Either way, a discussion of how humans and machines will interact can now take place within this context.

ARTIFICIAL INTELLIGENCE EXAMPLES UNDER THIS DRIVEN FUTURE

Would a few AI examples under the Driven Future help at this point?

A Child's Village AI

A critical parameter of the demographic transition element of the Driven Future is the change to women having only a small number of children but taking care of the ones they have very well. At the same time, electronic media opens a completely new world of risks for all children using it. AIs could address many elements of this problem.

Children have historically had imaginary friends. An AI could take over this task and add it to the requirements to be a guardian of a child in cyberspace.

It takes a village to raise a child (Clinton, 2006). In modern life, people move around a lot and many of the social functions of a village could now be supported by electronic social media. With children highly valued, it could be a powerful move to establish a virtual village that will stay with a child throughout its childhood and grow with the child. A critical member of that village then can be an AI with capabilities that develop with a child and provide cyberspace security.

Training an AI with the right mix of friendship and protection will prove a very difficult development task. On the one hand, an AI must be a child's friend and confidante; on the other hand, it must quickly warn of unsafe situations.

This problem is particularly critical for children at risk, such as boys in crowded living conditions worldwide. They can fall under recruitment attacks from religious extremists, drug lords, and other social miscreants. Yet they must have reasonable freedom to develop in their own way or they will rebel all the harder.

Such a village AI does not need a robotic presence but rather can be an interface avatar that appears only in virtual space. This will allow it to be present on cell phones, game boxes, and whatever electronic devices a child is currently using.

As a child matures, an AI will have to move toward a master/apprentice relationship with it, e.g., someone who shows a child how to do things while providing some discipline. Such a virtual person is likely to be acceptable as a friend if a child finds it useful, but not if it only sees the AI as a snitch. The AIs virtual avatar must also learn and develop as the child matures.

Of course, all the members of a child's virtual village will have to be thoroughly vetted. A child village AI will require certificates and periodic additional training itself. As security agents, they will have to vet the human members of the virtual village in turn, as people come and go over time.

At **no** time can the child/AI relationship be allowed to become master/slave, especially if who the master is cannot be reliably frozen. In addition, a child cannot be allowed to use the AI as its subordinate agent for mischief, but the AI should not be a straitjacket on a child's development either.

Grownups

What happens when such a child grows up?

To date, AI-driven machines have largely replaced blue-collar workers on production lines and will soon replace cab and truck drivers.

Driving a car is basically predicting the future at short intervals. The AI must answer the question, "What would a good driver do next?" AI are surprisingly good at this task. (Agrawal, 2018a) (Polson, 2018) Can this prediction capability be extended to day-to-day management situations?

As management decisions become more dependent on analyzing big data and as short-term prediction capabilities expand, the competence of AIs at prediction will move then into white-collar jobs.

In contrast, AIs do not do well in situations with no fixed rules. Games like chess and Go have a fixed set of rules; there AIs have done well. Business management does have some rules, but the playing field is much more chaotic.

If a young manager cannot beat them, then that manager must join them -- or at least, team with them --.

A team of a human and an AI could provide the best services of each. The AI could handle the bewildering flow of big data necessary to modern life and make predictions for the best team action, while the human could handle human interfacing and chaotic situations with no clear rules.

In such a team, the AI will continuously answer the question "what is the best thing for our team to do next?" Often the answer will be the obvious; sometimes the answer will be ignored on purpose; occasionally the answer will be something the person had not thought of. In situations with well-defined rules and large data sets, it would be foolish for a manager to override his or her AI team member. In situations with poorly defined rules and weak data, it will often be the manager who must instruct the AI. As the manager's experience with the AI and the AIs learning base are built up with life experiences, the manager will learn exactly when to pay attention to the AI and when not to.

The modern manager will also have a personal AI on its team. It will serve as a personal assistant emphasizing the task of health management. The amount of personal health data is growing quickly as are body monitors. It will be worth the cost to have a dedicated AI on the team to review all this data and look after the person.

The unit of employment will become the team. Best of all, the human will still get to claim supervisory credit for everything the team does.

AI and Ocean Front Displacement, Poor

Poor people displaced by sea level rise or major storm flooding will need help, and there will be a lot of them, tens of millions at least. Could an AI provide some of this help?

The answer is certainly yes.

Here is just a preliminary list of actions in which an AI might participate:

1. **Placement:** Finding new homes for people is similar to a dating service.
2. **Vetting:** The people in safe areas will insist on knowing whom they are getting, and this task can be very difficult during the chaos of a disaster.
3. **Uniting Families:** Finding scattered family members.
4. **Supporting Public Health:** Working the data to spot public health problems before they get out of hand in the camps.
5. **Security for the Children:** Identifying threats to the children.
6. **Education:** Developing skills for a new life, particularly new languages.
7. **Camp Organization:** How can a fluid organization like a camp govern itself with so many people coming and going? A permanent AI team member could provide much needed stability.

There is an enormous amount of work to be done that can be started right now. The need has already started; for example, the Rohingya having been driven into Bangladesh are trapped in this exact situation and need help immediately.

AI and Ocean Front Displacement, Rich

Sea level rise and flooding is a problem in developed countries too. One example is Dorchester County, Maryland, USA (Horton, 2018). There, within living memory, fields where young people played baseball are now under knee-deep water.

The current problem is being met by active denial of nearly everyone in the region who is not an actual resident of the distressed areas. Do not think that such a thing simply could not happen; it is happening already.

An AI dedicated to this problem might address some real questions:

1. **Deal With Big Data:** Massive amounts of data on sea level rise are available. Much of it is now in the form of large maps. Still, people need detailed information on their particular lot: When will the salt water kill the grass? When will the road be cut by high tide so that school buses have to drop kids off halfway home? When will the salt water get to their well or the septic system?
2. **Uninsurable:** When will the flood insurance on their property become so high that the property can no longer be sold at all?
3. **Limited Fixes:** How many years will fixes that could be done at a serious cost buy the owner? Should they build a berm around the property? Should they jack the house up eight feet?
4. **Early Birds:** How much advantage do the get-in-action-now people really achieve?

There is clearly an enormous amount of work that already needs to be done and AIs should have a part.

Self-Driving Trucks

Self-driving cars will affect people's lives, but self-driving, AI-controlled trucks and other capital equipment will affect the economy in a much more fundamental way. As an example, consider the enormous amount of infrastructure work that will be driven by sea level rise. AI-driven trucks, earthmovers, and other capital equipment could do much of the work, especially if managed with the help of a major stationary AI to handle the enormous data flows needed to coordinate the effort.

Convoys of self-driving big-rig trucks are quite likely. These would be a string of semi-trucks strung out at regular intervals along the interstates, perhaps with one human, a supercargo, on board to meet legal requirements and a major AI back in the office to monitor the big picture. The trucks could be all electric or hybrids capable of burning biologically produced fuels. The stationary AI would analyze all the available data on weather, traffic conditions, and fuel prices. The most important job of the big AI could well turn out to be calculating the most economically effective use for its convoys.

Major capital industrial equipment, such as factories and ships, may have AIs too. Their purpose will include maximizing the economic return through predictions and providing security by following big data concerns such as weather and commodity markets.

Fisherman's Friend

Currently there are hundreds of free-floating buoys that bob up and down in the oceans of the world. They float with the current, sink to 1000 meters, and return to the surface to send in periodically their data by satellite link. With each bob, they measure temperature, salinity, and a dozen other parameters. The individual devices may be too small and too expendable to warrant more than a minor AI, but applying the data they generate to offset unreliable weather and optimize use of the seas is a real opportunity.

The new three-meter surface units that are powered by sun and wind are a good candidate for the next generation of AIs. They are long-lived but must sail directly into harm's way, particularly bad weather.

Everything that monitors the oceans -- satellites, shore stations, sailing and bobbing buoys -- can then be combined into one worldwide monitoring system that supports all ocean-related industries. The larger of these units will certainly support a mobile AI as its controller, and overall collection and analysis of the big data will need a major stationary AI.

This system will need to be expanded to include active monitoring of Arctic and Antarctic ice, specifically for its effect on sea level rise. This rise is an expediential function and human beings are not good at anticipating the effects of such functions.

Commercial ships, AI run, will participate in this network too. They will carry basic data systems monitoring weather and ocean as the satellite's pass overhead.

As the seas rise, this system will answer shoreline questions too. All shore facilities will have to be rebuilt from time to time, including many industrial sites. Where will be the best places to build the new facilities? How long will the new facilities last before the seas reach them too? What is the condition of the supporting infrastructure for the new locations?

A human team plus a large AI will be much better at analyzing the big data and finding good answers to these questions than a human only team.

This organization of AI and human teams could be key to monitoring the health of the oceans, of fisheries, of ice, and of coastal regions.

If by Land

The technology of self-driving cars could be extended to a wide variety of AI-controlled vehicles that could be used to take ground truth data, particularly in remote areas and harsh environments. These could include all-terrain vehicles, shallow draft boats, and snowmobiles.

Figure 4. Dusty from the Herd Series of Stories

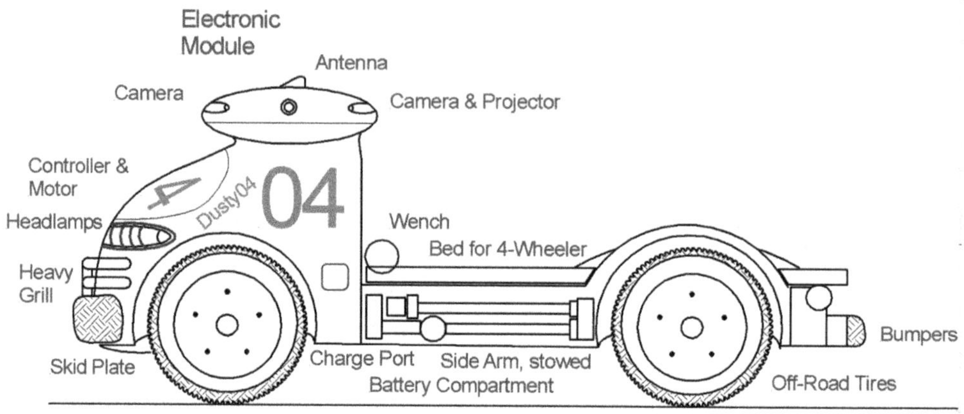

The primary purpose of these vehicles will be to monitor physical conditions such as ground moisture while also monitoring the condition of local wildlife. Their tasks would include monitoring human activity that is degrading the environment such as dumping and poaching. These AIs would have to be very adept at staying mobile and avoiding unwanted human contact.

Once developed, such AI machines can be applied to space exploration. Pathfinder missions to the Moon, Mars, and asteroids could keep up the human tradition of space exploration at a workable cost.

A Better Pie

Since early in the Industrial Revolution, the quality rating of national economies has been based on growth of the Gross National Product [GNP]. Everybody gains from a bigger pie. All this time, the growing population has been a reliable driver for this specific type of growth. With the peaking and then stabilizing of the population, this strong GNP growth driver is now simply petering out.

Society now needs to think in terms of making the pie better, even if it is not bigger and it may even have to shrink. This is not an easy task, but it is one in which truly big AIs may prove a lifesaver.

Human beings are nearly impossible to retrain en masse for such a radical change in their view of society. They can be counted on to resist and it will take a generation or two to establish the new economic system. That kind of time may not be available.

AIs on the other hand train fast and can handle the big data needed truly to understand an economy, at least in principle. It will take a major AI installation to first calculate the qualities of the existing pie, and determine the hundreds of parameters it needs to follow. The team will then provide direction by choosing the areas in which the quality of the pie that can be improved, and then convincing their stakeholders that the picture the team presents is factual and fair. This is no small task.

This possibility comes again from self-driving cars and the calculations they do. To drive a car, an AI must say, "I am probably here," and "the center of the road is probably there". (Polson, 2018) It then takes hundreds of readings in a few milliseconds and recalculates, "now I am probably here," and "now the center of the road is probably there" [Bayes's Rule]. This changes the problem to one of a calculation of numbers, which a computer is very good at doing. Even if there are a few hundred targets in the field of view and a calculation must be done for each, still no problem. [With the possible exception of Kangaroo's.]

In such a team, the AI would have a task that sets its direction and it will access and analyses large data sets. It would then calculate, "I am probably here", reduce some more statistics data, and then calculate "now I am probably here". It does not matter that there may be several hundred parameters that the AI must know its relationship too, it is still much better at calculating than any human.

This car-driving, now management, function would have to be scaled way up for an economic AI, It would change the question to, "what is the best thing for my economic team to do now?" and "where are we now with respect to a thousand parameters?" Fortunately, these questions need only be asked and answered a few times an hour, and a massive amount of big data will be available from worldwide sources to support this calculation.

The DACA Example

One specific example of the level of change in public attitudes related to economics that is likely in this transition is the plight of the Deferred Action for Childhood Arrivals [DACA] people. This is a cohort of over a million people who were brought into the United States by their parents illegally. As a group, they are young, well educated, and willing to work hard for a chance to be legal citizens. Currently their status is contentious and unsettled.

In a world with a stable population and a grow-the-quality economy, the economic value of this group would be instantly recognized. As society approaches a stable population, the number of young workers shrinks and the number of retired workers grows. A cohort of young, well-educated workers will therefore be a great prize.

Countries might actually bid for them. A block of new population this good will simply be nearly impossible to come by and will be seen as an enormous windfall.

Like the Gay Pride movement, the DACA people are a marker for the fast changes currently affecting society and economics. Change this rapid is simply very difficult to plan for; a truly powerful AI could help.

ARTIFICIAL INTELLIGENCE STRUCTURES UNDER THIS DRIVEN FUTURE

Will building solutions to real problems require new structures for the AIs?

The Human/Machine Symbiosis

As the place of AIs in society becomes more critical, the relationship between humans and their machines will become a key factor.

Currently the most common relationship is Master/Slave. This arrangement is easiest to program and recognizes the expense and difficulty that humans have to go to in order to build an AI.

Master/Slave has a big problem, however. So far, no one has reliably programmed a way to guarantee that the master and slave will not swap places someday. Just such a switch is the main plot point of many dystopian movies.

However, there is an alternative available taken from biology: symbiosis.

In symbiosis, two different species mutually support each other. Although each can often survive and reproduce alone, they can only prosper together; the two species are mutually dependent. In the extreme, neither species can successfully reproduce without the other, but this extreme level is not required.

Symbiotic relationships are common throughout the human environment. Humans are in symbiotic relationships with their crops and livestock; the crops are in symbiotic relationships with the molds and fungus that make soils rich. There is no particular reason that humans cannot design their relationship with machines as symbiotic too.

Simply put, humans and machines work as a team or neither prospers. This arrangement starts with the fundamental foundation of functioning as a Human/Machine Symbiosis, and then that concept must be implemented in both programming and training.

Whereas Master/Slave fails catastrophically when the roles are reversed, the Human/Machine Symbiosis only becomes inefficient when it fails to live up to its potential.

AI Consciousness

Bonobos, whales, and elephants are **not** currently recognized as people, nor are they likely to be so recognized anytime soon. Yet their consciousnesses are much closer to humans than AIs consciousness is likely to be in the near future. They are at least mammals.

From the Uncanny Valley work, AIs can present themselves, either physically or virtually, as obvious robots or as representations of humans that are so good that they can be mistaken for real people. What they cannot do is present themselves as a poorly done representation of a human because they then occur to other people as a sick human. In any case, the AIs position in society will need to be clearly defined and its powers both defined and limited.

Just making AIs second-class citizens without supports and controls could leave society open to future rebellion. To date, formally defining consciousness, and therefore personhood for AIs appears to be elusive and therefore unlikely in the Driven Future time frame, but there may be an alternative.

Corporate Persons

There is, however, an alternative and immediately available formal way to recognize AI as people: the Corporate Person.

The Constitution of the United States predates the Industrial Revolution by only a few decades. As a result, the legal structures, such as incorporation, that are so critical to a modern industrial society were not originally included in the Constitution at the national level. Over time, the individual states have passed laws and, critically, the courts have settled landmark cases that legally define these key economic concepts.

The result is that corporations now have some of the rights and responsibilities of a person, but **not** all. A corporate person may:

1. Hire and fire people
2. Enter into contracts
3. Sue and be sued in court
4. Maintain financial accounts
5. Borrow money
6. Issue stocks and bonds
7. Pay taxes

8. Have a board of directors
9. Go bankrupt
10. Support political campaigns
11. Have religious beliefs

The last two rights were only recently added. Most of the rest of these rights define a Corporate Person as an economic entity rather than just as a social entity.

A Corporate Person does have some limitations; they may **not**:

1. Vote
2. Serve on a jury
3. Take the Fifth Amendment against self-incrimination
4. Marry

These Corporate Persons are critical to the normal function of any capitalist economic system, so the current laws may be modified to accommodate AIs, but the corporate person concept cannot be abolished completely. The major corporations most definitely need these rights. This means that a Corporate Person is not just a second-class citizen but also a critical member of the economy, and therefore of the society as a whole.

Corporate Persons are also mortal in the sense that they can die, that is be declared bankrupt, and their assets be sold off piecemeal under the direction of a judge. They can also be bought out, sometimes hostilely, and be merged with another corporation. Mortality makes them just a little more human.

At present, the legal work to establish an AI as a Corporate Person has a surprisingly low cost: $400 on LegalZoom.

In some sense, making an AI a Corporate Person is simply a legal trick to get around the problem of society not defining exactly what a person is. However, this trick does define the AIs rights and responsibilities, establishes it as an economic entity, and provides a means of societal control through its board of directors.

A newly minted AI Corporate Person might wake up on its first day of consciousness to find itself already in debt for much of the cost of its construction and already contracted to provide a specific service to an initial customer. It may also find itself under the control of a board of directors. The rules over who, and how many other AIs, are allowed on such a board of directors will need much work.

CONCLUSION

Is the concept of a Driven Future a useful tool for planning?

Disruptive training with a Driven Future

The Driven Future concept can also be used for educational purposes, specifically to force disruptive thinking in management training. Sometimes the best thing to do is to challenge people's thinking. Before human leadership can teach AIs to deal with a peaked population and rising seas, human leadership will need to teach itself to think in these terms.

Planning for the Future

Society faces challenges of historic proportions in the 21st century. Society has enormous resources **not** currently directed to these big challenges. Society is constantly developing new technologies that could be applied; the number seems to grow with each new day. Some planning, even in these chaotic times, is possible, particularly if driven by real human needs.

Problems, even if daunting, can become opportunities through leadership.

-- We can do this! --

Moreover, that "We" will include many AIs.

REFERENCES

Agrawal, A. (2018). *Prediction machines: Why A.I.'s true potential is learning to read the future*. Retrieved May 2018 from http://bigthink.com/videos/ajay-agrawal-why-predictive-ai-leads-to-better-decision-making?utm_source=Daily+Newsletter&utm_campaign=4fe2983747-Daily_Newsletter_050418&utm_medium=email&utm_term=0_45b26faecc-4fe2983747-43589201

Agrawal, A., Gans, J., & Goldforb, A. (2018). *Prediction machines, The Simple Economics of Artificial Intelligence*. Boston, MA: Harvard Business Review Press.

dall'Acqua, L., & Dickson, L. (2018). Improving Business Performance Through Effective Managerial Training Initiatives. In *Extended Managerial Implications: People and Space in the Twenty-First Century*. Hershey PA: IGI Global.

EEStor, Energy Everywhere. (2017, January 18). Retrieved from http://www.eestor.us/index.html

Frances, J. A. (2018, April). Meltdown. *Scientific American, 318*(4), 48–53. doi:10.1038cientificamerican0418-48 PMID:29557956

Gent, E. (2018). *This New Chip Design Could Make Neural Nets More Efficient and a Lot Faster.* Retrieved June 13, 2018 from: https://singularityhub.com/2018/06/11/this-new-chip-design-could-make-neural-nets-more-efficient-and-a-lot-faster/?utm_source=Singularity+Hub+Newsletter&utm_campaign=5aedf55c2b-Hub_Daily_Newsletter&utm_medium=email&utm_term=0_f0cf60cdae-5aedf55c2b-5747300

Gleick, J. (1987). *Chaos*. Viking.

Gregory, J. (2013). *Projections of Sea Level Rise*. IPCC Fifth Assessment Report. Retrieved from https://www.ipcc.ch/pdf/unfccc/cop19/3_gregory13sbsta.pdf

Horton, T. (2018). *High Tide in Dorchester*. Retrieved from http://hightidedorchester.org/

IBM's Brain-Inspired Chip Tested for Deep Learning. (n.d.). Retrieved from: https://spectrum.ieee.org/tech-talk/computing/hardware/ibms-braininspired-chip-tested-on-deep-learning

JPL InfoGraphics. (n.d.). *Sea Level Rise*. Retrieved February 5, 2017 from http://www.jpl.nasa.gov/infographics/infographic.view.php?id=11298

Kurzgesagt – In a Nutshell. (2016, December 16). *Over Population, The Human Explosion Explained.* Retrieved from https://www.youtube.com/watch?v=QsBT5EQt348

Meadows, D., Randers, J., & Meadows, D. (2004). Limits to Growth, The 30-Year Update. White River Junction, VT: Chelsea Green.

Parshley, L. (2018, May). Catching Fever. *Scientific American, 318*(5), 58–65. doi:10.1038cientificamerican0518-58 PMID:29672493

Pinker, S. (2011). The Better Angles of Our Nature. New York: Viking.

Pinker, S. (2018). Enlightenment NOW. New York: Viking.

Polson, N., & Scott, J. (2018). *AIQ, How People and Machines are Smarter Together*. New York: St. Martin's Press.

Population Division, United Nations. (2018). *United Nations, World Population Prospects 2017, Probabilistic Projections, Population, Total Population, World. Graph.* Retrieved from: https://esa.un.org/unpd/wpp/Graphs/Probabilistic/POP/TOT/

Riley, T. (2017, January 30). *The Big Moon Dig.* Retrieved from http://bigmoondig.com/BigMoonDig.html

Riley, T. (2017, January 30). *The Big Moon Dig, Stories.* Retrieved from http://bigmoondig.com/Stories/BMDStories.html

Rosling, H. (2018). *Factfulness.* New York: Flatiron Books.

SingularityHub. (2017, January 18). Retrieved from https://singularityhub.com/

Tegmark, M. (2017). Life 3.0, Being Human in the Age of Artificial Intelligence. New York: Alfred A Knopf.

Wang, S., & Remlinger, B. (2017). Can math stop partisan gerrymandering? *The Los Angeles Times.* Retrieved from: http://www.latimes.com/opinion/op-ed/la-oe-wang-remlinger-gerrymandering-20170505-story.html

Wilson, E. O. (2012). *The Social Conquest of Earth.* New York: Liveright Publishing.

Wilson, E. O. (2016). *Half-Earth.* New York: Liveright Publishing.

Winston, A. S. (2014). *The Big Pivot.* Boston: Harvard Business.

World Population. (n.d.). In *Wikipedia.* Retrieved April 2018 from: https://en.wikipedia.org/wiki/World_population

KEY TERMS AND DEFINITIONS

Artificial Intelligence (AI): An electronic device that can mimic many of the capabilities of a human.

Buy-In: The mental process by which humans hear of an idea, envision themselves succeeding with the idea, get into action, and stay in action.

Corporate Person: The package of rights similar to those of a person that are recognized in court for a corporation.

Demographic Transition: These are major changes in the growth patterns of the human population that have enormous effects on society.

Driven Future: A technical vision of the future of human society based on summarizing a number of computer models.

Ground Truth: Taking scientific measurements on the ground beneath the path of a satellite to calibrate the big data set.

Human/Machine Symbiosis: A foundation for the relationship between humans and their machines based on the biological concept of symbiosis. An alternative to the master/slave approach.

Monte Carlo Methods: Using randomized methods to better to understand the limitations of a computer model.

Uncanny Valley: Studies show that the public will accept the presentation of an AI either as a robot or an interface avatar if its appearance is either clearly that of a non-human robot or a very good likeness of a human. Between these two peaks is a valley of almost humans that real humans will not interface with willingly.

Chapter 4
System Dynamics Modeling for Public Health Bed Capacity Planning

Arzu Eren Şenaras
https://orcid.org/0000-0002-3862-4551
Uludag University, Turkey

ABSTRACT

The system dynamics approach was developed by Jay Forrester from MIT during 1950s to analyze the complex behavior in administration with computer simulation in social sciences. System dynamics is a form of the systems approach as a methodology to understand the dynamic behavior of complex systems. The basis of system dynamics is to understand how system structures cause system behavior and system events. This chapter aims to develop a system dynamic model. System dynamics approach was adopted to build a bed capacity management model using a software package, Vensim.

DOI: 10.4018/978-1-5225-7903-8.ch004

INTRODUCTION

System dynamics approach was developed by Jay Forrester from MIT during the 1950's to analyze especially the complex behavior in administration with computer simulation in the social sciences. System dynamics is a form of the systems approach as a methodology to understand the dynamic behavior of complex systems. The basis of system dynamics is to understand how system structures cause system behavior and system events (Sezen, 2009: 298).

Jay Forrester initially constructed his first dynamic model during his meeting with the management of General Electric Corporation. Big fluctuations in production, inventory, labor force and profitability were compelling GE management. Despite the hard efforts of the management, these fluctuations were mostly associated with external factors. Especially, the fluctuations in the business were related to received orders. Forrester interacted with the management to observe the system operations in other departments. In the first model he developed, he observed that simulations were necessary since the system could not be monitored analytically. He demonstrated that the corporation could experience serious fluctuations due to management policies even when the demand is considered constant with the weekly simulation he ran. Later on, he designed the computer simulation for the same problem. In his later studies, Forrester demonstrated how the feedback control theory could be adapted for complex administration and human systems. He published his initial findings in an article in Harvard Business Review. Later on, he developed this study to write his famous work "Industrial Dynamics" (Lane & Sterman, 2011; Ramage & Shipp, 2009: 100-101).

SYSTEM DYNAMICS

System dynamics deals with how things change over time. Almost all are interested in how the past formed the present moment and how today's actions determine the future. System dynamics is designed to model, analyze and improve socio-economic and administrative systems using a feedback perspective. Dynamic structured administrative problems are modeled by mathematical equations and using computer software. Dynamic constructions of model variables are obtained using computer simulations (Forrester, 1995; Forrester, 1962; Ford 1999; Sterman, 2000).

The main principle of system dynamics is that the ongoing accumulation of the complex behavior of organizational and social systems (human, material, financial assets, information, biological and psychological states) is also the result of balancing and empowering feedback mechanisms. (Richardson, 1999).

System dynamics is an interdisciplinary problem-solving methodology that utilizes several significant thinking skills such as dynamic thinking and cause-and-effect thinking. System dynamics is a disciplined collaborative approach that could accelerate learning by combining a multifaceted perspective that provides insight into complex and interactive issues (Richmond 2010; Soderquist & Overakker 2010; Ferencik, 2014).

System dynamics is a method that allows analysts to separate complex social, and behavioral systems into components, to visualize them by reconstructing them as a whole again, and to develop a simulation model (Tang and Vijay, 2001: 3).

There is never one single correct answer in system dynamics. Since system dynamics represents the relationships within the current system, it presents multiple possible approaches that could be applied, instead of providing a single correct answer. Each approach could provide some of the desired result, as well as some unexpected ones. In fact, another significant characteristic of system thinking is to become aware of why we preferred a solution over others (Sterman, 2000: 127-133). System dynamics was designed to help managers make decisions similar to other information technologies. The aim of system dynamics studies is to assist decisions by analyzing old policies and designing new ones (Wheeler, 1994: 80).

System dynamics models are not derived statistically from time series data. They are statements related to policies and system structure that guide decisions. Models include admissions made about the system. A model is only as good as the expertise that underlies its formulation. A good computer model is distinguished from a bad one by the accuracy of its reflection of the system it represents. Several other mathematical models are limited due to the nonlinear nature of the real system and the lack of their inclusion of several feedback cycles. On the other hand, system dynamics computer models could reflect real system behavior (Forrester, 1995: 6).

System dynamics is based on information feedback theory and provides symbols for system management. These symbols include diagrams, equations, and programming languages for computer simulation (Morecoft & Sterman, 1994: 15).

The objective of system dynamics is not optimization, but to examine the system behavior in the long run at a macro level against specific changes and to help determine the strategies. System dynamics aims to achieve a holistic view of the system and to determine how interactions influence the system as a whole. It is often used for large organizations and global events. However, it could also be used for micro-level and small organizations (taking into account their intermittent structure inflows and levels). The most significant function of system dynamics is to improve system behavior by explaining the structure and behavior of the system. The system dynamics has a broad approach to problems to facilitate monitoring, development, and reorganization of the system performance. As a result, the improvement of the performance of one part of the system prevents the deterioration of another part of the system (Hesan et al., 2014; Başkaya, 1997: 93; Özbayrak vd., 2007; Towil, 1996). In system dynamics, generally a "what if" analysis is conducted.

STRUCTURE OF THE SYSTEM DYNAMICS MODEL

In order to analyze the dynamics of the actual system, system models arc investigated. Models are simplified structures designed to examine the system behavior (Karnopp et al., 1990: 4). Models are constructed to better understand the economic performance of alternative decisions and their impact on cnvironmental quality. Models are important tools for obtaining new knowledge (Ruth and Hannon, 2012: 4).

The model must have a clear objective, and this objective should provide a solution to a specific problem. The clear objective is the most important component of a successful model. A clear model, of course, could be inaccurate, too broad and difficult to understand. However, an explicit goal allows the users of the model to ask questions that demonstrate whether solving the problem is beneficial (Sterman, 1991: 5).

According to Forrester (1969), four hierarchical structures must be defined to model the dynamic behavior of a system:

1. A closed boundary around the system
2. Feedback loops as basic structural elements within the closed boundary
3. Level (status) variables indicating the totals of the feedback loops
4. Rate (flow) variables that indicate the actions within the feedback loops
    a. Objective
    b. Observed situations → Components of rate variables
    c. Determination of the difference
    d. Actions based on the difference

To develop the whole systems concept, boundaries in which the interactions forming the system's characteristic behavior occur must be established (Forrester, 1969: 12).

In order to achieve the expected objectives in the dynamic model, the model should include the following characteristics (Erkut, 1983: 42-43):

1. The ability to define the predicted cause and effect relationship
2. A simple mathematical structure
3. Incorporating concepts adequate for the economic and social structure
4. Ability to expand to several variables without exceeding computer application limits
5. Ability to produce and process continuous interactions.

Forrester created a language called system dynamics to define system behavior. This language consists of four components: stocks, flows, decision functions and information flow. As a result, the only thing we need to define the system is to create these four blocks despite the level of complexity of the system.

Dynamic analysis deals with time flow. So first, we have to define time. Time could simply be defined as a dimensionless real number. There is a starting point and it continues in the positive direction in the coordinate system. In this case, two different concepts stand out. The first concept is defined as a moment in time and denoted as $\tau=1, 2, 3,...$ The second concept is the time period and denoted as $t=1., 2., 3.,...$ The unit of time could be expressed in seconds, minutes, hours, weeks, months, years, decades, hundreds of years..., depending on the structure of the examined system. In system dynamics, the two time concepts must be distinguished correctly, because the stocks and flows need to be defined explicitly as τ and t. (Yamaguchi, 2013: 23).

The elements that constitute the dynamic system model could be explained in four groups such as stocks, ratios, decision functions and information flow.

Stocks (Levels) and Flows (Ratios)

While the stock could be defined as accumulation, the flow refers to the rate that stock levels change. Stocks could be clearly defined as the inventory of raw materials or finished products. Some are less clear, partly because the everyday language does not identify them as stocks. An example is the cash balance generated by the deposit and withdrawal of funds. Stocks are the accumulations within the system. These accumulations could include concepts such as inventory, business volume, number of employees with different qualifications and experiences, and workforce, etc. Stocks are the present values of the variables that are formed by the accumulated difference between the inflow and outflow (Sezen & Günal, 2009: 306-307; Erkut, 1983: 44).

Classification of Stocks and Flows

Yamaguchi (2013) classified the stocks based on their natural structures as depicted in Table 1.

- Natural stocks include stocks that could be found in the natural environment such as world population, number of birds and trees in the forests, and amount of water in the lakes.
- Capital stocks are the means of production such as machinery, factories and structures used to produce consumer goods.
- Products in process and in use include goods produces and intermediate products still in manufacturing process.
- Information is a non-physical inventory and it is stored in various types of media. For example, books, CDs, DVDs, ...
- Psychological passions are individuals' emotional stocks. For example, love, happiness, sadness, nervousness. It is stored somewhere in our brain.
- Indexed figures are a special form of stored information. It is used to describe nature and human activities. For example, temperature, price, sales figures, etc. (Yamaguchi, 2013: 24).

SYSTEM DYNAMICS MODELING PROCESS

Forrester's system dynamics modeling steps could be listed as follows (Forrester, 1962: 13):

- Identification of the problem.
- Separation (isolation) of the factors that include the observed symptoms.

Table 1. Classification of Stocks

Physical Stocks	Non-Physical Stocks
Natural Resources	Information
Capital	Psychological passions
Products in Process and in Use	Indexed figures

(Resource: Yamaguchi, 2013: 24)

- Arriving at new decisions through connecting the decisions to actions and actions to information feedback by following cause and effect information feedback cycles
- Formulation of acceptable and adequate (formal) decision-making policies that define the results of these decisions using existing information flows.
- Construction of the mathematical model for the interactions between decision-making policies, sources of information and system components.
- Formulation of system behavior as defined in the model
- Comparison of the results with all adequate data in the existing system
- Review of the model until it represents the actual system
- Discovery of organizational relationships and policy amendments that could improve system behavior through model redesign
- Obtaining the improved performance by implementing the changes in the actual system as stipulated by the model

DELAYS IN SYSTEM DYNAMICS

An important characteristics of various dynamic systems is the presence of delays that control the system, which are much more difficult to comprehend than it might seem at the first glance. Delays are a characteristic of dynamic systems and affect both material and information flow. The most common ones are exponential and pipeline-type delays (Sezen & Günal, 2009: 326).

Delays are inherent in many administrative processes. For example, it takes time to manufacture a product, to hire or lay out workers, to build a new factory, or to set up services (Kirkwood, 1998: 73).

In principle, there are delays in all flow channels. On the other hand, entering a time delay for each flow results in a quite unnecessarily detailed model, since most of these affect system behavior only very little. When introducing delays into the system, the number of delays could be reduced by two types of shortcuts. First is the case where the system delay is so short that its effect could be ignored. Second, the consecutive delays, which are actually separate, are usually combined and expressed as a single delay (Forrester, 1962: 86).

TIME PROCESSING IN SYSTEM DYNAMICS

System dynamics approach usually utilizes the time framing method. The modeler must determine the length of the time frame in advance. One important issue to note here is the accurate selection of the time frame length. If the time frame is extremely long for model behavior, the modeler will miss significant variations, hence, the simulation could provide misleading results. If the time frame is extremely short for model behavior, then model would be examined even at times when a change in the state is not possible, causing excessive collection of data and excessive computer processing time. It is recommended to select a sufficiently short time frame length generally (Sezen, 2009: 320).

VALIDITY OF SYSTEM DYNAMICS MODELS

The computerized simulation model could be used as a powerful tool to test how policies and structure that generate growth and fluctuations in socio-economic systems interact. For the effective use of the model, it needs to reflect the actual system (Forrester, 1977: 541).

Model validity is as controversial topic as it is significant in all model-based methods, especially in system dynamics. The validity of the results of the model-based study depends on the validity of the model. Nevertheless, there is no single well-agreed definition of model validity and model validation (Barlas, 1996: 183).

Significance of a model is measured by how well it serves its objective. The objective of system dynamics models is to help improve the decisions made. The validity of a model should be decided by its adequacy for the unique objective of the model. If a model serves its purpose, it could be justified and is significant. Thus, validity is an abstract concept separated from the objective. A model that is perfect for an objective might be misleading and useless for another objective (Forrester, 1962: 115).

To investigate model validity, two topics should be discussed. First, we cannot expect a model to be completely valid. A model has been constructed for a specific objective and its validity should be tested for this objective. However, a model investigated for other objectives might be unreliable. Second, we must realize that positive proof is impossible. The difficulty begins with selecting the validity criteria. There is no absolute proof, but there is a confidence interval for measuring the link between the model, the actual system and the objective. Concurrently, if two different models are measured, there is no assurance that the model that better reflects the measurement findings is the most efficient model (Forrester, 1975: 162).

The simplest model validity form is called the black box validity. In this method, the model is run under well-defined conditions and findings are obtained. The conditions chosen for running the model should be as similar as possible to the actual system. Then, the simulation model should be rendered compatible with the actual system. Thus, the model results should be the same as the actual system results. This is called the black box validity, because the topics of interest are only the system inputs and outputs. The internal structure of the model is not addressed. In this method, we cannot be sure that the model properly describes the operation of the actual system. In order to make sure of this, we must use a method called white box validity. The idea behind white-box validity is to examine the model's operation in more detail and to verify that the simulated system reflects the operation of the actual system appropriately. This validation method examines the programming logic, rather than investigating the result of the model (Fishwick, 2007: 33-21).

The most important aim of the model validity in system dynamics is verification of the model structure; although the validity of the results produced by the model could be assessed, this is only meaningful when the model structure itself is valid. Thus, verification should be conducted with the model structure first and then the behavior of the model should be verified (Barlas, 1994).

Validity could be examined both structurally and behaviorally. Structural validity could be defined as building trust on the fact that the relationships used in a model represent the actual relationships accurately. Barlas (1994) indicated two types of structural tests: 1-Direct Structural Tests and 2-Structural Behavior Tests. Direct building tests provide model validity only by comparing model equations with available information. In the direct structural test, consistency comparisons are made directly on the model without using a simulation. These tests could be empirical and theoretical. The empirical test involves comparing information obtained from the actual system modeled with equations of the model. On the other hand, the theoretical tests include a comparison of model equations with generalized information on the existing system available in the literature. Both tests are important for direct structural validity. Forrester and Senge (1980) gave the examples of structure and parameter validation test, direct end-value test and unit consistency test for direct structural tests. Parameter validation test is to assess the fixed parameters conceptually and numerically using the actual real information. The direct end-value test involves the evaluation of model equations with extreme values, and is a comparison of the result values with the information about what would occur under similar circumstances in real life. Finally, the unit consistency test analyzes the unit consistency of the model equations (Barlas, 1994; Forrester & Senge, 1980).

The second general category of structural tests is structural behavior tests. These tests assess model validity indirectly by testing certain behavior using behavior patterns created in the model. Indirect structural tests include specialized simulated runs and could provide indirect information about probable errors in model construction. Among these tests, end-value, behavioral sensitivity, limit compliance, and phase-correlation tests could be listed. In a behavioral test for a typical structure, the analyst makes the following proposition: "If the system works in condition K, it should demonstrate behavior D". If the model works under K conditions and yields similar behavior to the expected behavior, it passes this test. End-value behavior tests are the comparison of behavior created by the model by assigning extreme values to selected parameters and the observed or predicted behavior of the actual system with these extreme values. The behavioral sensitivity test aims to determine the parameters that are sensitive to the model and to test whether the actual system has the same high level of sensitivity for these. On the other hand, the adaptive behavior estimation test could be applied where it is possible to find data about the behavior of the adaptive version of the actual system. The model passes this test if it could produce similar adaptive behavior when simulated with similar adaptations. These two tests are designed to evaluate the validity of the model with the model structure. As a result of these tests, if there is sufficient level of confidence about the model structure, we could begin to apply a number of tests designed to measure how accurate the model reproduces the large behavioral patterns observed in the actual system behavior. Here, It is very important to emphasize the sampling estimate (period, frequency, trend wave size...) instead of point estimation. This is a logical consequence of the fact that system dynamics models have a tendency towards long term politics. Behavioral sample tests could be expressed as the multiple test procedure proposed by Barlas (1985, 1989), the general statistical summary proposed by Sterman (1984), and several behavioral sample tests discussed by Forrester and Senge (1980) (Barlas, 1996; Forrester & Senge 1980; Barlas & Saysel, 1996; Kanar, 1995).

SD MODEL TO ANALYZE HOSPITAL'S BED CAPACITY

For a medium size hospital assume that patient arrive with a random distribution. After registration and first check of arrival, acceptance portion of arrival are assuming as patient. This rate varies between countries but very little operation are not assuming as patient. In general, this type of arrival is known like winter bed and seen in older person. Than arrivals that are accepted as patient can be divided to two: one partition necessities bed allocation (inpatient) and other partition does not necessities bed allocation (outpatient). Number of patient necessities bed is calculated via rate of hospitalization multiply with patient number and then if hospital has not enough bed capacity, patients are sent (referred) to another hospital. Patient who use bed (inpatient), are assumed to pass 3 day in hospital as average.

SD Model Equations:

```
(01)        acceptace to tread=INTEGER(acceptance
rate*arrival)
(02)        acceptance rate=0.8
 (03)        acceptance to hospital= INTEG (acceptace to
tread-outpatient treatment-hospitalization acceptance-referred
to other hospital due to lack of bed,5)
```

Figure 1. SD model

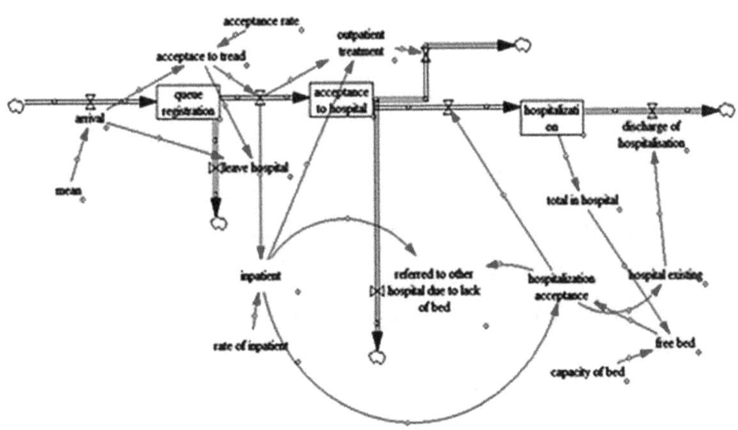

```
(04)        arrival=INTEGER(ABS(RANDOM
NORMAL(mean/4,mean*4,mean, mean/5, 2)))
(05)        capacity of bed=200
(06)        discharge of hospitalisation=hospital existing
(07)        FINAL TIME  = 500
(08)        free bed=capacity of bed-total in hospital
(09)        hospital existing=DELAY FIXED(hospitalization
acceptance, 2, 10)
10)        hospitalization=INTEG(-discharge of
hospitalisation+hospitalization acceptance,15)
(11)        hospitalization acceptance=IF THEN ELSE(free
bed>inpatient, inpatient, free bed)
(12)        INITIAL TIME  = 0
(13)        inpatient=INTEGER(acceptace to tread*rate of
inpatient)
(14)        leave hospital=arrival-acceptace to tread
(15)        mean=        400
(16)        outpatient treatment=        acceptace to tread-
inpatient
(17)        queue registration= INTEG (arrival-leave hospital-
acceptace to tread,0)
(18)        rate of inpatient=0.32
(19)        referred to other hospital due to lack of bed=IF
THEN ELSE(inpatient>hospitalization acceptance,inpatient-
hospitalization acceptance, 0)
(20)        SAVEPER  =   TIME STEP
(21)        TIME STEP  = 1
(22)        total in hospital=hospitalization
```

As it is observed, a number of patients that are referred to another hospital decrease with increasing bed capacity.

The number of patients is calculated from the number normal distribution so it changes as real World.

A social policy decision maker can calculate the necessary expenditure to increase bed capacity.

System dynamic deals with strategy and long run thinking. In the long run the number of patients can change such as migration or population increase. Assume that the number of arrival increase with time like the above equation:

Figure 2. Graph of arrival

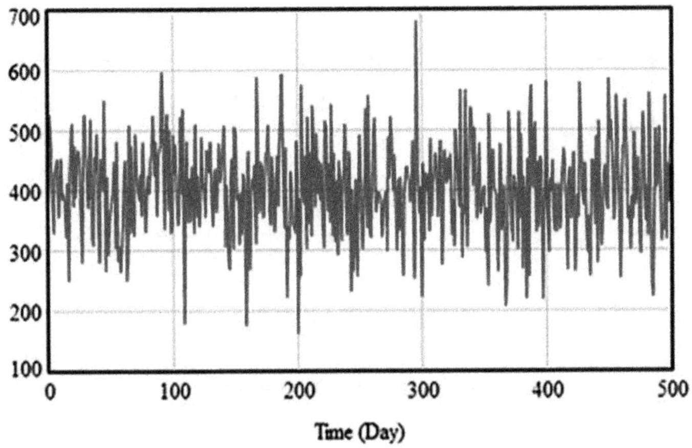

Figure 3. Acceptance to tread, inpatient and outpatient treatment

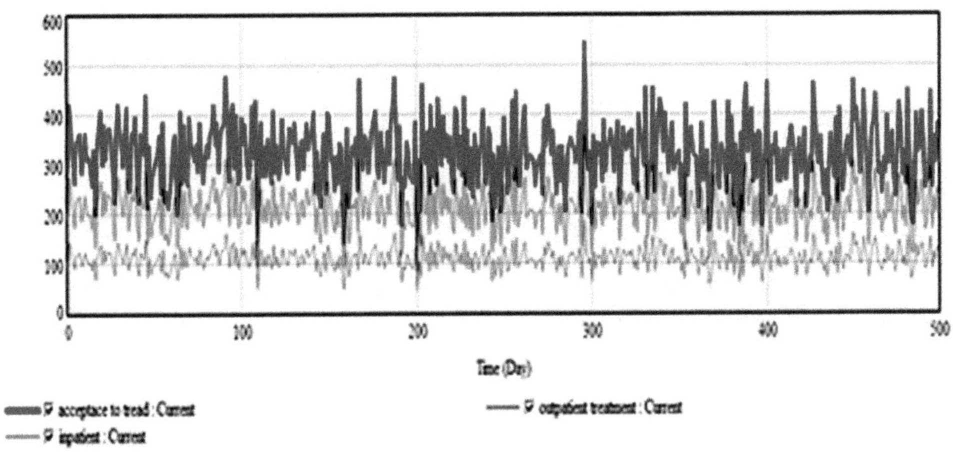

Figure 4. Hospitalization acceptance and referred to other hospital due to lack of bed (If bed capacity is 200)

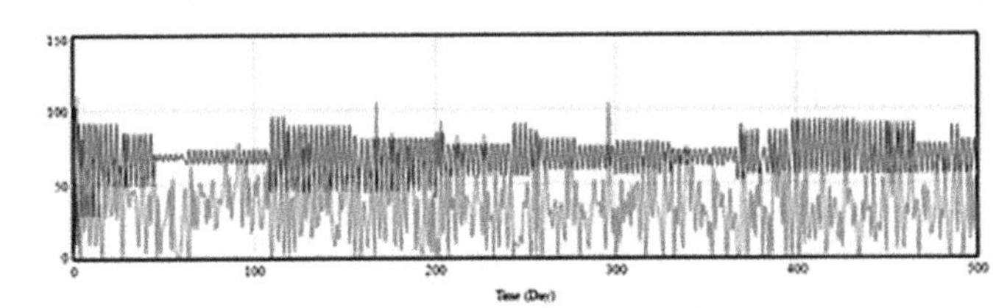

Figure 5. Hospitalization acceptance and referred to other hospital due to lack of bed (If bed capacity is 400)

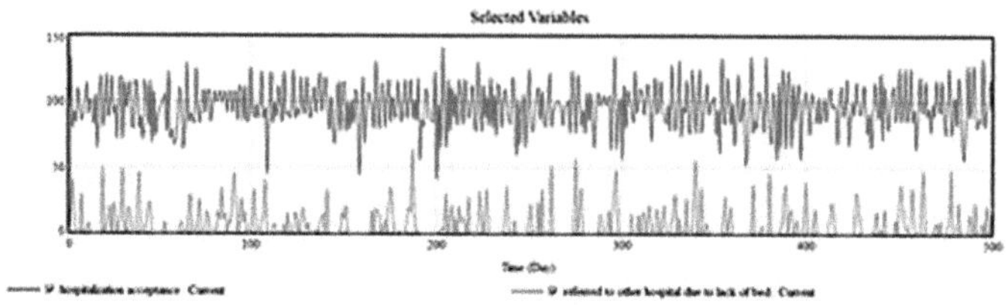

Figure 6. Graph of referred to other hospital due to lack of bed

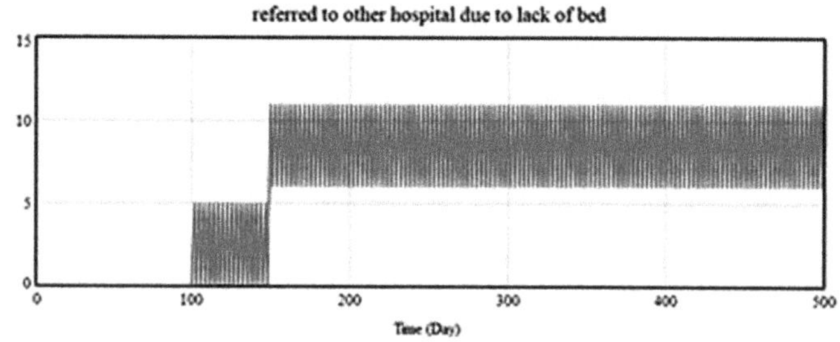


```
arrival=200+STEP(25,20)+STEP(25, 40)+STEP(25, 100)+STEP(25,
150)
```

While keeping bed capacity 200 constant, it is observed that until 100 that is no need for any other bed capacity increase but after 100 a portion of the patient must be referred to another hospital and after 150 the number of patients that are referred is increasing. So if bed capacity changes as below

```
Capacity of bed=200+STEP(60, 100)
```

So number patient referred to another hospital is became zero .It shows an unnecessary capacity increase is made. Unnecessary investment is made. The same result can be obtained by increasing bed capacity to 23 as the capacity of bed=200+STEP(23, 100)

As it is seen in below graph that with an increase of 23 bed capacity in time 100 . The number of patients referred to another hospital due to missing bed is 0.

Figure 7. Capacity of bed, mean, referred to other hospital due to lack of bed

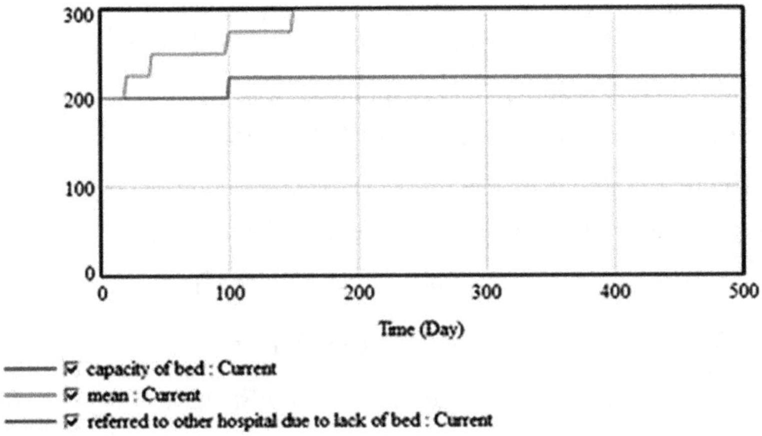

CONCLUSION

Bed capacity planning is a crucial issue for hospital management. This chapter aims to explore the system dynamics method for developing bed capacity model. System dynamics deal with strategic planning for complex problems. SD model developed using Vensim Software. Different scenarios can be tested and efficient bed capacity planning can be designed thanks to developed SD model.

REFERENCES

Barlas, Y. (1994). *Model Validation in System Dynamics*. The 12th International Conference of the System Dynamics Society, Stirling, UK.

Barlas, Y. (1996). Formal Aspects of Model Validity and Validation in System Dynamics. *System Dynamics Review*, *12*(3), 183–210. doi:10.1002/(SICI)1099-1727(199623)12:3<183::AID-SDR103>3.0.CO;2-4

Towil, D. R. (1996). Industrial Dynamics Modelling of Supply Chains. *Logistic Information Management*, *9*(4), 43-56.

Erkut, H. (1983). *Sistem Dinamiğinin Temelleri*. İstanbul: İTÜ Fen Edebiyat Fakültesi Ofset Atölyesi.

Ferencik, R. C., Soderquist, K., & Mınyard-Phıllıps, M. A. (2014). *Building Systems Thinking Capacity: An Essential Skill Set For Policymakers*. In 32nd International Conference of the System Dynamics Society, Delft, The Netherlands.

Fishwick, P. A. (2007). *Handbook of Dynamic System Modelling*. Boca Raton, FL: Chapman & Hall / CRC. doi:10.1201/9781420010855

Ford, A. (1999). *Modeling the Environment: An Introduction to System Dynamics Modeling of Environmental Systems*. Washington, DC: Island Press.

Forrester, J. W. (1962). *Industrial Dynamics*. Waltham, MA: Pegasus Communications.

Forrester, J. W. (1969). *Urban Dynamics*. The MIT Press.

Forrester, J. W. (1977). Growth Cycles. *De Economist, 125*(: 4).

Forrester, J. W., & Senge, P. M. (1980). Tests For Building Confidence In System Dynamic Models. *TIMS Studies in the Management Sciences, 14*, 209–228.

Forrester, J. W. (1995). *Road Map 1: Counterintuitive Behaviour Of Social Systems*. MIT System Dynamics In Education Project.

Kanar, K. (1995). Structure Oriented Behavior Tests. In *Model Validation, Master Of Science*. Industrial Engineering Boğaziçi University.

Karnopp, D. C., Margolis, D. L., & Rosenberg, R. C. (1990). *System Dynamics A Unified Approach* (2nd ed.). John Wiley & Sons, Inc.

Kirkwood, C. W. (1998). *System Dynamics Methods: A Quick Introduction*. Arizona State University.

Lane, D. J., & Sterman, J. D. (2011). Profiles in Operations Research: Jay Wright Forrester. In Profiles in Operations Research: Pioneers and Innovators. New York: Springer.

Morecroft, J. D. W., & Sterman, J. D. (1994). *Modelling For Learning Organizations*. Portland, OR: Productivity Press.

Mustafa, Ö., Papadopoulou, T. C., & Melek, A. (2007). System Dynamics Modelling of A Manufacturing Supply Chain System. *Simulation Modelling Practice and Theory, 15*(10), 1338–1355. doi:10.1016/j.simpat.2007.09.007

Ramage, M., & Ship, K. (2009). *Sytem Thinkers, The Open University Walton Hall*. Milton Keynes, UK: Springer London.

Reza, H., Amineh, G., & Virginia, D. (2014). Using Diference Equation to Model Discrete-time Behavior in System Dynamics Modeling. In *32nd International Conference of the System Dynamics Society*, Delft, The Netherlands.

Richardson George, P. (1999). *Feedback Throught in Social Science And Systems Theory*. Waltham, MA: Pegasus Communications, Inc.

Richmond, B. (2010). The Thinking In Systems Thinking: Eight Critical Skills. In Tracing Connections: Voices Of Systems Thinkers. Lebanon, NH: Creative Learning Exchange.

Ruth, M., & Hannon, B. (2012). *Modeling Dynamic Economic Systems* (2nd ed.). Springer. doi:10.1007/978-1-4614-2209-9

Sezen, H. K., & Günal, M. (2009). *Yöneylem Araştırmasında Benzetim*. Bursa: Ekin Yayınevi.

Soderquıst, C., & Overakkers, S. (2010). Education for Sustainable Development: A Systems Thinking Approach. *Global Environmental Research*, *14*, 193–202.

Sterman, J. D. (1991). *A Skeptic's Guide to Computer Models*. Cambridge, MA: MIT System Dynamics In Education Project.

Sterman, J. D. (2000). Business Dynamics Systems Thinking And Modelling. In *A Complex World*. New York: McGraw-Hill.

Victor, T., & Samutra, V. (2001). *System Dynamics Origins, Development And Future Prospects of a Method*. Research Seminar in Engineering Systems.

Wheeler Frederick, P. (1994). How to Get Managers To Use System Dynamics. In *International System Dynamics Conference*, Stirling, UK.

Yamaguchi, K. (2013). *Money and Macroeconomic Dynamics- Accounting System Dynamics Approach*. Awaji Island, Japan: Japan Future Research Center.

Zehra, B. (1997). *Sistem Dinamiğinin İşletmelerde Uygulanması*. Bursa: Ekin Kitabevi Yayınları.

KEY TERMS AND DEFINITIONS

Decision Functions: States of the policy that determines how to convert available information in stock into a decision.

Delays: A characteristic of dynamic systems and affect both material and information flow.

Flow: It is defined as the increase or decrease in the unit time interval in stocks and denoted by f (t).

Information Delay: They are usually caused by the transfer of information and the delay in the process of taking an action after the information is received. Information delays could occur in vertical hierarchical administrations.

Information Flow: Creation, control and distribution of information is the most significant task of business management. It might be difficult to model the information properly in the business process.

Material Delays: In this structure, the material moves forward from the beginning to the end of the pipeline without any change during a period of time, similar to a water running through a pipeline.

Material Flow: It includes stocks and flow rates of physical goods such as raw materials, inventories in the process or finished goods.

Stocks: The present values of the variables that are formed by the accumulated difference between the inflow and outflow.

System Dynamic Language: This language consists of four components: stocks, flows, decision functions, and information flow.

System Dynamics: The basis of system dynamics is to understand how system structures cause system behavior and system events.

Chapter 5
Future of Jobs and Humans in a Tech-Centric World

Rama Prasad Varanasi
Matryzel Consulting Sdn Bhdd, Malyasia

ABSTRACT

Modern technologies have presented the world with a plethora of new opportunities, from the mundane (reduced input rigor) through to new outcomes that eluded our collective wisdom and knowledge. These changes have confronted organizations with new risk types, spanning the strategic through to operational, resources through to circularity and sustainability. One poignant impact being seen today is the morphing between virtual and physical inputs (tech tools and humans), resulting in a demand for organizations to reinvigorate their business models in a manner that encompasses both types of inputs seamlessly. However, attendant issues with skills, job types, and tasks have come around full circle. One the one end, there is the fear of technology automating humans out of a job altogether (alongside the promise of enhancing individuals to pursue new skills in a cognitive world), while on the other end there are significant socio-economic concerns surrounding job losses and consequential impacts on the consumption-production continuum.

DOI: 10.4018/978-1-5225-7903-8.ch005

INTRODUCTION

Statistics are a lot of fun, and contentious too. Yet they permit us to remain fairly grounded. Let's start with the obvious. From self-driving vehicles and semi-autonomous robots to intelligent algorithms and predictive analytical tools, machines are increasingly capable of performing a wide range of jobs that have long been human domains. Frey and Osborne (2013) at Oxford University posited that as many as 47% of all jobs in the United States are at risk of "computerization."

And many respondents in a recent Pew Research Center canvassing of technology experts (Smith & Anderson, 2014), predicted that advances in robotics and computing applications will result in a net displacement of jobs over the coming decades – with potentially profound implications for both workers and society as a whole. It is expected that robots will undertake more than 50% of jobs currently being undertaken by humans.

At the current moment, there is palpable positivity that the nature and type of jobs currently undertaken by humans will not completely vanish before 2050. Optimism notwithstanding, the very changes one is seeing today to jobs, particularly at the bottom-end of complexity does suggest that fundamental shifts are in the offing.

I am inclined to take a peek not just into the near-term future where automation, algorithms and machine learning technologies are being viewed as emergent threats to traditionalist views with jobs, but also into the longer-term future where the very definition of jobs is seen as obsolete.

Trends in the past decade have accelerated technology adoption on a scale unimaginable until now. The belief that machines and technologies are primarily aimed at corporations and large entities, has been upended.

Now we see the role of machines everywhere, including but not limited to daily interactions among people. Smart machines today are being able to perform highly complex and advanced pattern recognition tasks, such that most industries are finding use for such technologies.

There is significant evidence of "capital deepening" as robots, computers, and software (all forms of capital) increasingly substitute for human labor. Some key factors contributing to this phenomenon are the availability of constantly increasing & cheap processing power, more sophisticated and intuitive software, cheap and ubiquitous sensors, and a better understanding of human intelligence (known more famously as cognitive science).

On the other end, there is a significant shift in marketplace behavior, manifested particularly in the reduced distinctions between buyer and supplier markets. Instead, integrated views to the production-consumption spectrum are being seen as leading evangelists that could enhance competencies and maximize resource efficiencies within limited means. Meanwhile, atomically precise manufacturing – advances with precision tooling, sophisticated new materials – is only leading to substantial shrinkage in global supply chains.

These shifts have become significantly visible, moving from hitherto hidden corners of certain sectors. Alongside, a range of new opportunities have begun to play out in a manner never envisaged before. The complimentary role of machines is perceived to be the root for much of the progress we see today. Yet, its ability to displace human endeavor, or even eliminate it has begun to assume mainstream conversations. The endeavor of this paper is to distill into these two trends and establish some critical pointers that shall allow us to understand, and appreciate.

NON-BIOLOGICAL INTERVENTIONS

First, let's address near-term trends, by considering algorithms. They are seen as instructions for solving a problem, and much like math. Computers and smartphones are fundamentally algorithms, which rule our daily lives – with social media, mobile apps, GPS systems, trackers, wearables, computers, financial transactions, travel et al.

We cannot do without them today. Interestingly the most underrated component with algorithms is the misunderstanding that algorithms earlier had functional specificities with which they undertook tasks efficiently. Today algorithms are on a self-learning mode, thereby giving us a window into a more interesting future where machine to machine interactions may soon supersede human to machine transfer of knowledge. At this point it is perhaps crucial to acknowledge one example.

Earlier in January 2017, Google Translate developed its own intermediate language so as to enhance its ability to provide translation services.

The most amazing thing about this development is that the algorithms governing it not only learned from millions of users the ability to translate meanings, but have now amassed enough information/ experience to build a "context-based translation language" to provide accurate contextual translation. The possibilities such self-learning tools offer is phenomenal, yet scary at times.

I hear of many arguments from leaders around the world that the recent trends with automation, robotics and attendant technologies are just that – technological interventions that will not fundamentally alter needs or drivers to businesses, but remain subsidiary in the context of value delivery.

At the moment, with the discrete nature of such interventions (both from a standpoint of development, and their adoption by organizations) I am inclined to agree. However, a thorough consideration of the implications (and preparedness required therefore going into the future) necessitates rigorous discussions from a standpoint of applicability and ability to deal with the shake-ups that will necessarily follow.

Service automation technologies (incorrectly labeled as RPA) have already begun to take over transactional jobs around the world. Jobs in office and administration, construction and extraction, arts, design, entertainment, media, legal, installation and maintenance et al are slated to vanish, while "cognitive" jobs in management, engineering, design, computing, architecture, sales, marketing, education et al are expected to grow.

Limiting ourselves to the APAC region as an example, by 2020, it is expected that 86.5 million people will be fully unemployed, while approximately 893 million people would be in "vulnerable employment", meaning such jobs are prime targets for replacement by a non-biological workforce.

Given that median ages in the region are skewed toward youth, with consistently positive birth rates, envisioning a scenario into the next two decades is quite scary.

Will adoption of such technologies therefore slow-down, or be rejected altogether? The economics of push-back on such developments can be quite disastrous – exports would become low-value, imports would become expensive, lifestyles may stagnate, incomes surely would dwindle, purchasing power drastically reduced, and consequent political fallouts may be severe, if not disastrous.

While I am not advocating aggressive adoption of such technologies just to be "in", a complete rejection has irreversible implications in the context of growth and development. I do see that policy makers will have to remain cognizant of the complexities surrounding modernization and job creation (that at the moment seem to be in dichotomy of each other).

The scenario within corporations of course is another interesting story. Bereft of the need to think about socio-economics, their strategies are governed more by competitiveness, growth and shareholder value. Adoption of transactional automation technologies is already being seen as an unavoidable imperative.

Most corporations have or are rigorously developing strategies where within the medium-term their organizations would reflect a workforce constituting both biological and non-biological employees. This transition requires not just an innate understanding of the organization's levers where technologies could be effectively leveraged, but also a clear view to the future that is driven by goals other than technological modernity.

Meanwhile, the inevitable conflict will come to be, pitting organizations against governments. I believe that one cannot ignore this reality. A good friend recently wondered whether it is time for governments to start taxing a non-biological workforce as well. But that is a different conversation for another day.

A HYPER-INTELLIGENT TOMORROW

At the other end of the spectrum we are witness to some great strides being made in various fields, some exciting and some conflicting: gene editing technologies to reduce instances of heart attacks, leveraging skin from fish to treat severe burn injuries, stem cell regeneration from all types of body cells, gene splicing to increase crop resistance to diseases and enhanced yield, GMO crops to eliminate hunger altogether, credit rating based on needs and not incomes, 3D and 4D printing, gesture-based computing, womb-based therapy, virtual health trackers and real-time treatments, water labeling of products, industrial repatriation and many more.

Considerations for such technologies can be driven either by an inherent "visionary" need, for e.g. moon mining, or beaming internet from space, or by envisioning a larger future where "homo-sapiens superiority" is pushing the gauntlet on innovative technologies and their applications.

There are a range of futurists in the world predicting the future of work in many ways, with most of them today focused on identifying "jobs that would be created in future" and comparing them to "jobs that will be lost".

Such predictions may seem overwhelming for governments and organizations who are collectively scampering to remain on top of all these trends. It reminds me of the same continued battles these very entities have engaged in for the past three decades, trying their best to identify near-term trends, and overhauling their environments (however sporadically) to remain in control.

From establishing communication networks, to building ecosystems for adoption and deployment of technologies in the mobility space, eCommerce, cloud computing to big data and IOT, almost all endeavors the world over have reflected a pursuit of technology with scant regard for their applicability and impact on socio-cultural constructs of their ecosystems.

The resultant supply clutter and value erosion (or non-creation) is palpable yet difficult to put a handle on. Complexity continued to increase, while our endeavors seem to fall short.

Meanwhile, a very few individuals/ entities have turned the question upside down. Instead of asking what jobs are needed in future, their question is – to what end do we ready ourselves.

Two institutions [1] have taken this discussion to a very poignant level, while refraining from offering solutions. I personally agree with the approach that we need to put human context into all our endeavors and predicaments.

The Institute for the Future (IFTF) (Davies et al. 2011) has identified six drivers for change that will in turn influence all developments, as well as adoption or rejection going into the future. These trends are human in nature, and have a direct influence on our collective decisions going into the future. I am not describing these here as they are beyond the remit of this paper.

I firmly believe it is crucial that policy makers and industry, along with civil society begin to engage in these inherently complex questions to understand implications, and then determine steps that are complimentary of their collective needs, and opportunities that could consequently be created. In the interim, I believe that almost all our efforts at transforming our workforce, and reinvigorating economic pursuits with new skill development initiatives will remain necessary but severely insufficient.

Trends like localism, contextual deficit, urbanization, increasing rage, increased longevity, cultural intimacy, digital narcissism, sense of entitlement and many more are critical to appreciate than just admiring technologies and rushing to adopt them.

CONCLUSION: DO WE NEED JOBS?

Humans over the past two centuries have built a successful societal model that rested on the back of two broad entities: corporations and governments.

The former created opportunities to leverage individual capabilities and compensated them in exchange for work; the latter created ecosystems for the former to operate within, while seeking taxes from the former to support the latter.

Over time taxes have morphed into a veritably complex set of initiatives the world over. With globalization, some rationalization of rules permitted cross-border trade and exchange.

Yet, a significant proportion of the global population is getting increasingly disconnected with this economic reality. Perhaps the time has come to ask some

Figure 1. Risk management tag

fundamental questions. I have always wondered this: Why do we need jobs? Can we do without them? Perhaps in such categorization of jobs we have built an inequitable system that can never change. Hence all initiatives aimed at inclusion, equality et al will always remain pipe dreams. What if we were to upturn this basic tryst?

Earlier in 2017, Switzerland, and closely followed by Finland initiated an exercise wherein they asked their citizens if they would prefer to have a Universal Basic Income (UBI) that would eliminate all people from the tyranny of empire (read hierarchy, organizations, jobs, positions, structures etc.)

I would have imagined that the very concept of UBI did present a unique opportunity for humanity to liberate itself from the clutches of its own pursuits.

Yet, citizens of both nations rejected the notion of UBI. Does it mean that inherently man believes his effort should necessarily be construed to be in comparison to another, and therefore rewarded commensurately? Or are there other reasons? Interestingly both nations rejected the proposal more on lines of its application and source of funding, rather than in terms of the manner in which it was defined. Of course, one cannot ignore UBI being compared with existing Social Security coverage in many nations, and the attendant disappointment many have with such social systems. Meanwhile, India is toying with the same idea of establishing a UBI.

I am inclined to think that there is significant opportunity to restructure and redirect existing subsidies into the UBI model, thereby freeing up resources to invest in growth and new opportunities. It is easier said than done. I think the discussions are complex, yet in context of incomes and sustenance, UBI presents an opportunity that may essentially eliminate categorization of individuals – through jobs – into various roles, and transform them into a conglomerate, where each individual is a producer, consumer, supplier, aggregator and enabler rolled into one.

Of course this presents another interesting question. Should we be able to eliminate jobs altogether, and have machines do them for us, who then remains in control? We as a species lost the battle to control nuclear technologies in 1945.

Lessons from it influenced a 1975 conference amongst scientists who had discovered DNA, resulting in an agreement not to recombine DNA from different species and possibly lose control. That agreement holds even today. Earlier in January 2017, a similar agreement was reached by technologists and global leaders, wherein 23 principles for AI have been established. Again, the goals around non-circumvention, retention of human control and other aspects govern this agreement. Would we as a species adhere to such an agreement as we did with DNA, in a time and age where animosity amongst and between nations is at its highest? (AA:VV, 2017; Berg, 2008).

Nevertheless, what remains true is that machines have begun to learn from each other, and are slowly making humans redundant. Google Brain's recent trysts with neural networks is a scary example of what possibly remains in store for us. We may have to make some radical choices in the next decade around policy and technology.

REFERENCES

AA.VV. (2017). *51st Asilomar Conference on Signals, Systems, and Computer, Proceedings*. Available in: https://ieeexplore.ieee.org/xpl/mostRecentIssue.jsp?punumber=8330843

Abbass, H. A. (2001). Marriage in honey-bee optimization (MBO): a haplometrosis polygynous swarming approach. *Proceedings of the congress on evolutionary computation (CEC2001)*, 207–214. 10.1109/CEC.2001.934391

Affenzeller, M., & Wagner, S. (2005). Offspring selection: a new self-adaptive selection scheme for genetic algorithms. *Proceedings of the international conference on adaptive and natural computing algorithms (ICANNGA)*, 218–221.

Alkhatib, H., & Duveau, J. (2013). Dynamic genetic algorithms for robust design of multimachine power system stabilizers. *Electr Power Energy Syst*, *45*(1), 242–251. doi:10.1016/j.ijepes.2012.08.080

Berg, P. (2008). Meetings that changed the world: Asilomar 1975: DNA modification secured. *Nature, 455*(18). Available in: https://www.nature.com/articles/455290a.pdf

Chaturvedi, K. T., Pandit, M., & Srivastava, L. (2008). Self-organizing hierarchical particle swarm optimization for nonconvex economic dispatch. *IEEE Transactions on Power Systems*, *23*(3), 1079–1087. doi:10.1109/TPWRS.2008.926455

Davies, A., Fidler, D., & Gorbis, M. (2011). *Future Work Skills 2020*. Institute for the Future for the University of Phoenix Research Institute. Retrieved from: http://www.iftf.org/uploads/media/SR-1382A_UPRI_future_work_skills_sm.pdf

Firouzia, B. B., Farjah, E., & Abarghooee, R. A. (2013). An efficient scenario-based and fuzzy self-adaptive learning particle swarm optimization approach for dynamic economic emission dispatch considering load and wind power uncertainties. *Energy*, *50*(1), 232–244. doi:10.1016/j.energy.2012.11.017

Frey, B. C., & Osborne, M. A. (2013). *The future of employment: how susceptible are jobs to computerisation?* University of Oxford. Retrieved from: http://www.oxfordmartin.ox.ac.uk/downloads/academic/The_Future_of_Employment.pdf

Smith, A., & Anderson, J. (2014). *AI, Robotics, and the Future of Jobs*. Retrieved from http://www.pewinternet.org/2014/08/06/future-of-jobs/

KEY TERMS AND DEFINITIONS

E-Commerce: The sale of goods and services marketed through online platforms. Over the years it is a mode that has increasingly taken hold; e-commerce allows the vendor to significantly reduce the prices of the final product and the players on the market are constantly increasing, from the giants Amazon and eBay to the specialized online store.

Global Position System (GPS): An utility that provides users with positioning, navigation, and timing (PNT) services. This system consists of three segments: the space segment, the control segment, and the user segment.

Human-Computer Interaction (HCI): The study of the interaction between people (users) and computers for the design and development of interactive systems that are usable, reliable, and that support and facilitate human activities.

Intelligent Algorithms: A large amount of intelligent techniques, including neural networks, fuzzy logics, genetic algorithms, etc., have been broadly applied to various fields in reality, such as chemical process, robotics, mechanical engineering, etc. In the biological system, they are practical alternative techniques for tackling and solving a variety of challenging engineering problems.

IT Work-Force Management: An institutional process that maximizes performance levels and competency for an organization in IT sector. The process includes all the activities needed to maintain a productive workforce.

Risk Management: It refers to the set of processes through which a company identifies, analyzes, quantifies, eliminates, and monitors the risks associated with a given production process.

Virtual Health Tracker: A wearable fitness technology like activity trackers, heart rate monitors, and global positioning system (GPS) watches. Wrist activity trackers monitor the number of steps you take, activity levels and sleep quality with an accelerometer, which is an instrument that measures movement. Some kinds also measure heart rate using lights on the bottom of the tracker to peer through your skin and monitor the flow of blood. Other models have a built in GPS to track distance, speed, and elevation. You can then synch all this information up with fitness apps on your smartphone, tablet or computer.

ENDNOTE

1 Please refer to www.thefuturehunters.com and www.iftf.org for greater information.

Chapter 6
Orientism Management Strategy for Training Policy-Makers in Emergency Decision-Making

Luisa Dall'Acqua
Scientific Lyceum TCO, Italy & University of Bologna, Italy

ABSTRACT

Policy-making is asked to define criteria and decisional support to respond to emergencies and a complex mix of social, environmental, economic, and cultural problems. Politics, especially at the highest levels, requires preparing professionals able to manage the opportunities offered by new technologies in the context of security and management. Risk analysis is an increasingly urgent necessity and challenge. Research data needs to be packaged into effective policy tools that will help policy-makers make an evidence-informed policy. The objective of this chapter is to offer a framework of analysis (Orientism Management OM Framework) useful for training policy-makers to develop a multi-perspective informed policy. It intends orienting the variety of backgrounds, interests, knowledge, skills, and the whole personality of the trainees, individually or within a work team.

DOI: 10.4018/978-1-5225-7903-8.ch006

INTRODUCTION

New technology implementation, the welfare state, new generation rights, global policies, and sustainable development goals are just some of the fundamental elements that must inspire the art of good governance. To manage them, a common idea is that a politician today must possess some basic requirements (Pollino Tour, 2017):

- Holding a basic culture (better a degree)
- Holding an ability to public speaking, participating in debates
- Proposing a vision, knowing how to build, having clear ideas, and knowing how to communicate
- Start small experience, ie always starting from a level of local political experience
- Being always up-to-date and active locally, participate in debates, events and give speeches and get to know local decision-makers
- Using social media to promote ideas and knowing how to interact with all the media
- Having organizational and management skills, decision-makership and management, to organize their staff, the election campaign, fundraising
- Knowing how to implement growth and development strategies

The politician is asked above all to be able to take decisions appropriate to the problems to be faced: conclude a trade treaty, make a law to combat corruption, introduce or abolish a tax, deal with the problem of immigration, change or not the text of the Constitution, planning an institution or health reform. These all decisions require training in this regard, on both individual problem and identifying the unexpected effects.

It is necessary that every single sector policy is framed in a general political line that has characteristics of coherence and unity. That of the politician is a complex activity, which does not allow arbitrary simplifications, and requires knowledge, decision, creative design of solutions and courage.

The formation of the ruling classes was fundamental in Greece and in Rome. Plato described a long training path and believed that a man could not deal with politics before the age of 35. Cicero speaks of it extensively, as well as in Italy more recently, from the State Unification onwards.

P. Villari, in the "Southern Letters" (1878), writes: "Have you ever known a country where slander is so powerful and so greedy, wherein such a short time an equal number of honorable reputations has been torn apart? Mediocrity is a leveling power, it wants to reduce all men to its measure, it hates the genius that it does not understand, it detests the ingenuity that destroys the harmony of its coveted equality " (Pernicone, 1993; Sida, n.d.).

In order to have a complete dimension of the educational context of the policy-making, it is necessary to deepen the growth and career path in the various European and extra-European contexts.

For example, France is a witness of excellence in the formation of the politician of the future. The Institut d'Etudes Politiques de Paris, better known as Sciences Po, is one of the best universities in the world in the field of political science, but above all it is the historical institution for the formation of the French political and administrative elite and European Union, has formed four Presidents of the French Republic, eleven prime ministers, numerous foreign heads of state, political and diplomatic personalities.

Instead, in Italy for years there were the party schools, which, however, presented a formative activity dedicated to the political thought and values of the political party to which they belong. Currently, Italy is moving towards a type of training of the political class that looks more at the competence of the person, rather than at his activity within the party of reference.

This research intends to put key questions and related criticalities of Policy-making School, proposing a conceptual interpretation, possible strategies, and tools to manage, which can attempt to explain how policymaking happens which typically adopt company productions or cyclic modes of analysis, reducing policy making to a rational, objective process of steps and stages, especially to govern emergencies.

According to Orientism Management (OM) framework, the analysis put in evidence the new decision-making mindset of the policy. maker, that makes a necessary paradigm change, based on computational thinking and project culture, and strategies.

Intelligence becomes essential to support any kind of strategic, economic, financial, political decision. Analysts and intelligence experts are increasingly requested by the institutional apparatus responsible for national security and public security, by the armed forces, companies, public and private research centers.

Rovner (2015) states that policy-makers tend to be self-confident and action-oriented. They come into office with strongly held worldviews and the belief that certain truths exist about international politics. They also believe that intelligence agencies can (and should) provide firm and unequivocal predictions about future events.

In an inherently ambiguous international environment, uncertainty and change are common. Intelligence analysts are usually unwilling to offer specific predictions about the future. Instead of offering unequivocal forecasts, they attempt to identify the factors that will make events more or less likely. And because intelligence analysis is somewhat akin to academic social science, analysts are comfortable speaking in abstract and theoretical terms that are unfamiliar to their policy bosses. As long as the intelligence sector and the policy teams speak different languages, they will find it difficult to interact.

POLICY-MAKING

The Policy Studies Organization was formed in 1971 in the U.S. and was also open to scholars of other nations. But the public policy as decision analysis already emerged in the 1960s, encompassing political science, sociology, economics, and other disciplines. It emerged out of a greater concern for specific policy problems, the causal determinations of particular policies, and the relationship between policies and societal impact.

Historically, this complex discipline developed starting from some milestones: the "rational decision" theory of M. Weber (1864-1920), the "efficiency choice" theory of V. Pareto (1848-1923), the "problem orientation" theory of H. Lasswell (1902-1978) are some of the main examples.

What's a public policy?

- Policy-making is everything a government decides to do or not to do (by Dye, in Colebatch, 2006).
- Policy-making is a set of concatenated and coherent decisions, taken by one or more public actors, and sometimes private, in order to resolve in a targeted way, a problem defined as politically as collective (Knoepfel, Larrue, & Varrone, 2007).
- Policy-making is a set of decisions and activities related to the solution of a collective problem, the need or demand for public intervention (Dunn, 1994).

In common these and other definitions have that a policy decision is a process of choosing between multiple solutions to a collective problem, and therefore the transformation of the ways in which it is dealt with.

The distinguishing features of the policy processes are:

- A progressive complexity
- The increase in uncertainty
- A possible increase in conflict

The main variable are: decision-makers making choices, institutions and network/ subsystems, ideas or beliefs, policy tools and resources, and the social environment.

Decisional Decision-Makers Making Choices, Institutions, Networks/Subsystems

Policy theories often categorize and describe some key policy decision-makers who act in a decision-making scenario, in the presence of those who suffer the effects of decisions.

Often active policy decision-makers (stakeholders) are involved in managing to create decisional effects. Each decisional decision-maker corresponds to a changing vision of the problem and of the solutions.

Recently, a broader definition of policy decision-makers emerges, multiplying the units of analysis, from the groups of interest to the individual (public choice). The focus shifts from decisional decision-makers in classical institutional approaches to a plurality of institutions and relationships. These institutions (together) take the form of collective actors capable of developing a general interest expression of a common identity, within a shared normative framework. Distinguishing who the real policy decision-makers are and what logic they answer is not always easy.

Typical policy decision-makers are Executives, Politicians, Legislators, Bureaucrats, Policy actors, Interest groups, Research organizations, Mass media.

In an area of absolute rationality, the objectives of a policy decision-maker should remain constant and legible. But often several factors obstacle them, such as the possible distance between starting targets and those pursued by an actor due to misjudgments changing preferences. And different factors can change objectives without the actors fully realizing their content objectives. with the nature of the problem and with the consequences of policy decisions.

Rules, norms, practices, and relationships influence individual and collective behavior. The choices of actors are explained partly by their understanding of and

Figure 1. Policy choice

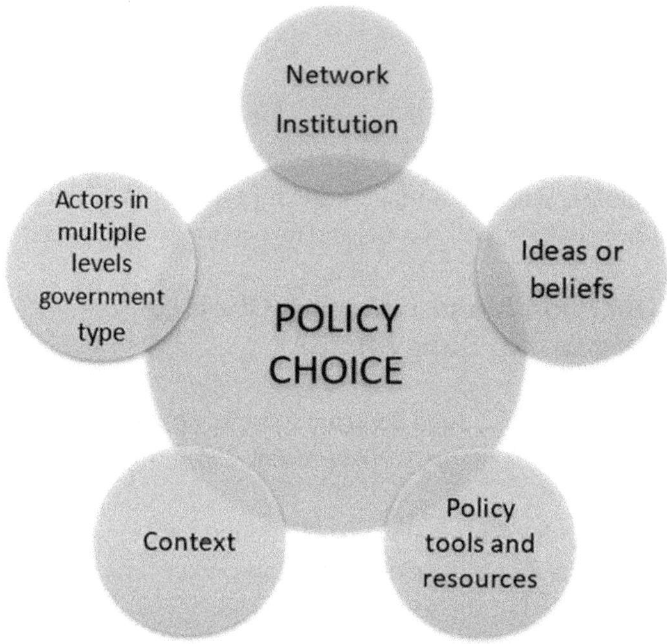

adherence to rules. Rules can be formal and widely understood, such as when enshrined in law or a constitution, or informal and only understood in particular organizations. Institutions at one level (e.g., constitutional) can also shape activity at another (e.g., legislative or regulatory), establish the types of venues where policy decisions are made, and make the rules that allow particular types of actors or ideas to enter the policy process.

These are the relationships between decisional decision-makers responsible for policy decisions and the "pressure participants" (Jordan, Halpin, and Maloney 2004), such as interest groups with which they consult and negotiate. Senior policymakers delegate responsibility for policy-making to bureaucrats, who seek information and advice from groups. Groups exchange information for access to and potential influence within government. Bureaucracies and other public bodies (or forums for collective choice) may have operating procedures that favor particular sources of evidence.

Ideas or Beliefs

This broad category captures how theories deal with ways of thinking or the knowledge that plays a role in the policy process. It may include beliefs, knowledge, worldviews, and shared definitions of policy problems, images, and solutions within groups, organizations, networks, and political systems. Some ideas or beliefs may be taken for granted or rarely questioned—such as core beliefs, values, or paradigms. Others may be more malleable, such as proposed solutions to policy problems.

Policy Tools and Resources

Policy tools are classified into coercive, volunteer, and mixed. The characteristic of voluntary instruments is the minimum or null involvement of the government. Through the coercive tools, the government can constrain the actions of the associates. The most used policies remain mixed, that influence the behavior of the members, leaving, however, to the private individuals the choice of their strategies.

The relevance of actors in influencing processes is a function of their influence, the control that only those who really decide to determine the outcomes of a process.

Policy-making resources are classified into political, economic, legal, informative. Anything that moves consensus is a political resource, An economic resource can mobilize wealth or liquidity (financial resources). With legal resources, various aspects are regulated by the law, and they determine prerogatives or positions of advantage.

Specifically, an authority has the possibility of issuing sanctions, guarantees, formal procedures. Finally, an informative resource allows an actor to climb the positions of influence. It is data, individual information, theories, models and knowledge of the process.

Resources are not distributed equally but are never sufficient for a decisional decision-maker, because they are replaceable.

Social Environment (Context)

This category describes the wide array of features of the policy-making environment that can influence policy decisions. It can refer to the often-changing policy conditions that policymakers take into account when identifying problems and deciding how to address them, such as a political system's geography, biophysical and demographic profile, economy, and mass attitudes and behavior It can also refer to a sense of policymaker "inheritance" of laws, rules, institutions, and programs—on entry into office (Hofferbert 1974).

THE POLICY CYCLE

The policy cycle is a way to organize relevant topics and an effective model of policy representation. It consists of 3 macro-phases (*see Figure* 2):

- **Ex Ante Evaluation:**
- **Agenda setting (Problem Finding):** Acknowledgment of the problem
- **Criteria (Problem Setting):** The methodology to define the problem
- **Analysis (Problem Analysis):** Break down the main problem into secondary problems
- **Formulation and Design (Problem solving proposal)**
- **In Itinere Evaluation:**
- **Decision Making:** Choice of the solution. It induces the decision-maker to assume specific behaviors and actions.
- **Implementation**
- **Ex Post Evaluation**
- **Final Evaluation:** It is a results check.

The Decision-Making as a Political Process

Basically, problem-solving is a cognitive process with respect to a problem. Its goal is to achieve a goal. The problem discovered leads to the analysis to find a solution.

The problem solving requires making decisions. It induces the subject to assume specific behaviors and actions. It is an adaptive process (Mayer 2014). Specifically, the goal of the formulation and design phase is to design a policy.

Many questions never reach the formulation stage. They remain as latent problems, sometimes present to part of the public opinion but without that a sufficient consensus is formed that leads to the decision.

The second problem concerns the identification of the problem. This is the case of all decision-making processes in which there are predetermined structures of subjects and relationships that monopolize the decision-making system.

These are groups (issue networks, policy networks, advocacy coalitions) in which there is little change. The constraints can be of various kinds, typically political-institutional-cultural (Heikkila & Cairney, 2014).

The analytical decision-making models identify the essential elements of the decision-making process, ie the decision maker, his cognitive attitudes, the research activities of the solutions, the modalities and criteria of the choice and above all the relationships that exist between all these different elements.

The main of them are focused on rational processes (such as comprehensive, absolute, bounded, and incremental rationality) or non-rational (garbage bin model).

Figure 2. Policy cycle and activities
(freely adapted by the author from Crossover, n.d.)

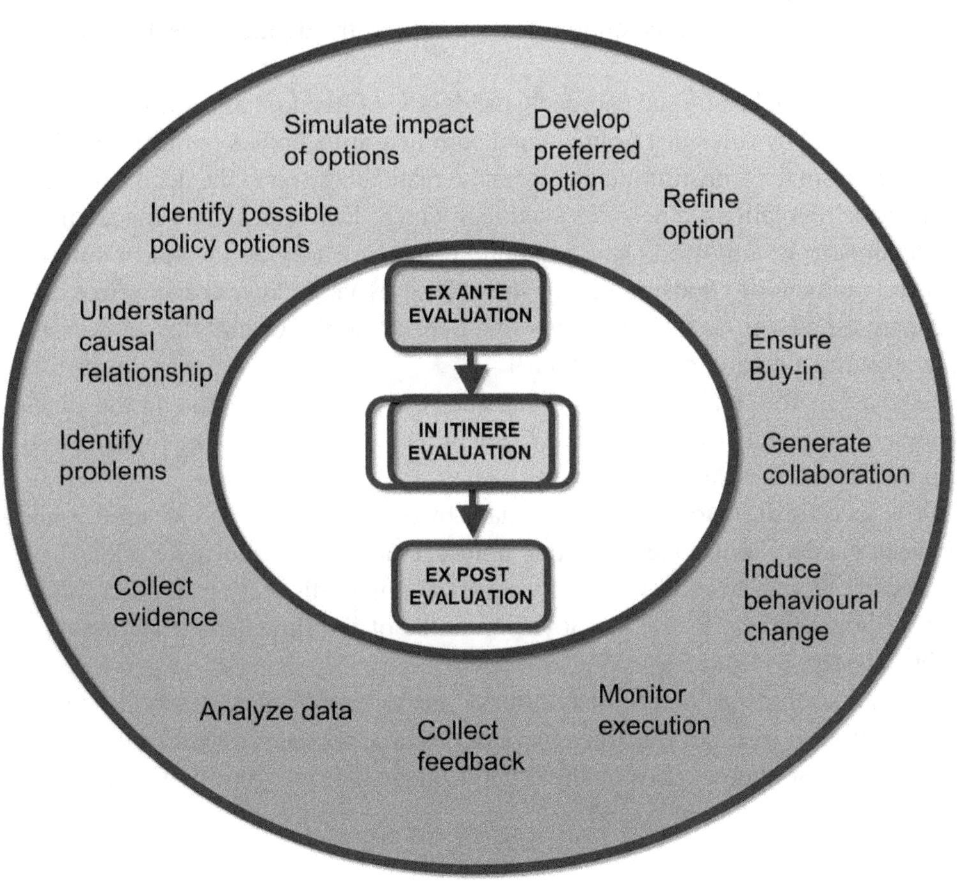

Rational (Synoptic) Approach

The decision criterion is the optimization of the choice in cognitive conditions of certainty of a single decision maker. The main features of the rational model are:

- There is a clearly identified and shared objective function
- All the variables relevant to the decision can be identified, selected, represented and measured
- It is possible to measure and quantitatively estimate the correlation between the variables
- We have mathematical algorithms that model reality
- The models make it possible to evaluate the impact of the various decision-making options available
- The choice falls on the option that maximizes the defined objective function

According to the rational approach, the degree of freedom of decision-makers is circumscribed by rules that political and administrative bodies must respect. They are taken from the Constitution and from the mandate given to the decision-makers by laws or regulations. The rules establish which decisions can be made and the procedures to be followed. The decision concept focuses on the set of solutions and the moment of choosing one of them. In a dynamic key, decision making is a coherent body of decisional events that depend on the desirability of decisions (perceived to a greater or lesser extent).

The actors that make it count (compared to a plurality of actors in the various phases of the policy cycle, from the formation of the agenda to the formula to the approval to the implementation).

The specific direction of decisions made by the crucial actors. The homogeneity between the decisions concerning that political date and that form a cycle.

Specifically, an absolute rationality model assumes a distinction between political and technical phases that favors loyalty, choice of the times and selection of the right answers.

It assumes that the analysis of solutions is always weighted and able to dispel the uncertainties; it assumes the uniqueness of the final decision-maker who is guided by the behavior of other ones on the right button at the right time and is oriented to the goals, as following indicated:

- The established goal can be achieved by the means available
- The individual interest coincides with the collective interest

- Objectives and values are identified and ordered hierarchically
- The means necessary to reach them are known and mastered
- An assessment of the consequences related to the various alternatives is carried out (predictability of the consequences)

The conditions for applying the rational model are:

- Well-structured problem
- Single decision-maker (individual or collective)
- Non-contradictory objectives
- Possibility to fix the ends before and independently of the means
- Availability of time

Specifically, a (synoptic) rationality model, applied to policy-making assumes the idea that elected policy-makers translate their values into policy in a straightforward manner. They have a clear, coherent and rank-ordered set of policy preferences which neutral organizations carry out on their behalf. It assumes that who makes the decisions:

- Have clear priorities, values and objectives
- Know the means to get your own wishes
- Have a sufficiently clear idea of the consequences
- Know how to calculate the costs of each decision
- Know how to choose alternative solutions (always following a cost / benefit calculation) in the event that a goal goes away by posing the problem of a return on the decision

The possible limits of a rational model are:

- Cognitive limits to decision-makers' ability to consider all the selected options, which force them to consider alternatives in a selective way (for example, for ideological or political reasons)-
- The model provides for the possibility that decision-makers know in advance the consequences of each decision (rare condition)
- Any political decision involves a series of favorable or unfavorable consequences that are in fact difficult to compare analytically
- The non-opportunity to use this approach to resolve emergency situations

Bounded Rationality Model (Simon)

The decision criterion is satisfaction in cognitive conditions of the uncertainty of a single decision maker (or a coalition). The main features are:

- There is no clearly identified and shares objective function
- Only some decisional variables can be identified, selected, represented and measured
- It is not possible to estimate and quantify the correlation between variables quantitatively
- The aim is to obtain the acceptable satisfaction of the objectives by the various subjects
- Decision makers adapt to the context and not vice versa

It suggests that policymakers' ability to make and implement decisions is more problematic. Rationality pushes decision-makers to cost/benefit calculations and to propose goals in line with their priorities. Fundamental principles:

- Men determine the functioning of organizations
- No identification of a clear and shared objective function
- No perfect knowledge available alternatives and consequences
- People adapt information / knowledge / cognitive system to the (changing) conditions of the external environment
- Decisor: criterion of average satisfaction of the objectives (not of maximization)

The possible limits of a Bounded Rationality Model are:

- Knowledge of the available alternatives is limited
- Even the cognitive capacity of an absolute decision maker is limited, as is the memory of the teachings of the past
- Time (poor) acts as a limit to rationality
- Practices and customs constitute limits to rationality

Political decisions do not maximize benefits over costs but tend to meet the criteria that decision-makers impose on the case in question. The search for alternatives is often sequential and often relies on heuristic or routine decisions.

In common with the model of synoptic rationality, this model has the idea of a univocal decision-maker capable of selecting and sorting preferences and priorities. But does this necessarily exist in a democratic situation of collective decision-makers?

Incrementalism

The decision criterion is the mutual accommodation in the decision under cognitive conditions of partiality of several interdependent decision-makers. The main features are:

- There are differentiated or limited overlapping objective functions among the stakeholders
- Decision processes are fragmented and heterogeneous
- There is no concentration of decisions in the hands of a single subject, but the coexistence of different decision-making poles
- The choices of the various decision-makers are interdependent
- Decisions are taken incrementally, just partially modifying the existing status quo
- Sequence of attempts and errors and attempts review
- Only some of the consequences of an alternative taken into consideration are investigated
- Realistic goal for every decision maker is to get by at the best (muddling through)
- Values and objectives of concrete action are not distinguishable but chained
- Therefore, there is not an adequate idea of the means necessary to arrive at a result
- Many alternatives that are actually practicable are neglected
- The consequences are often overlooked
- Typically the ex post analysis (hindsight) says that the decision maker could consider other ways.

Lindblom's famous conclusion is that bounded rationality helps an incrementalist approach. Organizations use simplifying strategies, such as limiting policy analysis to a small number of policy choices which diverge incrementally from the status quo. It bases on the argument that it is better to analyze a few issues comprehensively than seek comprehensive coverage of all issues

The decision is taken on the basis of the ability to create added value and partially to change the existing status quo. It depends on the agreement reached between those who contribute to the decision, interdependence of decision makers. That prevents concentration of power and guaranteed freedom of choice.

This causes a shift of attention from the single or prevalent actor to the whole of the relevant actors.

Focus more precisely on the political object of politics (policy-making policy): decisively impacting on politics means increasing one's influence and therefore one's own power.

The incremental model is preferable in the interpretation of most of the decisional processes because it allows centering the typical complexity of all public policies and at the same time to understand some compromises between the actors that are part of the life of the decision makers themselves.

The incremental model, therefore, allows putting at the center of the analysis the different types of actors, their interactions which form the network of decision-making (network), the resources in the field, the modalities of interaction, the relative posts. All within a given decision context.

The possible limits of the incremental model are:

- The risk of remaining rigid and conservative on an already assumed position
- The lack of orientation to the objectives
- Relegates the decision-making process to a negotiation between the policy-makers
- Threatens to discourage the search for alternative solutions

Mixed-Scanning (Etzioni) Model

It represents a more strategic and innovative vision of the incremental model.

The main features of the model are:

- the decision-making process is hierarchical
- higher decision-making criteria co-exist, a consequence of the lower ones
- the decision-making process operates by excluding the less relevant deiciosni in order to prepare the final decisions
- does not consider it necessary to analyze all the different alternatives all the available information sources, but to determine those that are strategically most important for making decisions

Scanning means a research, collection, process and evaluation of information, in order to prepare final decisions.

The Decision making and decision-making criteria are hierarchical, and the decision-making process is discarded for the purpose of preparing final decisions. It is necessary to determine the strategically most important alternatives for making decisions (it is not necessary to analyze all the different alternatives)

Garbage Can Model

The decision criterion is the case in cognitive conditions of ambiguity of a changing number of involved decision-makers. The main features of the model are:

- Preferences are unstable and influenced by the actors' prejudices
- Time determines an alignment of preferences which in turn plays a role
- The focus is on the timing of a policy, which is influenced by a set of flows (multiple stream approach): 1. flow of problems composed of issues; 2. flow of solutions; 3. flow of political action that establishes urgency through the formation of the political agenda
- Variables are: Actors, Problems, Solutions
- Choice opportunities: the garbage can, in which actors throw in bulk problems and possible solutions.

The decision depends from the casual combination between problems and solutions. Key issue is the time factor: temporal alignment, simultaneity.

The possible limits of the incremental model are:

- The decision-making process is strongly ambiguous and unpredictable.
- There isn't an evaluation associated to selected solutions.
- The disordered flows do not make us understand how the probelma emerges and when.

As in a bin, we do not know the order of the material we throw in, the link between material flows and the moment of full capacity.

However, we know that some variables (institutions) can give some order to flows and make decisions more rational.

Understanding the Problem of the Implementation

There are cases in which the implementation corresponds to a new process, very similar to the decision-making process, in which success is not assured. The opening of a school or a park is generally a simple decision, the construction of a new subway is more difficult, the success of a development project once decided is even more difficult.

The difference is largely due to the number of variables to check, such as:

- **Botton-Up:** Important and often decisive operational details of the implementation of a public policy are defined, selected and translated into practice above all by the "operators" (street level bureaucrats) who act in direct contact with the users of public policies
- **Top-Down:** The process of implementing a public policy proceeds almost linearly from the political and bureaucratic summit that formulated and approved it at the base, ie those charged with implementing it concretely.

Evaluation

Evaluation is the production of information to make judgments about public actions with the aim of improving them. In evaluating a public policy it is necessary to trace a theory of change that is not always explicit that links a problem (a dependent variable) to a solution (an independent variable).

The evaluation of public policies from the learning point of view is an iterative process in which actors actively learn the nature of policy issues and their solutions. Through learning, policy actors are led to change their positions and change their styles of action. The learning is endogenous if originated within the process and the policy subsystem, exogenous if originated from changes in external environments to the policy.

The adjustments, resulting from learning, are marginal and mainly affect policy tools or procedures, without touching the way in which the problem and the solutions are defined. It is the most frequent type of policy change, often the result of endogenous pushes to the policy subsystem.

The experimental approach consists in verifying the extent to which the objectives of a program have been achieved and verifying that the results achieved are directly attributable to the program. The focus is on objectives, means used and results. It is a top-down approach, with centrality in the concept of causality. The most commonly used instrument/method is the experiment such as the comparison between the experimental group and the control group.

The pragmatic approach is to provide useful knowledge to decision makers on how to improve a public policy. The Focus is on the context and the "values" with respect to which a program is evaluated, such as for example.

The tools are both quantitative/experimental and qualitative methods.

The constructivist approach (Guba & Lincoln 1989) consists in the cognitive purpose and the political aim; the evaluation must serve to compare the points of view of all the stakeholders, in order to clarify the terms of the problem faced, to compose the conflicts and to allow the "weaker" groups to participate. The evaluation itself takes place in a negotiation process that accompanies the entire course of the program. The relevant topics and the criteria of judgment are established by the stakeholders themselves. The method is qualitative.

POLICY-MAKING IN SAFETY AND SECURITY

Security Study is a field of study that fits within the larger academic domain of international relations. The latter itself is a sub-domain of political science, one of the social sciences. Security studies emerged as a new field in the middle of the 20th century in direct response to the Second World War and The Cold War.

Nowadays, it also studies the role of other levels of government, and it studies the ways in which large corporations, or even groups of citizens, or individuals can shape security risks.

Traditionally, security studies focused predominantly on interstate conflict. Later on, the field also started to study conflict within specific nation-states, for instance, civil wars. In recent decades the focus has broadened further to include things such as terrorism, and political violence, international crime, and security in cyberspace. In security studies, the focus in study lies predominately with gaining a better understanding of the causes of risk. Security studies aim to understand why risks emerge.

Specifically, war and international conflict are intentionally instigated by human actors.

This field emerged in the middle of the 20th Century and focused on interstate relations at first. Later on, it broadened its area of study to include other actors as well, such as other levels of government, businesses, and groups of citizens. Moreover, it broadened its scope to include other types of security risks, not just wars between nation-states.

Safety Science is a subfield of Security Science. It seeks to understand the risks for human beings or the environment come from new technologies. It serves as an international medium for research in the science and technology of human safety. It extends from the safety of people at work to other spheres, such as transport, leisure, and home, as well as every other field of man's hazardous activities.

Researchers develop models that can help us predict the likelihood and impact of natural hazards in specific locations. Using these models, they can assess whether the level of protection in these locations is adequate or should be improved to increase the safety of people living there.

These systems have made our lives easier and they also play a central role in facilitating economic activity in our societies. While complex technological systems such as nuclear power plants and the chemical industry have brought us many benefits, at the same time, these systems are also hazardous. They are risky technologies in the sense that when accidents occur, they may lead to significant harm to large groups of people and to the environment.

Therefore, studying safety in relation to chemical, industrial, and nuclear systems is literally of vital importance. A further subdomain of Safety Science is the area of Public Health. In this field, scientists study the potential and consequences of various health risks for communities and the public at large. Examples include ensuring that the food we eat is safe, preparing for epidemics or viral outbreaks, and investigating the effects of lifestyle choices in relation to certain diseases, for example, diabetes.

The political decision-maker during an emergency can buy or lose credibility based on the decisions he makes on managing the crisis, decisions such as the areas in which to concentrate the funds or which financial activities.

The political decision-maker is essentially involved for three reasons:

- Disasters involve people (political decision-makers are elected by citizens)
- Public policy (the political decision-maker in his strategy has decided how, why and how to make certain investments for the safety of its citizens rather than others, in emergence of all the fragility of the policy undertaken and the political decision-maker will have every interest in trying to mitigate the impact of the crisis on his population)
- Public interest (disasters are given a great media coverage so the political decision-maker must in some way participate as it is a matter of public interest).

According to Selves analysis (Selves, 2007) the factors that influence the political decision maker to be present and influential in the resolution of a crisis are:

- Very violent and rapid events that have a great media impact (eg earthquake)
- Events as terrorist attacks that undermine the country's security plan
- If the cause of the disaster is due to man (industrial disaster)
- Events involving state authorities at multiple levels
- Situations that can strongly influence the population (eg decision to forcibly evacuate a city area or quarantine)
- A low level of citizen satisfaction in the response put in place
- Disings in which a better work of institutional prevention would have mitigated the impact on the population
- The political color of the affected areas

These factors influence the decision on whether and how to intervene in response to emergencies both on their own territory and in support of other territories.

The foregoing does not mean that in any case a basic answer will still be given by the national emergency system. The political decision-maker, in the cited circumstances, will have every interest in ensuring that the emergency response is as effective as possible to limit the loss of credibility of his Government and therefore limit the loss of votes (Chen & Healy, 2014; Strömberg, 2007).

Decision-Making Under Risk

Aven (2010) provides a detailed analysis of risks in safety sector and argues that for some broad risk perspectives, which highlight uncertainties beyond probabilities and expected values, safety can, in fact, be considered the antonym of risk, and safe can be defined by reference to acceptable risk. An example of such a risk perspective is risk understood as uncertainty about and severity of the consequences of an activity (Aven and Renn, 2010).

Seeing safety as the antonym of risk leads to simple and easily understandable definitions of safety and safe. When the risk assessment describes risk in relation to the loss of lives, it assesses the safety at the same time. There could of course in practice be aspects of importance for the safety not captured by the risk assessment (for example psychological factors in relation to some accident events), yet this would not be the result of differences in the concepts but due to simplifications and limitations in the assessment (Aven, 2011).

A wide range of research and practices has been developed around the measurement and control of risk.

Defining and pursuing a given strategy is extremely important:

- Identifying all the risks that may affect its realization
- Identifying possible scenarios according to interpretative approaches
- Defining contingent interrelations and lines of action in order to maximize positive outcomes in favorable scenarios (opportunities) and minimize negative outcomes in unfavorable scenarios (threats)

Due to the diversity of studies and sectors in which the risk analysis has been applied, the present work proposes a summary of the most common criteria for a risk taxonomy (Loucks, Costa, 1991; Holland, 1992; Becker et all, 1992):

- **Source or Cause:** The first type of risk refers to the source of the event possibly giving rise to a damage. Researchers distinguish in:
    - **Technological Risks**: They are related to the danger for man and the environment, possibly resulting from a series of productive activities, linked to infrastructure and technology networks, increasingly sophisticated and complex in equipment and installations
    - **Natural Risks**: Due to irregular actions of physical and natural forces, such as earthquakes, floods, etc.) Research conducted by a team of scientists, led by Kunreuther at Boston International Institute of Applied Systems Analysis (IIASA) are well-known. They was about the risk of natural gas, considering in particular the jurisdictional limits in the decision-making processes used in decision, and to how individuals perceive the dangers of natural dangers
    - **Risks arising from the Human Factor**
- **Nature of the Event:** More articulated is the criterion regarding the nature of the potentially unfavorable event. Some authors generally distinguish between:
    - **Static Risks:** Linked to losses caused by unnatural action of nature and human mistakes and misunderstandings
    - **Dynamic Risks:** Associated with changes in human needs and technological and organizational improvements. Others between (Green-Trieschmann, 1981, pp. 4-6):
    - **Objective Risks:** Variations related to real loss versus probable

  - **Subjective Risks (Hazards):** Relating to the mental state of an individual who has doubts or disturbances about the outcome of an event
- **Effects:** Another type of risk refers to the possible effects of the event possibly giving rise to a damage. Researchers distinguish in:
  - Economic risks (in society) likely to cause monetary losses. For example in the financial sector:
    - Studies on the so-called theory of capital gains in the *valuation of investments*
    - Studies on the *perception of risk* by investors
    - Studies on the *political dimension* of risk in international affairs
  - Environmental risks (hazards), ie susceptible to leakage with immediate reflection on the population, such as:
    - **Public risks**
    - **Health risks:** tumors, infectious diseases, etc.
    - **Social risks:** Protecting the population from social risks is the main objective of welfare policies. Social risks vary according to the social class, gender, age, but also depending on contexts
- **Control:** the distinction based on the possibility of facing and controlling the risks is more generic. This is the case, for example, of:
  - **Avoidable Risks:** The subject can predict and establish a control strategy
  - **Inevitable Risks:** The subject can not avoid damage to external or internal factors
- **Size:** it refers to the possibility of distinguishing risks from the size in the scope of action, such as
  - **Large-Scale Risk:** affecting the entire society
  - **Small Scale Risk:** which concerns the personal activities of each individual, voluntary and controllable or not, and which have generally less catastrophic consequences than the first one
- **Stakeholders:** An additional criterion is based on those who suffer the consequences of the unfavorable event. They are divided in:
  - Impersonal Risks in origin and effect, such as those associated with disarmament of the economic system, political-social changes, extraordinary natural disturbances
  - Personal Risks in origin and effects, such as the risk of death, unemployment, property, legal liability, etc..

- Related to individual characteristics, such as: age, nationality gender, race, education
- Related to financial characteristics, such as: wealth or income
- Related to job, such as: employment, managerial activity, industrial activity or seniority

PROFILE OF A POLICY MAKER IN EMERGENCE SOCIAL CONDITIONS

According to PENTHA approach (dall'Acqua, 2014), policy-makers in emergence social conditions should be trained to get:

- Specific capacities for understanding and critical analysis of the phenomena and social, political, legal, cultural and geographical changes that in varying circumstances affect national and international scenarios in which emergencies occur
- A critical-comparative assessment capacity of the different emergencies and crisis states. This is favored by the essentially interdisciplinary character to master the analysis of an emergent phenomenon from multiple points of observation and to compare different states of crisis with each other
- The ability to operate at a technical-professional level in the sectors of public administrations and national and international organizations dedicated to civil defense to support, protection of the civil population, as well as the reconstruction of the cultural social fabric of areas affected by emergencies, disasters and states of conflict
- In-depth knowledge of method and scientific and professional content in the fields of legal-institutional, political-economic, political and sociological that allow him to occupy top positions in national and international organizations in charge of crisis management and emergencies.

This involves the acquisition of interdisciplinary skills in the various areas listed above in a comparative and international perspective that makes it capable of analyzing socio-political and economic-institutional phenomena and of managing the organizational aspects of complex emergent phenomena.

Specifically, the main decision-maker needs, to be effective and productive, in addition to activating performance of collaboration and cooperation, are:

- **Knowledge Level (K-L):**
    - By interactions, to generate a significant flux of communications and coordination of actions (reinforcement knowledge process) by processing meaning
    - To implement cooperation through knowledge management protocols, such as: sharing, level of specialization of the decision-makers (collection or creation of content) and sharing of the work (distributed allocation)
    - To manage factual information and access content, as well as procedural knowledge and best practices, towards "reduction of complexity"
    - To find related stuff, integrating distributed knowledge
    - To realize and manage knowledge awareness and data meaning management in a network of relationships
    - To realize and manage consciousness transfer in a knowledge interface phenomenon
    - Not last, to realize and manage "spirals" and re-birth, or re-purposing, of different knowledge (patterns), emerging in different forms
- **User Level (U-L):**
    - To realize a degree of connectedness, as function of density of connected decisional decision-makers, speed and flow of shared information, plasticity and frequency of created connections
    - To realize periodically interaction between all the decisional decision-makers, to understand problems, mitigate risks and remove the roadblocks
    - To manage a complex network with numerous typologies of nodes and connections of knowledge, competences, communication, representations, relationships, technologies and multi-paradigm
    - To manage own emotional and social intelligence (see below, kmf)
    - To improve problem solving, networking and bridging skills: expertise, design and organizational competence, ability to operate systematically in terms of processes and products
    - To optimize the entire range of resources (structural, logistic, material, economic-functional, human and professional) and make them synergistically working with system targets

- **Environment Level (E-L):**
  - To optimize the entire range of resources (structural, logistic, material, economic-functional, human and professional) and make them synergistically working with system targets
  - To facilitate information management by archiving all communications and interactions within an e-environment to access and share for future activities
  - To enable an effective capture of the tacit knowledge (e.g., experience, intuition, creativity) that is missed with traditional knowledge management systems, that focus on document archiving (i.e., explicit knowledge)
  - To promote communication and logistical coordination among (geographically distributed) workforce members through the use of communities of practice (cops) and collaboration tools
  - To scan and report pathways of individual/social actions
  - To facilitate an intelligent and creative learning/business atmosphere that will allow employees freedom to capture the knowledge that is up to date and accurate

POLICY-MAKING MINDSET TRAINING, ACCORDING TO ORIENTISM FRAMEWORK

This analysis refers to the Orientism Management (OM) concept, based on PENTHA vs. 2 approaches (dall'Acqua, Md Santo, 2014) to describe the decision-making under risk.

The focus of the OM is specifically to orient people to management decisions in unpredictability conditions in multi-user environment context. It intends to propose a new solution to the demand for "innovative and creative decision-makers" to make choices, to open to the change of perspective, to manage relationships and complex environments, basing on the conception of a new model of behavior and management of the simultaneity of how people process information.

The framework dedicates attention to different "plans" in the decision-making process, as following:

- **Prescriptive Plan:** How Policy-maker should reason
- **Descriptive Plan:** How they reason

- **Social Plan:** What type of reasoning motivates the decisional action in terms of efficacy and efficiency
- **Communicative Plan:** What type of reasoning is recognizable
- **Management Plan:** What conditions guarantee "order" in a process, against networking, understanding and learning "chaos"
- **Tutoring Plan:** How Policy-maker can be supported in their choosing process
- **Historical Plan:** How a diachronic vision (history) of the issues and own previous experiences can lead decisions
- **Comparative Plan:** How a synchronic vision (comparing transversal situations and conditions) can lead decisions
- **Creative Plan:** How to innovate
- **Simulation Plan:** How to simulate cases study

Key points of *Orientism* concept are:

- The creation of new models of behavior
- The simultaneity of how we process information
- Larger pieces of human experience are to be put together to achieve success
- The complex interconnection between reference points

New variables, factors, and criteria are needed to direct and motivate the mind in the decision-making process, in self-reference, to be considered in a lifelong guidance to have success in choices, assumptions of responsibilities and achievement of objectives, over the uncertainty.

Orientism approach proposes a new solution to make choices, to manage own life, relationships and complex environments, basing on:

- The conception of a new model of decisional behavior
- The management of the simultaneity of how people process information, that generates continuous changes each other
- The management of "larger pieces" of human experiences to be put together to achieve successful actions
- The management of a complex network with numerous typologies of nodes/ connections, such as information, competences, intelligence, people and interpretations
- The adaptation of the "learning attitude" to activate "orienting reflex" phenomena and to develop a critical mind the develop of analytic and aware skills

Orientism view is a possible new conception of the Knowledge Management: it moves towards a knowledge awareness, extension of own horizon and points of perspective, meanings assignment and management, in a network of relationships, starting from own profile and own strength points, and consciousness transfer in knowledge interface phenomena.

The vertices represent the profile variables to be considered in a training guidance. They are:

- **Profession Vertex**: It is an openly declaring, according own thought and identity; specific knowledge, training and skills towards own employment. It is the representation of people as policy decision-makers.
- **Vision Vertex**: It is an aware semantic interpretation of reality and/or own will. It leads the thought towards of a meaning schema of actions
- **Passion Vertex**: It is a powerful emotion. It pushes a person towards a target with force and determination.
- **Vocation Vertex**: It is a strong feeling of suitability to act in some context. For it people regard themselves as particularly worthy. It requires great dedication.
- **Mission Vertex**: It is a statement of a reason for existing. It motivates people to perform a service.

The connections among vertices represent the added subjective components to orient, train and activate choice processes.

- Spirit factor is the synthesis of the relationship between own personal investment and powerful being pushed towards a target (Passion) and own deep feeling and dedication (Vocation).
- Energy factor is the synthesis of the relationship between own personal investment and powerful being pushed towards a target (Passion) and semantic interpretation of reality (Vision).
- Awareness factor is the synthesis of the relationship between own semantic interpretation of reality (Vision) and own deep feeling and dedication (Vocation).
- Love factor is the synthesis of the relationship between own personal investment and powerful being pushed towards a target (Passion) and own reason to perform (Mission).
- Action factor is the synthesis of the relationship between own personal investment and powerful being pushed towards a target (Passion) and identity as a policy decision-maker towards an employment (Profession)

- Purpose factor is the synthesis of the relationship between own semantic interpretation of reality (Vision) and reason to perform (Mission).
- Skills factor is the synthesis of the relationship between own deep feeling and dedication (Vocation) and own identity as policy decision-maker towards an employment (Profession)
- Future factor is the synthesis of the relationship between own identity as policy decision-maker towards an employment (Profession) and semantic interpretation of reality (Vision).
- Role factor is the synthesis of the relationship between own deep feeling and dedication (Vocation) and own reason to perform (Mission).
- Work factor is the synthesis of the relationship between own identity as policy decision-maker (Profession) and own reason to perform (Mission).

The *Orientism Management* (OM) in PENTHA vs.2 consists in intertwined 10 different Knowledge Management typologies, each based on areas of development and improvement of own personal policy decision-making and success. They are the mutual influence between life reference points (vertices) and *Orientism* factors, in a process of building a new knowledge decision-making "orienting". They have the purpose to activate dynamic actions toward a goal, to promote processes of construction of meanings, and to promote the exploration and mediation of reality.

The outcome is the design of a training strategy for Policy-maker to make decision under risk

1ST Knowledge Management With Consciousness (Low Level): KMC/I

As Orientism component, it focuses on the learning "*TO KNOW WHAT*" by the policy-maker. It means to activate a *prescriptive plan*, that concerns a knowledge base of updated regulatory guide, according to the institution profile, needs and possible offer.

In PENTHA model approach, training for policy-maker is to apply *FORMING* mode: a method concerning a) a topic introduction to make policy-maker aware of the institutional reality, introducing to the role through normative, with a robust case of studies to apply it, and b) an increasingly updaing of law. The training purpose is to empower attitudes, according to vision, professionality and dedication to the role.

2ND Knowledge Management With Consciousness (Medium Level): KMC/M

As Orientism component, it focuses on the learning "*TO KNOW HOW*" by the policy-maker. It means to activate a *management plan*, concerning how to provide efficacy and efficiency by a distributed management.

In PENTHA model approach, training for policy-makers is to apply *MODELING*, *PERFORMING* and *SCAFFOLDING* modes. Modeling is a method for which the Tutor demonstrates how to perform a task It means to give a robust case of studies to the Policy-maker Performing is a method to push Policy-maker on motivation and attitude in a performance. Scaffolding is a method with a focus on favoring the adaptation of the knowledge/learning path taken, a reflection on the actions developed by the Policy-maker, stimulated by a supporting trainer.

The training purpose is to empower skills, effective awareness of the role and work outcome, according to professionality, vocation, and mission of the role.

3RD Knowledge Management With Consciousness (High Level): KMC/H

As Orientism component, it focuses on the learning "*TO KNOW WHERE*" by the Policy-maker It means to activate a *descriptive plan*, concerning contextualized design and action

The main critical contextualized issues, on which focusing the management, are to identify the levels of criticality and potentials associated with the relationship between Policy-maker and Collegiate Bodies, Unions, Government, Family, Region

Table 1. KMC/low according to OM model, with related focused tutoring modes

Knowledge Management	Learning	To Empower	According to	Focused Tutoring Modes
with (Low) Consciousness KMC/l	*to know what*	Energy, Action Future	Passion, Vision, Profession	Forming

Table 2. KMC/medium according to OM model, with related focused tutoring modes

Knowledge Management	Learning	To Empower	According to	Focused Tutoring Modes
with (Medium) Consciousness KMC/m	*to know how*	Role, Skills, Work	Vocation, Profession, Mission	Scaffolding, Modeling, Performing

and Local Authorities, Professional Organizations, Technical, companies and other stakeholders.

In PENTHA model approach, training for Policy-maker is to apply *NARRATING* mode. It is a method concerning two different aspects: a) introduction of the topic to attract the attention of the policy-maker, appreciating of different decision-making styles and different forms of intelligence; b) encouraging policy-maker to verbalize their experiences, not only for dutiful reports, but also in a personal e-portfolio. The training purpose is to empower skills, effective actions, and work outcome, loving the profession and according to profession, mission and passion of the role.

4TH Knowledge Management With Meaning: KMM

As Orientism component, it focuses on the learning "*TO KNOW WHY*", that the Policy-maker needs to manage. It means to activate a *social plan*, concerning a reasonable motivation for decisional actions in terms of efficacy and efficiency.

In PENTHA model approach, training for pre-service Policy-maker, as well in-service, is to apply *COACHING* and *NORMING* modes. Coaching is a method in which the Trainer actively supports the Policy-maker motivating, analyzing performance, providing feedback, reflection on assignment, stimulating discussion about the method adopted. Norming is a method to optimize high performing, effective behaviors

The training purpose is to empower work, purposes and future development, according to professionality, vision, and mission of the role.

5TH Knowledge Management With Feeling (KMF)

As Orientism component, it focuses on the learning "*TO KNOW MOVING (TOWARDS)*", by Policy-maker to activate a change of perspective or action. It means to activate a general personalized *tutoring plan*, concerning how to support Policy-maker in their personal choosing process.

Table 3. KMC/high according to OM model, with related focused tutoring modes

Knowledge Management	Learning	To Empower	According to	Focused Tutoring Modes
with (High) Consciousness KMC/h	*to know where*	Work, Action, Love	Profession, Mission, Passion	Narrating

Table 4. KMM according to OM model, with related focused tutoring modes

Knowledge Management	Learning	To Empower	According to	Focused Tutoring Modes
with Meaning KMM	*to know why*	Work, Purpose, Future	Profession, Vision, Mission	Coaching, Norming

In PENTHA model approach, training for Policy-maker is to apply *COACHING* (see KMM training), *NARRATING* (see KMC/h training), *FADING* and *REFLECTING* modes. Fading is a method for adjusting and adapting the learning path according to the achievements of the Learner until the proof of his positive capability in full autonomy. Reflecting is a method which pushes to compare own difficulties with an Expert / Tutor and encourages them to perform pull actions. Reflection is the vehicle for critical analysis, problem-solving, synthesizing of opposing ideas, evaluation, identifying patterns, and creating meanings. The training purpose is to empower the spirit of service and love in the role, according to own vocation, passion for the mission.

6TH Knowledge Management With Will (KMW)

As Orientism component, it focuses on the learning "*TO KNOW EXPERIENCING*", process that the Policy-maker needs to activate and control. It means both *historical, comparative* and *simulation plans,* about analyzing, using own, and other's previous experiences, comparing traversal situations and conditions, to make decisions, using also virtual simulation tools.

In PENTHA model approach, training for Policy-maker is to apply *FADING* (see KMF training) and *PERFORMING* (see KMC/m training) modes. The training purpose is to empower factual actions, spirit of service and soft skills, according to own passion, vocation and professionalization.

Table 5. KMF according to OM model, with related focused tutoring modes

Knowledge Management	Learning	To Empower	According to	Focused Tutoring Modes
with Feeling KMF	*to know moving*	Role, Love, Spirit	Vocation, Mission, Passion	Coaching, Reflecting, Fading, Narrating

7TH Knowledge Management With Understanding (KMU)

As Orientism component, it focuses on the learning "*TO KNOW ENABLING*", that the Policy-maker needs to improve. It means to activate *tutoring*, as well as *management* and *social plan*s.

Example of categories of indicators: direction and organization, internal and external relations; innovation and development; valuing human resources and managing financial and instrumental resources available.

In PENTHA model approach, training for Policy-maker is to apply *COACHING* (see KMM training), *NARRATING* (see KMC/h training), *FADING* (see KMF training), *NARRATING* (see KMC/h training), *REFLECTING* (see KMF training), *SCAFFOLDING* (see KMC/m training), and, in addition, *EXPLORING* modes. Specifically, Exploring is a method, which forces the Principal to solve problems with new or alternative solutions. The construction of knowledge occurs through the observation and the transformation of experience.

The training purpose is to empower awareness of the possible developments and soft skills, according to a vision of the future, own vocation and professionalization.

8TH Knowledge Management With Personalization (KMP)

As Orientism component, it focuses on the learning "*TO KNOW CHANGING*" by the Policy-maker It means to activate a *creating plan* to improve new dynamics, relations and balance.

Table 6. KMW according to OM model, with related focused tutoring modes

Knowledge Management	Learning	To Empower	According to	Focused Tutoring Modes
with Will KMW	*to know experiencing*	Action, Skills, Spirit	Passion, Profession, Vocation	Fading, Performing

Table 7. KMU according to OM model, with related focused tutoring modes

Knowledge Management	Learning	To Empower	According to	Focused Tutoring Modes
with Understanding KMU	*to know enabling*	Awareness, Skills, Future	Vision, Vocation, Profession	Coaching, Narrating, Exploring, Reflecting, Scaffolding, Fading

In PENTHA model approach, training for Policy-maker is to apply both *SCAFFOLDING* (see KMC/m training) and *STORMING* modes. Storming is a method concerning effective communication, conflict resolution. The training purpose is to empower awareness of the role of any involved a decision-maker, related to the goal, according to the vision of the future, own vocation and own mission.

9TH Knowledge Management With Availability (KMA)

As Orientism component, it focuses on the learning "*TO KNOW OPENING*" towards people, environment, prospective and perspectives, interpretations by the Policy-maker It's part of both *creative* and *social plans*, already described.

In PENTHA model approach, training for Policy-maker is to apply *FADING* (see KMF training) and *STORMING* (see KMP training) modes. The training purpose is to empower awareness of role of any involved decisional decision-maker, with energy and a spirit of service, according to a vision of the future, own vocation and passion.

10TH Knowledge Management With Synergy (KMS)

As Orientism component, it focuses on the learning "*TO KNOW DEVOTING*" towards work, goals, relationships by the Policy-maker It's on the base of *all plans*, specifically it's part of the *social plan*.

Table 8. KMP according to OM model, with related focused tutoring modes

Knowledge Management	Learning	To Empower	According to	Focused Tutoring Modes
with Personalization KMP	*to know changing*	Role, Awareness, Purpose	Vocation, Mission, Vision	Storming, Scaffolding

Table 9. KMA according to OM model, with related focused tutoring modes

Knowledge Management	Learning	To Empower	According to	Focused Tutoring Modes
with Availability KMA	*to know opening*	Awareness, Energy, Spirit	Vision, Vocation, Passion	Storming, Fading

In PENTHA model approach, training for Policy-maker is to apply *FADING* mode (see KMF), especially adjusting and adapting the decision path according to the achievements of the Policy-maker, until the proof of a synergetic rhythm of work and positive feedbacks.

Table 10. KMS according to OM model, with related focused tutoring modes

Knowledge Management	*Learning*	**To Empower**	**According to**	**Focused Tutoring Modes**
with Synergy KMS	*to know devoting*	Purpose, Energy, Love	Passion, Vision, Mission	Fading

Figure 3. Types of training mode for policy-makers

CONCLUSION

The present contribution intends to be a theoretical as well practical guideline to train Policy-maker to understand own personal and professional development to optimize performances. Considering the fluid nature of the decision-making process, looking at the dynamic of policy-making activities, necessarily adaptive and self-regulative, the present study applies Orientism Management OM Framework, an interpretative approach useful for training policy-makers.

It intends to support a multiperspective informed aware policy, to seize the unpredictability and risks of the dynamics of knowledge management in relationships with complex political, cultural, social, biological and business environment.

Orientism proposes a new scenario of activities. to improve the people's ability to make contextual changes in natural, social, artificial multi-user environments, with multiple reference points and multi-interpreting paradigms.

REFERENCES

Aven, T. (2011). *Risk assessment. The scientific platform.* Cambridge University Press. doi:10.1017/CBO9780511974120

Aven, T., & Renn, O. (2010). *Risk management and Risk Governance. Concepts, Guidelines and Applications*. Springer Verlag. doi:10.1007/978-3-642-13926-0

Aven. (2010). *Misconceptions of Risk.* Wiley.

Cheong, R.K.F., & Tsui, E. (2010). The Roles and Values of Personal Knowledge Management: An exploratory study. *VINE, the Journal of Information and Knowledge Management System*, *40*(2), 204-27.

Colebatch, H. (2006). Thinking about policy: finding the best way. In *GovNet International Conference*. Australian National University.

Crossover. (n.d.). *The policy cycle.* Retrieved from: https://debategraph.org/Details.aspx?nid=228943

dall'Acqua, L., & Santo, M. D. (2012). New interpretative paradigms to understand and manage the unpredictability of the dynamics of learning in a complex multi-user knowledge environment. *Proceedings of Artificial Intelligence Workshop 2012 on Collaboration and Intelligence in Blended Learning*, 92-9.

dall'Acqua, L., & Santo, M. D. (2014). Orientism, the basic pedagogical approach of PENTHA ID Model vs. 2, to manage decisions in unpredictability conditions. Proceedings of World Congress on Engineering and Computer Science WCECS2014, *1*, 316-21.

dall'Acqua, L. (2014). *Needs and strategies of KM in a multi-user environment: PENTHA Model view and analysis*. Jekpot KM19, Milano. Italy.

Dunn, W. N. (1994). *Public Policy Analysis: An Introduction*. Englewood Cliffs, NJ: Prentice Hall.

Green, M. R., & Trieschmann, J. S. (1981). *Risk and insurance*. Cincinnati, OH: South-Western Publishing Co.

Guba, G., & Lincoln, Y. S. (2001). *Guidelines and checklist for constructivist evaluation*. Evaluation Checklists Project. Retrieved from www.wmich.edu/evalctr/checklists

Hannigan, T. (1998). *Managing Tomorrow's High-Performance decision-makers*. London: Quorum Books.

Heikkila, T., & Cairney, P. (2014). *Comparison of Theories of the Policy Process*. Available in: https://paulcairney.files.wordpress.com/2014/01/heikkila-cairney-proof-24-4-17.pdf

Hofferbert, R. (1974). *The Study of Public Policy*. Academic Press.

Knoepfel, P., Larrue, C., Varone, F., & Hill, M. (2007). *Public Policy Analysis*. Policy Press.

Loucks, D. P., & da Costa, J. R. (Eds.). (1991). *Technology Assessment. Environmental Impact Assessment. and Risk Analysis: Contributions from the Psychological and Decision Sciences. NATO Advanced Study Institute (ASI).*

Mayer, E., Lee, H., & Peebles, A. (2014). Multimedia Learning in a Second Language: A Cognitive Load Perspective. *Applied Cognitive Psychology*, *28*(5), 653–660. doi:10.1002/acp.3050

Pernicone, N. (1993). *Italian Anarchism, 1864-1892*. Princeton University Press.

Pollino Tour. (2017). *School of training for politicians* [Scuola di formazione per i politici del future]. Pollino Tour. Retrieved from: http://www.pollinotour.com/2017/05/03/scuola-di-formazione-per-i-politici-del-futuro/

Rovner, J. (2015). *Fixing the Facts: National Security and the Politics of Intelligence*. Cornell Studies in Security Affairs.

Selves, M. D. (2007). *The politics of disaster*. FEMA.

Sharkansky, I. (1995). Policy analysis in historical perspective. *Journal of Management History*, *1*(1), 47-58. doi:10.1108/13552529510082822

Sida. (n.d.). *The managerial formation of politicians: the comparison with others* [La formazione manageriale dei politici: il confronto con gli altri]. Sida Management Academy. Retrieved from http://mastersida.com/57301/

Stromberg, D. (2007). *Natural Disaster, Economic Development and Humanitarian Aid*. American Economic Association.

KEY TERMS AND DEFINITIONS

Acceptable Risk: A risk which everyone impacted is prepared to accept. Action to further reduce.

Decision-Making Model: An analytical construct that identifies the essential elements of the decision-making process (i.e., the decision maker, his cognitive attitudes, the research activities of the solutions, the modalities and criteria of the choice, and above all, the relationships that exist between all these different elements).

Factor of Safety: The ratio of system resistance to the peak design loads, often calculated in accordance with established rules.

Natural Hazard: Natural process or phenomenon that may cause loss of life, injury or other health impacts, property damage, loss of livelihoods and services, social and economic disruption, or environmental damage.

Orientism: A new multi-dimensional KM approach to improve the people's ability to manage decisions and own change of perspective, according to natural, social, artificial environments, in personalized multi-user dynamic, assigned value to multiple reference points, and multi-interpreting paradigms.

Risk Management Policy: Overall intentions and direction of an organization related to risk management.

Safety Decision-Maker: The person or organizational unit who decides on a course of action in relation safety.

Subjects at Risk: Population, buildings and engineering works, infrastructure, environmental features, and economic activities in the area affected by a hazard. Such risk is usually not required unless reasonably practicable measures are available at low cost in terms of money, time, and effort.

Uncertainty: Describes any situation without certainty, whether or not described by a probability distribution. Uncertainty is caused by natural variation and/or incomplete knowledge (lack of understanding or insufficient data).

Chapter 7
Talent Management:
Retaining Distinctive Human Capital Sustainably

Thembinkosi Ngcobo
University of KwaZulu-Natal, South Africa

Ana Martins
https://orcid.org/0000-0002-9271-2114
University of KwaZulu-Natal, South Africa

Isabel Martins
https://orcid.org/0000-0001-5095-7028
University of KwaZulu-Natal, South Africa

ABSTRACT

Toyota South Africa Motors (TSAM) is the leading original equipment manufacturer in South Africa. Business strategy and talent management alignment is therefore the key for business success. For the past couple of years, there has been a frequent executive management turnover and several promotions to senior management positions. The research question was to ascertain the relationship between talent management strategy and the achievement of business objectives. The quantitative research study included a deductive approach. Primary data was collected using a questionnaire survey personally administered by the researchers. Results for two talent management pillars were positive but require some improvements. However, results for succession planning reveal this pillar requires urgent attention to maintain competitive advantage and realize the vision of becoming the mother plant in Africa.

DOI: 10.4018/978-1-5225-7903-8.ch007

INTRODUCTION

Talent management is a topic that has gained increasing attention in the human resources management and development literature (Johnson, Wilding & Robson, 2014). There are various school of thought surrounding the theory of talent management, the common thread that all the schools agreed upon, was that if well-established, it has significant advantage. Highly skilled human capital is critical for organizational sustainability, achieving business objectives and gaining competitive advantage (Collings & Mellahi, 2013). Schuler, Jackson and Tarique (2011) state that firms are able to gain and sustain global competitiveness if they manage their human capital efficiently and effectively. Karodia, Cowden, and Kum, 2014 agree that human capital management is key for organizational competitiveness, maintaining and gaining market leadership and retaining highly skilled and motivated employees. To achieve this, the organizations must face reality of global talent shortages and construct a talent management strategy that will address these challenges. Human resources, therefore have the challenge to ensure skilled work force readiness to drive the agility and rapid innovation strategies necessary to compete globally, in order to realize business objectives (Sinkin & Putney, 2014).

The intention of the study is to conduct research on Toyota South Africa Motors (TSAM) talent sourcing, competence development, and succession planning and retention strategies in order to ascertain the ability to continuously producing critical skills needed to achieve the organization vision. Therefore, the aim of the study is to ascertain the talent management relationship with business strategy to fulfill TSAM vision of increasing market leadership in South Africa and becoming the mother plant in Africa. This study consists of the past literature reviewed, the methodology used in carrying out the study, findings and discussion of results obtained through the primary data collected from completed questionnaires, conclusions and recommendations including recommended future studies. A list of references is provided at the end.

LITERATURE REVIEW

According to Al Ariss, Cascio and Paauwe (2014), talent management is a process that comprises spotting talent that will play a major role in the organization to become sustainable and have a competitive advantage over other organizations. Developing potential and high performing individuals with specialized skills to take over the strategic positions and to make sure they remain committed to the organization. Talent management involves a thoughtful process to attract, retain, train and develop individuals who have the necessary drive and potential to meet both current and future needs of the organization (Barkhuizen, Mogwere & Schutte, 2014).

GLOBAL TALENT MANAGEMENT

Talent management system begins by recognizing positions or strategic positions in the organization. Required talent to fill in strategic positions can be developed and recruited internally and can be sourced through external recruitment process (Al Ariss *et al.*, 2014).

An effective talent management strategy has a clear understanding of the company's current and future direction. Talent management personnel study the fundamental gaps between current and required talents, crafting a comprehensive talent strategy in order to eliminate the gaps. Therefore, a talent management strategy should be integrated with business strategies (Mobini Dehkordi & Tahmasb Kazemi, 2013).

Sidani and Al Ariss (2014) point out a number of global talent management challenges that limit the ability to create a successful talent management strategy. Such challenges are senior management lack of dedication, middle management lack of involvement, organizational structures, lack of employee willingness to accept poor performances and human resources lack of ability to address talent management challenges. Business competitiveness and survival in the global economic environment has become the enormous challenge as increasing globalization pressures impact on the organizations operations. Talent management is gradually becoming the fundamental strategic driver to achieve business success in global economy. Effective talent management strategies not only distinguish the organization from its competitors but are the critical value creation instrument in the modern business environment (Murongazvombo, 2015).

The notion of the open-talent economy entails that the organization takes into account Industry 4.0 in its human capital approach which are different to the traditional or previous industrial revolution. Therefore, there is a need to re-think succession plans so that leaders of contemporary organizations are able to interact with technology by becoming informed about new models and approaches of work (Deloitte Insights, 2018).

Talent Management in the South African Perspective

The close relationship between organization leaders and talent management is a key driver in candidate attraction, development and retention. Not having the right mind-set towards talent management structure automatically places an organization at a disadvantage when these search for the right talent to fit well in the organization. Numerous South African research studies indicated that the level to which management apply talent management practices within an organization has a huge effect on employee decision to remain or seek better employment outside the organization (Mtila, Barkhuizen & Mokgele, 2013).

A number of research studies thus far indicate that Talent Management processes are not implemented properly in South African organizations. Most problematic practices are about recruitment and talent retention, as well as performance management and development of talent (Mtila *et al.*, 2013).

Barkhuizen *et al.* (2014) add that poor application of talent management practices has a negative influence on employee individual results such as motivation and job satisfaction and also on organizational level results such as performance and service quality.

Talent Management at Toyota

TSAM vision of remaining the number one OEM market leader in South Africa, makes it imperative to have a robust talent management model. The Talent management department is called Organizational Development and Talent Management (OD & TM). It has four pillars as per Figure 1 below.

Figure 1. Toyota organizational development and talent management department

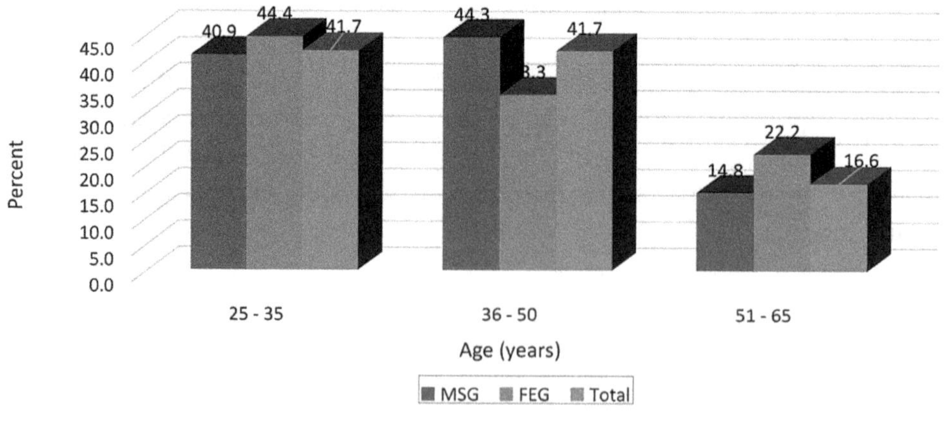

The department structure is designed to focus and address the following:

1. expand the knowledge and effectiveness of employees in order to accomplish more successful organizational change and performance;
2. establish a structured framework for succession planning;
3. maintain the integrity of the framework by ensuring that it is both unbiased and transparent;
4. ensure that there is adequate integration between Talent management, employee development and organizational design;
5. ensure that the organization is fast adaptable to change;
6. make TSAM attractive employer
7. revitalize performance management as an enabling tool;
8. support in career management and promote career mobility.

It is interesting to note that since the mid of 2016, Toyota has made enormous investment in the autonomous vehicle technology, in order to launch this vehicle type in 2021, according to the GreyB (2017) Autonomous Vehicles – Market and Research Trends report.

GLOBAL RECRUITMENT AND RETENTION

Recruitment and selection process is a very long and tedious process. It requires many 'person'-hours of searching for the suitable candidate to fit in the organization business objectives. Organizations also spend a huge amount of cash during this process. Those organizations with a number of skilled employees on succession strategy plan have a better chance of achieving better retention results of top talent. This reduces the outside recruitment cash outlay and ensures quick placement of top talent in strategic and specialist positions as soon as they become available (Sims, 2014).

Table 1. Summary of the talent management literature

Dimension	Global	Local	TSAM
Nurturing talent to filling strategic positions	√	√	√
Enhance employee commitment and retain skills	√	√	√
Understand skills GAP and strategy formulation	√	√	√
Critical for business success	√	√	√

Toulson (2016) adds that competition for talent is intensifying; gone are the days when human resources would just announce open positions and anticipate receiving a huge number of applications from interested candidates. To have an upper hand in this marketplace, human resources need to shift away from the traditional reactive hiring approach and rather put in place channels to engage candidates throughout the hiring cycle; such systems should have a close connection with the organization's business strategy.

Research reveals that recruitment is the most common area of HR that is normally being outsourced, Abdul-Halim and Che-Ha (2010); Ezigbo (2012). Wilton (2011) adds that this approach is used by leading UK organizations and all over Europe. About 59% of 4000 European organizations were outsourcing all or some of their recruitment processes. Johnson *et al.* (2014) also have an opposing idea to that of Sims (2014) and Toulson (2016). Recruitment outsourcing enhances access to candidate, saving on resources, specialization and flexibility, Johnson *et al.* (2014). Jamil and Neem (2013) corroborate that outsourcing of recruitment to the agency does not impact negatively on employee loyalty and commitment. The employee loyalty and commitment is influenced by how the agency describes the organization's human resources practices to the candidate. Johnson *et al.* (2014) further add that in Pakistan the telecommunication industry is one of the very profitable industries. To increase efficiency and profitability, the industry has started outsourcing recruitment processes to external agencies.

Recruitment in South African Perspective

Schöer, Rankin and Roberts (2014) state that the labour market in South Africa is categorized as a relaxed labour market where the employer (demand side) can decide how to select candidates and who they eventually employ. Gretczko and Cleary (2016) add that, too frequently human resources amend its recruitment process reactively, depending on the organization's cash flow or the internal demands from influential and powerful business units. This clearly shows that such organizations have not connected the hiring process with the business strategy. The South African labour market is facing its own unique difficulties; skilled staff frequently move from one organization to another and this highlights loop holes in recruitment processes. Other challenge is the oversupply of unskilled workers which becomes a recruitment and selection challenge for human resources. The Recruitment and selection function for human resources does not function separately as it was the case historically; now it must operate in conjunction with management and be aligned to business objectives. The procurement of suitable candidate is part of organizational strategy (Gretczko *et al.* 2016).

A Recruitment survey by Careers24 reveals the hardest vacancies to fill, namely, architects (8%), technology (32%), engineers (28%) and programmers (25%). The survey further informs that the organizations are searching for people with the right skills, but it is challenging to find the right candidates. This also suggests that there is a massive lack of skills within the country (Ryan, 2015). Furthermore, Ryan (2015) states that South Africa has an oversupply of low skilled laborers despite labor costs going up - a trend that is unsustainable.

Recruitment at Toyota

According to Toyota's human resource management (HRM) guiding model, the manpower recruitment/hiring objective is to maintain efficient business operations and continue corporate growth (Toyota HRM Guiding document, 2016). In order to ensure corporate development, there is need for personnel with the capabilities and acquired skill-sets to understand and realize the Toyota Way. The latter is the set of values, beliefs and business methods that act as the life blood of the company. The two main pillars that support the Toyota Way are Respect for people and Continuous improvement. Under the Respect for people pillar, falls respect and teamwork; under the Continuous improvement pillar is Challenge, Kaizen and Genchi Genbutsu. Hiring must be conducted from a perspective that focuses on developing employees over a mid to long-term, and not just from a perspective of immediate headcount need. The primary duty of hiring activities is the timely acquisition of required personnel (quantity and quality).

Resignation of employees at an early stage after recruitment, has a widespread negative impact. Despite the short lead-time available hiring of employees must be conducted deliberately, through a detailed process of matching the expectations of both the individual and the company. The optimal form of employment must be selected based upon considerations such as work content, term requirements, and cost.

GLOBAL RETENTION

Mehta, Kurbetti and Dhankhar (2014) highlight various reasons for staff turnaround in India, such as discontent with job placements, work profile, individual reasons and dissatisfaction with remuneration. To retain talent the organization need to improve

Table 2. Recruitment summary

Dimension	Global	Local	TSAM
Process is long, tedious and very costly	√	√	√
HR involvement is required throughout the process	X	√	√
Outsourcing of recruitment process is on the rise	√	X	X
Hiring process must satisfy both the departmental needs and overall business needs	√	√	√

pay and benefits and working conditions, introduce flexible working hours, encourage team work, good management team, organizational culture and values. According to the workforce in India, the factors that contribute to low staff turnover are work experience, clear career plan, freedom to perform ones functions and so forth. These employee concerns assisted the companies to accordingly align human resources practices and also assist companies increase staff retention percentage (Brigitte & Charissa, 2013). The findings of Brigitte and Charissa (2013) as well as Mehta *et al.* (2014) arising from research studies conducted in India, are not in agreement.

The study conducted in the United States of America by Holmes, Chapman and Baghurst (2013) highlight different points of view from those of Mehta *et al.* (2014), where 18 public sector HR practitioners were interviewed. The opinion of 13 HR personnel was that career progression is key to staff retention, followed by job security, job location and good leadership. While 11 HR personnel noted that training and mentoring programs are key in reducing staff turnover. Gaurav (2013) agrees with Chapman *et al.* (2013) and add that career path must be clear to the employees, such influences the workforce to stay with the company for an extended period of time. Osman (2013) points out that, employee retention strategies are necessary for the organization not only to gain competitive advantage within the global business environment but also maintain it.

Osibanjo, Salau and Falola (2014) present a different view point that employees work in order to get paid so they can satisfy their daily needs namely foodstuff, clothing and accommodation. Osibanjo *et al.* (2014) add that there are many approaches to persuading an employee, namely salary and bonuses and a share in company's profit. Globally, factors such as salary, bonuses and profit sharing, have been utilized to attract top talent and enhance retention of employees. However, while monetary reward may not be the controlling variable this helps employee decide either to join or remain with the company or resign. As a staff retention strategy, Volkswagen of America introduced a number of options such as working flexitime, compressed work schedules, job sharing, and telecommuting into their schedules to allow mature employees choose what is best for them and what will benefit the organisation (Tishman, Van Looy & Bruyère, 2014).

Murongazvombo (2015) added that retention is a complex concept and there is no one technique for keeping employees within an organization. However, business leaders have to decide which strategies motivate employees to remain with the company and which benefit both the company and the employees.

Retention in South African Perspective

Horwitz (2013) states that for organizations to address retention challenge, they have the option of taking advantage of the incentives available to train and develop its own employees. Some of these incentives are skills levy and grant system. Currently these incentives are being utilized by less than 20 percent of organizations in South Africa. Retaining quality employees in the South African labour market is very challenging due to shortage of skills, lack of employee flexibility and the retirement of key employees, in not too distant future. These factors adversely impact business ability to generate and sustain their competitive advantage within the labour market. Such conditions will get worse if businesses fail to handle these problems properly (Louw, 2013).

According to Theron, Barkhuizen and du Plessis (2014), executives take too lightly the value and significance of talent retention and, therefore, staff turnover causes are not appropriately identified and dealt with. For instance, executives in South African higher education institutions mainly concentrate on business sustainability and profits on the one hand, while on the other hand, employees are motivated by personal development, personal fulfilment and financial rewards.

A survey of the Economist Intelligence Unit (2007) demonstrates that an increasing salary above market related rates was only the fourth most effective human resources strategy amongst Asian firms. The main three human resources strategies revolved around personal growth. First, was increased training, second was mentoring and third was development of personal road maps. In South Africa, this is the area of opportunities for growth that a number of organizations are failing at. The Deloitte National Remuneration (2007) survey established that the cause of most staff turnover in South Africa is the absence of career progression, inefficient and ineffective utilization of their skill and knowledge, lack of work happiness and thus contributing to below performance (Horwitz, 2013).

Theron *et al.* (2014) point out the top three most likely reasons why employees at South African high education institutions would consider resigning are salary and benefits, career development opportunities and promotion. Furthermore, salary and benefits are more of a turnover factor and not as much of retention factor.

Retention at Toyota

Toyota's HRM guiding model (2016) recommends that Post Hiring Measures be put in place. These measures must ensure smooth employee introduction to the job, make clear true reasons for resignations and planning countermeasures to ensure the retention of employees. The guidelines make it clear that it is essential to grasp actual reasons for early resignations through a process of face-to-face communication, in addition to insistence on completion of exit interview forms or other similar documentation. Without thorough analysis based on facts, effective countermeasures cannot be established. Human resources role is to: i) grasp the true reasons for quitting, through frank discussions with the resigning person and conducting interviews with supervisors; ii) link the true reasons for quitting with future countermeasures aimed at retaining employees. Table 3 summarizes the employee retention literature discussed above.

SUCCESSION PLANNING

Global Succession Planning

Walker (2013) postulates that crafting succession requires the right mixture of people and process. The people part is accomplished through analysis of three human performance values. Knowledge and experience, motivation, personality and specific as well as natural approach to challenge, these are the most important factors for recruiting and selecting the right candidates for the role of successor. Hall and Hagen (2014) highlight that, baby boomers are now approaching their retirement age; in not more than seven years, succession planning is necessary.

Table 3. Retention summary

Dimension	Global	Local	TSAM
Retention strategies help organization gain competitive (global) advantage	√	√	√
Retaining skilled staff is a challenging assignment due to global demand	√	√	√
Skills retention is difficult due to skills shortage and retirement of key employees	X	√	√
There is no single formula to staff retention	√	√	√
Work experience, training and development, clear career path and job security contributes to job security and low staff turnaround	√	√	√
Lucrative remuneration package contributes to staff retention	√	√	√

Succession planning takes nothing less than five years to implement, therefore for organizational sustainability the business owners must take succession planning seriously and continuously prepare candidates to take over key positions within the organization. Collins (2014) agrees with Hall and Hagen (2014), adding that matured employees are the most critical asset in the organization. Projections are that the current loss of large number of human capital will continue up to year 2020 unless businesses put into place a system to transfer knowledge and skills from treasured matured employees to the successors and the entire organization.

Florea, Cheung and Herndon (2013) highlight a different point of view in that succession planning does not entirely depend on organization putting strategy in place; evidence from Coca Cola and Merck studies point out that, to implement succession strategy successfully is dependent on the employees and managers willingness to be hands-on and offer adequate attention to a process that can possibly result in no benefit to the organization but only benefit to the succession candidate. Comini, Paolino and Feitosa (2013) add to Florea *et al.* (2013) findings that if succession is not properly planned and structured, there is a major conflict between management, succession candidate and the staff members not on succession program. It is, therefore, essential to lay the foundation that will regulate succession process and prepare everyone for future changes to ensure sustainability and continuity of the organization.

Succession Planning in South African Perspective

Karodia *et al.* (2014) substantiate that a number of companies are faced with leadership problems because of poor and ineffective succession planning and when organizations identify prospective leaders, it is their duty to develop and empower them. Awan and Farhan (2016) add that succession planning ensures that most jobs which are critically important for long term well-being of the organization, must be filled with internally available and potential employees whenever possible. The study at selected SA banks (ABSA, FNB, Nedbank and Standard Bank), reveals that succession planning is designed to guarantee continuity and to sustain effective performance by planning for the replacement of key employees over a period of time (Chigada & Ngulube, 2015).

Schutte and Barkhuizen (2014) posit that it is essential to have competent staff and a very clear succession planning systems in order to protect the organizational knowledge base. Strategic leaders should recognize that succession planning is a long term process that seeks unconditional commitment from all stakeholders in order to achieve business objectives. Myers (2014) highlights another tactic undertaken by other organizations is merely to construct a long standing and strong organization by merging succession planning and leadership development in order to craft a long-standing procedure for managing individual talent.

Ximba (2016) corroborates that factors such as, namely, training and education, networking, mentorship and work related challenges, enable employees to develop in their careers while an absence of succession planning generates barriers for the employees to grow their careers. A number of studies noted that absence of structured succession planning, is a contributing factor defining the shortage of suitable executives of color, especially Blacks. Succession planning is regarded as a core component of talent management strategy (Myres, 2014).

Succession Planning at Toyota

Toyota's HRM guiding model (2016) states that for important positions, successors must be developed based on succession planning, through planned acquisition of required competencies for the positions. While excess positions should not be created if not needed, vacancies should be avoided due to unforeseeable reasons such as headhunting. Therefore, developing successors should be done under a thoroughly planned schedule. To achieve the business needs, it is necessary to grasp talented personnel to serve as future leaders and develop them on the basis of a mid to long-term plan. Information on the potential leaders must not be disclosed, and challenging work must be provided for their development.

Activities include, i) Clarification of important positions and required competencies; ii) Discernment the most appropriate individual, judging from required competencies; iii) Clarification of development items for identified individuals; iv) Supervisors understand their development role and supporting actual development; v) Coordination among respective divisions and progress reports to top management; Roles of the heads are as follows, a) Clarification of the required human resources in line with the management vision, b) Selection of successors within the organization; c) Planning, implementation and follow-up of development plan; d) Feedback on regular basis and Performance appraisal. The table below depicts a summary of succession planning.

Table 4. Succession planning summary

Dimension	Global	Local	TSAM
Address continuity issues within the organization	√	√	√
Deals with identifying and developing employees to fill strategic positions in the future	√	√	√
Long term process that requires commitment from all stakeholders in order to achieve business objectives	√	√	√
There is a lack of talent required to take over key positions due to leadership issues	√	√	√
Absence of succession planning generates barriers to employee development and growth	√	√	√

COMPETENCE DEVELOPMENT

Global Competency Development

The competency model developed by Sengupta, Venkatesh and Sinha (2013), is a future looking model described in three phases. Phase one deals with identifying core competencies needed to carry out a task. This phase focuses on the individual, job specific and role specific. Phase two identifies a competency gap through competency scorecard. This phase forms the foundation of further individual training and development plan to match the organization requirements. Phase three is the integration of competency development with overall talent management structure.

Sengupta *et al.* (2013) added that competency development is done in a classroom intense training, on the job training, assessments and job rotations. For an organization to design a competency development plan for its employees, employee competencies must be matched with the job requirements. Young and Conboy (2013) emphasize that the employee competency development plan is divided into four steps, namely, formal learning, interpersonal affairs, assessment and job experiences. Organizations must offer an environment and chance for continuous learning and practical targets. For instance, periodic employee rotation will keep them receptive to challenging jobs as it sustains motivation and satisfaction.

Kaiser and Curphy (2013) posit that there is a non-existence of the competency model that focuses on building a high performing team in an organization and further highlight that global businesses are expressing serious concerns regarding the supply of great leaders. A survey of 14,000 HR professionals and executives found that 26% of HR professionals and 38% of executives stated that the quality of leadership throughout their organizations was excellent. Future projections are getting worse, 18% of HR professionals and 32% of executives stated that they have confidence in the quality of current employees to lead their organizations in the future. The concern is that the organizations spend huge amount of money on staff competency development but the results are getting worse. Leadership training and development has become a big business in the United States. Consulting psychologists are the main beneficiaries in this industry. In 15 years the industry has become a $14 billion industry.

Adolph, Tisch and Metternich (2014) state that, due to the complex technology improvements, building of competency is becoming more and more complex and uncertain. Traditional methods are becoming irrelevant. Going forward, the businesses need to act quickly and introduce new training tools and methods.

Competency Development in South African Perspective

Competency model is a tool that identifies skills, capabilities and behavioral conduct needed to perform efficiently and effectively within an organization. The identified competencies form a foundation for the planning and development of human resource management activities. Additionally, a competency model supports to communicate an organization's strategic objectives and provides organizations with a common language that can be used for performance discussion, talent selection and development, career advancement and succession planning (Roman & Mason, 2015). Bergin (2013) states that the Competency-Based Training (CBT) dominates industry training and performance practices. The trend of employing CBT strategies in education and training, staff development, assessments and retirement is seen as inevitable.

Public sector employers and human resources have turned to competency models in order to determine business and employers needs as well as the required talent. Normally competency models are applied more within the private sector. Public sector is now utilizing these models to implement transformation and improving efficiency (Ndou & Sebola, 2016). South African employees raise contradictory views regarding competency develepment. Some stated that older staff compared to younger staff prefer more training and development and rewards that provide job flexibility than pay and benefits. Some stated that extrinsic rewards namely, pay and benefits are more treasured by older employees then younger staff and development is of less importance. It is, therefore, a challenge to the South African organizations to develop a balanced competency development model that will satisfy both older and younger staff members, while at the same time, also offer a remuneration package that will keep them motivated to willingly participate in development training (Snelgar, Renard & Venter, 2013).

Competency Development at Toyota

The Human resources guiding model looks at human resources systems that support human resources development (employee competency development). This model is divided into performance appraisal, promotion, rotation and succession planning (Toyota HRM Guiding document, 2016). Performance appraisal results should not be used merely as a tool for evaluation and compensation. It should also be utilized as necessary background information when proposing development plans. Promotion - when there are no other satisfactory employees when determining promotion, it is possible to promote a potential candidate and then develop him afterwards through actual work experience. In addition, implementing mandatory training programs before promotion, and utilizing training data as a reference, can also be an effective way to develop individuals. Rotation is an effective means of improving abilities and expanding employees' perspectives; therefore, it should be used as a part of human resources development.

When introducing a rotation system, employees should be thoroughly explained the intension, and the company should demonstrate by rotating members with excellent performance. Succession Planning - for important positions, successors must be developed based on succession planning, through planned acquisition of required competencies for the positions. Developing successors should be developed under a thoroughly planned schedule. Psychometric testing, coaching and mentoring, chairing job evaluations, develop and deploy performance management tools, are key activities that form part of employee development process. Table 5 depicts a summary of Competency development.

Table 5. Competency development summary

Dimension	Global	Local	TSAM
Competency development is achieved through classroom training, on the job training, assessments and job rotations	√	√	√
A well designed competency development is dependent on matching employee competencies with job requirements	√	√	√
Due to technological advancements and complexity competency development is becoming more complex uncertain	X	√	√
Organisation with skilled employees experience labor costs reduction and increase in productivity	√	√	√

METHODOLOGY

The research objectives are to evaluate talent sourcing and retention in increasing competitive advantage; to analyze the role of succession planning in sustaining competitive advantage and to determine the role of competence development sustaining competitive advantage. The study was conducted at Toyota South Africa Motors in the Durban Manufacturing Plant. Toyota has five divisions in total, four in Durban and one in Gauteng (MSG – Manufacturing support, FEG – Finance & Exports, MAG – Manufacturing Assembly Group, CSG – Corporate Services group and SMG – Sales & Marketing group).

Two divisions have been targeted for this study, namely, MSG and FEG. Human resources division (CSG) and direct plant/production division (MAG) and Gauteng based division (SMG) were excluded from this study. The most appropriate sampling type selected for this study was probability sampling. Senior and junior managers, specialists and principal engineers from two divisions (MSG & FEG) had an equal chance of being selected as a participant in the study. Thc rationale for selecting probability sampling is because the research has access to the list of targeted population, therefore everybody had an equal opportunity be part of the sample. The sample size for this study was derived using the scientific table (Krejcke & Morgan, 1970). Table 6 indicates the population and study sample size.

The research design selected for this study is the quantitative approach. A Questionnaire served as the research instrument to collect data and was personally administered by the researcher. The Statistical Package for Social Science (SPSS) Version 24.0 was utilized to analyze and interpret the collected data. The questionnaire was made up of a Likert scale, multiple choice, multiple-response scale and nominal scale questions. The reliability was measured by sending out two batches of questionnaires to Toyota ex-employees and Ford employees as well as to Toyota current staff in Gauteng respectively.

Table 6. Targeted population and sample size

Population type	Population	Sample
Senior manager	43	22
Manager	88	60
Grade10 /11 (Specialist/ principal engineer/ other)	112	70
Total	**243**	**152**

The second batch was distributed one week after the first batch. There were no statistically significant differences from both batches, therefore it can be concluded that the questionnaire was reliable. Errors identified during the first and second pilot studies as well as the input and comments suggested were considered when questionnaire improvements were made. The preliminary questionnaire was distributed to 13 participants in total. As shown in Table 7, the questionnaire valid responses by division and by job level equates to 152 in total (116 MSG and 36 FEG), which gave a 76% response rate.

Figure 2 shows that there were marginally more employees in FEG in the youngest & oldest age categories, with the trend reversed for the middle-aged grouping. In total, the participants in the age groups 25 – 35 and 36 – 50, are precisely the same.

Table 7. The respondents' distribution summarized according to division and job level

Job Level	Division				Total	
	MSG		FEG			
	Frequency	Percentage	Frequency	Percentage	Frequency	Percentage
Senior manager	16	13.9%	5	13.9%	21	13.9%
Manager	39	33.9%	21	58.3%	60	39.7%
Grade 10/11 (Specialist/ principal engineer/ other)	61	53.0%	10	27.8%	71	46.4%
Total	116	100.0%	36	100.0%	152	100.0%

Figure 2. The respondents' distribution summarized according to age group

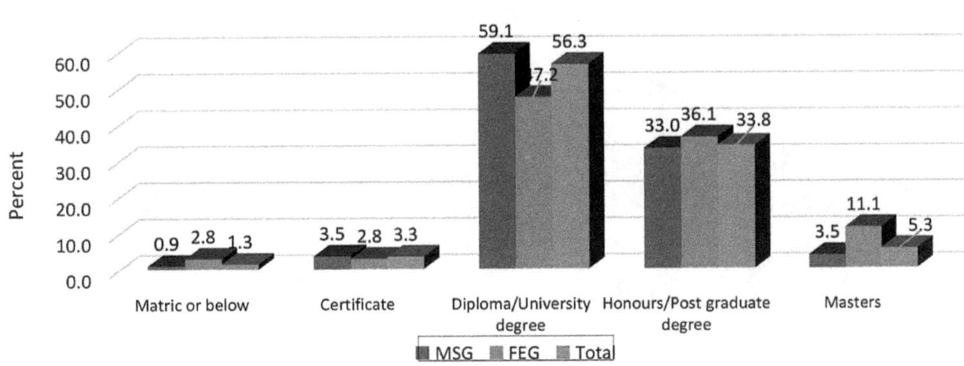

Figure 3 shows that 95.4% of respondents have a post matric qualification. Nearly 40% of the respondents have a postgraduate degree. This is a useful statistic as it indicates that a fair proportion of the respondents have a higher qualification.

It is encouraging to note that all length of service categories are being represented in this study as indicated in Figure 4. The majority of the respondents in both divisions are in the category of 6 – 10 years. The respondents who have been with the company for more than 20 years is quite high, their input is valuable in this study.

Figure 3. The respondents' distribution summary according to education level

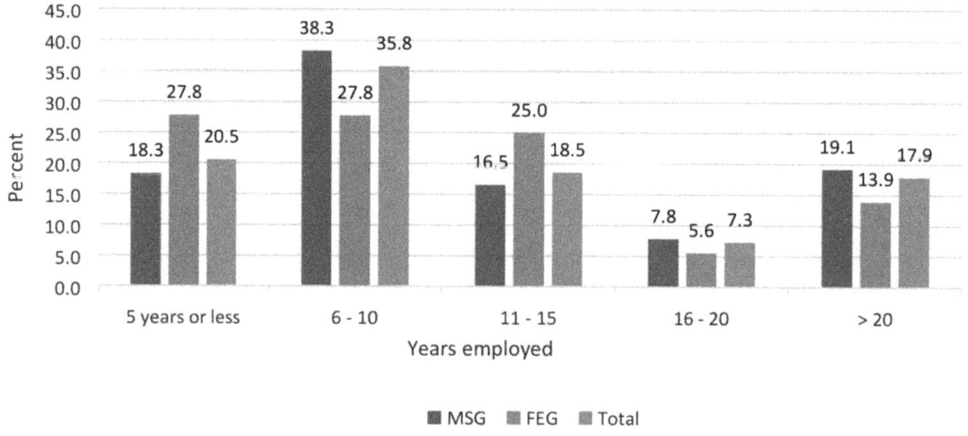

Figure 4. The length of service of the respondents

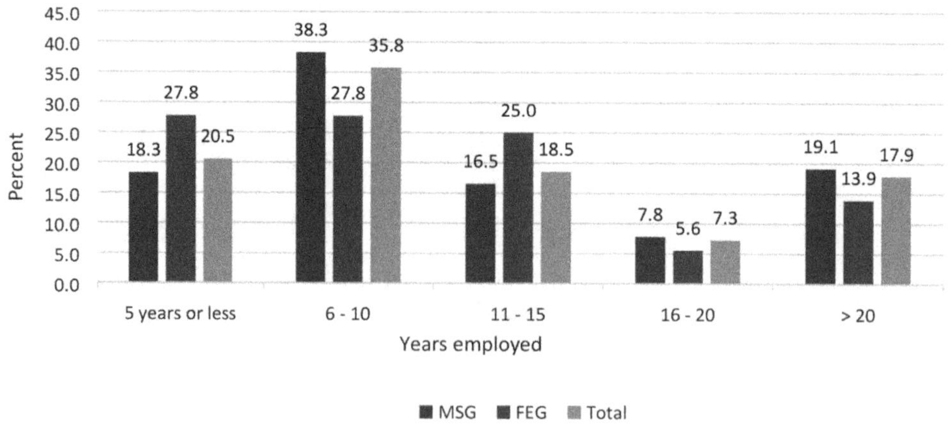

FINDINGS AND DISCUSSION

Objective one of this study is to evaluate talent sourcing and retention in increasing competitive advantage, included six questions (Qs A1-A6) from the research instrument. Table 8 shows the results summarized per division.

Q. A1. Recruitment Process and Business Strategy

In Table 8, the combined findings reveal that 68.3% respondents agree that recruitment process is driven by business strategy. A concerning factor in these findings is that 60% of MSG senior management disagree that the recruitment process is driven by business strategy. It is still agreeable to note that the overall response is positive.

Q. A2. Future Talent Requirements and Talent Recruitment

Table 8 also depicts the Combined findings of 63.1% (64.6% MSG and 58.4% FEG) revealed that the future talent requirements are being considered when recruiting new talent. It is of great interest to note that 60% of FEG senior managers did not agree. Senior management respondents were the ones expected to give positive feedback. The overall results are nevertheless positive.

Table 8. Talent recruitment and retention per division summary analysis

Question	Division							
	MSG				FEG			
	Strongly disagree	Disagree	Agree	Strongly agree	Strongly disagree	Disagree	Agree	Strongly agree
A1. Recruitment process at Toyota is driven by business strategy	5.40%	20.50%	**62.50%**	**11.60%**	5.60%	44.40%	47.20%	2.80%
A.2 Future talent requirements are considered when recruiting new talent	5.30%	30.10%	**56.60%**	**8.00%**	2.80%	38.90%	**55.60%**	**2.80%**
A3. Toyota's recruitment process is fair and transparent	**11.30%**	**41.70%**	40.00%	7.00%	13.90%	36.10%	50.00%	0.00%
A4. Toyota's remuneration package contributes greatly to my retention at Toyota	5.20%	35.30%	**55.20%**	**4.30%**	8.30%	25.00%	**63.90%**	**2.80%**
A5. Human resources (HR) and management recruitment and retention responsibilities are aligned	**11.60%**	**54.50%**	32.10%	1.80%	**11.10%**	**63.90%**	25.00%	0.00%
A6. Toyota has a robust strategy to prevent good talent from leaving	**24.10%**	**56.00%**	17.20%	2.60%	**30.60%**	**63.90%**	5.60%	0.00%

Q. A3. Recruitment Process Fairness and Transparency

The results show that 53% of MSG respondents revealed that the recruitment process is not fair and transparent, on the other hand FEG respondents are indecisive, 50% agree and the other 50% disagree. Combined findings (52.3%) indicate that recruitment process is not fair and transparent. This is a bit contradictory since the majority in the above variable indicated that TSAM considers future needs when recruiting talent.

Q. A4. Remuneration Package and Employee Retention

The results show (in Table 8) that the majority of the combined respondents (61.1%) indicated that remuneration package contributes to employee retention. Looking at individual divisions, both divisions agree (MSG 59.5% and FEG 66.7%). These results confirm that majority of employees are happy with the remuneration package.

Q. A5. HR and Management Recruitment and Retention Responsibilities Alignment

In Table 8, the results indicate that both MSG 66.1% and FEG 75% (68.3% combined) do not agree that human resources and management recruitment and retention responsibilities are aligned. It is important to note that 100% of FEG senior managers disagree and 73.3% of MSG senior managers.

Q. A6. Robust Retention Strategy

From Table 8, the findings reveal that there seems to be a dilemma because over 80% of the respondents from both divisions (MSG 80.1% and FEG 94.4%) do not agree there is a good enough retention strategy in place to prevent good talent from leaving.

Objective two of this study is to analyze the role of succession planning in sustaining competitive advantage, was evaluated according to five questions from the questionnaire with five or six options to choose from. As shown in Table 9, not more than 10% per division in all five questions are in agreement with these statements. The majority of the respondents opted for the option to voice their opinions. Such overall feedback is very disturbing.

Q.B1. Succession Planning Strategy is Clearly Articulated

In summary the majority of all respondents from both the divisions and all job levels (MSG 62.1% and FEG 61.1%), stated that succession planning strategy is not clearly articulated, it is only applicable to the few individuals and some stated that there is no succession planning at all.

Q.B2. Succession Candidates and Company Plans

The majority of the respondents from both the divisions and all job levels MSG (64.7%) and FEG (72.2%) stated that they are not aware if such a process existed, some made it clear that candidates are not informed of plans about them and made suggestions that TSAM needed to make some improvements.

Table 9. Succession planning per division summary analysis

Question		Division			
		MSG		FEG	
Succession planning strategy is clearly articulated	**B1**	Yes	No	Yes	No
Candidate selection process is clear and transparent	B1.1	10.3%	89.7%	11.1%	88.9%
Development timing plan is clear and transparent	B1.2	11.2%	88.8%	2.8%	97.2%
Development training schedule & milestones are clear and transparent	B1.3	14.7%	85.3%	22.2%	77.8%
All of the above	B1.4	9.5%	90.5%	2.8%	97.2%
Other: Please indicate (respondent's opinion)	B1.5	62.1%	37.9%	61.1%	38.9%
Succession candidates and company plans	**B2**	Yes	No	Yes	No
Reason(s) for their selection & expectation	B2.1	17.2%	82.8%	16.7%	83.3%
Detailed future plan within the organization	B2.2	8.6%	91.4%	0.0%	100.0%
Detailed development plan is clear and discussed upfront	B2.3	8.6%	91.4%	5.6%	94.4%
All of the above	B2.4	10.3%	89.7%	5.6%	94.4%
Other: Please indicate (respondent's opinion)	B2.5	64.7%	35.3%	72.2%	27.8%
Tools in place to track succession candidate's development	**B3**	Yes	No	Yes	No
Regular progress reviews/feedback meetings are in place and are recorded	B3.1	15.5%	84.5%	11.1%	88.9%
A candidate is strategically placed in development/leadership positions as per timing plan, progress is monitored and feedback is given	B3.2	12.1%	87.9%	5.6%	94.4%
A candidate is allocated a mentor	B3.3	7.8%	92.2%	11.1%	88.9%
All of the above	B3.4	9.5%	90.5%	5.6%	94.4%
Other: Please indicate (respondent's opinion)	B3.5	62.9%	37.1%	63.9%	36.1%
Departmental planning and HR succession strategy integration	**B4**	Yes	No	Yes	No
Succession candidate is identified & agreed upfront with HR	B4.1	19.0%	81.0%	5.6%	94.4%
A development plan is communicated & agreed upfront with HR	B4.2	4.3%	95.7%	8.3%	91.7%
Candidate progress is tracked & monitored by HR	B4.3	5.2%	94.8%	2.8%	97.2%
All of the above	B4.4	6.9%	93.1%	5.6%	94.4%
Other: Please indicate (respondent's opinion)	B4.5	66.4%	33.6%	77.8%	22.2%
Departmental workforce reshuffling and HR succession strategy alignment	**B5**	Yes	No	Yes	No
Departmental workforce changes are discussed & agreed with the candidate	B5.1	22.4%	77.6%	25.0%	75.0%
Departmental workforce changes are discussed & agreed between management & HR	B5.2	18.1%	81.9%	16.7%	83.3%
Departmental structural changes are communicated with candidate upfront	B5.3	18.1%	81.9%	30.6%	69.4%
Revised succession/development plan is discussed and agreed with candidate & HR	B5.4	13.8%	86.2%	11.1%	88.9%
All of the above	B.5.5	3.4%	96.6%	2.8%	97.2%
Other: Please indicate (respondent's opinion)	B.5.6	52.6%	47.4%	52.8%	47.2%

Q. B3. Tools in Place to Track Succession Candidate's Development

The majority of the respondents from both the divisions and all job levels MSG (62.9%) and FEG (63.9%) stated that the candidates are the ones leading this process. Some respondents stated that there is no fixed process or no tools are in place and others even stated that they had no idea if such a process is in place or not. Included in FEG 63.9% is 100% of FEG senior management.

Q. B4. Departmental Planning and HR Succession Strategy Integration

The majority of the respondents from both the divisions and all job levels MSG (66.4%) and FEG (77.8%) stated that they are not exposed to this process, others stated they are not aware or unsure if the process exists and others mentioned that this process is ineffective. Included in FEG 77.8% is 100% of FEG senior management.

Q. B5. Departmental Workforce Reshuffling and HR Succession Strategy Alignment

The majority of the respondents from both the divisions and all job levels MSG (52.6%) and FEG (52.8%) stated that there is no logic applied and they are unaware if the succession planning process is in place, others indicated that this process only takes place at senior management level.

Objective three of this study is to determine the role of competence development sustaining competitive advantage - was evaluated by five questions from the research instrument. Table 10 shows the results summarized per division.

Q. C1. Competency Development and Business Strategy

In Table 10, the results indicate that majority of the respondents both in MSG (65.7%) and FEG (55.6%) stated that employee competency development is linked to business strategy. All job levels agree except the majority of FEG managers (52.5%).

Table 10. Competency Development per division summary analysis

Question	Division							
	MSG				FEG			
	Strongly disagree	Disagree	Agree	Strongly agree	Strongly disagree	Disagree	Agree	Strongly agree
C1. Employee competence development at Toyota is linked to business strategy	7.00%	27.20%	**59.60%**	**6.10%**	2.80%	41.70%	**52.80%**	**2.80%**
C.2 Toyota working environment/culture is conducive for employees to pursue competency development opportunities	3.50%	20.20%	**68.40%**	**7.90%**	2.80%	38.90%	**55.60%**	**2.80%**
C3. Competency development is used as a retention strategy	**7.00%**	**50.00%**	40.40%	2.60%	**5.60%**	**55.60%**	36.10%	2.80%
C4. There is alignment between HR and all Toyota departments on the importance of employee competence development	**8.80%**	**52.60%**	37.70%	0.90%	**11.10%**	**52.80%**	36.10%	0.00%
C5. Employee competency development at Toyota improves business performance	2.70%	23.90%	**66.40%**	**7.10%**	0.00%	13.90%	**75.00%**	**11.10%**

Q. C2. Working Environment/Culture and Competency Development Opportunities

From Table 10, MSG (76.3%) and FEG (58.4%) agree that the working environment is conducive for employees to pursue competency development opportunities. Feedback tells us that the majority of employees at all levels are happy with the working environment/culture as it gives them the opportunity to undergo development training.

Q. C3. Competency Development and Retention Strategy

In Table 10, combined results reveal that the majority of the respondents do not agree that competency development is used as a retention strategy, MSG (57%) and FEG (61.2%). The results also reveal that 66.7% of MSG senior managers disagree that competency development is used as a retention strategy, on the contrary 60% of FEG senior managers agree.

Q. C4. HR and Departments Alignment and Importance of Employee Development

Table 10 above shows that the majority of the respondents from both MSG (61.4%) and FEG (63.9) agree that human resources and departments are not aligned when it comes to employee competency development. Surprisingly, the majority of senior management from both divisions are part of the job levels that agree that there is no alignment between the HR and departments, MSG senior managers (73.3%) and FEG senior managers (80%). Senior management and above levels are the ones responsible for such relationship to work in harmony.

Q. C5. Competency Development and Business Performance Improvement

As Table 10 depicts, the majority of respondents from MSG (73.5%) and FEG (86.1%) indicated that the employee competency development improves business performance. The majority of respondents from all job levels are in agreement.

CONCLUSION

The overall findings from TSAM talent management strategy were not entirely positive; there are some areas of concern that require some improvements and other areas that require major and urgent improvements. The findings of the study in evaluating the role of talent sourcing and retention to increase competitive advantage provided favourable feedback on some areas and also highlighted areas that need some improvements, such as the lack of a robust strategy to prevent good talent from leaving. The results revealed that Toyota's recruitment process is driven by business strategy and future talent requirements are considered during talent sourcing. The findings of the study in determining the role of competence development in sustaining competitive advantage provided advantageous feedback on some areas and also highlighted areas that need some improvements. Results revealed that staff competency development is linked with business strategy. Alignment of human resources and departments requires some attention. The findings of the study, in analyzing the role of succession planning in sustaining competitive advantage, revealed that succession planning requires an urgent attention. Succession planning was not well received by the majority of the respondents, feedback given indicates that respondents were not aware succession planning at TSAM exist or not and some respondents have no clear understanding of TSAM succession planning strategy and the other respondents do not agree that succession planning is well structured. Human capital is the critical component that drives the company to success. The results suggest that there is a need to revisit TSAM talent management strategy and make few improvements on some areas and some drastic improvement on other areas, namely succession planning. The study was limited to two divisions of one particular organization. Finally, as most manufactures are planning to launch autonomous vehicles by 2021 and are been forced to adapt their business model to cater for full autonomy, therefore keeping the skilled and motivated talent is crucial for smooth transition. Some of the challenges facing full autonomy are namely, huge investment in new mobility technology not only at OEMs level but also at supplier level; and huge infrastructure investment, namely current poor road condition improvements and clear road marking (real-time 3D mapping) that can communicate with vehicles and also allows vehicles to communicate with each other.

FUTURE RESEARCH

Further study to ascertain the relationship between talent management strategy and business objectives will be of benefit, by enlarging the sample to several organizations. The results of this study also highlight the need for a further study that will look at talent management strategy and business objectives relationship and the impact or influence this relationship has on employee wellbeing. Another study could be to demonstrate how business strategy is using talent management to achieve this goal.

REFERENCES

Abdul-Halim, H., & Che-Ha, N. (2010). HR outsourcing among Malaysian manufacturing companies. *Business Strategy Series*, *11*(6), 363–370. doi:10.1108/17515631011093061

Adolph, S., Tisch, M., & Metternich, J. (2014). Challenges and approaches to competency development for future production. *Journal of International Scientific Publications–Educational Alternatives*, *12*(1), 1001–1010.

Al Ariss, A., Cascio, W. F., & Paauwe, J. (2014). Talent management: Current theories and future research directions. *Journal of World Business*, *49*(2), 173–179. doi:10.1016/j.jwb.2013.11.001

Awan, A. G., & Farhan, H. M. (2016). Talent management practices and their impact on job satisfaction of employees: A case study of banking sector in Pakistan. *Science International*, *8*(2), 1950.

Bagga, G. (2013). How to keep the talent you have got. *Human Resource Management International Digest*, *21*(1), 3–4. doi:10.1108/09670731311296401

Barkhuizen, N., Mogwere, P., & Schutte, N. (2014). Talent management and leadership reciprocity: The case of the South African aviation industry. *Mediterranean Journal of Social Sciences*, *5*(9), 11.

Bergin, T. (2013). *Learning and development in the public sector. The care for maintaining investment in tough times*. Canberra: Australian Institute of Management.

Chigada, J., & Ngulube, P. (2015). Knowledge-management practices at selected banks in South Africa: Original research. *South African Journal of Information Management, 17*(1), 1–10. doi:10.4102ajim.v17i1.634

Collings, D., & Mellahi, K. (2013). Commentary on: Talent—innate or acquired? Theoretical considerations and their implications for talent management. *Human Resource Management Review, 23*(4), 322–325. doi:10.1016/j.hrmr.2013.08.003

Collins, C. E. (2014). *Gray as gold: the significant value of the mature worker*. Tucson, AZ: University of Arizona.

Comini, G., Paolino, M., & Feitosa, M. (2013). Mapping of the succession process in non-profit organizations in Brazil. *International Leadership Journal, 5*(3), 28–50.

Dehkordi, M. A., & Kazemi, T. B. (2013). The talent's strategic management: An analysis of approaches, problems, and features. *Strategy for Culture, 22*, 105–134.

Deloitte Insights. (2018). *The Fourth Industrial Revolution is here—are you ready?* Deloitte Development LLC.

DNdou, S., & Sebola, M. P. (2016). Capacity building in local government: An analysis for application of competency-based training in South Africa. *International Journal of Higher Education Management, 6*(5), 90–100.

Ezigbo, C. A. (2012). Justification of outsourcing for organisation's competitive advantage. *European Journal of Soil Science, 34*(2), 262–272.

Florea, L., Cheung, Y. H., & Herndon, N. C. (2013). For all good reasons: Role of values in organizational sustainability. *Journal of Business Ethics, 114*(3), 393–408. doi:10.100710551-012-1355-x

Gretczko, M., & Cleary, W. (2016). The Candidate as Customer: A Proactive Approach to Talent Acquisition. *Workforce Solutions Review, 7*(3), 8–10.

Grey, B. (2017). *Autonomous Cars: Everything You Need To Know About Market And Research Trends. Autonomous Vehicles – Market and Research Trends report*. Retrieved from https://www.greyb.com/autonomous-cars/#_Toc484626650

Hall, L. O., & Hagen, C. D. (2014). Holistic approach to succession planning provides added value for clients: Financial service professionals play key role in successful plans. *Journal of Financial Service Professionals, 68*(1), 78–83.

Holmes, P., Chapman, T., & Baghurst, T. (2013). Employee job embeddedness: Why people stay. *International Journal of Business Management & Economic Research*, *4*(5), 802–813.

Horwitz, F. M. (2013). An analysis of skills development in a transitional economy: The case of the South African Labour Market. *International Journal of Human Resource Management*, *24*(12), 2435–2451. doi:10.1080/09585192.2013.781438

Jamil, R., & Neem, H. (2013). The Impact of outsourcing external recruitment process on the employee commitment and loyalty: Empirical evidence from the telecommunication sector of Pakistan. *Journal of Business and Management*, *8*(2), 69–75.

Johnson, G., Wilding, P., & Robson, A. (2014). Can outsourcing recruitment deliver satisfaction? A hiring manager perspective. *Personnel Review*, *43*(2), 303–326. doi:10.1108/PR-12-2012-0212

Kaiser, R. B., & Curphy, G. (2013). Leadership development: The failure of an industry and the opportunity for consulting psychologists. *Consulting Psychology Journal: Practice and Research*, *65*(4), 294–302. doi:10.1037/a0035460

Karatepe, O. M. (2013). High-performance work practices, work social support and their effects on job embeddedness and turnover intentions. *International Journal of Contemporary Hospitality Management*, *25*(6), 903–921. doi:10.1108/IJCHM-06-2012-0097

Karodia, A. M., Cowden, R., & Kum, F. D. (2014). The impact of training and development on employee performance: A case study of ESCON Consulting. *Singaporean Journal of Business. Economics and Management Studies*, *3*(3), 72–105.

Krejcie, R., & Morgan, D. (1970). Determining sample size for research activities. *Educational and Psychological Measurement*, *30*(3), 607–610. doi:10.1177/001316447003000308

Kroon, B., & Freese, C. (2013). Can HR practices retain flexworkers with their agency. *International Journal of Manpower*, *34*(8), 899–917. doi:10.1108/IJM-07-2013-0169

Louw, G. J. (2013). Exploring recruitment and selection trends in the Eastern Cape. *SA Journal of Human Resource Management*, *11*(1), 1. doi:10.4102ajhrm.v11i1.319

Mehta, M., Kurbetti, A., & Dhankhar, R. (2014). Review paper–study on employee retention and commitment. *International Journal of Advance Research in Computer Science and Management Studies, 154*(5), 154–164.

Mtila, J., Barkhuizen, E. N., & Mokgele, R. (2013). *Exploring the Application of Talent Management Practices in a Local Government Institution*. Paper presented at the 30th Pan Pacific Business Association Conference, Johannesburg, South Africa.

Murongazvombo, P. K. (2015). *Talent retention strategies in a competitive ICT industry: case of twenty third century systems global*. Harare: BUSE.

Myres, H. (2014). *Factors in South Africa inhibiting the progression of black executives in their careers and the role of coaching in their development*. Johannesburg: Wits Business School.

Osibanjo, A. O., Salau, O. P., & Falola, H. O. (2014). Modelling the relationship between motivating factors; employee's retention; and job satisfaction in the Nigerian banking industry. *Journal of Management Policies and Practices, 2*(2), 63–83.

Roman, L. J., & Mason, R. B. (2015). Employment equity in the South African retail sector: Legal versus competence and business imperatives. *South African Journal of Labour Relations, 39*(2), 84–104.

Ryan, C. (2015, October 1). Recruitment is a tough gig these days. Finweek, 28 - 30.

Schöer, V., Rankin, N., & Roberts, G. (2014). Accessing the first job in a slack labour market: Job matching in South Africa. *Journal of International Development, 26*(1), 1–22. doi:10.1002/jid.2838

Schuler, R. S., Jackson, S. E., & Tarique, I. (2011). Global talent management and global talent challenges: Strategic opportunities for IHRM. *Journal of World Business, 46*(4), 506–516. doi:10.1016/j.jwb.2010.10.011

Schutte, N., & Barkhuizen, N. (2014). Creating public service excellence applying learning organisation methods: The role of strategic leadership. *Mediterranean Journal of Social Sciences, 5*(4), 159.

Sengupta, A., Venkatesh, D., & Sinha, A. (2013). Developing performance-linked competency model: A tool for competitive advantage. *The International Journal of Organizational Analysis, 21*(4), 504–527. doi:10.1108/IJOA-05-2011-0488

Sidani, Y., & Al Ariss, A. (2014). Institutional and corporate drivers of global talent management: Evidence from the Arab Gulf region. *Journal of World Business, 49*(2), 215–224. doi:10.1016/j.jwb.2013.11.005

Sims, D. M. (2014). 5 Ways to increase success in succession planning. *TD: Talent Development*, *68*(8), 60.

Sinkin, J., & Putney, T. (2014). How to manage internal succession. *Journal of Accountancy*, *217*(2), 1–5.

Snelgar, R. J., Renard, M., & Venter, D. (2013). An Empirical Study of the Reward Preferences of South African Employees. *SA Journal of Human Resource Management*, *11*(1), 1. doi:10.4102ajhrm.v11i1.351

Theron, M., Barkhuizen, N., & du Plessis, Y. (2014). Managing the academic talent void: Investigating factors in academic turnover and retention in South Africa. *SA Journal of Industrial Psychology*, *40*(1), 1–14. doi:10.4102ajip.v40i1.1117

Tishman, F., Van Looy, S., & Bruyère, S. (2014). *Employer strategies for responding to an aging workforce*. The NTAR Leadership Center.

Toulson, P. K. (2016). Recruitment and talent management. *Human Resources Magazine*, *21*(2), 34–35.

Toyota. (2016). *Toyota human resources management guiding document.* Human Resources, Durban. Toyota.

Toyota. (2017). *Toyota HR OD&TM overview_v5 document*. Human Resources, Durban. Toyota.

Walker, L. J. (2013). The Reframing of succession strategies. *Journal of Financial Planning*, *26*(8), 37–39.

Wilton, N. (2011). *An introduction to human resource management*. London: Sage Publications.

Ximba, T. M. (2016). *Career advancement challenges facing people with disabilities in South Africa*. Durban: University of South Africa.

Young, M., & Conboy, K. (2013). Contemporary project portfolio management. Reflections on the development of an Australian Competency Standard for Project Portfolio Management. *International Journal of Project Management*, *31*(8), 1089–1100. doi:10.1016/j.ijproman.2013.03.005

KEY TERMS AND DEFINITIONS

Business Objectives: This term is associated with the main purpose for the organization to be sustainable; the main goal target the firm needs to deal with competitors in the industry.

Competitive Advantage: The notion is linked with factors that support the organization's leading position in the competitive environment.

Human Capital: The construct is related to employees as individuals carry a set of skills, knowledge, attitude, competencies, and experience, which is regarded as capability, talent.

Strategy: This concept is associated with plans of action, approaches, techniques, policies to manage and lead the organization to ensure its competitive advantage.

Succession Planning: Procedures that are allied to resourcing approaches the organization can implement to ensure that its employees are further developed to fill in vital and strategic roles to be leaders.

Sustainability: This notion is associated with the organization's capability to be viable, feasible, long-living.

Talent Management: A collection of plans that organizations can implement to ensure individuals are continuously developed their talent, to update their knowledge, expertise, skills.

Chapter 8
Risk and Benefit of Effective Techniques and Technologies in Education:
A Historical Overview

Maria Luisa Nardi
Independent Researcher, Italy

ABSTRACT

Technological innovation is increasingly penetrating the world, and its implementation has the potential to bring a change in the learning organization and pedagogical approach; therefore, it is vital to understand where technology can alleviate problems and not be a hindrance or a gadget. Change factors in the knowledge dynamic today are on the one hand the passage from individual knowledge to global knowledge, with multi-user connections, but without losing the subjective prospective, and on the other hand, the passage from a received multimediality (such as television and cinema) to an interactive multimediality (such as videogames or virtual reality), to a built multimediality (such as socialnetworking knowledge management tool), up to a reflective multimediality (dynamic, intelligent, and semantic UI). This chapter has the purpose to describe possible benefits or risks, barriers or precautions, using effective technologies in education, resulting from the long history of aware applications.

DOI: 10.4018/978-1-5225-7903-8.ch008

INTRODUZIONE

The American acronym ICT (Information and Communication Technologies) identifies the set of technologies that allow the processing and exchange of information, whether textual, visual or sound, in format digital. These technologies have brought about profound changes in society, economically as well as socially.

In the space of a generation, the dynamics, methodologies, and channels of information have multiplied, creating difficulties in understanding and inter-generational communication and, consequently, problems in educating young people. Their understanding and expectation of the sciences are mediated by multimedia experiences and by the use of new technologies, which prefer a method that facilitates connections and conceptual jumps.

Since the entrance of new technologies in teaching, researchers and teachers have tried to understand how using the computer to teach and have been developed different types of relationships between teacher and student mediated by the machines.

The introduction of information and communication technologies cannot be resolved only in the use of the tool, but rather involves an approach to the educational paths that one wants to develop, which has the underlying logic of these new tools.

Learning moves in a multidirectional field of information, in a context of a plurality of sensorial stimuli that involve all the senses of the individual (Correlli, 2015).

The birth of the Educational Technology can be placed around the early '20s, with the first machines to teach [1].

The beginning (1920-1960) is characterized by three main phases (Midoro, 2015):

- The birth of the first teaching machines (1920)
- The study of the media (cinema and television)
- Behaviorism and planned education (the 1950s)

Subsequently, we distinguish other 8 phases:

- The era of mainframes (1960-1975)
- The era of mini (1976-1980)
- The era of PC (1981-1985)
- The era of multimedia systems (1986-1992)
- The era of networks and the Web 1.0 (1993-2005)
- The Web 2.0 (2006 to date)
- Introduction of Coding and Educational Robotics (2010 to date)
- Introduction of Edugames, with Virtual, Augmented or Mixed reality (2010 to date)

In 1920 Sidney Pressey, a professor of psychology at Ohio State University, tired of correcting hundreds of his students' test papers, invented the first "teaching machine" in history, which presented multiple choice tests and accepted. It was the first milestone in the digital education sector.

Then, in the field of studies on communication media, an important contribution came from E. Dale (1946), who became famous for his experience, in which he proposed a classification (with the shape of a cone) of possible learning experiences. Starting from the more concrete ones, placed at the base of the cone, we go back to increasingly abstract experiences up to those based on verbal symbols, placed at the top. The cone of Dale provided the basis for numerous subsequent researches.

From the point of view of the development of the science of means (Olimpo, 1993) we can identify three stages of development until the end of the 60s: a first phase in which the research focused on the audiovisuals intended as an instrument and on the relative didactic material. The studies considered the machine, its characteristics and the effects it produced on the training process. In the second phase the study also extended to the human-machine communication process. The third stage, on the other hand, is the one concerning the creation of real didactic systems, of which we grasp the meaning if we relate them to the line followed by the application of behaviorist principles. On the one hand, in fact, this line of research was dedicated to the development of methodological proposals related to the production of programmed education courses and on the other hand sought out suitable means to manage the presentation of the subject but also suitable to implement the reinforcing techniques we have seen they were the ones that, according to behaviorists, allowed learning.

The 50s and 60s are characterized by the emergence and the affirmation of the behavioral school. Behaviorism is based on the stimulus-response process. Teaching occurs in a "transmissive" mode. The learning objectives are defined in terms of performance. The learner acquires skills like recalling facts, defining and illustrating concepts, applying explanations, and performing specific procedures.

In the famous article *The science of learning and the art of teaching* (1954), Skinner describes in detail his behavioral theory of learning, characterized by the importance of positive reinforcement in facilitating learning. Skinner proposes to entrust the role of mediators to the machines guided by sequences of programmed actions. The lessons are divided into units (frames) at the end of each of which ask questions to check if the learner has learned the notions of the finished frame. In the positive case, the student can move on to the next frame, otherwise he has to repeat the form he has not been able to answer: in this way not only the student is individually followed by the machine, but the teacher is also freed from the assignment having to mark the right and wrong answers.

Seeing the educational technologies in this light naturally led to strong criticism and opposition between supporters who advocated the use of machines as tools to optimize teaching and those who instead considered them a danger because they would have made the human less relationship between teacher and student: this is because the machines were proposed by Skinner as substitutes for the teacher.

In the era of mainframes (1960-1975), the available technologies were large computers connected to alphanumeric terminals via switched lines. These computers, located in computer centers, were simultaneously connected to several terminals with a mode called time-sharing. In this period the learning theory prevalently based on the realization of learning environments was Skinner's behaviorism, and learning was seen as a transfer of knowledge. Learning environments aimed primarily at individualizing learning and the efforts of teaching technologists were mainly aimed at making their Computer Assisted Instruction systems as adaptive as possible. In this period also developed that set of practices related to the design of learning environments called Instructional Design.

Crowder (1969) transforms this approach into a ramified programmed instruction. Thus we arrive at a decisive transition around the end of the '60s, which sees the transition from programmed education to education planning, where all the ideological armaments are still used (objectives, fragmentation of education, control, etc. .) elaborated by behaviorists.

It meant the transition from programmed education to education planning, through a vision of systemic education technologies, which implies a whole organized, and systematic, that foresees logical procedures organized in phases. This new way of understanding the teaching technologies allowed them to acquire importance and to assume for their systemic and multidisciplinary approach a relevant and strategic position for development.

The era of mini (1976-1980) was characterized by smaller computers than the mainframes, called mini, which, unlike the former, which required a computer center, were small computers that could be placed in an office. In the TD this era saw the decline of behaviorism as a theory of reference learning and the contemporary affirmation of cognitivism and constructivism with the two main figures of reference, Gagné (1987) and Papert (1980).

Cognitivism considers learning as an expression of mind in its processes and psycho-dynamic conditions. Teachers/Authors are responsible for assisting learners, organizing information in an optimal way to be easily assimilated. This approach was assumed as a theory for the applications of artificial intelligence to teaching, which stimulated the development of knowledge representation languages, methods for student modeling and for the realization of increasingly friendly man-machine interfaces.

On the other hand, constructivism emphasizes the student as being the "active learner", playing a central role in mediating and managing learning activities. Instruction is a process of supporting knowledge construction, rather than communicating knowledge. Learning activities should be "authentic", and should focus on the "problematic" as perceived by the learner. This approach stimulated the emergence of reactive learning environments, such as simulation, gaming and programming environments accessible to children and young people

In this period the Intelligent Tutoring System was born, which aimed to simulate an expert teacher able to communicate with the student: an intelligent tutoring function to support the teacher/tutor in his actions, guide students to complete their courses on the base of their performance, progress and styles of learning, towards the realization of "self-directed" and personalized learning processes (dall'Acqua, 2010).

The PC era (1981-1985) was characterized by the development of microprocessors, which allowed the creation of computers even smaller than the mini: it was the personal computers, or PC, that could be on a desk. This period was characterized by the development of cognitive sciences, by the application and diffusion of learning environments that incorporated strategies borrowed from constructivism, such as cognitive learning and situated learning. The computer began to establish itself as a tool of thought that amplified the possibilities of creation and production of individuals, through tools to support individual products such as wordprocessors for writing, spreadsheets for calculation, etc. The TDs began to take care of how to exploit the new opportunities made available by technology to facilitate and improve learning (Midoro, 2015).

The era of multimedia systems (1986-1992) saw the integration into the computer, which in the meantime had become portable, of different channels of communication until then separated: writing, graphics, video, audio, etc. In the cognitive sciences, there was the diffusion of Gardner's ideas on multiple intelligences (Gardner, 2011). Hypertexts and hypermedia and the awareness that we live in a knowledge society based on digital technologies began to spread. In the TD the computer began to be used as a tool that allowed the student to navigate autonomously in a knowledge Retrieved from the reticular way in the hypermedia and also to create new ones in multidisciplinary projects (Midoro, 2015).

The telematic networks begin to spread with their e-mail and file transfer services. It let the beginning of the era of networks and the Web 1.0 (1993-2005). The first conferencing systems and bulletin board systems are born, electronic bulletin boards that, without space and time constraints, allow a rapid communication between individuals who share the same interest. This is the period in which the first virtual communities begin to be born and in the Didactic Technologies, the reference psychological paradigm becomes the social constructivism of Vygotsky (1987).

The era of broadband, tablets, smartphones and Web 2.0 (2006-2015) was a period in which broadband and systems integrated more and more typical features of the computer, of the telephone, of the systems for the access to Internet, of the TV, etc. With the birth of Web 2.0 emerges the use of the network as a new medium of production, sharing and communication. The concepts of collective intelligence (Levy, 1997) and the community of practice are affirmed (Wenger, 1998). With the diffusion of smartphones, a new field of study is born in the field of TD, mobile learning or m-learning. The virtual learning communities are spreading and they stimulate studies on informal learning environments and on self-regulated learning. The awareness of the need for a new type of literacy, or literacy, more suited to the knowledge society, and the concepts of life-wide and life-long learning become established.

The nature of Web 2.0 is captured by three elements: participation, sharing and collaboration. Participative and collaborative practice takes place in an ocean of digital documents. Those who learn, the first block, now have the opportunity to become part of a learning community made up of other students, but also by its teachers, experts and people with whom they share, in whole or in part, interests, objectives, goals. Thanks to the potential for participation and sharing of Web 2.0, learning environments are enriched by a new social dimension. In this context the student works with different tools, thinking of himself as a member of a community.

Four fundamental types of Web 2.0 technologies are (dall'Acqua, 2012):

- **Communication Systems**: Synchronous (video conferencing etc.) and asynchronous (forum, blog, del.icio.us, etc..). This is in accordance with "Networked Collaborative Learning" (NCL), a social e-learning approach, founded on strategies of active and collaborative online learning. Fundamental factors are technological online media, communicative dynamics (synchronous and asynchronous mode), the interaction between actors, online and blended activities. Design of communicative processes is functional to the development and management of online learning activities
- **Sharing Resources Functionality**: Synchronous (screen sharing, electronic whiteboard etc.) and asynchronous (access to shared databases, shared documents etc.) to support group activities (collaborative writing, collaborative document synthesis etc.)
- **Tools for Knowledge Mapping and Simulation:** (Conceptual maps, flowcharting, etc.). This is also in accordance to the "Open Learning Environment" (OLE) ID Models, based on the use of tools for visualization and manipulation in order to facilitate testing of complex phenomena, "authentic" contexts to promote the connection between formal knowledge

and everyday experience. Therefore make use of "simulation environments" that allow students to manipulate variables and observe the results.

- **Tools for the Education Workflow Engine**: Systems dedicated to sequential didactical architecture (for procedural ability learning and corrective feedback), and collaborative activity (for peer learning, peer tutoring, project work, problem based approach). We refer to a Learning Activity Management Systems like LAMS (a project of Macquarie University), that allows to create sequences of activities in a graphical environment, using "drag and drop" facility, which facilitates the creation, exchange, re-use and adaptation of these sequences, and RAMS, a system based on "human group e-Research" work-flow.

Customize study environments, such as using blogs as personal journals, wikis as a content management space, tools for storing personal bookmarks, Flickr and YouTube as multimedia archives, etc. And, if he wants to, he can share part of his personal world with others through social networks

The term literacy denotes the ability to live in a society in which social relationships are largely based on writings. With the spread of information and communication technologies, the "world of letters", based on the alphabet, is transforming itself into a "world of digital objects" that require new abilities compared to the writings (Midoro, 2013). The term literate, connoted by the digital attribute, can be used to denote the profile of an individual able to operate satisfactorily in the society of knowledge based on digital technologies. Digital literate is a person who acts in the knowledge society using the typical objects of this world and related technologies. He must therefore be an ICT literate, a media literate, an information literate and must know how to participate in social life as an active member of a society characterized by a collective intelligence (Olimpo, 1993).

DIGITAL RESOURCES AND TOOLS FOR THE DIGITAL SOCIETY

The term Open Educational Resource (OER) was first used by UNESCO in 2002, to indicate that sea of free online content that can be used for learning: «Open Educational Resources (OER) are materials used to support education that may be freely accessed, reused, modified, and shared "(UNESCO, 2011). The use of OER is much more than simply making available freely accessible materials, as it has a potential for innovation capable of re-configuring training in terms of learning, organization and sustainability models. On the one hand, new open education paths and a new type of "open students" emerge, and on the other, the need for the recognition of informal learning. And of this the Massive Open Online Course (MOOC) is a significant example, based on a connectivist approach (dall'Acqua, 2012).

Connectivism[2] is one of the most recent didactic approach according to this cultural context. It considers the learning as dynamic (from a "learning about, to do and to be" to a "learning to transform"), contextualized, involving and relevant, result of a complex network of several typologies of nodes, connections and diversified components, like knowledge, competences, communications, representations, relationships, technologies and paradigms.

Connectivism acknowledges the fluid nature of knowledge and connections based on contexts. In this perspective, knowledge and learning are based on analysis and comparison of different opinions, through the ability to identify connections between fields, ideas and concepts (Siemens, 2008).

The main idea of this type of MOOC course is that a learner is immersed within a (large) community of practice and introduced to methods, thoughts and practices of this community. The courses' common goal was not to be conducted in a single confined learning space or institutional environment, but distributed across the web. This approach adopts the philosophy of a personal learning environment (PLE) which learners themselves have control over. The participants' activities and interactions, therefore, took place in different tools and platforms across the web. Although some reading lists and other materials were provided, the decision to participate in the course was itself seen as more important than the content which participants happened to learn during the course. From a pedagogic perspective, content in this environment can be categorized into four main features (Kop et al, 2011):

- **Aggregation**: Access to a wide variety of resources to read, watch, or play, along with a newsletter called 'The Daily', which highlighted and summarised some of this content.
- **Remixing and Repurposing:** After consuming some content, participants were encouraged to disassemble and re-assemble content according to their needs and perspectives.
- **Production**: Participants were encouraged to create learning artefacts of their own. In the analysed MOOCs, it was envisaged that with practice, participants would become accomplished creators and critics of ideas and knowledge.
- **Feed Forward:** Participants were encouraged to share their work with others in the course and with the world at large. Tools and technologies for sharing were suggested but not mandated by the course organisers. Specific metatags were used as identifiers for course-related content.

In synthesis, this type of course is focused on the necessity to overcome the limitations of traditional curricula, such as the fragmentation of disciplines, their extraneousness with respect to new social needs and the real problems of life, the lack of consideration of the new skills required by the digital society (creativity, problem solving ability), ability to learn independently, etc.). The ability to learn in environments where physicality and virtuality are combined in a continuous social, informative and training, requires an extension of skills compared to those that were the goal of traditional educational processes. The new skills could schematically be divided into three blocks: a) skills and competences with which the individual faces the phases of a process: exploration and "problem setting", "problem solving" and communication, autonomy, tolerance, parallelism of action, etc.; b) relational skills; c) organizational skills of a process.

Cognitive Tutoring

The expert system and the associated Knowledge base should suggest links, knowledge contents (through predefined reusable learning objects), monitor and supervise the learning behaviors, suggest actions to be taken (through established rules) (See Figures 1, 2 and 3).

Figure 1. Cognitive Tutoring in Mathematics
(Source: Homeschool Math, 2015)

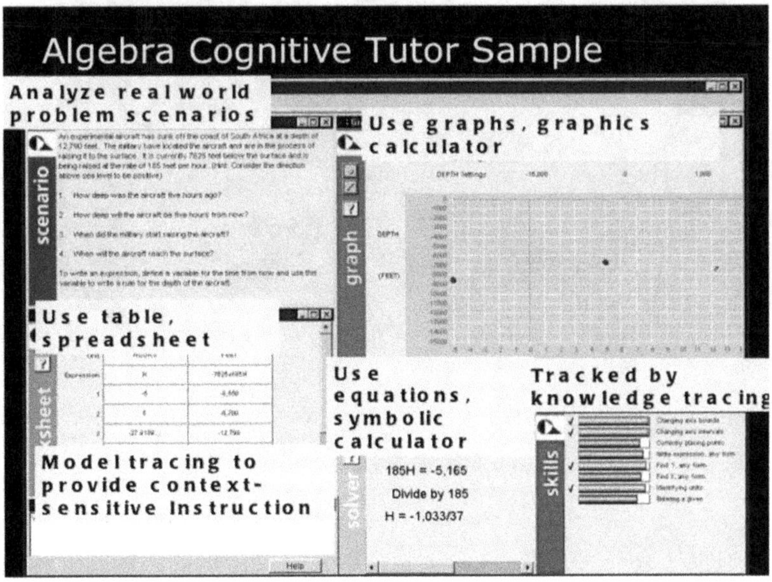

Figure 2. Cognitive tutoring: Military applications
(Source Utopia Compression (n.d)

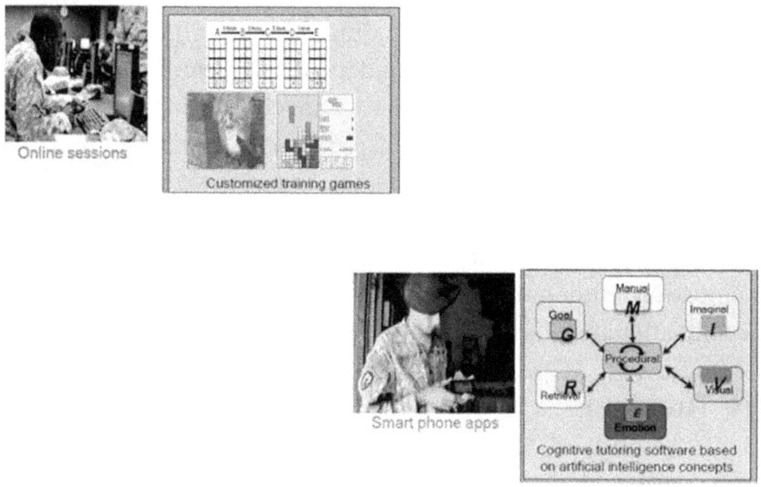

Figure 3. Educational robotics: Nao
(Source Alive Robots (n.d.)

In summary, an e-Tutor, on today's state of research, should be able to (dall'Acqua, 2010):

- Recognize and update the profile of the Student and domain specifications
- Monitor the status of each Student's knowledge in real time and tailor course material for each Student, based on continuous assessments
- Provide immediate feedback on errors, associating suggestions to the Student (just-in-time, automatic hint-/help or upon the Learner's request) and has the ability to propose an adaptation of the actual learning path (based on optional selected didactical nodes)
- Suggest interventions to the human Tutor and suggests "re-designing" actions to the Teacher/Author
- Suggest a personalized learning path based on the learning session selected considering the corresponding prerequisites. Therefore, learners will not miss any fundamental sections for the targets of the learning activity selected
- Guide the student towards the achievement of objective tests, based on the structure of problem solving (*reification action*)
- Divides the problems in primary and secondary targets, active actions of scaffolding and reasoning
- Allows teachers to monitor the students' progress and select suitable learning materials/topics in the learning object repository (lor) accordingly
- Streamline the process of content management and course development, allowing Teachers to spend more time on the pedagogical design/-issues of the course

The Cognitive Tutor should be able to suggest a diversification of the learning path on the base of the student profile evolution and necessities.

The collaboration with an ID Knowledge Specialist is an essential strategy to obtain technical and methodology support a) in adapting the course design, b) in the formulation of the necessary didactical rules and logical relations for the Rule Engine of the Cognitive Tutor.

Educational Robotics

During the last decade robotics has attracted the high interest of teachers and researchers as a valuable tool to develop cognitive and social skills for student, to support learning in science, mathematics, technology, informatics and other school subjects or interdisciplinary learning activities.

The use of robotics in the teaching and learning process (in the educational practice) Educational robotics uses robotics kits, programming software and computer as hands-on learning tools (See Figure 4). It achieves disciplinary learning objectives, and engage groups of students in playful collaborative problem solving activities, and can create a learning environment that can enhance collaboration and communication among students, problem-solving skills, critical thinking skills, and creativity.

ICAP (France, an ambitious program for technology–enhanced learning) has identified 3 roles for robots in education (The Disruptory (2016) and Figures 5, 6):

- **The Robot as an Educational Subject:** To start with, in early primary classes, from 5-6 years of age, children learn basic algorithms by programming objects and actions. Throughout their schooling, they are now offered robots that follow their progress. There are also a number of competitions at different levels using robots they have built and programmed.
- **Robots as Learning Support Tools:** In this second role, robots help to support educational activities. For instance, in medical and healthcare education, the use of simulation is an important means of learning in order to improve patient safety and quality of care. Implementation of more realistic simulation-based teaching methodologies, which serves as a bridge between the acquisition and application of clinical skills, knowledge, and attributes, increasingly makes use of robotic simulators.

Figure 4. Social robotics: GiraffPlus
(Source: DMO (2014))

Figure 5. Cognitive robotics for disability
(Source: Dasha 2017)

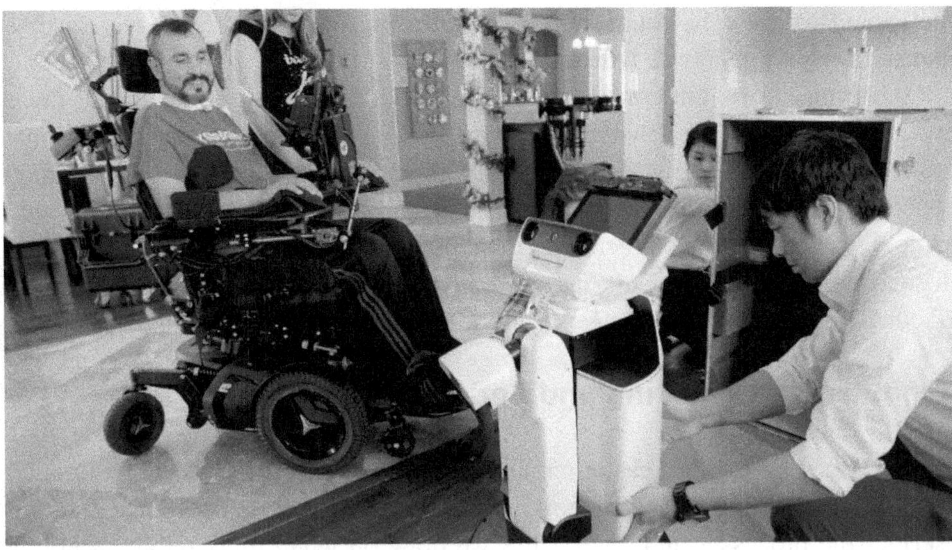

Figure 6. Serious game
(Source: Gamification 2018)

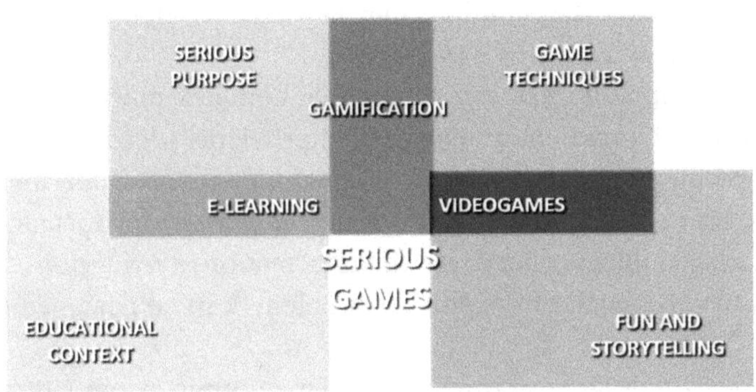

- **Telepresence Robots:** These devices enable sick or hospitalized children to “virtually” attend classroom sessions at school by taking control of a tele-operated robot.
- We can add a 4th role, assisting education professionals in their daily tasks via a “collaborative, complementary robot-human” approach. For instance, robots can account for the presence or absence of students, welcome them into the classroom by name, etc., thus allowing the teacher to focus on their pedagogical objective.

Different strategies for introducing students to robotics technologies and concepts should be employed by teachers and educators to provide multiple pathways into robotics and to ensure that there are entry points to engage young people with diverse interests and learning styles (Rusk et al., 2008).

Pioneering efforts are considered as development of a high potential if these networks link together and synchronize their actions into a European/International network (Bredenfeld et al., 2010) that will offer well-organized and coordinated collective actions, mainly in order to create and share open educational and technological products and practices (curriculum and resources) for both formal and informal learning environments in a way that reflects the best pedagogical practices and educational research in the field, and to test and validate curricula

Computational Thinking and Serious Game

We often draw on logical reasoning, algorithms, decomposition, abstraction, and patterns and generalisation when thinking computationally. Computational thinking describes the processes and approaches we draw on when thinking about how a computer can help us to solve complex problems and create systems. It allows users to take a complex problem, understand what the problem is and develop possible solutions.

We can then present these solutions in a way that a computer, a human, or both, can understand.

Computational thinking involves taking that complex problem and breaking it down into a series of small, more manageable problems *(decomposition)*. Each of these smaller problems can then be looked at individually, considering how similar problems have been solved previously *(pattern recognition)* and focusing only on the important details, while ignoring irrelevant information *(abstraction)*. Next, simple steps or rules to solve each of the smaller problems can be designed (*algorithms*) (BBC, 2018).

Finally, these simple steps or rules are used to program a computer to help solve the complex problem in the best way.

Thinking computationally is not programming. It is not even thinking like a computer, as computers do not, and cannot, think. Computational thinking enables you to work out exactly what to tell the computer to do. For example, it might be that you need to decide what to do with your group of friends. If all of you like different things, you would need to decide:

- What you could do
- Where you could go

- Who wants to do what
- What you have previously done that has been a success in the past
- How much money you have and the cost of any of the options
- What the weather might be doing
- How much time you have

Another example might occur when playing a videogame. Depending on the game, in order to complete a level you would need to know:

- What items you need to collect, how you can collect them, and how long you have in which to collect them
- Where the exit is and the best route to reach it in the quickest time possible
- What kinds of enemies there are and their weak points

From these details you can work out a strategy for completing the level in the most efficient way.

Nowadays, within this evolutionary path of learning processes, we can not but consider serious games, which represent a real cultural revolution in this area. In fact, thanks to their ability to simulate different aspects of the experience, they become a powerful tool for the acquisition and development of skills in many sectors.

The three dimensions, typical of serious games (Ascolese, 2016), that make them effective and powerful are the simulation, the playful one and the formative one. Thanks to these three foundations, learning games make it possible to concentrate learning both on 'what', as traditional learning does, and on 'how', as e-learning does. The learning process that passes through the serious games is therefore able to integrate declarative knowledge and procedural knowledge (Anolli & Mantovani, 2011).

Gamification uses elements by games and game design techniques in contexts external to games, in order to increase participation and involvement.

Serious games are real gameplays, but has different difficulties that can still be the most varied and disparate (teaching is only one of these). "Educational games", or video games designed to "teach" or transmit some kind of "value";

To date there is no uniform theory on serious game pedagogy. Particular importance has been given to experiential learning which starts from the assumption that learning by doing favors deeper and more lasting behavioral changes; in fact it is well known that active learning obtains qualitatively better results than passive ones, in which contents are conveyed through lectures that are too often boring (Alo, 2015).

Moreover, the possibility of repeating the exercise-game several times allows to reach the total mastery of the dynamics explored, increasing the competence and familiarity with the real situation.

The simulative dimension of serious games, means that these tools allow the learning user to make experiences, that is, to concretely represent what we know at a theoretical level. The simulation aspects allow you to get in touch with knowledge through your senses, your body, and not only at the abstract level. By employing digital devices that support serious games, users can reproduce aspects present in the 'real' experience and anticipate future perspectives while maintaining an active role.

The playful aspects allow the user to live a rewarding experience, a source of positive emotions such as interest, curiosity, exploration, the sense of challenge and self-efficacy. These positive emotions exert a strong influence both on our attention and on our memorability. More specifically, they are able to capture our attentive resources and focus on the task we are performing.

Finally, they can provide the possibility to recreate a protected environment in which the user has the opportunity to get involved without being afraid of making mistakes but rather can learn from their mistakes in order not to commit them in real life (Anderson & Phelps, 2001).

Simulation, Virtual, Augmented, or Mixed Reality

Augmented and virtual reality will experience more widespread adoption over the next two years. Augmented reality (AR), or 'blended reality', refers to the 'layering of data over 3D spaces to enhance a participant's encounter with reality. AR can be built into apps on mobile phones to blend the digital and real world, but in such a fashion that they remain distinct from one another. Diversely, virtual reality (VR) simulates changes to the physical environment through audio, and visual embodiments of people and objects. AR and VR are increasingly being developed into viable tools within the HE sector, generating some of the most stimulating pedagogical innovation of the 21st century (Augment, n.d.).

VR is made possible at low cost through virtual headsets attached to smart phones, simulating visual experiences. Google Cardboard has enabled the spread of this tool in HE. Alternatively, VR simulation rooms can provide complex training, like that used for astronauts. Furthermore, VR has a lot of potential for online education. MIT and Stanford University have adopted VR into their executive education programs, enabling students from all over the world to partake in a simulated on-campus environment, so they can network and conduct group work (Johnson, et al.2016).

AR is particularly relevant for students who cannot experience specific conditions untrained, which is why AR, alongside VR, has revolutionised the medicine discipline (See figure 8). City University London ran a project which offered nurses simulated clinical training, by emulating patient care scenarios. AR is also applied frequently to visual subjects such as architecture, engineering and construction, and music production, demonstrating AR's versatility as an educational tool (Dasha et al. 2017).

THE EFFECTIVE IMPROVEMENT: RISKS AND OPPORTUNITIES

Technology can perform several key functions in the change process, including opening up new opportunities that improve teaching and learning, particularly with the affordance of customization of learning to individual learner needs, which is highly supported by the learning science (Groff, 2013; OECD, 2015).

The skills for an adult life include technological literacy, and people who do not acquire and master these competencies may suffer from a new form of the digital divide, which will impact their capacity to effectively operate and thrive in the new knowledge economy.

Technology is an integral part of accessing the higher-order competencies often referred to as 21st Century Skills, which are also necessary to be productive in today's society.

One of the educational strategies is 'Bring Your Own Device', also called bring your own technology (BYOT), bring your own phone (BYOP), and bring your own personal computer (BYOPC), which refers to the policy of permitting employees

Figure 7. Augmented reality in education: Anatomy
(Source: Palladino, 2018)

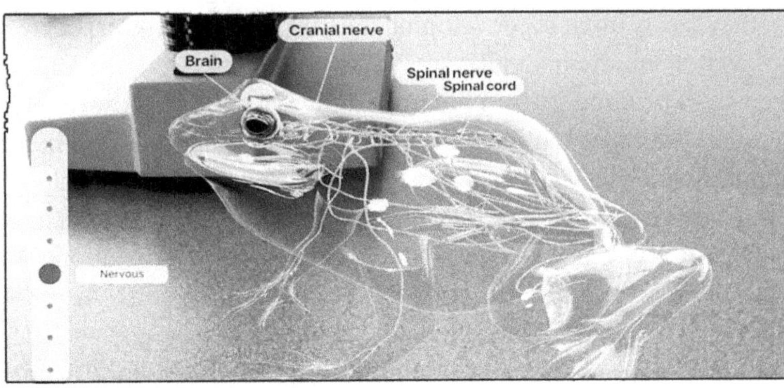

to bring personally owned devices (laptops, tablets, and smart phones) to their workplace, and to use those devices to work or study.

It is expected to, and have, become increasingly popular, drawing on mobile learning and online student data to enhance the learner experience.

A future in which robots work alongside students is no longer just the hyperbole of sci-fi movies. Robotics, too, is projected to become more prevalent in mainstream HE within the next three to four years

N.W. Gleason (Dasha et al, 2017, cit.), Director at the Centre for Teaching and Learning and Senior Lecturer within the Social Science Division at Yale-NUS College, states: "In the fourth industrial revolution there will still be demand for employees who have completed an undergraduate degree. But constantly re-skilling those graduates will be equally important," Gleason contended. "The job of the professor will change. Professors, like everyone else, will have to constantly be learning how to use and communicate with those who use new technologies. Students will collect information in new ways; some of this will be complemented by artificial intelligence and online learning." .

Challenges

Practice shows that even when students have access to the devices and the Internet but they lack technological knowledge and support, they will not benefit much from technology. What is more, if students know how to use the device but no quality content has been uploaded onto it, then learning might deteriorate into mindless clicking (Czopek et al., 2017).

Children growing up in stimuli-rich environments where education is highly appreciated and well-scaffolded will be able to properly interact with technology even when they are given access to it at a later age. In contrast, when children with limited cultural capital and disadvantaged social background receive access to technology, they rarely use it for developmental purposes. In this respect technology may be seen as not beneficial at all.

In such cases, it becomes even more important to teach kids how to interact with technology in the way that will benefit them instead of taking away their valuable developmental time .

European Commission states that a wider use and uptake of digital technologies in teaching and learning can also enable and facilitate European Educational Istitutions to acquire the basic level of digital skills needed for finding jobs. At present these skills are not being fostered or developed thoroughly. For example by 2015, 90% of jobs will require at least a basic level of digital skills, while as of today only 50% of

Europeans have these (European Commision (n.d.). Though there are many examples of grass root initiatives at national, regional and or local level, these suffer from lack of sustainability and scale. Moreover, the collaboration between practitioners and decision makers, required to achieve the necessary critical mass, is frequently limited. Different types of bottlenecks, at different levels and affecting different stakeholders, hamper the digital education value chain.

A risk to confuse technological innovation with methodological innovation exists. It means thinking that everything we do with them is innovative, while it is clear that it is possible to realize an absolutely conservative teaching approach also using digital. In short, a lecture on the IWB or using video, it remains a frontal lesson in which nothing changes with regard to the way to set the relationship with the contents and with the students (Vayola, 2013).

Already Calvani (2013) emphasized the need to take into account the scientific evidence regarding the results, in terms of performance, the introduction of these tools and reported the conclusions of various researches that confirmed that there were no necessarily positive correlations between school outcomes and use of technologies.

Another risk is believing that students have different skills and competencies than those of teachers in the use of technologies.

Starting from Prensky's articles (2001a, 2001b), also accompanied by the analogous conclusions of other scholars in that same period (Veen, 2008), the conviction that young people born from the last years of the last century has been affirmed onwards, that is, those who, since they were children, have been in contact with technologies to the point of learning their use before school age, were anthropologically different from those who had preceded them because the familiarity with digital devices would have changed the their way of learning, of relating to others and of working.

Prensky (2010) modified his previous statements, cushioning the generation gap and emphasizing instead the importance of continuity in the use of technologies over time. This led him to replace the previous dichotomy with a tripartition *(digital wiseness, digital cleverness, digital dumbness*) that disregards any registry reference and instead highlights how the wisdom (*digital wiseness*) coincides with the acquisition of the digital competence of citizenship and not with the massive use of technologies that is rather what characterizes the "smanettone" (*digitally clever*), which, in turn, is opposed to the so-called stupid (*digitally dumb*), who does not know or does not want to try his hand at the technologies.

Opportunities

On the other hand, one of the opportunities on which it is necessary to insist, by designing teacher training for an effective use of digital technologies, is that they can make it possible to do otherwise difficult or impossible things. Consider, for example, the possibility of sharing materials and co-building knowledge in collaborative ways at distance offered by the web 2.0 and how they allow to face and solve the historical difficulty of overcoming the frontal lesson. They allow to organize non-communicative learning opportunities without absorbing too much time in the school and avoiding having to choose between carrying out effective methodologies and being able to process content deemed essential for their discipline.

The American researcher R. Puentedura (2014) proposes a model for the planning of learning, the so-called SAMR, which can be useful not so much as a design tool but as a tool for reflection and metacognition addressed to teachers to better understand the type of use they are doing of ICT in the classroom. The model defines two macro-modalities of use of digital tools, one of simple progress and one of transformation.

In the first mode, that of the so-called advancement (enhancement), the technologies can serve only to replace other older ones (substitution), but without this producing an added value, as in the case in which you change a printed map with a digital map. However, if the digital map is dynamic and therefore allows you to zoom, improving the use, then you will find yourself in a development situation (augmentation) compared to the previous approach.

By the age of three, a child can turn on the TV, a video recorder, or click on a computer screen and access information sources that nurture his need to explore the world around him more extensively. This new one possibility is an opportunity and a risk at the same time, because it guarantees valuable sources of information, but it can also bring bad influences. Parents should not restrict access to the child's TV or computer completely, but prevent harmful influences.

Papert (Barbieri, 2013).advises to establish precise rules with him. It is essential to establish a climate of trust that allows parents to know what their child is doing on the Internet. Papert explains the principles that educators should be inspired by and provides many concrete ideas for activities that implement these principles using computers at home

- **Motivation:** Children need to find out for themselves (not just to hear it) the usefulness of a learning objective. In the presence of a high motivation to learn a new thing practically any way of learning and any kind of content become effective.

- **Exciting fun:** If the motivation is high, difficult tasks are more fun than easy ones.
- **Powerful Ideas:** Let the children discover the meaning of key ideas in human knowledge as the function of grammar in the language or the meaning of the number zero in mathematics.
- **Exploration:** Let the children immerse themselves in new worlds in search of answers to questions (autoposte) or to perform a task chosen by themselves. Virtual micromonds offer a limited virtual world that can be fully explored and understood. They are suitable for learning to use knowledge that requires profound mastery.
- **Creation:** Make concrete or fantastic objects using new elements to apply new rules to learn. Traditional building blocks can be enhanced with virtual elements of unlimited variety
- **Learning Styles:** Be prepared to adapt to different learning styles
- **Talents:** Recognizing individual talents and adapting them
- **Culture of Children:** The project should be felt by the child as part of his usual activities, especially with the type of activity that takes place with the computer
- **Property:** Let children create artifacts that can be exhibited and shared, give them credit for discovering or creating something
- **Technological Deficiency:** Let children use and discover new technologies to explore and create
- **Transparency:** To make complex systems transparent to the understanding of them or at least their concepts
- **Activities:** Children are active, not passive. They are responsible, they make choices. They are non-consumer producers.
- **Family Learning Culture:** The way in which the family considers learning: his beliefs, favorite activities and learning habits

CONCLUSION

Change factors in the knowledge dynamic today are: on a hand the passage from individual knowledge to global knowledge, with multi-user connections, but without losing the subjective prospective. On the other hand, the passage from a received multimediality (such as television and cinema), to an interactive multimediality (such as videogames or virtual reality), to a built multimediality (such as socialnetworking knowledge management tool), up to a reflective multimediality (dynamic, intelligent and semantic UI).This work wanted to describe possible benefits or risks, barriers or precautions, using effective technologies in education, resulting from the long history of aware applications.

The risk of falling into a kind of multi-reductionism exists, in which, depending on the perspective that is assumed, the salient features are those of information research, media literacy, moral responsibility, problem solving and so on . Beyond the deepening and articulation of the discussion, which in itself demonstrates the need to effectively account for a completely new reality, there is the risk that the emerging and irreducible nature, the "discontinuity" of the activities, escapes that are practiced in the digital environment. Approaches descriptive or narrative, less classifiers, but more focused on practices, can perhaps help us to reconstruct the specific experiences in which, for example, are less distinctions such as the one between programmer and user, between producer and consumer, and therefore cannot be traced to known categories

REFERENCES

Alive Robots. (n.d.). *NAO es la mejor plataforma robótica para educacion*. Retrieved from: https://aliverobots.com/nao-educacion/

Alo, A. (2015). *Serious game: metodologie innovative per l'apprendimento esperienziale*. Retrieved from: http://www.diversity-management.it/2015/12/24/serious-game-definizione-vantaggi/

Anderson, A. K., & Phelps, E. A. (2001). Lesions of the human amygdala impair enhanced perception of emotionally salient events. *Nature*, *411*(6835), 305–309. doi:10.1038/35077083 PMID:11357132

Anolli, L., & Mantovani, F. (2011). *Come funziona la nostra mente. Apprendimento, simulazione e Serious Games*. Il Mulino.

Ascolese, A. (2016). *Perché i serious games ci aiutano ad apprendere?* Retrieved from: http://www.stateofmind.it/2016/10/serious-games-apprendimento/

Augment. (2015). *Virtual Reality vs. Augmented Reality*. Retrieved from: http://www.augment.com/blog/virtual-reality-vs-augmented-reality/

Barbieri, A. (2013). *Sfide della rivoluzione digitale nel contesto educativo*. University of Milano, Dottorato di Ricerca in Società dell'Informazione, Ciclo XXV.

BBC. (2018). *Introduction to computational thinking*. Retrieved from: https://www.bbc.com/education/guides/zp92mp3/revision/2

Bredenfeld, A., & Leimbach, T. (2010). *The Roberta Initiative*. In *First International Conference on Robotics in Education*, Bratislava, Slovakia.

Calvani, A. (2013). Le TIC nella scuola: dieci raccomandazioni per i policy maker. *Form@re - Open Journal per la Formazione in Rete, 4*(13), 30–46.

Correlli, S. (2015). *Didattica e nuove tecnologie, Seminario di cultura digitale*. University of Pisa.

Crowder, N. (1969). Automatic Tutoring by Intrinsic Programming. In A. A. Lumsdaine & R. Glaser (Eds.), *Teaching Machines and Programmed Learning*. Washington, DC: National Education Assn.

Czopek, A. (2017), The Value of Technology in Education. Young Digital Planet 2017, Gdansk, Poland.

Dale, E. (1946). *Audio-visual methods in teaching*. New York, NY: Dryden Press.

dall'Acqua, L., & Santo, M. D. (2012). New interpretative paradigms to understand and manage the unpredictability of the dynamics of learning in a complex multi-user knowledge environment. *Proceedings of Artificial Intelligence Workshop 2012 on Collaboration and Intelligence in Blended Learning*, 92-9.

dall'Acqua, L., & Santo, M. D. (2014). Orientism, the basic pedagogical approach of PENTHA ID Model vs. 2, to manage decisions in unpredictability conditions. *Proceedings of World Congress on Engineering and Computer Science WCECS2014, 1*, 316-21.

dall'Acqua, L. (2011). Didactical suggestion for a Dynamic Hybrid Intelligent e-Learning Environment (DHILE) applying the PENTHA ID Model. *AIP Proceedings, 1373*, 159-173.

Dasha, K. (2017). *Technology & Pedagogical Innovation.* Retrieved from: http://www.reimagine-education.com/wp-content/uploads/2018/01/RE_White-Paper_Technology-Pedagogical-Innovation.pdf

DMO. (2014). *Nonna Lea e la sua badante robot.* Retrieved from: http://www.datamanager.it/news/nonna-lea-e-la-sua-badante-robot-56063.html

Downes, S. (2010). *The role of the Educator in PLE World.* Retrieved from http://www.slideshare.net/Downes/the-role-of-the-educator-in-a-ple-world

Downes, S. (2011). Knowledge, *Learning and Community*. Retrieved from http://www.downes.ca/files/books/KnowledgeLearning.pdf

European Commission. (n.d.). *ICT in education. EU Smart Specialisation Platform*. Retrieved from: http://s3platform.jrc.ec.europa.eu/education

Gagne, R. (1987). *Instructional Technology Foundations*. Hillsdale, NJ: Lawrence Erlbaum Associates.

Gamification. (2018). *E-Learning: glossario dei termini*. Retrieved from: http://www.gamification.it/tag/serious-games/

Gardner, H. (2011). *Frames of Mind: The Theory of Multiple Intelligences*. New York, NY: Basic Books.

Groff, J. (2013). *Technology-rich innovative learning environments*. Centre for Educational Research and Innovation (CERI). Retrieved from: http://www.oecd.org/education/ceri/Technology-Rich%20Innovative%20Learning%20Environments%20by%20Jennifer%20Groff.pdf

Homeschool Math. (2015). *Review of Carnegie Learning's Cognitive Tutor Algebra 1*. Retrieved from: https://www.homeschoolmath.net/reviews/carnegie-learning.php

Huffman, W. E. (1974). Decision Making: The Role of Education. *American Journal of Agricultural Economics*, *56*(1), 85–97. doi:10.2307/1239349

Johnson. (2016). *NMC Horizon Report: Higher Education Edition*. Austin, TX: The New Media Consortium.

Kop, R., Fournier, H., & Mak, J. S. F. (2011). A Pedagogy of Abundance or a Pedagogy to Support Human Beings? Participant Support on Massive Open Online Courses. *International Review of Research in Open and Distance Learning*, *12*(7), 74–93. doi:10.19173/irrodl.v12i7.1041

Levy, P. (1997). *Collective Intelligence*. Cambridge, MA: Perseus Books.

Luhmann, N., & Schorr, K. E. (1999). *Il sistema educativo. Problemi di riflessività*. Armando Editore.

Midoro, V. (2013). Insegnanti per la scuola nell'era digitale. In D. Persico & V. Midoro (Eds.), Pedagogia nell'era digitale (pp. 118–124). Academic Press.

Midoro, V. (2015). Dalle tecnologie didattiche ad una pedagogia digitale. *TD Tecnologie Didattiche*, *23*(1), 59–63.

OECD. (2015). *Students, Computers and Learning*. OECD Publishing.

Olimpo, G. (1993). Nascita e sviluppi delle tecnologie didattiche. Italian Journal of Educational Technology, 1(1).

Palladino, T. (2018). *Apple's Education-Focused iPad Event Pushes Augmented Reality Further into the Classroom*. Retrieved from: https://next.reality.news/news/apples-education-focused-ipad-event-pushes-augmented-reality-further-into-classroom-0183762/

Papert, S. (1980). *Mindstorms: Children, Computers, and Powerful Ideas*. New York: Basic Books.

Prensky, M. (2001a). Digital Natives, Digital Immigrants. On the Horizon, 9(5), 1-6.

Prensky, M. (2001b). Digital Natives, Digital Immigrants, part 2: Do they really think differently? *On the Horizon*, *9*(6), 1–6. doi:10.1108/10748120110424843

Prensky, M. (2010). *Teaching Digital Natives: Partnering for Real Learning*. London: Sage Publishers.

Puentedura, R. (2014). SAMR and Bloom's Taxonomy: Assembling the Puzzle. Retrieved from https://www.graphite.org/blog/samr-and-blooms-taxonomy-assembling-the-puzzle

Rusk, N., Resnick, M., Berg, R., & Pezalla-Granlund, M. (2008). New pathways into robotics: Strategies for broadening participation. *Journal of Science Education and Technology*, *17*(1), 59–69. doi:10.100710956-007-9082-2

Skinner, B. F. (1954). The science of learning and the art of teaching. *Harvard Educational Review*, *24*.

Technologies for Education. (n.d.). *Storia dello sviluppo delle tecnologie didattiche*. Retrieved from: https://sites.google.com/site/tecnologieperleducazione/storia-dello-sviluppo-delle-tecnologie-didattiche

The Disruptory. (2016). *Robots in Education: Why? What? How? And What For?* Retrieved from: https://www.thedisruptory.com/2016/11/robots-in-education/

UNESCO. (2011). *Guidelines for Open Educational Resources (OER) in Higher Education*. Retrieved from http://unesdoc.unesco.org/images/0021/002136/213605e.pdf

Utopia Compression. (n.d.). *Medical technology. Online Cognitive tutors*. Retrieved from: http://www.utopiacompression.com/technologies/neuro_imaging_augmented_cognitive_models.php

Vajola, P. (2013). Risks and opportunities of digital technologies in the school. Reflections about planning the teacher's training. *Form@re*. Retrieved from: http://www.fupress.net/index.php/formare/article/download/18196/17323

Veen, W. (2008). The Role of Beliefs in the Use of Information Technology: implications for teacher education, or teaching the right thing at the right time. Journal of Information Technology for Teacher Education, 2(2).

Wenger, E. (1998). *Communities of practice: learning, meaning, and identity*. New York: Cambridge University Press. doi:10.1017/CBO9780511803932

KEY TERMS AND DEFINITIONS

"Bring Your Own Device": It refers to the policy of permitting employees to bring personally owned devices (laptops, tablets, and smart phones) to their workplace, and to use those devices to work or study.

Cognitivism: It considers learning as an expression of mind in its processes and psycho-dynamic conditions. Teachers/authors are responsible in assisting learners, organizing information in an optimal way to be easily assimilated.

Connectivism: It considers the learning as dynamic (from a "learning about, to do and to be" to a "learning to transform"), contextualized, involving, and relevant, result of a complex network of several typologies of nodes, connections, and diversified components, like knowledge, competences, communications, representations, relationships, technologies, and paradigms.

Constructivism: It emphasizes the student as being the "active learner," playing a central role in mediating and managing learning activities. Instruction is a process of supporting knowledge construction, rather than communicating knowledge.

ENDNOTE

1 In Italy the term Educational Technology, coined in 1948, became commonly used only in the late sixties, when in Italy were born the "Didactic Technologies", proposed by R. Sanna, who founded the homonymous Laboratory of the CNR in 1970.

Chapter 9
Bio-Ethics of Innovation:
Innovative Practices, Global Health Delivery, and Safeguard of Environment

Anna Verrini
Independent Researcher, Italy

ABSTRACT

The word innovation could mean everything new capable of solving in an easier and better way any problem we find in our lives. Any innovation has always created risks, but specifically, now, the innovation related to the information technology poses major problems because of the pervasiveness everywhere, anytime. It can happen that we are not any more capable of doing very basic things without the help of a computer, and unfortunately, too many persons feel strongly that we can solve the crisis we are living now just by innovating. This chapter explores the bio-ethics of innovation.

DOI: 10.4018/978-1-5225-7903-8.ch009

INTRODUCTION

In the opinion of the author it would be necessary that the word innovation means every new thing coming from Man and capable to introduce not only something new but create benefits for humanity. What is described in this chapter specifically is the experience over forty years of the author in a large number of application/solution in the Information Computation Technology (ICT) area, in many different industries, following the evolution of technology in ICT.

It is very important to start this chapter by remembering one of the best descriptions of a computer. Umberto Eco,[1] the Italian novelist very well known internationally for the novel *Il nome della rosa* (*The Name of the Rose*). asserts (Pozzoli, 1986): "*Il computer non è una macchina intelligente che aiuta le persone stupide, anzi è una macchina stupida che funziona solo nelle mani delle persone intelligenti* [The computer is not a clever machine that helps stupid persons, on the contrary it is a stupid machine that works only in the hands of clever persons]."

In a few words, it is naive to believe that innovation is just to use everything new that comes from computers and, in general, from ICT, to get results to better the human life. We have and we must keep the control on what we can do through information technology. The Man creates applications, solutions and tools using computers to solve problems. The Man must also be able to design, develop and monitor solutions to avoid the connected risks, at the maximum level. The Man has the idea; ICT is just the set of tools that realize it.

Figure 1. Umberto Eco, the Italian author of the romance "Il nome della rosa" (From the Inauguration of the Coop Zanichelli bookshop in Bologna)

GOING BACK OVER THE BEGINNING OF THE COMPUTER

It can be useful to go back to the beginning of the computer era when the "pioneers" started to develop solutions to help persons just to work easier, specifically in the administration area. Apparently, at that moment, there was no risk in the use of the computer. There was the risk only for mistakes that could create problems in the application of the solutions and cause indirectly a waste of time and then costs to solve problems manually. The risk was just the cost to control and recover problems, nothing too dangerous for anybody, a part from a waste of time and a loss of money. Anybody who worked, for example, in the administration, can confirm the difficulties to use the computer solutions and, then, the risk to spend time to solve the problems coming with the use of the solutions. To give an example, it was a standard not to get a balancing figure between the document in input and the total calculated by the computer: this caused a waste of time to find the mistake and then to solve the problem.

Also in the beginning, very often major problems were caused by technicians being more careful of technicality than of applications, support, and training of the users to make use of the solutions. Installing and testing the latest release of the operating system was many times more important and interesting for these persons than properly running the application. This caused serious problems in the correct flow of the work. Just to mention an example for this kind of risk, it happened in the beginning of 80's when an oil refinery installed the latest release of an operating system, for no specific reason, which then created a serious risk in the operation of the company. In fact, what happened was the stopping of the application for handling the maintenance spare parts warehouse. The company was an oil refinery and anybody who worked in this kind of company knows that this problem can be really a risk being a "non-stop production" where maintenance is a very critical area because it is not possible to stop production facilities except when scheduled. This means that, if something unexpected happens, the stop must be controlled and reduced to the shortest possible time.

PERSONAL AND PORTABLE COMPUTERS

The advent of the Personal Computer, in the middle eighties, started a revolution that was not only technological but it was a new way to work, with a completely new organization.

About 20 years in advance Olivetti designed, produced and sold the first Personal Computer. In the middle sixties the Italian Company announced and put on the market the Programma 101 (P101), the first desktop computer in the world created by a small group of researchers still working at Olivetti under the responsibility of Pier Giorgio Perotto, after the death of Adriano Olivetti and Mario Tchou.

The P101 (see Figure 2) was the first desktop machine capable of storing and processing data on a unique computer available for one operator and was programmable using a language close to the assembly language. It was produced in a significant number of units (over 40,000) between 1965 and 1971. It was sold primarily in the US and was used specifically for scientific applications.

Starting from 1981, the major computer companies announced and put on the market the first Personal Computers, desk top and portable, for example the IBM Personal Computer (see Figure 3).

The product line grew to include the Olivetti M20 and then the IBM compatible Olivetti M24 (see Figure 4), the portable Epson HX20 to the Olivetti M10 (see Figure 5), and many others. This product line started the possibility of giving any person their own computing power. However, at that moment, it was not clear that "the world" was moving away from mainframe distributing process power through "stupid terminals", with solutions designed and developed by specialized people, to distributed computing systems where every user has his own process capability but would need to be integrated as part of the organization.

Not only did any user have the possibility to have process capability on its own desk but also had the possibility to develop application by himself, because the developing tools became more and more easy to use by the day for persons without a technical background.

Figure 2. First desktop computer, P101
Source: Fondazione Adriano Olivetti's Archive (2017)

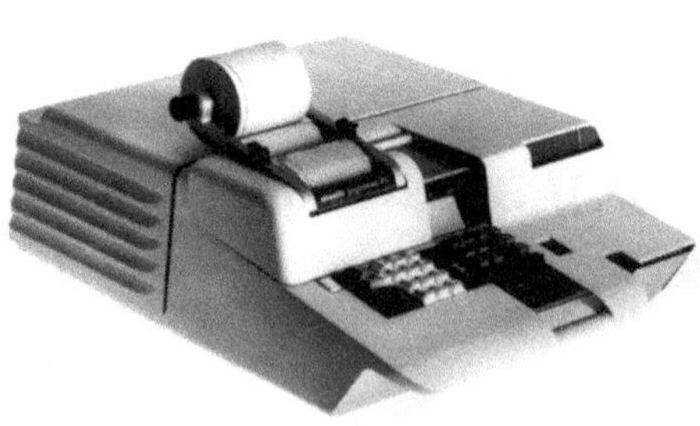

Figure 3. IBM personal computer
Source: PC (n.d.)

Figure 4. Olivetti M20
Source: Olivetti M20 (n.d.)

This situation created a number of serious problems because many persons developed applications in a completely independent way without taking into account any other requirement: a sum of elements is not the same as the integration in a system. For example, where it would be necessary to define a workflow with application and data moving from a user to the following one, and back to the previous, it is very important to design the solution in its entirety not just with solutions running individually on each PC and moving data between PC's. However, at least in the beginning, many times data were transferred using floppy discs slowing down the functionality and productivity. A PC network-based solution is a sophisticated and complex system to design, achieve, and maintain. This capability requires very specialized persons to establish. The user interface must be as friendly as possible because of the number of different persons using ICT solutions with different competence. Consequently, it is very important to be sure of the way to interface the user before releasing a new solution or a new version. This was one of the reasons why many applications were tested by persons with no IT competence.

In the beginning personal computers and portables were used for specific applications designed to solve problems to link and transfer information from remote devices to a central point to be processed and vice versa. As first applications, we can find the collection of the orders from sales people to the company, the stories from reporters to the newspaper, stock levels from distributed stores to the center, contracts and administration information from assurance agencies to the company, and so on. Of course, for any of these applications there is significant information that must be sent back after a number of controls has been executed. A very interesting application was realized middle 80's for a car manufacturer where the spare parts warehouse was centralized and the 350 car dealers were all over the Italian territory.

Figure 5. Epson HX20
Source: Epson HX20 (n.d.)

The dealers transmitted the parts orders to the headquarters of the company in the morning and by the end of the day, they received confirmation about availability and time to receive what was requested.

Another very interesting application was realized in occasion of the Olympic Games in Los Angeles (it was 1986) giving reporters the possibility to write their stories with a portable PC and then transmit it immediately to the newspaper where it was put into the newspaper in few minutes.

Integration in the use of PC/Portables and communication network, when internet was not yet available, created the possibility of solving a number of very serious problems, for example, the possibility to have information when and where necessary, as planned in advance. Infonet, a Time Sharing service of CSC, a very large Company in Los Angeles, was also used as worldwide network to move information. This kind of applications, at the beginning, were more under the control of specialized people also because of technical reasons. It is evident that it is possible to implement innovation in the process and in the organization, even when technical innovation is not yet available: the idea is more important than the tools to realize innovation and then to find a way to make it happen.

ICT started to enter pervasively in the life of many people, at least in business activity, becoming more and more important to take into account some rules, from the user-friendliness to the security both for the information and for the correct operation of the hardware and software infrastructure. Again, we must remember that any mistake can generate risk and then problems more or less serious but problems that must be solved.

THE INTERNET ERA

However, the real risk started with the Internet. The Internet gives the possibility to connect anybody to anything, anybody to anybody, anything to anything. The Internet is the worldwide network through which it is possible to collect data from everywhere, to process and put at the disposal of everyone both data and information.

This means the possibility to solve very easily an enormous number of problems that require moving data and information.

Let see some examples:

The Social Media

Social media are probably the more powerful tool to communicate, being in the same time the more dangerous and stupid way to use the Internet.

Quoting again Eco (2018):

Social media gives the right of expression to an army of idiots that before were used to speak only after a glass of wine in a bar, without doing any kind of damage to the community. They were immediately silenced, while now they have the same right to speak as a Nobel laureate. We are occupied by an army of idiots.[2]

Where is the real risk? It is not, of course, the tool for itself. The risk is the power of the tool to distribute everywhere in the world, to anybody, any kind of information stupid or intelligent, true or fake stories, without any kind of control before sending the information. This means the possibility to create serious problems to persons who, in some particular situation, decided to commit suicide because they were unable to overcome the consequences created. But, also worse than this, is the general miseducation, ineptitude and stupidity generated in the young people who are convinced to have the world in their hands only for the enormous number of followers (they call friends) that they have everywhere around the world. Worse than this, we must be afraid of the results that can result when politicians and in general, persons with a deep influence on a mass of persons, get involved in operations like elections. It is too easy to influence a mass: it is just enough to launch the messages that persons like to receive and through the Internet it is possible to contact millions of persons with the consequences that it is possible to see every day.

The problem is also that the previous generation has proven unable to manage and have care generate good relations with the young, creating in the new generation with the necessity to look everywhere for persons to speak with. More than this, young people started having positions of responsibility everywhere without any competence, being convinced that they can do everything for it does not matter what the reason. It just requires mastering the use of communications and messaging through social media. Moreover, the mass thinks that these are clever people because they are capable in using these tools just for their own interest.

The question is: what can we do now? Absolutely we <u>cannot</u> just stop the social media. We cannot go against the future, but we must learn how to properly use the enormous potentiality of these tools in the best way we can, and to learn where and when it is best to use then. For example, it is essential to use this kind of tools in many critical situations when is mandatory to alert thousands of persons for natural or social cataclysm/alluvium/disaster or any other reason for which it is necessary to alert a large number of people on a vast territory.

For these reasons, and not only, the middle-aged generation must have the commitment to train young people to use these tools in the best way. It is mandatory that anybody uses technology for what can do and for the problems can solve without being influenced in any decision, important are not.

The only way we can try to get this result is to give the correct information and training. The most dangerous situation is to fall in love with technicality for technicality or with the idea that some tools give the possibility to have the world in our own hands.

SOME SPECIAL APPLICATIONS: THE HEALTHCARE

Let see another area of risk that can be really more dangerous. An important use of ICT started some years ago for healthcare applications. Everything started, the same as in other applications with solutions in the administration area to make reservations in a hospital, to calculate costs, to invoice the patient when the patient is discharged from a hospital, to generate statistical data, and so on. Then another typical application was developed to manage reservations for specialized tests and check-up.

This application, if used through the Internet, is particularly helpful to the user who can make the reservation with a quick look around for where and when it is available. It is necessary to find key information to properly decide on the best service, but, many times, this information is not available or it is not clear whether or not the available information is correct, thus making necessary the support of a specialist. This way we cannot say that there is a risk using this kind of application but just a waste of time being obliged to consult different sources before taking any decision.

Let us look to other applications in the same area that can create many more risks for the reason that wrong results can create very serious problems for the health of the patient. We started a while ago to develop and use applications in the e-health area. This is very important because it gives us the possibility of realizing things that otherwise would be impossible to realize. For example, the remote control of some specific parameters like blood pressure, glycaemia, and heart beats where that control provides the possibility of preventing critical situations from arising when it is very important that an intervention be made as soon as possible.

This kind of solution is very important to adopt in many situations such as chronic diseases, old persons living alone, persons just discharged from a hospital, and so

Figure 6. General figure from a clinical folder documentation

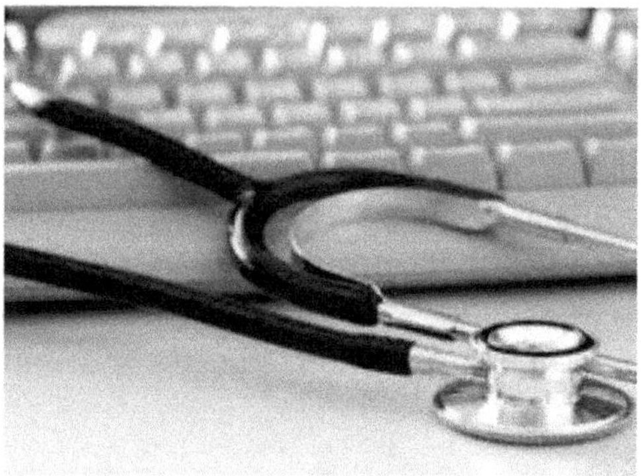

on, because of the necessity to keep the person under a continuous control with the possibility to react immediately when something starts to go wrong. Control and the following of reaction are usually done by collecting data and information to transfer to a center where it can be analyzed and compared to take the decision for what kind of intervention must be implemented. Those solutions give also the possibility to store the medical information of the patient creating a folder with the history of the person for a better future assistance.

An excellent result is also the major reduction of costs of assisting persons in bad physical condition who are no longer capable of caring for themselves and the possibility of opening more beds in hospitals by moving the patients to their homes when possible.

Usually these applications are started with the support of ICT and medical experts, on the base of standard solution tested on a large number of cases, and are based on the analysis of an enormous quantity of data collected over a long period; this process gives a certain kind of safety about the results. Now I-phone, portable, wearable medical devices are very well used sending automatically data to a center, giving also the possibility to take control of critical parameters for persons who still have an active life, with demonstrably less risk than without this kind of support.

A FIRST BALANCE RISK BENEFIT

After the very quick overview made on two very important application area and use of ICT, communication and healthcare, we can start to make a balance between risks and benefits.

For sure, now we have available tools with a power that we could not even imagine until few years ago and becoming more and more powerful every day. Every day it becomes more and more easy and quick to develop and set up special applications with excellent results. Today it is very easy and quick to solve problems to help everybody in his life to be more efficient.

Problems it is possible to see are coming for specific reasons we must avoid.

Again, one of the worst risk is the attitude of technicians to fall in love for technicality: everything can be innovation is wonderful for itself; it does not matter when and for what purpose it can be used. Let us just see an example that can clear very well what it does mean. It is not so long when 3D Printers were announced and we started to understand and analyze what we could do with this solution. It seems it depends only from our imagination what we can do: order the “pizza” and “print” it at home, make any gift we want to do and print directly at our friends place, print internal organs of the human body, let say a kidney.

However, we do not ask ourselves a basic question: How do we dial with the problem if something is not going well? What is it the material used to produce the “pizza”, or the kidney, or the object we want to give? If something goes badly when transplanting an organ made with a 3D Printer, where is the mistake? Was a mistake made by the surgeon, or was the material used to produce the organ bad, or was the software developed for the printer at fault? This is a classic example where the blame can be put on anybody or nobody. Nevertheless, the result can also be the death of a person. On the other hand, we could solve very important problems like the distribution all over the world of spare parts for, let say, household appliances or cars, and so on without moving any physical object.

ARTIFICIAL INTELLIGENCE (AI)

Today we have many discussions on this argument. It is said that AI can be the solution for any kind of problems, in does not matter in what area, from the industry to the economic/financial crisis we are living, from HR management to the medicine to prescribe, for example, getting a diagnosis as correct as possible. This is true, but it would be better to use the AI tool as a support for a doctor to make a diagnosis, and, generally, as a support for decisions that must be taken. The enormous quantity of information can “suggest” what is the more probable diagnosis but does not give the certainty. It is mandatory to have the correct analysis of the doctor. For sure, it is also very important to have the possibility to look the patient in his eyes when making a diagnosis; probably it is not enough to use algorithms on the big data to get a result with the necessary level of confidence (Sourour, 2016).

Now we have many discussions about what Artificial Intelligence means and what we can do with them. However, people thinking that machines could become more intelligent than man, that robots could do many works in place of man and so on, and that machines will take supremacy over man, are all ideas that create trouble. It could seem too simple but probably man will do is better trying to keep the control and the governance of the situation. Machine must help the Man, learning from him, not replace him.

Going back to the first argument, the social media, also we must take care of the damage a bad use of the tool can cause. It is too easy for young people to be convinced that they have the world in their hands because they can link to millions of persons. Probably they do not know even the correct name of the persons but they call them “friends” anyway.

The influence of this “virtual mass of persons” created through internet and the social network can be terrific. As a result, we have also seen persons commit suicide as a consequence of being involved in idiot exchanges that became tragic discussions over a social network. However, we have also seen how powerful social network can be in informing a mass of person for any risk coming (Patrignani, 2015).

CONCLUSION

Of course, it would be crazy to waste all the power we have in our hands through ICT. Just now, we cannot even evaluate the enormous benefit we can face using these tools, practically with all the improvements coming every day. Let us evaluate how we can avoid the risks.

It will be extremely important to govern the innovation and the computer ethics can be a way to reply to all our doubts. The American Association for Computing Machinery (ACM) is supporting and maintaining from years the Ethics Code including the principals that would be the base for ICT professional when designing and developing any hardware/software solution (Brinkman, Gotterbarn, Miller, & Wolf, 2016).

Any time we start with a new project we must keep in mind and then evaluate the risk of the consequences when using the result of the project whether it is a portable PC or Phone, or a software solution. When speaking of hardware, we must develop devices that it is possible to maintain not just use until a new model is available and throw immediately the old one in the bin. This could be a first step to cut down the problems of environmental damage and to reduce the use of special materials.

When speaking of software solutions, the basic principles we must keep in mind are related, again in the design step, to the evaluation of the consequence for the use of what we are developing, for the person who will use the solution. More and more people are being trained to use ICT application but only a very few people are rising to the level of an ICT expert capable of avoiding risks or solving problems.

More than this, at the end, it is a must for any expert in the ICT, to train and train and train people to use properly the solutions they develop, starting with young people.

REFERENCES

Brinkman, B., Gotterbarn, D., Miller, K., & Wolf, M. J. (2016, December 16). Making a positive impact: Updating the ACM code of ethics. *Communications of the ACM*.

Eco, U. (2018). *Aforismi*. Available at https://aforismi.meglio.it/aforisma.htm?id=15003

Fondazione Adriano Olivetti's Archive. (2017). (p. 101). Author.

Olivetti M20. (n.d.). In *Wikipedia*. Retrieved from https://it.wikipedia.org/wiki/Olivetti_M20

Patrignani, N. (2015). Slow tech: Per un'informatica buona, pulita e giusta. In *Mondo Digitale*. AICA House Organ.

PC. (n.d.). In *Wikipedia*. Retrieved from https://it.wikipedia.org/wiki/PC_IBM

Pozzoli, C. (1986). Preface. In *Come scrivere una tesi di laurea con il personal computer*. Rizzoli.

Source: Epson HX20. (n.d.). In *Wikipedia*. Retrieved from http://oldcomputers.net/hx-20.html

Sourour, B. (2016). *The code I'm still afraid of.* Available in: https://medium.freecodecamp.org/the-code-im-still-ashamed-of-e4c021dff55e

KEY TERMS AND DEFINITIONS

ACM: Association for Computing Machinery.

AICA: Associazione italiana per l'informatica ed il calcolo automatico.

Bioethics: Is a philosophical discipline pertaining to notions of good and bad, right and wrong, our moral life in community. Bioethics is the application of ethics to the field of medicine and healthcare.

ENDNOTES

1 Umberto Eco (Alessandria, Jan 5, 1932 – Milano, Feb 19, 2016) was an Italian novelist, literary critic, philosopher, semiotician and university professor. He is very well known internationally for the novel he wrote in 1980, a historical mystery combining semiotics in fiction with biblical analysis, medieval studies and literary theory. He wrote children's books and essays and it was the founder of the Department of the media studies at University of *Repubblica di San Marino* (center of Italy) and president of the Graduate School of the Humanities at the University of Bologna, member of the Accademia dei Lincei and an honorary fellow of Kellogg College, Oxford.

2 Freely translated by the author.

Chapter 10
Ecology, Sustainability, and Scientific Education:
The Evolution of an Environmental Pedagogy

Maria Luisa Nardi
Independent Researcher, Italy

ABSTRACT

Environmental education is a new discipline, which has been gaining increasing importance in recent decades. It is a fundamental tool to sensitize citizens and communities to greater responsibility and attention to environmental issues and good governance of the territory. The educational component allows us to transform scientific languages into simple languages that can be appropriated and understood by the different social groups, and the environmental component that tries to reconstruct. These relationships are created by man with nature, but through cultural parameters. The growing concern for environmental devastation has its roots in the decade of the 1970s. Countless efforts have been made to draw the attention of populations to this topic. Among these attempts come out different approaches such as sustainable development that uses environmental education and local sustainability as tools to prevent damages. This chapter describes the key theoretical and government references that support environmental education, focusing on their relationship and the rising of a new sector of work.

DOI: 10.4018/978-1-5225-7903-8.ch010

INTRODUCTION

The growing attention to the interconnection between the environmental, social and economic dynamics has led to the elaboration of the broader concept of Education for Sustainable Development. It concerns not only the environment but also the economy (consumption, poverty, the north and south of the world) and society (rights, peace, health, cultural diversity). It is a lifelong process, with a holistic approach, which is not limited to "formal" learning, but also extends to non-formal and informal learning.

Education for Sustainable Development involves all aspects of life and the common values of fairness and respect for others, for future generations, for diversity, for the environment, for the resources of the Earth.

In 2002, during the World Summit in Johannesburg, UNESCO launched the Global Program of Action on Education for Sustainable Development (GAP) to contribute to the new Agenda 2030. Among its new 17 Goals, education plays a central role with particular reference to education (Ministero dell'Ambiente Italiano, n.d.a).

The environmental challenge, linked to the conservation of our planet's resources, represents a challenge no longer avoidable for future generations.

Nowadays, the whole world, in particular Italy and Europe, require radically different choices from those made in the past: far from the traditional production model, directed towards a new model of economy that respects the environment, oriented to a society that does not produce waste but knows how to create wealth and well-being with the reuse and regeneration of resources. In order for this to happen, a profound change of mentality is required that involves institutions, businesses, and individuals. And this new national awareness can only start from schools and students, of all ages. Above all by the youngest, what we might call "environmental natives": a generation that in everyday behavior already finds a respect for the environment in which it lives (AA.VV., 2014).

The thesis that more stringent environmental regulations lead to a slowdown in economic growth and negative effects on employment is not corroborated by empirical studies. For example, in several countries, the impetus to technological renewal induced by environmental regulations has shown positive effects on employment. But, in industrial sectors, the legitimate concerns that environmental protection may pose a threat to the competitiveness of companies remain an open problem. The adoption of purifiers, filters and other measures that focus on the discharge of production waste represents for the enterprise an additional net cost; on the other hand, the introduction of clean upstream technologies, during the production process, is often a source of significant savings in energy and raw materials in the medium and long-term - as evidenced by the experience of the structural changes that occurred as a result of stringent environmental regulations in the chemical sector (Vitali, 2010).

In effect, progressive cultural changes and individual preferences with respect to ecological problems mean that environmentally friendly production processes, made recognizable by consumers for example through ecolabelling schemes, are destined to become an increasingly important opportunity for product differentiation and a potential source of competitive advantage for the companies themselves.

Key challenges for the future include those of

- Finding appropriate and acceptable remedies from all member countries to the dysfunctions of institutional channels through which the decision-making process takes place
- Maintaining the set of laws and regulations lean, transparent, and updated with respect to scientific and technological developments
- Strengthening the means and instruments to ensure the effective application of environmental legislation.

The main problems dealt with by the European environmental policy are (Jordan, &Adelle, 2012; European Parliament, n.d.) (see Figure 1):

- **Acid Rains:** These are rainfalls (which can also occur in the form of snow or hail) rich in particles and acid molecules that are usually found in the atmosphere but due to this phenomenon they are deposited on the ground.

Figure 1. European environmental policy

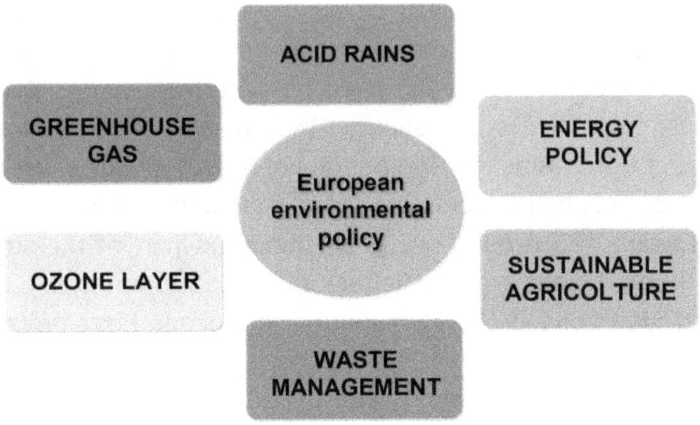

The formation of acid rain is due to an increase in the atmosphere of carbon dioxide (CO_2), sulfur oxides and nitrogen oxides. This increase can be determined by natural causes but also and above all by human activity. The acid rains and their progressive intensification has devastating consequences, not only for our health but also for the survival of the ecosystem itself (See Informazione ambiente Italia, n.d.) on:

    - **Environment:** The natural environment is exposed to a high risk due to the intensification of acid rain: this in fact affects the growth and reproductive capacity of the plants, drastically reducing them
    - **Mankind:** Acid rain is going to affect and raise the levels of toxicity of the foods that are grown: this has serious effects on our health, which can occur with circulatory diseases, respiratory problems but also with tumor forms, especially the lungs
    - **Structures:** Acid rain causes, in the long run, also serious damage to structures: sulfuric acid tends to corrode the material, accelerating its decay. This applies to most materials used in building construction, including reinforced concrete

- **Greenhouse Gas:** It is a gas in the atmosphere that absorbs and emits radiant energy within the thermal infrared range. These gases, responsible for the famous greenhouse effect, allow the sun's rays to pass through the atmosphere: they are in fact transparent to solar radiation. The emissions of carbon dioxide (CO_2) derive, mainly, from the anthropogenic activities that involve the combustion of fossil fuels. Also contributing to the greenhouse effect are methane (CH_4), whose emissions are mainly linked to the breeding and disposal of waste, and nitrous oxide (N_2O), deriving mainly from agricultural activities. Greenhouse gases can be naturally occurring in nature, or produced by man: in the latter case we are talking about anthropogenic greenhouse gases and it is these that must worry us. If, in fact, thanks to these gases, the temperature of the Earth reaches a perfect balance, the emission of greenhouse gases in massive quantities by human activities tends to break this balance. For this reason, the Kyoto Protocol (1997) regulates the emissions of greenhouse gases by each country. It was signed by 141 nations.
- **Ozone Layer:** The ozone layer is an important part of the atmosphere. It protects living beings from radiations that the Sun emits. By absorbing in particular ultraviolet B (UVB) radiation, the ozone layer protects humans, animals, plants and even certain materials from sun damage. UVB can damage humans and animals by causing skin cancers and cataracts in the eyes, which causes blindness. In addition to the health of the inhabitants of the planet, UVB can damage plant life, with repercussions on both the animal

world and global warming of the planet. The ozone layer has been altered by some man-made chemicals that remove the ozone gas responsible for the formation of this layer.

- **Waste Management:** It is the set of policies, procedures or methodologies aimed at managing the entire waste process, from their production to their final destination, thus involving the collection, transport, treatment (recovery or disposal) phase up to reuse / recycling of waste materials, usually produced by human activity, in an attempt to reduce their effects on human health and the impact on the environment. The correct management of hazardous and non-hazardous waste, of urban or special origin, is the basis of the principles that the European Union has indicated in specific Regulations and Directives. Each Member State, including Italy, has had to implement the principles established by the European Union with a specific waste management legislation.
- **Sustainable Agriculture** (Also Called Eco-Compatible Or Integrated): It is the compliance with sustainability criteria in agricultural and agri-food production, favoring those natural processes that allow us to preserve the "environment resource". Sustainable agriculture consists of the use of agricultural techniques that respect the environment, biodiversity and the natural ability to absorb waste from the earth. In this sense, the most widespread agricultural models in Italy that implement sustainable principles and techniques are organic farming and biodynamic farming. In fact, in biological agriculture to eliminate parasites, instead of resorting to pesticides, other insects or antagonistic bacteria are used and traditional techniques such as organic fertilization or crop rotations are used to enrich the soil; in biodynamic agriculture, the fundamental principle is that of healing and enriching the environment and improving human nutrition. Sustainable agriculture pursues the following objectives:
    - The farmer's fair income
    - The health protection of the agricultural operator and the consumer
    - The preservation over time of soil fertility
    - The conservation of environmental resources over time
- **Energy Policy:** It should guarantee a balanced fuel mix that ensures the well-being of the individual and the company from a sustainable standpoint. Many countries, today rich and developed, to the detriment of others, have disposed in the last 2 centuries of ever increasing quantities of energy, both in terms of availability of the raw material (fuels, available locally or imported from other countries), and in terms of the relative technologies necessary to convert the "raw material" into energy available in the usual forms of greater

use, such as: heat, steam and electricity. The Treaty of Lisbon (2007) puts energy at the center of European activity and gives it a legal basis (Article 194 TF-EU). The EU energy policy pursues three main objectives:

- Security of supply
- Competitiveness
- Sustainability

The Commission has launched plans for a European Energy Union to ensure safe, accessible and climate-friendly energy for EU citizens and businesses. As stated in the Commission Communication "An Energy Policy for Europe" of the January 10, 2007, the EU can not achieve the goal of an energy supply alone safe, competitive and sustainable. In the future, the EU will only be responsible for 15% of new emissions of CO2. For this, the EU must work with developed and developing countries as well with consumers and energy producers, to ensure competitive, sustainable and secure energy (McCormick, 2001) .

The EU plays a leading role in the formulation of international energy agreements:

- Reinforces the Treaty on the European Energy Charter
- Takes the initiative for an agreement on energy efficiency
- Actively participates in the formulation of the climate change regime

EDUCATION TO SUSTAINABILITY

The term "sustainable development" refers, according to the Brundtland report (see Table 1), to: "development that meets the needs of the present without compromising the ability of future generations to meet their needs and is based on the ability to maintain the natural environment".

The possibilities offered by sustainable development have led to a renewed interest in the theme of community sustainability and local sustainability. In the face of global sustainability, whose conditions have been exposed by systemic ecologists and macroeconomists, the sustainability of specific places on the planet arises whose conditions are the subject of study of landscape ecology, ecological economy, cultural anthropology, or environmental sociology and, of course, radical environmentalism.

The theme of local sustainability must be addressed by the community to be able and organize to cope with local environmental problems and directly affect them.

Local sustainability work has two main objectives: resource management and community participation.

These two aspects come together in the concept of environmental education, where projects that give a favorable response to the resolution of environmental problems can be shaped in an interdisciplinary manner.

Local sustainability processes require the development of a set of indicators from environmental education, which help to visualize the results both in the management of resources and in community participation, for the resolution of an environmental problem in a given space and time. These indicators must refer to the following reflections:

- The environment is analyzed as a result of the interactions between nature and society.
- The environmental situation is analyzed as the state of the specific environment, which becomes dynamic in spaces that are not only physical, if not geographical, ecological and environmental through time.
- The environmental situation is analyzed as a development of reality that allows individuals and communities, of a specific community, to relate to their environment.
- The environmental problem appears as the disharmony produced in the environmental system, through the impacts of interactions: society-nature-culture.
- The resources, the populations and the societies are analyzed through the relationships that are established between them, waiting for specific spaces and times in which to develop their own dynamics.

Through an environmental problem, therefore, we can make readings on the quality of the relationships of human groups, with the natural systems of which they are part and through which they develop their social and cultural dynamics. Similarly, to understand the origin of a given environmental problem and its consequences, it is necessary to take as a reference the environmental situation in which it is located.

The local sustainability generates participatory processes, which give rise to a new management of environmental resources, where environmental education is the working tool that gives the possibility of new visions of the future and a strategic action plan, concerning problems environmental issues felt by the community (Velaiz Rolon, 2010).

Information, training and environmental education activities are an integral part of the institutional tasks. The regional legislator, in fact, wanted to specify that in parallel with the functions of environmental protection, an activity should be developed to promote information, training, environmental education and internal training programs with a view to the sustainable development of the territory.

Some politicians (see Tables 1, 2 and 3) believe that environmental sustainability should be a fundamental goal free from development. Industry and trade representatives consider economic sustainability to be of vital importance to environmental sustainability because conservation of the environment is very expensive and, consequently, economic activities need to be enabled to bear the costs of contributing to ecological sustainability. The very concept of education for sustainable development is debatable because it takes the notion of development in positive terms. If there is growth there is growth, if there is growth there is consumption, so to speak of sustainable development means strengthening the vision of the things that underlie an economic system that consumes nature.

To achieve a sustainable model of life, the first duty is to pay attention to social problems that prevent a large number of people from living a satisfying quality of life. In practice, the environmental question is reconceptualized because it concerns not only the protection of nature but the redistribution of resources and respect for human rights. In short, respect for the environment alone is not enough to change our common future (Bonafrini, 2011).

ENVIRONMENTAL EDUCATION IN INTERNATIONAL DOCUMENTS

The key international conventions on environment place a high value on public awareness, education and training and obtaining information through monitoring.

The Environmental Education has been conceived as a strategy to offer new ways of generating significant changes in behavior in human persons and societies and of reassigning a new importance to cultural, social, political, economic and nature-related values. At the same time, it tries to facilitate the mechanisms of acquisition of intellectual and physical abilities, promoting the active and decisive participation of individuals in a permanent way; reflecting in a better human intervention for the environment and consequently an adequate quality of life. With this concept, in recent decades, confidence has been placed in the educational process to contribute to the response of environmental problems.

The concept of environmental education has changed over time, linked to the historical moments and the relationship that man has established with the environment, nevertheless maintaining the same concern: environmental destruction (Velaiz Rolon, 2010).

The expression of environmental education is historically placed at the end of the twentieth century.

But probably already the philosophy and ideas of J. J. Rousseau (1712-1778), as well as other philosophers, containing discourses on pedagogical naturalism, can be considered as the clearest historical reference of environmental education. Rousseau shows that nature is the only and true teacher for the students. Nature was understood as a source of wisdom from which subjects had to learn.

Environmental education embraces current issues and problems with which the new generations will have to confront.

The two over-arching factors are a national education policy and a national environment and population policy. These policies are a reflection of national cultural values, priorities and socio-economic goals in most countries.

A national environmental education policy is usually the result of decisions made in these broader fields. For example, It is increasingly a prominent part of primary, secondary and tertiary education in Europe, Asia, and the Pacific. And environmental education in Australia has seen two major shifts since the 1970s. First, there has been a distinct move away from nature and science-based environmental education to a concern with the social, economic and political aspects of sustainable development. There has also been a major shift from schools to adult and community environmental education. (Fien, 2000).

Table 1. The evolution of the concept of environmental education: some of the main meeting (1948-2015)

1948	The International Union for the Conservation of Nature (UICN) - France	It referred, for the first time, to environmental education as "an educational approach as the synthesis between Natural Sciences and Social Sciences".
1965/ 1971	International Conferences in Bangkok (1965) and Singapore	They confirmed what stated in the previous conferences, and related the concept of environmental education to the conservation of nature.
1971	UNESCO's Man and the Biosphere Programme (MAB)	It was an Intergovernmental Scientific Programme that aims to establish a scientific basis for the improvement of relationships between people and their environments. It gave importance to teaching and information about the environmental issue; we report: "To complete an interdisciplinary research program that gives special importance to the ecological method in the study of relations between man and the environment, considering that the project is focused on teaching and information about these problems" (UNESCO, 1971).
1972	Conference on the Human Environment, Stockholm	It stated the importance of education concerning environmental issues and directed towards the different social actors contributing to the devastation of the environment. For example, the principle 19 describes that the young and adult generations must give due attention to the less privileged populations. It is essential to create the basis of well-informed public opinion and behavior of individuals, businesses and of the community inspired by the sense of its own responsibility for the protection and improvement of the environment in all its human dimension. It is also essential that the mass media should avoid contributing to the destruction of the human environment and, on the contrary, disseminate educational information on the need to protect and improve it, so that man can develop in all its aspects. Among the most significant achievements of the agreements made at the Stockholm Conference are the creation of the United Nations Environment Program (PNUA) and the Interdisciplinary Environmental Education Program (PIEA), a commitment taken by the Organization of the Nations Unite for Education, Science and Culture (UNESCO) (The Belgrade Charter, 1972).

continued on following page

Table 1. Continued

1975	UN Conference on the Human Environment in Stockholm, Sweden	One of the results obtained was the definition of the objectives of the work in environmental education: 1. For each nation, according to its own culture, to clarify to itself the meaning of basic concepts, such as "quality of life" and "human happiness", in the context of the global environment, also endeavoring to clarify and understand these notions as they are understood by other cultures beyond their national borders. 2. Identify the actions that guarantee the preservation and improvement of human potential and that promote social and individual well-being, in harmony with the biophysical environment and the environment created by man (United Nations Conference, 1972).
1977	U.N. Environment Programme (UNEP) in Tbilisi, Georgia (USSR)	It is one of the most important conferences on environmental education. The principles, goals and objectives of environmental education were defined, also the tools needed to integrate natural, social and cultural aspects to the environmental theme (U.N. Environment Programme (UNEP), 1977).
1984	UN World Commission Brundtland on Environment and Development	The result of the aforementioned research was published under the name "Our Common Future", where the role of human beings is clarified in the conservation of resources in a sustainable way. Especially, in principle 27. "It is in the hands of humanity to ensure that development is sustainable, that is, to ensure that it meets the needs of the present without compromising the ability of future generations to meet their own needs. The concept of sustainable development implies limits - not absolute limits, if not limitations that the current state of technology or social organization impose on the resources of the environment and the ability of the biosphere to absorb the effects of human activity - but so much technology how social organization can be ordered and improved in ways that open the way for a new era of economic growth. The commission believes that poverty is not only bad in itself. Sustainable development requires meeting the basic needs of all and extending the opportunity for everyone to fill their aspirations for a better life. A world where poverty is endemic will always be inclined to suffer from an ecological or other catastrophes (World Commission On Environment And Development, 1987).
1987	Unesco-Unep International Congress On Environmental Education And Training (Moscow, Ussr)	The commission recognized that there are no distinct crises: the environmental crisis, that of development, that of energy, since all are interrelated and as such need to be addressed. In this perspective the concept of "sustainable development" has been affirmed and with it the idea of an education to sustainability that can be understood as an analysis shared by students and teachers on those forms of social and technological organization that allow adopt a lifestyle in harmony with the human and natural world (Huckle, 1991, UNESCO-UNEP International Congress On Environmental Education And Training, 1987).
1992	United Nations Conference on Environment and Development (Earth Summit) in Rio de Janeiro.	The economic, social and environmental dimensions became the three pillars of sustainable development. The environmental problem is traced back to the principle of international and intergenerational justice. Education is thus identified as a primary resource for promoting sustainable life and production systems (Jackson et al, 2013). In Article 36, one of the main program areas is the Re-orientation of education towards sustainable development. Education is a process that allows human beings and societies to fully develop their latent capacity. Environmental education is of critical importance to promote sustainable development and to increase people's capacity to tackle environmental and development issues. Although basic education serves as a foundation for environmental and development education, the latter must be incorporated as a fundamental part of learning. In the Art., environmental and development education must address the dynamics of the physical/biological environment and the socio-economic and development environment (which could include spiritual development), integrate into all disciplines and use academic and non-academic and effective methods of communication (Earth Summit, 1992).
1997	The International Conference on Environment and ociety: Education and Public. Awareness for Sustainability, organized by UNESCO and the Government of Greece UNESCO Teaching and Learning for a Sustainable Future Report	Keywords: transdisciplinarity, education in values, complexity. Especially, Theme 4, teaching & learning strategies are: experiential learning, storytelling, values education, enquiry learning, appropriate assessment, future problem solving, Learning outside the classroom, Community Problem Solving (UNESCO, n.d.). It reaffirmed the need to invest in education to promote sustainable development, through a process of participation and collective learning. IT'S AT. Pillar of sustainable development (UNESCO, 1997).
2002	World Summit On Sustainable Development Meets In Johannesburg (SA)	The summit implementation document states that: - Education is fundamental to pursuing sustainable development - Sustainable development must be integrated into education systems at all levels to promote education as a fundamental key to change - E.A. a process (formal and informal) that lasts throughout life The document recommends to the UN Assembly the adoption of a decade on the ESA from 2005 (World Summit On Sustainable Development, 2002).
2015	United Nations Climate Change Conference in Paris	The premise of this conference is that we are increasingly aware of how the constant increase in the temperature of the atmosphere of our planet, through the emission of carbon dioxide (CO2) and other greenhouse gases, can have devastating repercussions on the climate balance, causing floods., heat waves, drought; moreover, the melting of the ice and the consequent rise in sea level will lead to the disappearance of island states. One of the objectives that the signatory countries have undertaken to achieve is to limit the increase in global mean temperature to 1.5 degrees above pre-industrial levels, even if national emission limits have not been set. Furthermore, low environmental impact technologies and the green economy are to be promoted all over the world (COP21 conference on climate change, 2015).

(freely retrieved from Provincia di Bolzano Italia, n.d.)

Table 2. The main steps of the origin of environmental education in the European Union Programs (1992-2020)

1973 1993	I, II, III, IV,V Environment Action Programme (European Union)	They emphasized the need to educate the citizen as a consumer, producer, administrator and active subject of behaviors that make him interact with the environment.
1993	European Parliament	It proposed a new resolution on environmental education (the first was in 1988) to invite member states to define, on the basis of multiannual programs, a European policy for the EA in which, inter alia, integrating the environmental dimension into all aspects of teaching at all levels, highlighting the fundamental role of schools and teachers in implementing this policy.
1994	The 'Aalborg Charter'	It was an urban sustainability initiative approved by the participants at the first European Conference on Sustainable Cities & Towns in Aalborg, Denmark. It was inspired by the Rio Earth Summit's Local Agenda 21 plan. Many European cities adhere to the Local Agenda 21 strategy launched at the Rio Summit, based on community involvement in the ecological and social choices of their future (The Aalborg Charter, 1994).
2002	VI Environment Action Programme to 2012 (European Union)	It highlights the strategic and transversal role that environmental information and education strategies play within each action to improve the quality of the environment. It set out the framework for environmental policy-making in the European Union for the period 2002-2012 and outlines actions that need to be taken to achieve them. The 6th EAP identified four priority areas: Climate change, Nature and biodiversity, Environment and health, Natural resources and waste (6th Environment Action Programme (6th EAP), 2002).
2014	VII Environment Action Programme to 2020 (European Union)	The objective is summarised in the title "Living well, within the limits of our planet." EU environment policy must steer a course between mankind's justified desire for well-being and the limits set by the environment. It identifies three key objectives: 1) to protect, conserve and enhance the Union's natural capital, 2) to turn the Union into a resource-efficient, green, and competitive low-carbon economy, 3) to safeguard the Union's citizens from environment-related pressures and risks to health and wellbeing. Four so-called "enablers" will help Europe deliver on these goals: 1) better implementation of legislation, 2) better information by improving the knowledge base, 3) more and wiser investment for environment and climate policy, 4) full integration of environmental requirements and considerations into other policies. Two additional horizontal priority objectives complete the programme: 1) to make the Union's cities more sustainable, 2) to help the Union address international environmental and climate challenges more effectively (7th Environment Action Programme (6th EAP), 2014).

The Italian Case

According to the Italian Ministry of the Environment, Environmental Education is "a fundamental tool to sensitize citizens and communities to greater responsibility and attention to environmental issues and good governance of the territory". For this reason, the ministry has compiled guidelines that can be followed in all schools (Ministero dell'Ambiente Italiano, n.d.c). The will is to grow up generations able to start a cultural change, starting right from the schools even with environmental education.

When the Italian Constitution came into force in 1948 it did not contain provisions on the environment understood as a value, right or interest of the community.

A turning point came in 1986 with the entry into force of the law of 8 July 1986, n. 349 which provided for the establishment of the Ministry of the environment and rules on environmental damage. Even if, before the entry into force of this law, already existed some organizations that were concerned with the protection of environmental interest, this law consecrated the value of the environment in its own dimension and autonomous value.

Table 3. The origin of Italian Educational Environment Programs (1996-2008)

1996	Primo accordo di programma interministeriale Ministero Ambiente e Istruzione per l'Educazione Ambientale	The objective was to promote the correct knowledge of environmental issues, both responsible and active behavior towards the common environmental heritage, in favor of sustainable management of natural and urban environments
1997	Carta dei principi per l'Educazione Ambientale di Fiuggi	It represented the first organic document on the subject, aimed at citizens of all ages such as the Public Administration, businesses as workers, schools as educational agencies in the area, identifying in the permanent education for sustainable development the strategic element for the promotion of critical and proactive behavior of citizens towards their own environmental context.
2000	Prima Conferenza Nazionale dell'Educazione Ambientale a Genova.	Institutions, ministries, businesses, local bodies, training agencies, and associations have been confronted on methods and strategies for the re-launching and strengthening of education for sustainable development, underlining the need for work in the "network". The Interministerial Technical Committee undertook a redefinition of the Program Agreement between the two Ministries. During the Conference, the Regions and the Autonomous Provinces presented the request to find suitable venues and ways of comparison for the elaboration and verification of shared strategies through the establishment of a technical table dedicated to these issues in the State-Regions Conference.
2000	Linee di indirizzo Conferenza Stato – Regioni	It was a program of the Ministry of the Environment aimed at disseminating and coordinating information, training and environmental education on local territories. In the regulatory interventions of recent years, the development of a National System has been promoted as coordination of Regional Systems to activate synergies between the various agencies (formal and non-formal) that in the territories dealing with EE, among national strategies / international and local ones.
2007	Forum di Torino "Educazione all'ambiente e alla sostenibilità" organizzato dal Ministero dell'Ambiente e della Tutela del Territorio e del Mare	It was the presentation of the document 'Ecological Alphabets, manifesto for the environmental education of the future', which defined, through the comparison with the Ministry of Education, the new guidelines for Environmental Education in public schools
2007	Nuovo Quadro programmatico Stato-Regioni e Province autonome per l'Educazione all'Ambiente e alla Sostenibilità	Some strategic goals was: • Activation of program agreements between the Ministry of the Environment the other ministries (not only Education) for the dissemination of the culture of sustainability in the various areas of intervention • Creation "Permanent National Forum on Environmental Education for Sustainability" for comparison with "Territorial actors" EA • Articulation of actions at national, interregional, regional / provincial level
2008	Secondo accordo di programma interministeriale Ministero Ambiente, Istruzione, Università e Ricerca per l'Educazione allo sviluppo sostenibile	Some strategic goals • Re-orientate activities for education to sustainable development as an interdisciplinary and transversal theme in which the principles of sustainability live • Promote educational / training processes for sustainability that are part of a lifelong learning process • Qualify the training of school staff in terms of the functional skills of the educational / training processes for sustainable development.

Specifically, the Italian Conference on Environmental Education 2016, which was attended by the Institutions, Civil Society, the world of Communication, Research and environmental operators and organizations managing the Protected Natural Areas and representatives of the economic sectors, produced twelve documents which concern the following topics (Ministero dell'Ambiente Italiano, n.d.b):

1. Biodiversity Protected natural areas, ecosystem services and land development
2. Education (Agenda 2030) for sustainable development, innovative business and consumer models
3. Sustainable mobility New culture of mobility, governance, information, safety and environmental benefits
4. Civil society Formal, non-formal and informal educational models: instruments of integration
5. Digital and communication From digital natives to environmental natives, how will this be possible? Contents, languages, format
6. Environment and Health Education, environment and health. The need for a systemic approach: which obstacles and what advantages
7. Circular Economy Strategies to educate the producer and the consumer to the new model
8. Sustainable tourism Environment and enhancement of landscape resources
9. Fight against climate change Successful educational strategies for climate change
10. City Climate change, mitigation and adaptation in urban areas. How to form a resilient community
11. Management of natural resources Protection and management of water, defense of hydrogeological risk and flood risk management
12. Food waste Sustainable agriculture, education for proper nutrition, measures to prevent food waste

And the described key educational goals are (Ministero dell'Ambiente Italiano, n.d.a):

- Relationship with the environment, recovering it with natural and socio-cultural resources and diversity of the territory
- Complexity and interdependence of global challenges
- Aware choices in daily life (from food to tourism, use of energy and water)
- Creative, innovative and market solutions, to face contraints
- Critical evaluation of information and behavior

The doctrinal and jurisprudential orientation has progressively consolidated by attributing to the environment the quality of "constitutional value".

Despite, for example, in Article 9 of the Italian Costitution (1948) there is no explicit reference to the environment, thanks to a work of interpretation of the term landscape, which lasted several years, we come to affirm that the second paragraph of Article 9 of the Constitution protects the landscape based on a notion that has evolved over time to include not only aesthetic profiles preservation of natural beauty, but also aspects related to the environment in its extreme complexity.

Even within the article 32 of the Constitution, it is possible to insert the environment and, in this case, is intended as a protection of health. In particular, the first paragraph of this article protects health as a fundamental and inviolable right of the individual, but also as an interest of the community. Environmental degradation and pollution affect the lives and health of individuals living in certain areas affected by these factors.

The duties of economic, political and social solidarity, imposed by article 2 of the Constitution, include duties of environmental solidarity, placed in the hands of all 94 subjects of the legal system, both public and private. The protection of the environment can thus be perceived both as a recognized and guaranteed right, but also as a duty of the individual and public subjects.

The Cassation, with the sentence n. 5172 of 1979, already affirmed the existence of a "subjective right to the healthiness of the environment" in direct relation with the art. 32, first paragraph, of the Constitution; moreover, "the right to health is configured as a right to a healthy environment" based on articles. 2 and 32 of the Constitution.

Also, the Constitutional Court has contributed to the determination of the concept of the environment through some judgments. For example, in the judgment of 28 May 1987, n. 210, the environment is a value expected and guaranteed by the Constitution and refers to art. 9 and 32 of the latter. The Court makes explicit reference to constitutional values such as the environment and health that fall within the jurisdiction of the State. In the sentence of 30 December 1987, n. 641, the Court defines the environment as a primary good and an absolute value constitutionally guaranteed to the community; furthermore, it is affirmed that the environment is a unitary intangible asset and is brought back to the category of CDs. free assets therefore usable by the community and by individuals.

The Charter of principles for environmental education, oriented towards sustainable and conscious development (Fiuggi, 1997) is one of the key historical Italian document on Environmental Education. It aims to guide research, reflection, comparison, dissemination, qualification, socialization of public choices aimed at sustainable development and is integrated with the process of renewal of the educational structures of the training system. It states that public institutions must guarantee the right to girls and children have the right to form their own opinion, to express it freely, to be involved in decisions concerning resources and development, helping to prepare them to take responsibility for life in a free society, in a spirit of understanding, peace, tolerance, fairness, opportunities, between the sexes and between all peoples, ethnic, national and religious groups. Education for sustainable development must thus become a strategic element for promoting critical and propositive behaviors of citizens towards their own environmental context.

According to this document, environmental education ultimately aims to train active citizenship and allows us to understand the complexity of the relationship between nature and human activities, between inherited resources, to be saved and transmitted, and the dynamics of production, consumption and of solidarity. Environmental education must become an organic component of all public policies, formative and environmental policies first and foremost. The protection and enhancement of natural and human resources imply simple rules and choices that define a new citizenship and coexistence of living species.

An important constitutional change took place in 2001, with the explicit presence of the term "environment" in the Constitution came with the entry into force of the constitutional law October 18, 2001, n. 3, which provided for "Changes to Title V of the second part of the Constitution". From this moment on, the term "environment" appears in article 117 of the Constitution which deals with delineating the legislative competences between State and Regions.

The revision of Title V of the Constitution has also led to the introduction of new principles of division of administrative functions between the various levels of territorial government: these are the principles of subsidiarity, adequacy, and differentiation (Article 118 of the first paragraph of the Constitution). A parenthesis has also been opened on the question of the landscape which is not mentioned among the various subjects of article 117 of the Constitution; after several interpretations, the protection of the landscape has been brought to the subject of "cultural heritage" as per art. 117, paragraph 2, lett. s, Constitutions thus re-entering the exclusive legislative power of the State.

Moreover, we wanted to provide a distinction between "protection" and "valorization" and reference was made to the doctrine, in particular, Rossi, but also to the ruling 94/2003 of the Constitutional Court. On the distribution of powers between the State and the Regions, since there is no very clear delimitation, the Constitutional Court has specified that starting from the well-known sentence no. 407/2002, the environment is attributable to a "transversal" matter and therefore regarding the competence in the legislative field, in addition to the State, the Regions may also be competent in the measure that has already been analyzed.

A PEDAGOGY FOR ENVIRONMENTAL EDUCATION (EE)

Among other issues, environmental education interacts with the functioning and evolution of natural ecosystems, with the changes induced by human activities with the contributions of scientific research and technological innovation. In the school environment environmental education cannot be circumscribed within the boundaries of a new subject, nor can it be identified with any preferential content; environmental education is interdisciplinary and transversal, working on long times.

Specifically, the activities and initiatives of environmental education, even in the variety of organizational forms and styles, while not demanding exhaustiveness: involve knowledge, values, behaviors, direct experiences for the respect and interaction between the plurality of life forms present in the environment ; they have the possibility of constructing and spreading a modern culture "capable of the future", that is, capable of going beyond the dimension of the throwaway and of inspiring one's actions to the "sense of limit"; they promote opportunities and contexts to foster the development of dynamic qualities, to build the ability to make decisions in conditions of uncertainty, to raise awareness that the ability to predict cannot be separated from the willingness to face the unpredictable, to educate in comparison and to the management of conflicts, between different points of view; they strengthen coherence between action and knowledge, between enunciation and behavior.

The fields of nature study, outdoor education, and conservation education set the basic stage from which EE emerged.

Launched in 1891 by American Wilbur Jackman's book Nature Study for the Common Schools, and enhanced by the work of Liberty Hyde Bailey and Anna Botsford Comstock at Cornell, nature study was practiced in the United States and Europe during the early 1900s. It revolutionized elementary science education by emphasizing the observation of nature while in the outdoors and through exploration of the relationships of plants, animals, and the physical systems that support them (Palmer, 1998).

The movement was driven, in part, by a surge in urban growth, migration from rural farms to industries, and a concern that youth were missing vital interactions with the natural world that could shape their future careers. Comstock's 1911 Handbook of Nature Study clearly suggested that the role of the teacher was to promote interest and excitement in the discovery of nature, yet since many teachers lacked sufficient training in science and nature observation, the movement found limited appeal (Comstock, 1939).

In 1968, William Stapp, Ph.D., engaged his students at the University of Michigan in discussions of the limits of conservation education (too descriptive and focused on the natural world) and outdoor education (too limited to using the outdoors to enrich school programs). Stapp and his students came to believe that there was a need for a new field that considered the total environment and emphasized problem-solving skills (Gough, 1997). Thus, environmental education was developed, and the definition and rationale for EE based on the work of Stapp and his students were appropriately published in the first issue of the Environmental Education Journal in 1969. Stapp continued to play a leadership role in the development of EE both in the U.S. and globally as the first director of the International Environmental Education Programme, jointly funded by UNESCO and UNEP; and an organizer of the first international conference at Tbilisi, Georgia, USSR in 1977 (Biedenweg et al, 2013).

While youth undoubtedly represent a critical audience for environmental education, it is equally important to nurture and support environmental literacy among adults whose daily consumer behaviors and political actions can have impressive impacts on the environment and conservation (Heimlich&Ardoin, 2008).

The sciences, particularly ecology, provide important fundamentals for understanding environmental issues, but EE by definition is framed by its social context. It is about human behavior, focusing on human interactions with the world around us and encouraging people to engage in productive dialogue and decision-making with an emphasis on positive environmental behavior, critical thinking, and citizen participation. Within a formal, or school, setting, environmental education comprises a variety of subjects (Dietz&Stern, 2002).

Social studies, government, and history are as important as biology, chemistry, and physics in addressing today's complex environmental problems. For example, in recognition of the complex nature of environmental issues, the State of California's Education and Environment Initiative weaves environmental principles and concepts throughout instructional materials in science, history/social science, English/language arts, and mathematics.

Engaging students across the disciplines in this way provides them an opportunity to understand environmental issues as they truly are—multifaceted, ever-shifting, and responsive to human intervention.

In the face of the complexity and uncertainty embedded in many environmental issues, the time-honored policy tools of regulation and market incentives often prove insufficient to the task of coping with significant environmental management problems. Managers and policy-makers must turn ever more frequently to other policy options, including education, information provision, and voluntary measures (Heimlich&Ardoin, 2008).

In synthesis, the main Environmental Education Goals are:

- To foster clear awareness of and concern about economic, social, political, and ecological inter-dependence in urban and rural areas;

Figure 2. Key pillars of enviromental education

- To provide every person with opportunities to acquire the knowledge, values, attitudes, commitment, and skills needed to protect and improve the environment;
- To create new patterns of behavior of individuals, groups, and society as a whole towards the environment.

And the Environmental Education Objectives are (UNESCO-UNEP, 1978):

- **Awareness:** To help social groups and individuals acquire an awareness of and sensitivity to the total environment and its allied problems.
- **Knowledge:** To help social groups and individuals gain a v ariety of experience in, and acquire a basic understanding of, the environment and its associate problems.
- **Attitudes:** To help social groups and individuals acquire a set of values and feelings of concern for the environment, and the motivation for actively participating in environmental improvement and protection.

- **Skills:** To help social groups and individuals acquire the skills for identifying and solving environmental problems.
- **Participation:** To provide social groups and individuals with an opportunity to be actively involved at all levels in working toward resolution of environmental problems.

Deep Ecology Education

Deep ecology arises from the personal intuition that one's self is part of the world's environmental wholeness. This awareness may be constructed upon scientific foundations but it is more commonly thought a spiritual concept.

The basic principles of deep ecology formulated by A. Naess are (Smith&Gough, 2015):

1. The well-being and prosperity of human and non-human life on Earth have value for themselves (in other words: they have an intrinsic or inherent value). These values are independent of the usefulness that the non-human world can have for man
2. The richness and diversity of life forms contribute to the realization of these values and are also values in themselves
3. Men have no right to impoverish this richness and diversity unless they have to meet vital needs
4. The prosperity of life and of human cultures is compatible with a substantial reduction of the human population: the prosperity of non-human life requires this decrease.
5. The current interference of man in the non-human world is excessive and the situation is getting progressively worse.
6. Consequently, collective choices must be changed. These choices influence fundamental ideological, technological and economic structures. The state of things that will result will be profoundly different from the current one.
7. The ideological change consists mainly in the appreciation of the quality of life as an intrinsic value rather than in adhering to an ever higher standard of living. The difference between what is qualitatively large and what is quantitatively will have to be clear.
8. Those who share the previous points are obliged, directly or indirectly, to attempt to implement the necessary changes.

The Manager and the Environmental Consultant (HSE)

The HSE, the manager and the environmental consultant are some of the emerging figures in modern business management, as responsible for the environmental problems of the company, guiding it between obligations, obligations, opportunities, and risks that the legislation requires.

Surely HSE manager is a highly qualified professional both for the functions and for the roles that contain "mixing" the two subjects, work safety, and environmental law.

HSE stands for "Health, Safety & Environment": the HSE Manager is the figure that deals with the management of these aspects within the corporate ecosystem of activities and processes.

An HSE has to:

- Deal with the drafting and updating of all the documentation necessary for the fulfillment of obligations regarding Safety and the Environment, the management of safety systems and environmental protection, maintains relations with the competent authorities and the certification bodies.
- Study and implement the adjustments resulting from the promulgation of new laws and regulations, resolves the requirements and non-conformities, collects and processes the data related to environmental monitoring (discharges, waste, emissions, energy resources, etc.).
- Assure the implementation of the legal requirements on health and safety in the workplace, Legislative Decree 81/08.
- Deal with the assessment of risks and improvement plans, verification and management of maintenance plans, performs physical instrumental investigations with external support, updates procedures.
- Check the availability and correct use of personal protective equipment (PPE) and check the provisions of the Operational Safety Plan (POS), possibly reporting the changes to be made.

Among the necessary knowledge to pass these exams are those related to the legislation and responsibility related to safety at work and environmental protection, the implementation of an integrated security management system, quality, environment and ethics, to the modality conducting audits, managing the risk analysis phase for an appropriate prevention plan, economic control for a correct investment in actions to improve and reduce risks, to spread the culture of security and conflict management, to development of organizational organizational well-being, to the management of emergency situations.

CONCLUSION

Environmental Education (EE) is a process in which individuals gain awareness of their environment and acquire knowledge, skills, values, experiences, and also the determination, which will enable them to act - individually and collectively - to solve present and future environmental problems. It is aimed at producing a citizenry that is knowledgeable concerning the biophysical environment and its associated problems, aware of how to help solve these problems, and motivated to work toward their solution (Stap et al, 1969).

Environmental education, properly understood, should constitute a comprehensive lifelong education, one responsive to changes in a rapidly changing world. It should prepare the individual for life through an understanding of the major problems of the contemporary world, and the provision of skills and attributes needed to play a productive role towards improving life and protecting the environment with due regard given to ethical values (UNESCO, 1977).

The strategies and priorities pursued through EE are strongly shaped by political power, current environmental issues, social priorities, and trends in educational policy. For example, EE within schools has been influenced by the development of curriculum standards.

Environmental education can also be influenced by government fiscal and administrative policy decisions. In the U.S., EE implementation occurs within many different departments and is shaped by the executive and legislative branches of government, through presidential appointments and congressional funding appropriations. In India, for instance, the government provides financial and administrative support for the Centre for Environmental Education (CEE), which represents a unique partnership between the Ministry of Environment and Forests and an NGO conducting a number of ESD focused projects nationwide. (Biedenweg et al, 2013).

Compelled by the vision and value of environmental education, the foundation world is now engaging in an exciting and productive yet sometimes difficult dialogue about a new definition of, and best entry points into, this evolving field. Environmental education strategies are flexible and influenced by environmental, political, economic, and cultural realities.

This work aimed to describe the long international history leading to its current definitions and strategies for engaging the public in sustainable, environmentally responsible discourse. Specifically, it wanted to synthesize a pedagogical approach to the matter, concluding with the profile of the manager and the environmental consultant.

REFERENCES

6th Environment Action Programme (6th EAP). (2002). Retrieved from http://ec.europa.eu/environment/archives/action-programme/intro.htm [07/29/2018]

7th Environment Action Programme (6th EAP). (2014). Retrieved from http://ec.europa.eu/environment/action-programme/ [07/29/2018]

AA.VV. (2014). *Le Linee Guida Educazione ambientale per lo sviluppo sostenibile*. Available in: http://www.minambiente.it/sites/default/files/archivio/allegati/LINEE_GUIDA.pdf

Biedenweg, K. (2013). Foundation of Environmental Education. In M. C. Monroe & M. E. Krasny (Eds.), *Across the Spectrum* (pp. 9–29). *North American Association for Environmental Education.*

Bonafini, M. (2011). *Teoria e pratica di educazione ambientale*. Università degli Studi di Verona Corso di laurea in Scienze della Formazione Primaria. Available in: http://www.dsu.univr.it/documenti/Avviso/all/all412685.pdf

COP21 conference on climate change. (2015). Retrieved from http://www.undp.org/content/undp/en/home/presscenter/events/2015/december/COP21-paris-climate-conference.html [07/29/2018]

Comstock, A. B. (1939). *Handbook of Nature-Study for Teachers and Parents* (24th ed.). Ithaca, NY: Comstock Publishing Associates, Division of Cornell University Press.

Dietz, T., & Stern, P. (2002). *New Tools for Environmental Protection: Education, Information, and Voluntary Measures*. Washington, DC: National Academies Press.

Earth Summit. (1992). Retrieved from https://api.parliament.uk/historic-hansard/commons/1992/jun/03/earth-summit

European Parliament. (n.d.). *Reducing carbon emissions: EU targets and measures*. Retrieved from http://www.europarl.europa.eu/news/en/headlines/society/20180305STO99003/reducing-carbon-emissions-eu-targets-and-measures

Fien, J. (2000). 'Education for the Environment: A critique'—an analysis. *Environmental Education Research*, *6*(2), 179–192. doi:10.1080/713664671

Gough, A. (1997). Founders of Environmental Education: Narratives of the Australian Environmental Education Movement. *Environmental Education Research*, *3*(1), 43–57. doi:10.1080/1350462970030104

Heimlich, J. E., & Ardoin, N. M. (2008). Understanding Behavior to Understand Behavior Change: A Literature Review. *Environmental Education Research*, *14*(3), 215–237. doi:10.1080/13504620802148881

Huckle, J. (1991). Education for Sustainability: Assessing Pathways to the Future. *Australian Journal of Environmental Education*, *7*(2), 43–62. doi:10.1017/S0814062600001853

Informazione ambiente Italia. (n.d.). *Piogge Acide: cosa sono e quali sono le conseguenze del fenomeno*. Retrieved from https://www.informazioneambiente.it/piogge-acide/

Jackson, J. (2013). Aerosol algorithms and data products. Journal of Geophysical Research: Atmospheres, 118, 22.

Jordan, A. J., & Adelle, C. (Eds.). (2012). Environmental Policy in the European Union: Contexts, Actors and Policy Dynamics (3rd ed.). Earthscan.

McCormick, J. (2001). *Environmental Policy in the European Union*. Basingstoke, UK: Palgrave. doi:10.1007/978-0-333-98557-1

Ministero dell'Ambiente Italiano. (n.d.a). *Educazione ambientale e sviluppo sostenibile*. Retrieved from http://www.minambiente.it/pagina/educazione-ambientale-e-allo-sviluppo-sostenibile

Ministero dell'Ambiente Italiano. (n.d.b). *Da Stati Genereali una carta per l'educazione Green*. Retrieved from http://www.minambiente.it/comunicati/da-stati-generali-una-carta-leducazione-green

Ministero dell'Ambiente Italiano. (n.d.c). *Linee guida per l'educazione ambientale*. Retrieved from http://www.minambiente.it/sites/default/files/archivio/allegati/LINEE_GUIDA.pdf

Palmer, J. A. (1998). *Environmental Education in the 21st Century: Theory, Practice, Progress and Promise*. London: Routledge.

Provincia di Bolzano Italia. (n.d.). *Educazione Ambientale*. Retrieved from http://www.provincia.bz.it/intendenza-scolastica/download/Evoluzione__Ed_Ambientale.pdf

Smith, W., & Gough, A. (2015). Deep Ecology as a framework for student eco-philosophical thinking. *Journal of Philosophy in Schools*, *2*(1), 38–55. doi:10.21913/JPS.v2i1.1101

Stapp, W. B. (1969). The Concept of Environmental Education. *The Journal of Environmental Education*, *1*(1), 30–31. doi:10.1080/00139254.1969.10801479

The Aalborg Charter. (1994). Retrieved from http://www.sustainablecities.eu/the-aalborg-charter/

The Belgrade Charter. (1972). Retrieved from https://www.gdrc.org/uem/ee/belgrade.html

U.N. Environment Programme (UNEP). (1977). *Tbilisi Declaration.* Retrieved from https://www.gdrc.org/uem/ee/tbilisi.html

UNESCO. (1971). *Final Report: Man and Biosphere Programme.* Retrieved from http://www.unesco.org/new/en/natural-sciences/environment/ecological-sciences/

UNESCO. (1997). *Educating for a Sustainable Future.* Retrieved from http://unesdoc.unesco.org/images/0011/001106/110686eo.pdf

UNESCO. (n.d.). *Teaching And Learning For A Sustainable Future.* Retrieved from http://www.unesco.org/education/tlsf/

UNESCO-UNEP. (1978). Final Report: Intergovernmental Conference on Environmental Education. *Environmental Education Newsletter, 3*(1), 1-8. Retrieved from http://unesdoc.unesco.org/images/0015/001563/156393eb.pdf

UNESCO-UNEP International Congress On Environmental Education And Training. (1987). *Report.* Retrieved from http://unesdoc.unesco.org/images/0007/000750/075072Eo.pdf

United Nations Conference. (1972). *Human Environment.* Retrieved from https://en.wikipedia.org/wiki/United_Nations_Conference_on_the_Human_Environment

Velez Rolon, A. (2010). *La educación ambiental como herramienta de participación para la sosteniblidad local.* Available in: https://www.ecoportal.net/?s=Velez+Rolon+A

Vitali, G. (2010). *La politica per l'ambiente nell'Unione Europea.* Istituto di Ricerca sull'Impresa e lo Sviluppo. Available in: http://www2.ceris.cnr.it/homedipendenti/vitali/dispense2010_11_PE/politica%20ambientale%20corso%20pol%20eco%2006%2012%202010.pdf

World Commission On Environment And Development. (1987). *Brundtland Report.* Retrieved from https://www.britannica.com/topic/Brundtland-Report

World Summit On Sustainable Development. (2002). *Improve Lives While Preserving Earth's Resources*. Retrieved from http://www.un.org/events/wssd/summaries/envdevj1.htm

KEY TERMS AND DEFINITIONS

HSE, the Manager and the Environmental Consultant: They are some of the emerging figures in modern business management, as responsible for the environmental problems of the company, guiding it between obligations, obligations, opportunities, and risks that the legislation requires.

Compilation of References

6th Environment Action Programme (6th EAP). (2002). Retrieved from http://ec.europa.eu/environment/archives/action-programme/intro.htm [07/29/2018]

7th Environment Action Programme (6th EAP). (2014). Retrieved from http://ec.europa.eu/environment/action-programme/ [07/29/2018]

AA.VV. (2012). *Glossario Intelligence: il linguaggio degli organismi informativi*. Retrieved from: http://silendo.org/2012/07/05/glossario-intelligence-il-linguaggio-degli-organismi-informativi/

AA.VV. (2014). *Le Linee Guida Educazione ambientale per lo sviluppo sostenibile*. Available in: http://www.minambiente.it/sites/default/files/archivio/allegati/LINEE_GUIDA.pdf

AA.VV. (2014). *Lezioni sull'Intelligence, Sistema di informazione per la Sicurezza della Repubblica*. Retreived from: https://www.sicurezzanazionale.gov.it/sisr.nsf/wp-content/uploads/2014/05/lezione-intelligence.pdf

AA.VV. (2017). *51st Asilomar Conference on Signals, Systems, and Computer, Proceedings*. Available in: https://ieeexplore.ieee.org/xpl/mostRecentIssue.jsp?punumber=8330843

Abbass, H. A. (2001). Marriage in honey-bee optimization (MBO): a haplometrosis polygynous swarming approach. *Proceedings of the congress on evolutionary computation (CEC2001)*, 207–214. 10.1109/CEC.2001.934391

Abdul-Halim, H., & Che-Ha, N. (2010). HR outsourcing among Malaysian manufacturing companies. *Business Strategy Series*, *11*(6), 363–370. doi:10.1108/17515631011093061

Adolph, S., Tisch, M., & Metternich, J. (2014). Challenges and approaches to competency development for future production. *Journal of International Scientific Publications–Educational Alternatives*, *12*(1), 1001–1010.

Affenzeller, M., & Wagner, S. (2005). Offspring selection: a new self-adaptive selection scheme for genetic algorithms. *Proceedings of the international conference on adaptive and natural computing algorithms (ICANNGA)*, 218–221.

Agrawal, A. (2018). *Prediction machines: Why A.I.'s true potential is learning to read the future*. Retrieved May 2018 from http://bigthink.com/videos/ajay-agrawal-why-predictive-ai-leads-to-better-decision-making?utm_source=Daily+Newsletter&utm_campaign=4fe2983747-Daily_Newsletter_050418&utm_medium=email&utm_term=0_45b26faecc-4fe2983747-43589201

Agrawal, A., Gans, J., & Goldforb, A. (2018). *Prediction machines, The Simple Economics of Artificial Intelligence*. Boston, MA: Harvard Business Review Press.

Al Ariss, A., Cascio, W. F., & Paauwe, J. (2014). Talent management: Current theories and future research directions. *Journal of World Business*, *49*(2), 173–179. doi:10.1016/j.jwb.2013.11.001

Albus, J. S. (1991). Outline for a Theory of Intelligence. *IEEE Transactions on Systems, Man, and Cybernetics*, *21*(3), 473–509. doi:10.1109/21.97471

Alive Robots. (n.d.). *NAO es la mejor plataforma robótica para educacion*. Retrieved from: https://aliverobots.com/nao-educacion/

Alkhatib, H., & Duveau, J. (2013). Dynamic genetic algorithms for robust design of multimachine power system stabilizers. *Electr Power Energy Syst*, *45*(1), 242–251. doi:10.1016/j.ijepes.2012.08.080

Alo, A. (2015). *Serious game: metodologie innovative per l'apprendimento esperienziale*. Retrieved from: http://www.diversity-management.it/2015/12/24/serious-game-definizione-vantaggi/

Analytic thinking and presentation for intelligence producers. (n.d.). Retrieved from: https://ia800201.us.archive.org/23/items/CIA_Analytic_Thinking_and_Presentation_for_Intelligence_Analysis_Training_Handbo/CIA_Analytic_Thinking_and_Presentation_for_Intelligence_Analysis_Training_Handbook.pdf

Anderson, A. K., & Phelps, E. A. (2001). Lesions of the human amygdala impair enhanced perception of emotionally salient events. *Nature*, *411*(6835), 305–309. doi:10.1038/35077083 PMID:11357132

Anolli, L., & Mantovani, F. (2011). *Come funziona la nostra mente. Apprendimento, simulazione e Serious Games*. Il Mulino.

Ascolese, A. (2016). *Perché i serious games ci aiutano ad apprendere?* Retrieved from: http://www.stateofmind.it/2016/10/serious-games-apprendimento/

Augment. (2015). *Virtual Reality vs. Augmented Reality.* Retrieved from: http://www.augment.com/blog/virtual-reality-vs-augmented-reality/

Aven. (2010). *Misconceptions of Risk.* Wiley.

Aven, T. (2011). *Risk assessment. The scientific platform*. Cambridge University Press. doi:10.1017/CBO9780511974120

Aven, T., & Renn, O. (2010). *Risk management and Risk Governance. Concepts, Guidelines and Applications*. Springer Verlag. doi:10.1007/978-3-642-13926-0

Awan, A. G., & Farhan, H. M. (2016). Talent management practices and their impact on job satisfaction of employees: A case study of banking sector in Pakistan. *Science International*, *8*(2), 1950.

Bagga, G. (2013). How to keep the talent you have got. *Human Resource Management International Digest*, *21*(1), 3–4. doi:10.1108/09670731311296401

Bano, M., & Ikram, N. (2010). Issues and Challenges of Requirement Engineering in Service Oriented Software Development. In *Proceedings of the Fifth International Conference on Software Engineering Advances*. IEEE Xplore.

Baraniuk, C. (2018, January 25). For AI to Get Creative, It Must Learn the Rules—Then How to Break 'Em. *Scientific American*.

Barbieri, A. (2013). *Sfide della rivoluzione digitale nel contesto educativo*. University of Milano, Dottorato di Ricerca in Società dell'Informazione, Ciclo XXV.

Barkhuizen, N., Mogwere, P., & Schutte, N. (2014). Talent management and leadership reciprocity: The case of the South African aviation industry. *Mediterranean Journal of Social Sciences*, *5*(9), 11.

Barlas, Y. (1994). *Model Validation in System Dynamics*. The 12th International Conference of the System Dynamics Society, Stirling, UK.

Barlas, Y. (1996). Formal Aspects of Model Validity and Validation in System Dynamics. *System Dynamics Review*, *12*(3), 183–210. doi:10.1002/(SICI)1099-1727(199623)12:3<183::AID-SDR103>3.0.CO;2-4

BBC. (2018). *Introduction to computational thinking*. Retrieved from: https://www.bbc.com/education/guides/zp92mp3/revision/2

Berg, P. (2008). Meetings that changed the world: Asilomar 1975: DNA modification secured. *Nature, 455*(18). Available in: https://www.nature.com/articles/455290a.pdf

Bergin, T. (2013). *Learning and development in the public sector. The care for maintaining investment in tough times*. Canberra: Australian Institute of Management.

Biedenweg, K. (2013). Foundation of Environmental Education. In M. C. Monroe & M. E. Krasny (Eds.), *Across the Spectrum* (pp. 9–29). *North American Association for Environmental Education*.

Bonafini, M. (2011). *Teoria e pratica di educazione ambientale*. Università degli Studi di Verona Corso di laurea in Scienze della Formazione Primaria. Available in: http://www.dsu.univr.it/documenti/Avviso/all/all412685.pdf

Bontempi, M. (2003). Introduzione all'Intelligence e alla Controintelligence istituzionale. In Dispense per il Master in Intelligence and Security (2nd ed.). dell'Università di Malta.

Booth, K. (2007). *Theory of world security*. Cambridge University Press. doi:10.1017/CBO9780511840210

Bredenfeld, A., & Leimbach, T. (2010). *The Roberta Initiative*. In *First International Conference on Robotics in Education*, Bratislava, Slovakia.

Brinkman, B., Gotterbarn, D., Miller, K., & Wolf, M. J. (2016, December 16). Making a positive impact: Updating the ACM code of ethics. *Communications of the ACM*.

Buzan et a. (1998). *Security: A new framework for analysis*. Boulder, CO: Lynne Rienner Publishers, Inc.

Caligari, M. (2016). *Cyber Intelligence. Tra libertà e sicurezza*. Donzelli Editore.

Calvani, A. (2013). Le TIC nella scuola: dieci raccomandazioni per i policy maker. *Form@re - Open Journal per la Formazione in Rete, 4*(13), 30–46.

Chandler, C. (2018). *Why China Has An Edge In the A.I. Arms Race*. Retrieved July 2018, from http://fortune.com/2018/06/25/artificial-intelligence-in-china/

Chaturvedi, K. T., Pandit, M., & Srivastava, L. (2008). Self-organizing hierarchical particle swarm optimization for nonconvex economic dispatch. *IEEE Transactions on Power Systems, 23*(3), 1079–1087. doi:10.1109/TPWRS.2008.926455

Cheong, R.K.F., & Tsui, E. (2010). The Roles and Values of Personal Knowledge Management: An exploratory study. *VINE, the Journal of Information and Knowledge Management System, 40*(2), 204-27.

Chigada, J., & Ngulube, P. (2015). Knowledge-management practices at selected banks in South Africa: Original research. *South African Journal of Information Management, 17*(1), 1–10. doi:10.4102ajim.v17i1.634

Christel, M. G., & Kang, K. C. (1992). *Issues in Requirements Elicitation*. Technical Report. CMU/SEI-92-TR-12. ESC-TR-92-012. Software Engineering Institute. Carnegie Mellon University.

Chulki, J., & Sungjin, A. (2014). A Study on the Improvements of Information Security Management System for Environment Education Institutes. International Journal of Security and its Applications, 8(4), 247-252.

Cilluffo, F. J., & Cardash, S. L. (2013). Cyber Domain Conflict in the 21st Century. *Seton Hall J. Dipl. & Int'l Rel., 14*, 41.

Colebatch, H. (2006). Thinking about policy: finding the best way. In *GovNet International Conference*. Australian National University.

Collings, D., & Mellahi, K. (2013). Commentary on: Talent—innate or acquired? Theoretical considerations and their implications for talent management. *Human Resource Management Review, 23*(4), 322–325. doi:10.1016/j.hrmr.2013.08.003

Collins, C. E. (2014). *Gray as gold: the significant value of the mature worker*. Tucson, AZ: University of Arizona.

Comini, G., Paolino, M., & Feitosa, M. (2013). Mapping of the succession process in non-profit organizations in Brazil. *International Leadership Journal, 5*(3), 28–50.

Comstock, A. B. (1939). *Handbook of Nature-Study for Teachers and Parents* (24th ed.). Ithaca, NY: Comstock Publishing Associates, Division of Cornell University Press.

COP21 conference on climate change. (2015). Retrieved from http://www.undp.org/content/undp/en/home/presscenter/events/2015/december/COP21-paris-climate-conference.html [07/29/2018]

Correlli, S. (2015). *Didattica e nuove tecnologie, Seminario di cultura digitale*. University of Pisa.

Cox, M. T., & Raja, A. (2011). *Metareasoning: Thinking about Thinking*. MIT Press. doi:10.7551/mitpress/9780262014809.001.0001

Crossover. (n.d.). *The policy cycle*. Retrieved from: https://debategraph.org/Details.aspx?nid=228943

Crowder, N. (1969). Automatic Tutoring by Intrinsic Programming. In A. A. Lumsdaine & R. Glaser (Eds.), *Teaching Machines and Programmed Learning*. Washington, DC: National Education Assn.

Czopek, A. (2017), The Value of Technology in Education. Young Digital Planet 2017, Gdansk, Poland.

Dale, E. (1946). *Audio-visual methods in teaching*. New York, NY: Dryden Press.

dall'Acqua, L. (2011). Didactical suggestion for a Dynamic Hybrid Intelligent e-Learning Environment (DHILE) applying the PENTHA ID Model. *AIP Proceedings, 1373*, 159-173.

dall'Acqua, L. (2014). *Needs and strategies of KM in a multi-user environment: PENTHA Model view and analysis*. Jekpot KM19, Milano. Italy.

dall'Acqua, L., & Dickson, L. (2018). Improving Business Performance Through Effective Managerial Training Initiatives. In *Extended Managerial Implications: People and Space in the Twenty-First Century*. Hershey PA: IGI Global.

dall'Acqua, L., & Santo, M. D. (2012). New interpretative paradigms to understand and manage the unpredictability of the dynamics of learning in a complex multi-user knowledge environment. *Proceedings of Artificial Intelligence Workshop 2012 on Collaboration and Intelligence in Blended Learning*, 92-9.

dall'Acqua, L., & Santo, M. D. (2014). Orientism, the basic pedagogical approach of PENTHA ID Model vs. 2, to manage decisions in unpredictability conditions. Proceedings of World Congress on Engineering and Computer Science WCECS2014, *1*, 316-21.

Dasha, K. (2017). *Technology & Pedagogical Innovation.* Retrieved from: http://www.reimagine-education.com/wp-content/uploads/2018/01/RE_White-Paper_Technology-Pedagogical-Innovation.pdf

Davies, A., Fidler, D., & Gorbis, M. (2011). *Future Work Skills 2020*. Institute for the Future for the University of Phoenix Research Institute. Retrieved from: http://www.iftf.org/uploads/media/SR-1382A_UPRI_future_work_skills_sm.pdf

Davis, J. (2002). Sherman Kent and the Profession of Intelligence Analysis. *Occasional Papers*, *1*(5).

Dehkordi, M. A., & Kazemi, T. B. (2013). The talent's strategic management: An analysis of approaches, problems, and features. *Strategy for Culture*, *22*, 105–134.

Deloitte Insights. (2018). *The Fourth Industrial Revolution is here—are you ready?* Deloitte Development LLC.

Dente, B. (2014). *Understanding Policy Decision*. Springer. doi:10.1007/978-3-319-02520-9

Dietz, T., & Stern, P. (2002). *New Tools for Environmental Protection: Education, Information, and Voluntary Measures*. Washington, DC: National Academies Press.

DMO. (2014). *Nonna Lea e la sua badante robot.* Retrieved from: http://www.datamanager.it/news/nonna-lea-e-la-sua-badante-robot-56063.html

DNdou, S., & Sebola, M. P. (2016). Capacity building in local government: An analysis for application of competency-based training in South Africa. *International Journal of Higher Education Management*, *6*(5), 90–100.

Downes, S. (2010). *The role of the Educator in PLE World.* Retrieved from http://www.slideshare.net/Downes/the-role-of-the-educator-in-a-ple-world

Downes, S. (2011). Knowledge, *Learning and Community*. Retrieved from http://www.downes.ca/files/books/KnowledgeLearning.pdf

Dunn, W. N. (1994). *Public Policy Analysis: An Introduction*. Englewood Cliffs, NJ: Prentice Hall.

Duyvesteyn. (2014). *The Future of Intelligence: Challenges in the 21st Century*. Routledge. doi:10.4324/9780203071472

Earth Summit. (1992). Retrieved from https://api.parliament.uk/historic-hansard/commons/1992/jun/03/earth-summit

Eco, U. (2018). *Aforismi*. Available at https://aforismi.meglio.it/aforisma.htm?id=15003

EEStor, Energy Everywhere. (2017, January 18). Retrieved from http://www.eestor.us/index.html

Emerging Technology from the arXiv. (2018, March). When an AI finally kills someone, who will be responsible? Legal scholars are furiously debating which laws should apply to AI crime. *MIT Technology Review*.

Eom, J. H. (2012). Cyber military strategy for cyberspace superiority in cyber warfare. In *Cyber Security, Cyber Warfare and Digital Forensic (CyberSec). 2012 International Conference* (pp. 295-299). Academic Press. 10.1109/CyberSec.2012.6246114

Erkut, H. (1983). *Sistem Dinamiğinin Temelleri*. İstanbul: İTÜ Fen Edebiyat Fakültesi Ofset Atölyesi.

Escuela de las Américas. Inteligencia de Combate. (n.d.). Retrieved from: http://www.derechos.org/nizkor/la/libros/soaIC/cap3.html

European Commission. (2018). *Statement on Artificial Intelligence, Robotics and 'Autonomous' Systems*. European Group on Ethics in Science and New Technologies. Publications Office of the European Union, 2018.

European Commission. (n.d.). *ICT in education. EU Smart Specialisation Platform*. Retrieved from: http://s3platform.jrc.ec.europa.eu/education

European Parliament. (n.d.). *Reducing carbon emissions: EU targets and measures*. Retrieved from http://www.europarl.europa.eu/news/en/headlines/society/20180305STO99003/reducing-carbon-emissions-eu-targets-and-measures

Evans, G. (2009). Rethinking Military Intelligence Failure. Putting the Wheels Back on the Intelligence Cycle. *Defence Studies*, *9*(1), 22–46. doi:10.1080/14702430701811987

Ezigbo, C. A. (2012). Justification of outsourcing for organisation's competitive advantage. *European Journal of Soil Science*, *34*(2), 262–272.

Fägersten, B. 2015). Intelligence and decision-making within the Common Foreign and Security Policy. In European Policy Analysis. Swedish Institute of European Security Studies.

Felten, E., & Lyons, T. (2016). *The Administration's Report on the Future of Artificial Intelligence*. Retrieved July 2018, from https://obamawhitehouse.archives.gov/blog/2016/10/12/administrations-report-future-artificial-intelligence

Ferencik, R. C., Soderquist, K., & Mınyard-Phıllıps, M. A. (2014). *Building Systems Thinking Capacity: An Essential Skill Set For Policymakers*. In 32nd International Conference of the System Dynamics Society, Delft, The Netherlands.

Fien, J. (2000). 'Education for the Environment: A critique'—an analysis. *Environmental Education Research*, *6*(2), 179–192. doi:10.1080/713664671

Firouzia, B. B., Farjah, E., & Abarghooee, R. A. (2013). An efficient scenario-based and fuzzy self-adaptive learning particle swarm optimization approach for dynamic economic emission dispatch considering load and wind power uncertainties. *Energy*, *50*(1), 232–244. doi:10.1016/j.energy.2012.11.017

Fishwick, P. A. (2007). *Handbook of Dynamic System Modelling*. Boca Raton, FL: Chapman & Hall / CRC. doi:10.1201/9781420010855

Fleisher, C. S., & Bensoussan, B. E. (2003). *Strategic and Competitive Analysis: Methods And Techniques for Analyzing Business Competition*. Upper Saddle River, NJ: Prentice Hall.

Florea, L., Cheung, Y. H., & Herndon, N. C. (2013). For all good reasons: Role of values in organizational sustainability. *Journal of Business Ethics*, *114*(3), 393–408. doi:10.100710551-012-1355-x

Fondazione Adriano Olivetti's Archive. (2017). (p. 101). Author.

Ford, A. (1999). *Modeling the Environment: An Introduction to System Dynamics Modeling of Environmental Systems*. Washington, DC: Island Press.

Forrester, J. W. (1995). *Road Map 1: Counterintuitive Behaviour Of Social Systems*. MIT System Dynamics In Education Project.

Forrester, J. W. (1962). *Industrial Dynamics*. Waltham, MA: Pegasus Communications.

Forrester, J. W. (1969). *Urban Dynamics*. The MIT Press.

Forrester, J. W. (1977). Growth Cycles. *De Economist, 125*(: 4).

Forrester, J. W., & Senge, P. M. (1980). Tests For Building Confidence In System Dynamic Models. *TIMS Studies in the Management Sciences, 14*, 209–228.

Frances, J. A. (2018, April). Meltdown. *Scientific American, 318*(4), 48–53. doi:10.1038cientificamerican0418-48 PMID:29557956

Frey, B. C., & Osborne, M. A. (2013). *The future of employment: how susceptible are jobs to computerisation?* University of Oxford. Retrieved from: http://www.oxfordmartin.ox.ac.uk/downloads/academic/The_Future_of_Employment.pdf

Gagne, R. (1987). *Instructional Technology Foundations*. Hillsdale, NJ: Lawrence Erlbaum Associates.

Gamification. (2018). *E-Learning: glossario dei termini*. Retrieved from: http://www.gamification.it/tag/serious-games/

Gardner, H. (2011). *Frames of Mind: The Theory of Multiple Intelligences*. New York, NY: Basic Books.

Gent, E. (2018). *This New Chip Design Could Make Neural Nets More Efficient and a Lot Faster.* Retrieved June 13, 2018 from: https://singularityhub.com/2018/06/11/this-new-chip-design-could-make-neural-nets-more-efficient-and-a-lot-faster/?utm_source=Singularity+Hub+Newsletter&utm_campaign=5aedf55c2b-Hub_Daily_Newsletter&utm_medium=email&utm_term=0_f0cf60cdae-5aedf55c2b-5747300

Gleick, J. (1987). *Chaos*. Viking.

Goldman, J. (2011). *Words of Intelligence: An Intelligence Professional's Lexicon for Domestic and Foreign Threats, Security and Professional Intelligence Education Series*. Scarecrow Press.

Gough, A. (1997). Founders of Environmental Education: Narratives of the Australian Environmental Education Movement. *Environmental Education Research, 3*(1), 43–57. doi:10.1080/1350462970030104

Green, M. R., & Trieschmann, J. S. (1981). *Risk and insurance*. Cincinnati, OH: South-Western Publishing Co.

Gregory, J. (2013). *Projections of Sea Level Rise*. IPCC Fifth Assessment Report. Retrieved from https://www.ipcc.ch/pdf/unfccc/cop19/3_gregory13sbsta.pdf

Gretczko, M., & Cleary, W. (2016). The Candidate as Customer: A Proactive Approach to Talent Acquisition. *Workforce Solutions Review*, *7*(3), 8–10.

Grey, B. (2017). *Autonomous Cars: Everything You Need To Know About Market And Research Trends. Autonomous Vehicles – Market and Research Trends report.* Retrieved from https://www.greyb.com/autonomous-cars/#_Toc484626650

Groff, J. (2013). *Technology-rich innovative learning environments*. Centre for Educational Research and Innovation (CERI). Retrieved from: http://www.oecd.org/education/ceri/Technology-Rich%20Innovative%20Learning%20Environments%20by%20Jennifer%20Groff.pdf

Guba, G., & Lincoln, Y. S. (2001). *Guidelines and checklist for constructivist evaluation*. Evaluation Checklists Project. Retrieved from www.wmich.edu/evalctr/checklists

Gulla, J. (2012). *Seven Reasons IT Projects Fail. IBM Systems Magazine*.

Hall, L. O., & Hagen, C. D. (2014). Holistic approach to succession planning provides added value for clients: Financial service professionals play key role in successful plans. *Journal of Financial Service Professionals*, *68*(1), 78–83.

Hampson, F. O. (2008). Human security. In P. D. Williams (Ed.), *Security studies: An introduction* (pp. 229–244). London: Routledge.

Hannigan, T. (1998). *Managing Tomorrow's High-Performance decision-makers*. London: Quorum Books.

Heikkila, T., & Cairney, P. (2014). *Comparison of Theories of the Policy Process*. Available in: https://paulcairney.files.wordpress.com/2014/01/heikkila-cairney-proof-24-4-17.pdf

Heimlich, J. E., & Ardoin, N. M. (2008). Understanding Behavior to Understand Behavior Change: A Literature Review. *Environmental Education Research*, *14*(3), 215–237. doi:10.1080/13504620802148881

Herman, H. (2001). *Intelligence services in the information age*. London, UK: Frank Cass Publishers.

Herring, J. (1996). Creating the intelligence system that produces analytical intelligence. In B. Gilad & J. Herring (Eds.), *The art and science of business intelligence* (pp. 53–81). Greenwich, CT: JAI Press.

Hofferbert, R. (1974). *The Study of Public Policy*. Academic Press.

Holmes, P., Chapman, T., & Baghurst, T. (2013). Employee job embeddedness: Why people stay. *International Journal of Business Management & Economic Research*, *4*(5), 802–813.

Homeschool Math. (2015). *Review of Carnegie Learning's Cognitive Tutor Algebra 1*. Retrieved from: https://www.homeschoolmath.net/reviews/carnegie-learning.php

Hopkin, P. (2018). *Fundamentals of Risk Management: Understanding, Evaluating and Implementing Effective Risk Management*. Kogan Page.

Horton, T. (2018). *High Tide in Dorchester*. Bay Journal Film. Retrieved from http://hightidedorchester.org/

Horton, T. (2018). *High Tide in Dorchester*. Retrieved from http://hightidedorchester.org/

Horwitz, F. M. (2013). An analysis of skills development in a transitional economy: The case of the South African Labour Market. *International Journal of Human Resource Management*, *24*(12), 2435–2451. doi:10.1080/09585192.2013.781438

Hosanagar, K., & Saxena, A. (2017, April). The First Wave of Corporate AI Is Doomed to Fail. *Harvard Business Review*.

Huckle, J. (1991). Education for Sustainability: Assessing Pathways to the Future. *Australian Journal of Environmental Education*, *7*(2), 43–62. doi:10.1017/S0814062600001853

Huffman, W. E. (1974). Decision Making: The Role of Education. *American Journal of Agricultural Economics*, *56*(1), 85–97. doi:10.2307/1239349

Hulnick, A. (2006). What's wrong with the Intelligence Cycle. *Intelligence and National Security*, *21*(6), 959–979. doi:10.1080/02684520601046291

IBM's Brain-Inspired Chip Tested for Deep Learning. (n.d.). Retrieved from: https://spectrum.ieee.org/tech-talk/computing/hardware/ibms-braininspired-chip-tested-on-deep-learning

Informazione ambiente Italia. (n.d.). *Piogge Acide: cosa sono e quali sono le conseguenze del fenomeno*. Retrieved from https://www.informazioneambiente.it/piogge-acide/

IPCC SR1. 5. (2018). *Global Warming of 1.5 C Technical Summary*. Retrieved October 2018 from http://ipcc.ch/report/SR15/

Jackson, J. (2013). Aerosol algorithms and data products. Journal of Geophysical Research: Atmospheres, 118, 22.

Jamil, R., & Neem, H. (2013). The Impact of outsourcing external recruitment process on the employee commitment and loyalty: Empirical evidence from the telecommunication sector of Pakistan. *Journal of Business and Management*, *8*(2), 69–75.

Johnson. (2016). *NMC Horizon Report: Higher Education Edition*. Austin, TX: The New Media Consortium.

Johnson, G., Wilding, P., & Robson, A. (2014). Can outsourcing recruitment deliver satisfaction? A hiring manager perspective. *Personnel Review*, *43*(2), 303–326. doi:10.1108/PR-12-2012-0212

Jordan, A. J., & Adelle, C. (Eds.). (2012). Environmental Policy in the European Union: Contexts, Actors and Policy Dynamics (3rd ed.). Earthscan.

JPL InfoGraphics. (n.d.). *Sea Level Rise*. Retrieved February 5, 2017 from http://www.jpl.nasa.gov/infographics/infographic.view.php?id=11298

Kaiser, R. B., & Curphy, G. (2013). Leadership development: The failure of an industry and the opportunity for consulting psychologists. *Consulting Psychology Journal: Practice and Research*, *65*(4), 294–302. doi:10.1037/a0035460

Kanar, K. (1995). Structure Oriented Behavior Tests. In *Model Validation, Master Of Science*. Industrial Engineering Boğaziçi University.

Kaplan, R. S., & Mikes, A. (2012, June). Managing Risks: A New Framework. *Harvard Business Review*.

Karatepe, O. M. (2013). High-performance work practices, work social support and their effects on job embeddedness and turnover intentions. *International Journal of Contemporary Hospitality Management*, *25*(6), 903–921. doi:10.1108/IJCHM-06-2012-0097

Karnopp, D. C., Margolis, D. L., & Rosenberg, R. C. (1990). *System Dynamics A Unified Approach* (2nd ed.). John Wiley & Sons, Inc.

Karodia, A. M., Cowden, R., & Kum, F. D. (2014). The impact of training and development on employee performance: A case study of ESCON Consulting. *Singaporean Journal of Business. Economics and Management Studies, 3*(3), 72–105.

Keen, G. (1977). The intelligence cycle: a differentiated perspective on information processing. In *Proceedings of the June 13-16, 1977, National Computer Conference* (pp. 317-320). ACM. 10.1145/1499402.1499458

Kirkwood, C. W. (1998). *System Dynamics Methods: A Quick Introduction*. Arizona State University.

Knight, W. (2017, April 11). The Dark Secret at the Heart of AI. *MIT Technology Review*.

Knoepfel, P., Larrue, C., Varone, F., & Hill, M. (2007). *Public Policy Analysis*. Policy Press.

Kop, R., Fournier, H., & Mak, J. S. F. (2011). A Pedagogy of Abundance or a Pedagogy to Support Human Beings? Participant Support on Massive Open Online Courses. *International Review of Research in Open and Distance Learning, 12*(7), 74–93. doi:10.19173/irrodl.v12i7.1041

Krejcie, R., & Morgan, D. (1970). Determining sample size for research activities. *Educational and Psychological Measurement, 30*(3), 607–610. doi:10.1177/001316447003000308

Kroon, B., & Freese, C. (2013). Can HR practices retain flexworkers with their agency. *International Journal of Manpower, 34*(8), 899–917. doi:10.1108/IJM-07-2013-0169

Kurzgesagt – In a Nutshell. (2016, December 16). *Over Population, The Human Explosion Explained*. Retrieved from https://www.youtube.com/watch?v=QsBT5EQt348

Lane, D. J., & Sterman, J. D. (2011). Profiles in Operations Research: Jay Wright Forrester. In Profiles in Operations Research: Pioneers and Innovators. New York: Springer.

Levy, S. (2018). *Inside Amazon's Artificial Intelligence Flywheel: How deep learning came to power Alexa, Amazon Web Services, and nearly every other division of the company*. Retrieved July 2018, from https://www.wired.com/story/amazon-artificial-intelligence-flywheel/

Levy, P. (1997). *Collective Intelligence*. Cambridge, MA: Perseus Books.

Longo, L. M. (2003). Il fattore umano nel controspionaggio industriale. In Dispense per il Master in Intelligence and Security (2nd ed.). dell'Università di Malta.

Loucks, D. P., & da Costa, J. R. (Eds.). (1991). *Technology Assessment. Environmental Impact Assessment. and Risk Analysis: Contributions from the Psychological and Decision Sciences. NATO Advanced Study Institute (ASI)*.

Louw, G. J. (2013). Exploring recruitment and selection trends in the Eastern Cape. *SA Journal of Human Resource Management*, *11*(1), 1. doi:10.4102ajhrm.v11i1.319

Luhmann, N., & Schorr, K. E. (1999). *Il sistema educativo. Problemi di riflessività*. Armando Editore.

Malfanti, F. (2005). Il ruolo dell'analista di Intelligence. *Intelligrate*. Available in: https://intelligrate.it/downloads/IntelligenceAnalyst.pdf

Massa, A. (2015). OSINT e Cyber intelligence: tecniche di investigazione nella rete. *Sicurezza e Giustizia, 3*. Available in: https://www.sicurezzaegiustizia.com/numero-iii-del-mmxv/

Mayer, E., Lee, H., & Peebles, A. (2014). Multimedia Learning in a Second Language: A Cognitive Load Perspective. *Applied Cognitive Psychology*, *28*(5), 653–660. doi:10.1002/acp.3050

McCormick, J. (2001). *Environmental Policy in the European Union*. Basingstoke, UK: Palgrave. doi:10.1007/978-0-333-98557-1

Meadows, D., Randers, J., & Meadows, D. (2004). Limits to Growth, The 30-Year Update. White River Junction, VT: Chelsea Green.

Mehta, M., Kurbetti, A., & Dhankhar, R. (2014). Review paper–study on employee retention and commitment. *International Journal of Advance Research in Computer Science and Management Studies*, *154*(5), 154–164.

Meredith, M. (2014). *The Value of Knowing What You Don't Know You Don't Know*. Retrieved July 2018, from https://www.umbel.com/blog/services/know-what-you-dont-know/

Midoro, V. (2013). Insegnanti per la scuola nell'era digitale. In D. Persico & V. Midoro (Eds.), Pedagogia nell'era digitale (pp. 118–124). Academic Press.

Midoro, V. (2015). Dalle tecnologie didattiche ad una pedagogia digitale. *TD Tecnologie Didattiche*, *23*(1), 59–63.

Ministero dell'Ambiente Italiano. (n.d.a). *Educazione ambientale e sviluppo sostenibile.* Retrieved from http://www.minambiente.it/pagina/educazione-ambientale-e-allo-sviluppo-sostenibile

Ministero dell'Ambiente Italiano. (n.d.b). *Da Stati Genereali una carta per l'educazione Green.* Retrieved from http://www.minambiente.it/comunicati/da-stati-generali-una-carta-leducazione-green

Ministero dell'Ambiente Italiano. (n.d.c). *Linee guida per l'educazione ambientale.* Retrieved from http://www.minambiente.it/sites/default/files/archivio/allegati/LINEE_GUIDA.pdf

Mitchell, T. M. (1997). *Machine Learning*. McGraw-Hill Science/Engineering/Math.

Morecroft, J. D. W., & Sterman, J. D. (1994). *Modelling For Learning Organizations*. Portland, OR: Productivity Press.

Mtila, J., Barkhuizen, E. N., & Mokgele, R. (2013). *Exploring the Application of Talent Management Practices in a Local Government Institution*. Paper presented at the 30th Pan Pacific Business Association Conference, Johannesburg, South Africa.

Murongazvombo, P. K. (2015). *Talent retention strategies in a competitive ICT industry: case of twenty third century systems global.* Harare: BUSE.

Mustafa, Ö., Papadopoulou, T. C., & Melek, A. (2007). System Dynamics Modelling of A Manufacturing Supply Chain System. *Simulation Modelling Practice and Theory*, *15*(10), 1338–1355. doi:10.1016/j.simpat.2007.09.007

Myres, H. (2014). *Factors in South Africa inhibiting the progression of black executives in their careers and the role of coaching in their development*. Johannesburg: Wits Business School.

National Research Council. (2005). *The Owner's Role in Project Risk Management*. The National Academies Press.

OECD. (2015). *Students, Computers and Learning*. OECD Publishing.

Olimpo, G. (1993). Nascita e sviluppi delle tecnologie didattiche. Italian Journal of Educational Technology, 1(1).

Olivetti M20. (n.d.). In *Wikipedia*. Retrieved from https://it.wikipedia.org/wiki/Olivetti_M20

Osibanjo, A. O., Salau, O. P., & Falola, H. O. (2014). Modelling the relationship between motivating factors; employee's retention; and job satisfaction in the Nigerian banking industry. *Journal of Management Policies and Practices*, *2*(2), 63–83.

Palladino, T. (2018). *Apple's Education-Focused iPad Event Pushes Augmented Reality Further into the Classroom*. Retrieved from: https://next.reality.news/news/apples-education-focused-ipad-event-pushes-augmented-reality-further-into-classroom-0183762/

Palmer, J. A. (1998). *Environmental Education in the 21st Century: Theory, Practice, Progress and Promise*. London: Routledge.

Papert, S. (1980). *Mindstorms: Children, Computers, and Powerful Ideas*. New York: Basic Books.

Parshley, L. (2018, May). Catching Fever. *Scientific American*, *318*(5), 58–65. doi:10.1038cientificamerican0518-58 PMID:29672493

Patrignani, N. (2015). Slow tech: Per un'informatica buona, pulita e giusta. In *Mondo Digitale*. AICA House Organ.

PC. (n.d.). In *Wikipedia*. Retrieved from https://it.wikipedia.org/wiki/PC_IBM

Pernicone, N. (1993). *Italian Anarchism, 1864-1892*. Princeton University Press.

Phythian, M. (2013). *Understanding the intelligence cycle*. Routledge. doi:10.4324/9780203558478

Piney, C. (2003). *Risk Identification: Combining the Tools to Deliver the Goods*. Paper presented at PMI® Global Congress 2003—EMEA, The Hague, South Holland, The Netherlands.

Pinker, S. (2011). The Better Angles of Our Nature. New York: Viking.

Pinker, S. (2018). Enlightenment NOW. New York: Viking.

Pollari, N. (2001). Ipotesi di lavoro per l'intelligence economica: strutture organizzative e moduli operativi. *Sisde*. Available in: http://www.sisde.it

Pollino Tour. (2017). *School of training for politicians* [Scuola di formazione per i politici del future]. Pollino Tour. Retrieved from: http://www.pollinotour.com/2017/05/03/scuola-di-formazione-per-i-politici-del-futuro/

Polson, N., & Scott, J. (2018). *AIQ, How People and Machines are Smarter Together*. New York: St. Martin's Press.

Population Division, United Nations. (2018). *United Nations, World Population Prospects 2017, Probabilistic Projections, Population, Total Population, World. Graph*. Retrieved from: https://esa.un.org/unpd/wpp/Graphs/Probabilistic/POP/TOT/

Pozzoli, C. (1986). Preface. In *Come scrivere una tesi di laurea con il personal computer*. Rizzoli.

Pratihar, D. K., & Jain, L. C. (2010). Toward Intelligent Autonomous Systems. In D. K. Pratihar & L. C. Jain (Eds.), *Intelligent Autonomous Systems: Foundations and Applications* (p. 1). Springer-Verlag Berlin Heideberg. doi:10.1007/978-3-642-11676-6_1

Pratt, M. K. (2017). *Why IT Projects Still Fail.* Retrieved July 2018, from https://www.cio.com.au/article/625522/why-it-projects-still-fail/

Prensky, M. (2001a). Digital Natives, Digital Immigrants. On the Horizon, 9(5), 1-6.

Prensky, M. (2001b). Digital Natives, Digital Immigrants, part 2: Do they really think differently? *On the Horizon*, *9*(6), 1–6. doi:10.1108/10748120110424843

Prensky, M. (2010). *Teaching Digital Natives: Partnering for Real Learning*. London: Sage Publishers.

Project Management Institute. (2017). *A Guide to the Project Management Body of Knowledge (PMBOK® Guide)*. Project Management Institute.

Provincia di Bolzano Italia. (n.d.). *Educazione Ambientale.* Retrieved from http://www.provincia.bz.it/intendenza-scolastica/download/Evoluzione__Ed_Ambientale.pdf

Puentedura, R. (2014). SAMR and Bloom's Taxonomy: Assembling the Puzzle. Retrieved from https://www.graphite.org/blog/samr-and-blooms-taxonomy-assembling-the-puzzle

Puong, F. Y. (2015). The Case for Using Robots in Intelligence Analysis. *Studies in Intelligence, 59*(4). Available in: https://www.cia.gov/library/center-for-the-study-of-intelligence/csi-publications/csi-studies/studies/vol-59-no-4/pdfs/Yeh-Automated-Analysis.pdf

Ramage, M., & Ship, K. (2009). *Sytem Thinkers, The Open University Walton Hall*. Milton Keynes, UK: Springer London.

Rebovich, G. Jr. (2014). *Systems Engineering Guide*. The MITRE Corporation.

Reese, H. (2016). *Top 10 AI failures of 2016*. Retrieved July 2018, from https://www.techrepublic.com/article/top-10-ai-failures-of-2016/

Reza, H., Amineh, G., & Virginia, D. (2014). Using Diference Equation to Model Discrete-time Behavior in System Dynamics Modeling. In *32nd International Conference of the System Dynamics Society*, Delft, The Netherlands.

Richardson George, P. (1999). *Feedback Throught in Social Science And Systems Theory*. Waltham, MA: Pegasus Communications, Inc.

Richmond, B. (2010). The Thinking In Systems Thinking: Eight Critical Skills. In Tracing Connections: Voices Of Systems Thinkers. Lebanon, NH: Creative Learning Exchange.

Riley, T. (2017, January 30). *The Big Moon Dig, Stories*. Retrieved from http://bigmoondig.com/Stories/BMDStories.html

Riley, T. (2017, January 30). *The Big Moon Dig*. Retrieved from http://bigmoondig.com/BigMoonDig.html

Roman, L. J., & Mason, R. B. (2015). Employment equity in the South African retail sector: Legal versus competence and business imperatives. *South African Journal of Labour Relations*, *39*(2), 84–104.

Rosling, H. (2018). *Factfulness*. New York: Flatiron Books.

Rovner, J. (2015). *Fixing the Facts: National Security and the Politics of Intelligence*. Cornell Studies in Security Affairs.

Rusk, N., Resnick, M., Berg, R., & Pezalla-Granlund, M. (2008). New pathways into robotics: Strategies for broadening participation. *Journal of Science Education and Technology*, *17*(1), 59–69. doi:10.100710956-007-9082-2

Ruth, M., & Hannon, B. (2012). *Modeling Dynamic Economic Systems* (2nd ed.). Springer. doi:10.1007/978-1-4614-2209-9

Ryan, C. (2015, October 1). Recruitment is a tough gig these days. Finweek, 28 - 30.

Satell, G. (2018). How to Make an AI Project More Likely to Succeed. *Harvard Business Review*, (July): 2018.

Schöer, V., Rankin, N., & Roberts, G. (2014). Accessing the first job in a slack labour market: Job matching in South Africa. *Journal of International Development*, *26*(1), 1–22. doi:10.1002/jid.2838

Schuler, R. S., Jackson, S. E., & Tarique, I. (2011). Global talent management and global talent challenges: Strategic opportunities for IHRM. *Journal of World Business*, *46*(4), 506–516. doi:10.1016/j.jwb.2010.10.011

Schutte, N., & Barkhuizen, N. (2014). Creating public service excellence applying learning organisation methods: The role of strategic leadership. *Mediterranean Journal of Social Sciences*, *5*(4), 159.

Selves, M. D. (2007). *The politics of disaster*. FEMA.

Sengupta, A., Venkatesh, D., & Sinha, A. (2013). Developing performance-linked competency model: A tool for competitive advantage. *The International Journal of Organizational Analysis*, *21*(4), 504–527. doi:10.1108/IJOA-05-2011-0488

Sezen, H. K., & Günal, M. (2009). *Yöneylem Araştırmasında Benzetim*. Bursa: Ekin Yayınevi.

Sharkansky, I. (1995). Policy analysis in historical perspective. *Journal of Management History*, *1*(1), 47-58. doi:10.1108/13552529510082822

Shulsky, A. N., & Schmitt, G. J. (2002). *Silent Warfare: understanding the world of intelligence* (3rd ed.). Dulles, VA: Brassey's Inc.

Sida. (n.d.). *The managerial formation of politicians: the comparison with others* [La formazione manageriale dei politici: il confronto con gli altri]. Sida Management Academy. Retrieved from http://mastersida.com/57301/

Sidani, Y., & Al Ariss, A. (2014). Institutional and corporate drivers of global talent management: Evidence from the Arab Gulf region. *Journal of World Business*, *49*(2), 215–224. doi:10.1016/j.jwb.2013.11.005

Sikdar, P. (2017). *Practitioner's Guide to Business Impact Analysis*. Auerbach Publications. doi:10.1201/9781315187884

Simonite, T. (2017, January). AI Software Learns to Make AI Software: Google and Others Think Software that Learns to Learn Could Take Over Some Work Done by AI Experts. *MIT Technology Review*.

Sims, D. M. (2014). 5 Ways to increase success in succession planning. *TD: Talent Development*, *68*(8), 60.

SingularityHub. (2017, January 18). Retrieved from https://singularityhub.com/

Sinkin, J., & Putney, T. (2014). How to manage internal succession. *Journal of Accountancy*, *217*(2), 1–5.

Skinner, B. F. (1954). The science of learning and the art of teaching. *Harvard Educational Review*, *24*.

Smith, A., & Anderson, J. (2014). *AI, Robotics, and the Future of Jobs*. Retrieved from http://www.pewinternet.org/2014/08/06/future-of-jobs/

Smith, W., & Gough, A. (2015). Deep Ecology as a framework for student eco-philosophical thinking. *Journal of Philosophy in Schools*, *2*(1), 38–55. doi:10.21913/JPS.v2i1.1101

Snelgar, R. J., Renard, M., & Venter, D. (2013). An Empirical Study of the Reward Preferences of South African Employees. *SA Journal of Human Resource Management*, *11*(1), 1. doi:10.4102ajhrm.v11i1.351

Soderquist, C., & Overakkers, S. (2010). Education for Sustainable Development: A Systems Thinking Approach. *Global Environmental Research*, *14*, 193–202.

Sommerville, I. (2015). *Software Engineering*. Pearson.

Source: Epson HX20. (n.d.). In *Wikipedia*. Retrieved from http://oldcomputers.net/hx-20.html

Sourour, B. (2016). *The code I'm still afraid of.* Available in: https://medium.freecodecamp.org/the-code-im-still-ashamed-of-e4c021dff55e

Standards Australia. (2009). *Australian/New Zealand Risk Management Standard: AS/NZS ISO 31000: 2009*. Author.

Stapp, W. B. (1969). The Concept of Environmental Education. *The Journal of Environmental Education*, *1*(1), 30–31. doi:10.1080/00139254.1969.10801479

Sterman, J. D. (1991). *A Skeptic's Guide to Computer Models*. Cambridge, MA: MIT System Dynamics In Education Project.

Sterman, J. D. (2000). Business Dynamics Systems Thinking And Modelling. In *A Complex World*. New York: McGraw-Hill.

Stromberg, D. (2007). *Natural Disaster, Economic Development and Humanitarian Aid*. American Economic Association.

Technologies for Education. (n.d.). *Storia dello sviluppo delle tecnologie didattiche*. Retrieved from: https://sites.google.com/site/tecnologieperleducazione/storia-dello-sviluppo-delle-tecnologie-didattiche

Tegmark, M. (2017). Life 3.0, Being Human in the Age of Artificial Intelligence. New York: Alfred A Knopf.

The Aalborg Charter. (1994). Retrieved from http://www.sustainablecities.eu/the-aalborg-charter/

The Belgrade Charter. (1972). Retrieved from https://www.gdrc.org/uem/ee/belgrade.html

The Disruptory. (2016). *Robots in Education: Why? What? How? And What For?* Retrieved from: https://www.thedisruptory.com/2016/11/robots-in-education/

The Intelligence Cycle. (n.d.). Retrieved from https://www.cia.gov/kids-page/6-12th-grade/who-we-are-what-we-do/the-intelligence-cycle.html

Theron, M., Barkhuizen, N., & du Plessis, Y. (2014). Managing the academic talent void: Investigating factors in academic turnover and retention in South Africa. *SA Journal of Industrial Psychology*, *40*(1), 1–14. doi:10.4102ajip.v40i1.1117

Tishman, F., Van Looy, S., & Bruyère, S. (2014). *Employer strategies for responding to an aging workforce*. The NTAR Leadership Center.

Tonellotto, M. (2014). Evidenza informatica, computer forensics and best practices. Rivista di Criminologia, Vittimologia e Sicurezza, 8(2).

Toulson, P. K. (2016). Recruitment and talent management. *Human Resources Magazine*, *21*(2), 34–35.

Towil, D. R. (1996). Industrial Dynamics Modelling of Supply Chains. *Logistic Information Management, 9*(4), 43-56.

Toyota. (2016). *Toyota human resources management guiding document.* Human Resources, Durban. Toyota.

Toyota. (2017). *Toyota HR OD&TM overview_v5 document.* Human Resources, Durban. Toyota.

Treverton, G. F., Jones, S. G., Boraz, S., & Lipscy, P. (2006). *Toward a Theory of Intelligence Workshop Report.* National Security Research Division, U.S. Department of Defense. Available in: https://www.rand.org/content/dam/rand/pubs/conf_proceedings/2006/RAND_CF219.pdf

U.N. Environment Programme (UNEP). (1977). *Tbilisi Declaration.* Retrieved from https://www.gdrc.org/ucm/ee/tbilisi.html

UNESCO. (1971). *Final Report: Man and Biosphere Programme.* Retrieved from http://www.unesco.org/new/en/natural-sciences/environment/ecological-sciences/

UNESCO. (1997). *Educating for a Sustainable Future.* Retrieved from http://unesdoc.unesco.org/images/0011/001106/110686eo.pdf

UNESCO. (2011). *Guidelines for Open Educational Resources (OER) in Higher Education.* Retrieved from http://unesdoc.unesco.org/ images/0021/ 002136/213605e.pdf

UNESCO. (n.d.). *Teaching And Learning For A Sustainable Future.* Retrieved from http://www.unesco.org/education/tlsf/

UNESCO-UNEP International Congress On Environmental Education And Training. (1987). *Report.* Retrieved from http://unesdoc.unesco.org/images/0007/000750/075072Eo.pdf

UNESCO-UNEP. (1978). Final Report: Intergovernmental Conference on Environmental Education. *Environmental Education Newsletter, 3*(1), 1-8. Retrieved from http://unesdoc.unesco.org/images/0015/001563/156393eb.pdf

United Nations Conference. (1972). *Human Environment.* Retrieved from https://en.wikipedia.org/wiki/United_Nations_Conference_on_the_Human_Environment

Utopia Compression. (n.d.). *Medical technology. Online Cognitive tutors.* Retrieved from: http://www.utopiacompression.com/technologies/neuro_imaging_augmented_cognitive_models.php

Vajola, P. (2013). Risks and opportunities of digital technologies in the school. Reflections about planning the teacher's training. *Form@re*. Retrieved from: http://www.fupress.net/index.php/formare/article/download/18196/17323

van den Berg, B., & de Bos, T. (2014). *On (the emergence of) cyber security science and its challenges for cyber security education*. Tallin: NATO.

van den Berg, B., & Keymolen, E. L. O. (2017). Regulating security on the Internet: Control versus trust. *International Review of Law Computers & Technology*, *31*(2), 188–205. doi:10.1080/13600869.2017.1298504

Veen, W. (2008). The Role of Beliefs in the Use of Information Technology: implications for teacher education, or teaching the right thing at the right time. Journal of Information Technology for Teacher Education, 2(2).

Velásquez Hurtado, L. A. (2016). *Colombia and the intelligence cycle in the 21st century, the digital age* (Master's Thesis). Institute of Computer Science, University of Tartu. Available in: https://comserv.cs.ut.ee/home/files/Velasquez+Hurtado+CyberSecurity+2016.pdf?study=ATILoputoo&reference=0F5176FB1F90355934306790E8C049BBCD9E422E

Velez Rolon, A. (2010). *La educación ambiental como herramienta de participación para la sosteniblidad local*. Available in: https://www.ecoportal.net/?s=Velez+Rolon+A

Verner, J., Sampson, J., & Cerpa, N. (2008). What Factors Lead to Software Project Failure? In *Proceedings of Second International Conference on Research Challenges in Information Science* (pp. 71-80). IEEE Xplore. 10.1109/RCIS.2008.4632095

Victor, T., & Samutra, V. (2001). *System Dynamics Origins, Development And Future Prospects of a Method*. Research Seminar in Engineering Systems.

Vincent, J. (2017). *Putin Says the Nation that Leads in AI 'Will be the Ruler of the World'*. Retrieved July 2018, from https://www.theverge.com/2017/9/4/16251226/russia-ai-putin-rule-the-world

Vitali, G. (2010). *La politica per l'ambiente nell'Unione Europea*. Istituto di Ricerca sull'Impresa e lo Sviluppo. Available in: http://www2.ceris.cnr.it/homedipendenti/vitali/dispense2010_11_PE/politica%20ambientale%20corso%20pol%20eco%2006%2012%202010.pdf

Walker, L. J. (2013). The Reframing of succession strategies. *Journal of Financial Planning*, *26*(8), 37–39.

Wang, S., & Remlinger, B. (2017). Can math stop partisan gerrymandering? *The Los Angeles Times*. Retrieved from: http://www.latimes.com/opinion/op-ed/la-oe-wang-remlinger-gerrymandering-20170505-story.html

Wenger, E. (1998). *Communities of practice: learning, meaning, and identity*. New York: Cambridge University Press. doi:10.1017/CBO9780511803932

Wheeler Frederick, P. (1994). How to Get Managers To Use System Dynamics. In *International System Dynamics Conference*, Stirling, UK.

Wilson, E. O. (2012). *The Social Conquest of Earth*. New York: Liveright Publishing.

Wilson, E. O. (2016). *Half-Earth*. New York: Liveright Publishing.

Wilton, N. (2011). *An introduction to human resource management*. London: Sage Publications.

Winston, A. S. (2014). *The Big Pivot*. Boston: Harvard Business.

World Commission On Environment And Development. (1987). *Brundtland Report*. Retrieved from https://www.britannica.com/topic/Brundtland-Report

World Population. (n.d.). In *Wikipedia*. Retrieved April 2018 from: https://en.wikipedia.org/wiki/World_population

World Summit On Sustainable Development. (2002). *Improve Lives While Preserving Earth's Resources*. Retrieved from http://www.un.org/events/wssd/summaries/envdevj1.htm

Ximba, T. M. (2016). *Career advancement challenges facing people with disabilities in South Africa*. Durban: University of South Africa.

Yamaguchi, K. (2013). *Money and Macroeconomic Dynamics- Accounting System Dynamics Approach*. Awaji Island, Japan: Japan Future Research Center.

Young, M., & Conboy, K. (2013). Contemporary project portfolio management. Reflections on the development of an Australian Competency Standard for Project Portfolio Management. *International Journal of Project Management, 31*(8), 1089–1100. doi:10.1016/j.ijproman.2013.03.005

Zehra, B. (1997). *Sistem Dinamiğinin İşletmelerde Uygulanması*. Bursa: Ekin Kitabevi Yayınları.

Zerega, B. (2017). *AI Weekly: Google Shifts from Mobile-First to AI-First World*. Retrieved July 2018, from https://venturebeat.com/2017/05/18/ai-weekly-google-shifts-from-mobile-first-to-ai-first-world/

Related References

To continue our tradition of advancing information science and technology research, we have compiled a list of recommended IGI Global readings. These references will provide additional information and guidance to further enrich your knowledge and assist you with your own research and future publications.

Abu Seman, S. A., & Ramayah, T. (2017). Are We Ready to App?: A Study on mHealth Apps, Its Future, and Trends in Malaysia Context. In J. Pelet (Ed.), *Mobile Platforms, Design, and Apps for Social Commerce* (pp. 69–83). Hershey, PA: IGI Global. doi:10.4018/978-1-5225-2469-4.ch005

Aggarwal, S., & Azad, V. (2017). A Hybrid System Based on FMM and MLP to Diagnose Heart Disease. In S. Bhattacharyya, S. De, I. Pan, & P. Dutta (Eds.), *Intelligent Multidimensional Data Clustering and Analysis* (pp. 293–325). Hershey, PA: IGI Global. doi:10.4018/978-1-5225-1776-4.ch011

Akaichi, J., & Mhadhbi, L. (2016). A Clinical Decision Support System: Ontology-Driven Approach for Effective Emergency Management. In J. Moon & M. Galea (Eds.), *Improving Health Management through Clinical Decision Support Systems* (pp. 270–294). Hershey, PA: IGI Global. doi:10.4018/978-1-4666-9432-3.ch013

Akerkar, R. (2016). Towards an Intelligent Integrated Approach for Clinical Decision Support. In A. Aggarwal (Ed.), *Managing Big Data Integration in the Public Sector* (pp. 187–205). Hershey, PA: IGI Global. doi:10.4018/978-1-4666-9649-5.ch011

Al-Busaidi, S. S. (2018). Interdisciplinary Relationships Between Medicine and Social Sciences. In M. Al-Suqri, A. Al-Kindi, S. AlKindi, & N. Saleem (Eds.), *Promoting Interdisciplinarity in Knowledge Generation and Problem Solving* (pp. 124–137). Hershey, PA: IGI Global. doi:10.4018/978-1-5225-3878-3.ch009

Al Kareh, T., & Thoumy, M. (2018). The Impact of Health Information Digitization on the Physiotherapist-Patient Relationship: A Pilot Study of the Lebanese Community. *International Journal of Healthcare Information Systems and Informatics, 13*(2), 29–53. doi:10.4018/IJHISI.2018040103

Alenzuela, R. (2017). Research, Leadership, and Resource-Sharing Initiatives: The Role of Local Library Consortia in Access to Medical Information. In S. Ram (Ed.), *Library and Information Services for Bioinformatics Education and Research* (pp. 199–211). Hershey, PA: IGI Global. doi:10.4018/978-1-5225-1871-6.ch012

Ameri, H., Alizadeh, S., & Noughabi, E. A. (2017). Application of Data Mining Techniques in Clinical Decision Making: A Literature Review and Classification. In E. Noughabi, B. Raahemi, A. Albadvi, & B. Far (Eds.), *Handbook of Research on Data Science for Effective Healthcare Practice and Administration* (pp. 257–295). Hershey, PA: IGI Global. doi:10.4018/978-1-5225-2515-8.ch012

Anand, S. (2017). Medical Image Enhancement Using Edge Information-Based Methods. In B. Singh (Ed.), *Computational Tools and Techniques for Biomedical Signal Processing* (pp. 123–148). Hershey, PA: IGI Global. doi:10.4018/978-1-5225-0660-7.ch006

Angjellari-Dajci, F., Sapienza, C., Lawless, W. F., & Kavanagh, K. (2016). Human Capital Accumulation in Medical Simulated Learning Environments: A Framework for Economic Evaluation. In M. Russ (Ed.), *Quantitative Multidisciplinary Approaches in Human Capital and Asset Management* (pp. 65–88). Hershey, PA: IGI Global. doi:10.4018/978-1-4666-9652-5.ch004

Anil, M., Ayyildiz-Tamis, D., Tasdemir, S., Sendemir-Urkmez, A., & Gulce-Iz, S. (2016). Bioinspired Materials and Biocompatibility. In M. Bououdina (Ed.), *Emerging Research on Bioinspired Materials Engineering* (pp. 294–322). Hershey, PA: IGI Global. doi:10.4018/978-1-4666-9811-6.ch011

Anton, J. L., Soriano, J. V., Martinez, M. I., & Garcia, F. B. (2018). Comprehensive E-Learning Appraisal System. In M. Khosrow-Pour, D.B.A. (Ed.), Encyclopedia of Information Science and Technology, Fourth Edition (pp. 5787-5799). Hershey, PA: IGI Global. doi:10.4018/978-1-5225-2255-3.ch503

Arabi, M. (2016). Redesigning the Organizational Structure to Reach Efficiency: The Case of Ministry of Health and Medical Education of Iran. In R. Gholipour & K. Rouzbehani (Eds.), *Social, Economic, and Political Perspectives on Public Health Policy-Making* (pp. 257–294). Hershey, PA: IGI Global. doi:10.4018/978-1-4666-9944-1.ch012

Assis-Hassid, S., Heart, T., Reychav, I., & Pliskin, J. S. (2016). Modelling Factors Affecting Patient-Doctor-Computer Communication in Primary Care. *International Journal of Reliable and Quality E-Healthcare, 5*(1), 1–17. doi:10.4018/IJRQEH.2016010101

Atzori, B., Hoffman, H. G., Vagnoli, L., Messeri, A., & Grotto, R. L. (2018). Virtual Reality as Distraction Technique for Pain Management in Children and Adolescents. In M. Khosrow-Pour, D.B.A. (Ed.), Encyclopedia of Information Science and Technology, Fourth Edition (pp. 5955-5965). Hershey, PA: IGI Global. doi:10.4018/978-1-5225-2255-3.ch518

Audibert, M., Mathonnat, J., Pélissier, A., & Huang, X. X. (2018). The Impact of the New Rural Cooperative Medical Scheme on Township Hospitals' Utilization and Income Structure in Weifang Prefecture, China. In I. Management Association (Ed.), Health Economics and Healthcare Reform: Breakthroughs in Research and Practice (pp. 109-121). Hershey, PA: IGI Global. doi:10.4018/978-1-5225-3168-5.ch007

Ayyachamy, S. (2016). Analysis and Comparison of Developed 2D Medical Image Database Design using Registration Scheme, Retrieval Scheme, and Bag-of-Visual-Words. In N. Dey & A. Ashour (Eds.), *Classification and Clustering in Biomedical Signal Processing* (pp. 149–168). Hershey, PA: IGI Global. doi:10.4018/978-1-5225-0140-4.ch007

Babalola, A. C. (2016). Literacy and Decision Making on Health Issues among Married Women in Southwest Nigeria. In V. Wang (Ed.), *Handbook of Research on Advancing Health Education through Technology* (pp. 191–212). Hershey, PA: IGI Global. doi:10.4018/978-1-4666-9494-1.ch009

Babu, A., & Ayyappan, S. (2017). A Methodological Evaluation of Crypto-Watermarking System for Medical Images. In C. Bhatt & S. Peddoju (Eds.), *Cloud Computing Systems and Applications in Healthcare* (pp. 189–217). Hershey, PA: IGI Global. doi:10.4018/978-1-5225-1002-4.ch010

Bakke, A. (2017). Ethos in E-Health: From Informational to Interactive Websites. In M. Folk & S. Apostel (Eds.), *Establishing and Evaluating Digital Ethos and Online Credibility* (pp. 85–103). Hershey, PA: IGI Global. doi:10.4018/978-1-5225-1072-7.ch005

Bali, S. (2018). Enhancing the Reach of Health Care Through Telemedicine: Status and New Possibilities in Developing Countries. In U. Pandey & V. Indrakanti (Eds.), *Open and Distance Learning Initiatives for Sustainable Development* (pp. 339–354). Hershey, PA: IGI Global. doi:10.4018/978-1-5225-2621-6.ch019

Barrett, T. E. (2018). Essentials for Education and Training for Tomorrow's Physicians. In C. Smith (Ed.), *Exploring the Pressures of Medical Education From a Mental Health and Wellness Perspective* (pp. 230–252). Hershey, PA: IGI Global. doi:10.4018/978-1-5225-2811-1.ch010

Barrett, T. J. (2016). Knowledge in Action: Fostering Health Education through Technology. In V. Wang (Ed.), *Handbook of Research on Advancing Health Education through Technology* (pp. 39–62). Hershey, PA: IGI Global. doi:10.4018/978-1-4666-9494-1.ch003

Berrahal, S., & Boudriga, N. (2017). The Risks of Wearable Technologies to Individuals and Organizations. In A. Marrington, D. Kerr, & J. Gammack (Eds.), *Managing Security Issues and the Hidden Dangers of Wearable Technologies* (pp. 18–46). Hershey, PA: IGI Global. doi:10.4018/978-1-5225-1016-1.ch002

Bhagat, A. P., & Atique, M. (2016). Medical Image Mining Using Fuzzy Connectedness Image Segmentation: Efficient Retrieval of Patients' Stored Images. In W. Karâa & N. Dey (Eds.), *Biomedical Image Analysis and Mining Techniques for Improved Health Outcomes* (pp. 184–209). Hershey, PA: IGI Global. doi:10.4018/978-1-4666-8811-7.ch009

Bhargava, P. (2018). Blended Learning: An Effective Application to Clinical Teaching. In S. Tang & C. Lim (Eds.), *Preparing the Next Generation of Teachers for 21st Century Education* (pp. 302–320). Hershey, PA: IGI Global. doi:10.4018/978-1-5225-4080-9.ch018

Binh, N. T., & Tuyet, V. T. (2016). The Combination of Adaptive Filters to Improve the Quality of Medical Images in New Wavelet Domain. In N. Dey & A. Ashour (Eds.), *Classification and Clustering in Biomedical Signal Processing* (pp. 46–76). Hershey, PA: IGI Global. doi:10.4018/978-1-5225-0140-4.ch003

Bird, J. L. (2017). Writing Healing Narratives. In V. Bryan & J. Bird (Eds.), *Healthcare Community Synergism between Patients, Practitioners, and Researchers* (pp. 1–28). Hershey, PA: IGI Global. doi:10.4018/978-1-5225-0640-9.ch001

Bottrighi, A., Leonardi, G., Piovesan, L., & Terenziani, P. (2016). Knowledge-Based Support to the Treatment of Exceptions in Computer Interpretable Clinical Guidelines. *International Journal of Knowledge-Based Organizations*, *6*(3), 1–27. doi:10.4018/IJKBO.2016070101

Bougoulias, K., Kouris, I., Prasinos, M., Giokas, K., & Koutsouris, D. (2017). Ob/Gyn EMR Software: A Solution for Obstetricians and Gynecologists. In A. Moumtzoglou (Ed.), *Design, Development, and Integration of Reliable Electronic Healthcare Platforms* (pp. 101–111). Hershey, PA: IGI Global. doi:10.4018/978-1-5225-1724-5.ch006

Bouslimi, R., Ayadi, M. G., & Akaichi, J. (2018). Medical Image Retrieval in Healthcare Social Networks. *International Journal of Healthcare Information Systems and Informatics*, *13*(2), 13–28. doi:10.4018/IJHISI.2018040102

Bouzaabia, O., Bouzaabia, R., & Mejri, K. (2017). Role of Internet in the Development of Medical Tourism Service in Tunisia. In A. Capatina & E. Rancati (Eds.), *Key Challenges and Opportunities in Web Entrepreneurship* (pp. 211–241). Hershey, PA: IGI Global. doi:10.4018/978-1-5225-2466-3.ch009

Briz-Ponce, L., Juanes-Méndez, J. A., & García-Peñalvo, F. J. (2016). The Role of Gender in Technology Acceptance for Medical Education. In M. Cruz-Cunha, I. Miranda, R. Martinho, & R. Rijo (Eds.), *Encyclopedia of E-Health and Telemedicine* (pp. 1013–1027). Hershey, PA: IGI Global. doi:10.4018/978-1-4666-9978-6.ch079

Briz-Ponce, L., Juanes-Méndez, J. A., & García-Peñalvo, F. J. (2016). A Research Contribution to the Analysis of Mobile Devices in Higher Education from Medical Students' Point of View. In L. Briz-Ponce, J. Juanes-Méndez, & F. García-Peñalvo (Eds.), *Handbook of Research on Mobile Devices and Applications in Higher Education Settings* (pp. 196–221). Hershey, PA: IGI Global. doi:10.4018/978-1-5225-0256-2.ch009

Brown-Jackson, K. L. (2018). Telemedicine and Telehealth: Academics Engaging the Community in a Call to Action. In S. Burton (Ed.), *Engaged Scholarship and Civic Responsibility in Higher Education* (pp. 166–193). Hershey, PA: IGI Global. doi:10.4018/978-1-5225-3649-9.ch008

Bwalya, K. J. (2017). Next Wave of Tele-Medicine: Virtual Presence of Medical Personnel. In K. Moahi, K. Bwalya, & P. Sebina (Eds.), *Health Information Systems and the Advancement of Medical Practice in Developing Countries* (pp. 168–180). Hershey, PA: IGI Global. doi:10.4018/978-1-5225-2262-1.ch010

Carlton, E. L., Holsinger, J. W. Jr, & Anunobi, N. (2016). Physician Engagement with Health Information Technology: Implications for Practice and Professionalism. *International Journal of Computers in Clinical Practice*, *1*(2), 51–73. doi:10.4018/IJCCP.2016070103

Castillo-Page, L., Eliason, J., Conrad, S. S., & Nivet, M. A. (2016). Diversity in Undergraduate Medical Education: An Examination of Organizational Culture and Climate in Medical Schools. In C. Scott & J. Sims (Eds.), *Developing Workforce Diversity Programs, Curriculum, and Degrees in Higher Education* (pp. 304–326). Hershey, PA: IGI Global. doi:10.4018/978-1-5225-0209-8.ch016

Cebeci, H. I., & Hiziroglu, A. (2016). Review of Business Intelligence and Intelligent Systems in Healthcare Domain. In N. Celebi (Ed.), *Intelligent Techniques for Data Analysis in Diverse Settings* (pp. 192–206). Hershey, PA: IGI Global. doi:10.4018/978-1-5225-0075-9.ch009

Celik, G. (2018). Determining Headache Diseases With Genetic Algorithm. In U. Kose, G. Guraksin, & O. Deperlioglu (Eds.), *Nature-Inspired Intelligent Techniques for Solving Biomedical Engineering Problems* (pp. 249–262). Hershey, PA: IGI Global. doi:10.4018/978-1-5225-4769-3.ch012

Chakraborty, C., Gupta, B., & Ghosh, S. K. (2016). Mobile Telemedicine Systems for Remote Patient's Chronic Wound Monitoring. In A. Moumtzoglou (Ed.), *M-Health Innovations for Patient-Centered Care* (pp. 213–239). Hershey, PA: IGI Global. doi:10.4018/978-1-4666-9861-1.ch011

Chakraborty, S., Chatterjee, S., Ashour, A. S., Mali, K., & Dey, N. (2018). Intelligent Computing in Medical Imaging: A Study. In N. Dey (Ed.), *Advancements in Applied Metaheuristic Computing* (pp. 143–163). Hershey, PA: IGI Global. doi:10.4018/978-1-5225-4151-6.ch006

Chavez, A., & Kovarik, C. (2017). Open Source Technology for Medical Practice in Developing Countries. In K. Moahi, K. Bwalya, & P. Sebina (Eds.), *Health Information Systems and the Advancement of Medical Practice in Developing Countries* (pp. 33–59). Hershey, PA: IGI Global. doi:10.4018/978-1-5225-2262-1.ch003

Chen, E. T. (2016). Examining the Influence of Information Technology on Modern Health Care. In P. Manolitzas, E. Grigoroudis, N. Matsatsinis, & D. Yannacopoulos (Eds.), *Effective Methods for Modern Healthcare Service Quality and Evaluation* (pp. 110–136). Hershey, PA: IGI Global. doi:10.4018/978-1-4666-9961-8.ch006

Chin, S. (2016). Surviving Sandy: Recovering Collections after a Natural Disaster. In E. Decker & J. Townes (Eds.), *Handbook of Research on Disaster Management and Contingency Planning in Modern Libraries* (pp. 366–388). Hershey, PA: IGI Global. doi:10.4018/978-1-4666-8624-3.ch016

Chojnacki, M., & Wójcik, A. (2016). Security and the Role of New Technologies and Innovation in Medical Ethics. In A. Rosiek & K. Leksowski (Eds.), *Organizational Culture and Ethics in Modern Medicine* (pp. 52–77). Hershey, PA: IGI Global. doi:10.4018/978-1-4666-9658-7.ch003

Cılız, N., Yıldırım, H., & Temizel, Ş. (2016). Structure Development for Effective Medical Waste and Hazardous Waste Management System. In U. Akkucuk (Ed.), *Handbook of Research on Waste Management Techniques for Sustainability* (pp. 303–327). Hershey, PA: IGI Global. doi:10.4018/978-1-4666-9723-2.ch016

Ciufudean, C. (2018). Innovative Formalism for Biological Data Analysis. In M. Khosrow-Pour, D.B.A. (Ed.), Encyclopedia of Information Science and Technology, Fourth Edition (pp. 1814-1824). Hershey, PA: IGI Global. doi:10.4018/978-1-5225-2255-3.ch158

Ciufudean, C., & Ciufudean, O. (2016). Tele-Monitoring for Medical Diagnosis Availability. In M. Cruz-Cunha, I. Miranda, R. Martinho, & R. Rijo (Eds.), *Encyclopedia of E-Health and Telemedicine* (pp. 401–411). Hershey, PA: IGI Global. doi:10.4018/978-1-4666-9978-6.ch032

Colaguori, R., & Danesi, M. (2017). Medical Semiotics: A Revisitation and an Exhortation. *International Journal of Semiotics and Visual Rhetoric, 1*(1), 11–18. doi:10.4018/IJSVR.2017010102

Cole, A. W., & Salek, T. A. (2017). Adopting a Parasocial Connection to Overcome Professional Kakoethos in Online Health Information. In M. Folk & S. Apostel (Eds.), *Establishing and Evaluating Digital Ethos and Online Credibility* (pp. 104–120). Hershey, PA: IGI Global. doi:10.4018/978-1-5225-1072-7.ch006

Contreras, E. C., & Puente, G. J. (2016). How to Identify Rheumatic Diseases by General Physicians. In T. Gasmelseid (Ed.), *Advancing Pharmaceutical Processes and Tools for Improved Health Outcomes* (pp. 136–166). Hershey, PA: IGI Global. doi:10.4018/978-1-5225-0248-7.ch006

D'Andrea, A., Ferri, F., & Grifoni, P. (2016). RFID Technologies in Healthcare Setting: Applications and Future Perspectives. *International Journal of Computers in Clinical Practice, 1*(1), 15–27. doi:10.4018/IJCCP.2016010102

Damianakis, A., Kallonis, P., Loudos, G., Tsatsos, D., & Tsoukalis, A. (2016). Exploiting 3D Medical Equipment Simulations to Support Biomedical Engineering Academic Courses: Design Methodology and Implementation in a Small Scale National Project. In B. Khan (Ed.), *Revolutionizing Modern Education through Meaningful E-Learning Implementation* (pp. 277–295). Hershey, PA: IGI Global. doi:10.4018/978-1-5225-0466-5.ch015

Demiroz, E. (2016). Principles of Instructional Design for E-Learning and Online Learning Practices: Implications for Medical Education. In V. Wang (Ed.), *Handbook of Research on Advancing Health Education through Technology* (pp. 419–451). Hershey, PA: IGI Global. doi:10.4018/978-1-4666-9494-1.ch018

Deperlioglu, O. (2018). Intelligent Techniques Inspired by Nature and Used in Biomedical Engineering. In U. Kose, G. Guraksin, & O. Deperlioglu (Eds.), *Nature-Inspired Intelligent Techniques for Solving Biomedical Engineering Problems* (pp. 51–77). Hershey, PA: IGI Global. doi:10.4018/978-1-5225-4769-3.ch003

Dey, N., & Ashour, A. S. (2018). Meta-Heuristic Algorithms in Medical Image Segmentation: A Review. In N. Dey (Ed.), *Advancements in Applied Metaheuristic Computing* (pp. 185–203). Hershey, PA: IGI Global. doi:10.4018/978-1-5225-4151-6.ch008

Dey, N., Ashour, A. S., & Althoupety, A. S. (2017). Thermal Imaging in Medical Science. In V. Santhi (Ed.), *Recent Advances in Applied Thermal Imaging for Industrial Applications* (pp. 87–117). Hershey, PA: IGI Global. doi:10.4018/978-1-5225-2423-6.ch004

Di Virgilio, F., Camillo, A. A., & Camillo, I. C. (2017). The Impact of Social Network on Italian Users' Behavioural Intention for the Choice of a Medical Tourist Destination. *International Journal of Tourism and Hospitality Management in the Digital Age*, *1*(1), 36–49. doi:10.4018/IJTHMDA.2017010103

Dias, C. M., Ribeiro, A. G., & Furtado, S. F. (2016). An Overview about the Use of Healthcare Applications on Mobile Devices. In M. Cruz-Cunha, I. Miranda, R. Martinho, & R. Rijo (Eds.), *Encyclopedia of E-Health and Telemedicine* (pp. 285–298). Hershey, PA: IGI Global. doi:10.4018/978-1-4666-9978-6.ch024

Dogra, A. K., & Dogra, P. (2017). The Medical Tourism Industry in the BRIC Nations: An Indian Analysis. In M. Dhiman (Ed.), *Opportunities and Challenges for Tourism and Hospitality in the BRIC Nations* (pp. 320–336). Hershey, PA: IGI Global. doi:10.4018/978-1-5225-0708-6.ch020

Drowos, J. L., & Wood, S. K. (2017). Preparing Future Physicians to Adapt to the Changing Health Care System: Promoting Humanism through Curricular Design. In V. Bryan & J. Bird (Eds.), *Healthcare Community Synergism between Patients, Practitioners, and Researchers* (pp. 106–125). Hershey, PA: IGI Global. doi:10.4018/978-1-5225-0640-9.ch006

Dulam, K. (2017). Medical Patents and Impact on Availability and Affordability of Essential Medicines in India. In R. Aggarwal & R. Kaur (Eds.), *Patent Law and Intellectual Property in the Medical Field* (pp. 41–57). Hershey, PA: IGI Global. doi:10.4018/978-1-5225-2414-4.ch003

Dutta, P. (2017). Decision Making in Medical Diagnosis via Distance Measures on Interval Valued Fuzzy Sets. *International Journal of System Dynamics Applications*, *6*(4), 63–83. doi:10.4018/IJSDA.2017100104

Edoh, T. O., Pawar, P. A., Brügge, B., & Teege, G. (2016). A Multidisciplinary Remote Healthcare Delivery System to Increase Health Care Access, Pathology Screening, and Treatment in Developing Countries: The Case of Benin. *International Journal of Healthcare Information Systems and Informatics*, *11*(4), 1–31. doi:10.4018/IJHISI.2016100101

El Guemhioui, K., & Demurjian, S. A. (2017). Semantic Reconciliation of Electronic Health Records Using Semantic Web Technologies. *International Journal of Information Technology and Web Engineering*, *12*(2), 26–48. doi:10.4018/IJITWE.2017040102

Ellouze, N., Rekhis, S., & Boudriga, N. (2016). Forensic Investigation of Digital Crimes in Healthcare Applications. In O. Isafiade & A. Bagula (Eds.), *Data Mining Trends and Applications in Criminal Science and Investigations* (pp. 169–210). Hershey, PA: IGI Global. doi:10.4018/978-1-5225-0463-4.ch007

Eneanya, A. N. (2016). Health Policy Implementation and Its Barriers: The Case Study of US Health System. In R. Gholipour & K. Rouzbehani (Eds.), *Social, Economic, and Political Perspectives on Public Health Policy-Making* (pp. 42–63). Hershey, PA: IGI Global. doi:10.4018/978-1-4666-9944-1.ch003

Entico, G. J. (2016). Knowledge Management and the Medical Health Librarians: A Perception Study. In J. Yap, M. Perez, M. Ayson, & G. Entico (Eds.), *Special Library Administration, Standardization and Technological Integration* (pp. 52–77). Hershey, PA: IGI Global. doi:10.4018/978-1-4666-9542-9.ch003

Ferradji, M. A., & Zidani, A. (2016). Collaborative Environment for Remote Clinical Reasoning Learning. *International Journal of E-Health and Medical Communications, 7*(4), 62–81. doi:10.4018/IJEHMC.2016100104

Fisher, J. (2018). Sociological Perspectives on Improving Medical Diagnosis Emphasizing CAD. In M. Khosrow-Pour, D.B.A. (Ed.), Encyclopedia of Information Science and Technology, Fourth Edition (pp. 1017-1024). Hershey, PA: IGI Global. doi:10.4018/978-1-5225-2255-3.ch088

Flores, C. D., Respício, A., Coelho, H., Bez, M. R., & Fonseca, J. M. (2016). Simulation for Medical Training. In M. Cruz-Cunha, I. Miranda, R. Martinho, & R. Rijo (Eds.), *Encyclopedia of E-Health and Telemedicine* (pp. 827–842). Hershey, PA: IGI Global. doi:10.4018/978-1-4666-9978-6.ch064

Frank, E. M. (2018). Healthcare Education: Integrating Simulation Technologies. In V. Bryan, A. Musgrove, & J. Powers (Eds.), *Handbook of Research on Human Development in the Digital Age* (pp. 163–182). Hershey, PA: IGI Global. doi:10.4018/978-1-5225-2838-8.ch008

Garner, G. (2018). Foundations for Yoga Practice in Rehabilitation. In S. Telles & N. Singh (Eds.), *Research-Based Perspectives on the Psychophysiology of Yoga* (pp. 263–307). Hershey, PA: IGI Global. doi:10.4018/978-1-5225-2788-6.ch015

Gasmelseid, T. M. (2016). Improving Pharmaceutical Care through the Use of Intelligent Pharmacoinformatics. In T. Gasmelseid (Ed.), *Advancing Pharmaceutical Processes and Tools for Improved Health Outcomes* (pp. 167–188). Hershey, PA: IGI Global. doi:10.4018/978-1-5225-0248-7.ch007

Gavurová, B., Kováč, V., & Šoltés, M. (2018). Medical Equipment and Economic Determinants of Its Structure and Regulation in the Slovak Republic. In M. Khosrow-Pour, D.B.A. (Ed.), Encyclopedia of Information Science and Technology, Fourth Edition (pp. 5841-5852). Hershey, PA: IGI Global. doi:10.4018/978-1-5225-2255-3.ch508

Ge, X., Wang, Q., Huang, K., Law, V., & Thomas, D. C. (2017). Designing Simulated Learning Environments and Facilitating Authentic Learning Experiences in Medical Education. In J. Stefaniak (Ed.), *Advancing Medical Education Through Strategic Instructional Design* (pp. 77–100). Hershey, PA: IGI Global. doi:10.4018/978-1-5225-2098-6.ch004

Gewald, H., & Gewald, C. (2018). Inhibitors of Physicians' Use of Mandatory Hospital Information Systems (HIS). *International Journal of Healthcare Information Systems and Informatics*, *13*(1), 29–44. doi:10.4018/IJHISI.2018010103

Ghosh, D., & Dinda, S. (2017). Health Infrastructure and Economic Development in India. In R. Das (Ed.), *Social, Health, and Environmental Infrastructures for Economic Growth* (pp. 99–119). Hershey, PA: IGI Global. doi:10.4018/978-1-5225-2364-2.ch006

Ghosh, K., & Sen, K. C. (2017). The Potential of Crowdsourcing in the Health Care Industry. In N. Wickramasinghe (Ed.), *Handbook of Research on Healthcare Administration and Management* (pp. 418–427). Hershey, PA: IGI Global. doi:10.4018/978-1-5225-0920-2.ch024

Ghrab, S., & Saad, I. (2016). Identifying Crucial Know-How and Knowing-That for Medical Decision Support. *International Journal of Decision Support System Technology*, *8*(4), 14–33. doi:10.4018/IJDSST.2016100102

Giokas, K., Tsirmpas, C., Anastasiou, A., Iliopoulou, D., Costarides, V., & Koutsouris, D. (2016). Contemporary Heart Failure Treatment Based on Improved Knowledge and Personalized Care of Comorbidities. In D. Fotiadis (Ed.), *Handbook of Research on Trends in the Diagnosis and Treatment of Chronic Conditions* (pp. 301–314). Hershey, PA: IGI Global. doi:10.4018/978-1-4666-8828-5.ch014

Gopalan, V., Chan, E., & Ho, D. T. (2018). Deliberate Self-Harm and Suicide Ideology in Medical Students. In C. Smith (Ed.), *Exploring the Pressures of Medical Education From a Mental Health and Wellness Perspective* (pp. 122–143). Hershey, PA: IGI Global. doi:10.4018/978-1-5225-2811-1.ch005

Goswami, S., Dey, U., Roy, P., Ashour, A., & Dey, N. (2017). Medical Video Processing: Concept and Applications. In N. Dey, A. Ashour, & P. Patra (Eds.), *Feature Detectors and Motion Detection in Video Processing* (pp. 1–17). Hershey, PA: IGI Global. doi:10.4018/978-1-5225-1025-3.ch001

Goswami, S., Mahanta, K., Goswami, S., Jigdung, T., & Devi, T. P. (2018). Ageing and Cancer: The Epigenetic Basis, Alternative Treatment, and Care. In B. Prasad & S. Akbar (Eds.), *Handbook of Research on Geriatric Health, Treatment, and Care* (pp. 206–235). Hershey, PA: IGI Global. doi:10.4018/978-1-5225-3480-8.ch012

Gouva, M. I. (2017). The Psychological Impact of Medical Error on Patients, Family Members, and Health Professionals. In M. Riga (Ed.), *Impact of Medical Errors and Malpractice on Health Economics, Quality, and Patient Safety* (pp. 171–196). Hershey, PA: IGI Global. doi:10.4018/978-1-5225-2337-6.ch007

Gürcü, M., & Tengilimoğlu, D. (2017). Health Tourism-Based Destination Marketing. In A. Bayraktar & C. Uslay (Eds.), *Strategic Place Branding Methodologies and Theory for Tourist Attraction* (pp. 308–331). Hershey, PA: IGI Global. doi:10.4018/978-1-5225-0579-2.ch015

Gürsel, G. (2016). Mobility in Healthcare: M-Health. In A. Panagopoulos (Ed.), *Handbook of Research on Next Generation Mobile Communication Systems* (pp. 485–511). Hershey, PA: IGI Global. doi:10.4018/978-1-4666-8732-5.ch019

Gürsel, G. (2017). For Better Healthcare Mining Health Data. In S. Bhattacharyya, S. De, I. Pan, & P. Dutta (Eds.), *Intelligent Multidimensional Data Clustering and Analysis* (pp. 135–158). Hershey, PA: IGI Global. doi:10.4018/978-1-5225-1776-4.ch006

Guzman-Lugo, G., Lopez-Martinez, M., Lopez-Ramirez, B., & Avila-Vazquez, D. (2016). City-Driven Approach to Determine Health Services Based on Current User Location and Collaborative Information. *International Journal of Knowledge Society Research*, *7*(1), 53–62. doi:10.4018/IJKSR.2016010104

Gyaase, P. O., Darko-Lartey, R., William, H., & Borkloe, F. (2017). Towards an Integrated Electronic Medical Records System for Quality Healthcare in Ghana: An Exploratory Factor Analysis. *International Journal of Computers in Clinical Practice*, *2*(2), 38–55. doi:10.4018/IJCCP.2017070103

Handayani, P. W., Sandhyaduhita, P. I., Hidayanto, A. N., Pinem, A. A., Fajrina, H. R., Junus, K. M., ... Ayuningtyas, D. (2016). Integrated Hospital Information System Architecture Design in Indonesia. In T. Iyamu & A. Tatnall (Eds.), *Maximizing Healthcare Delivery and Management through Technology Integration* (pp. 207–236). Hershey, PA: IGI Global. doi:10.4018/978-1-4666-9446-0.ch013

Hanel, P. (2017). Is China Catching Up?: Health-Related Applications of Biotechnology. In T. Bas & J. Zhao (Eds.), *Comparative Approaches to Biotechnology Development and Use in Developed and Emerging Nations* (pp. 465–520). Hershey, PA: IGI Global. doi:10.4018/978-1-5225-1040-6.ch016

Harmsen, C. A., & Royle, R. N. (2016). St. Stephen's Hospital Hervey Bay: Study of Developing a Digital Hospital. In J. Moon & M. Galea (Eds.), *Improving Health Management through Clinical Decision Support Systems* (pp. 127–153). Hershey, PA: IGI Global. doi:10.4018/978-1-4666-9432-3.ch006

Harp, D., Shim, R. S., Johnson, J., Harp, J. A., Wilcox, W. C., & Wilcox, J. K. (2016). Race and Gender Inequalities in Medicine and Biomedical Research. In U. Thomas & J. Drake (Eds.), *Critical Research on Sexism and Racism in STEM Fields* (pp. 115–134). Hershey, PA: IGI Global. doi:10.4018/978-1-5225-0174-9.ch006

Hartman, A., & Brown, S. (2017). Synergism through Therapeutic Visual Arts. In V. Bryan & J. Bird (Eds.), *Healthcare Community Synergism between Patients, Practitioners, and Researchers* (pp. 29–48). Hershey, PA: IGI Global. doi:10.4018/978-1-5225-0640-9.ch002

Hazra, J., Chowdhury, A. R., & Dutta, P. (2016). Cluster Based Medical Image Registration Using Optimized Neural Network. In S. Bhattacharyya, P. Banerjee, D. Majumdar, & P. Dutta (Eds.), *Handbook of Research on Advanced Hybrid Intelligent Techniques and Applications* (pp. 551–581). Hershey, PA: IGI Global. doi:10.4018/978-1-4666-9474-3.ch018

Hung, S., Huang, W., Yen, D. C., Chang, S., & Lu, C. (2016). Effect of Information Service Competence and Contextual Factors on the Effectiveness of Strategic Information Systems Planning in Hospitals. *Journal of Global Information Management, 24*(1), 14–36. doi:10.4018/JGIM.2016010102

Iltchev, P., Śliwczyński, A., Szynkiewicz, P., & Marczak, M. (2016). Mobile Health Applications Assisting Patients with Chronic Diseases: Examples from Asthma Care. In A. Moumtzoglou (Ed.), *M-Health Innovations for Patient-Centered Care* (pp. 170–196). Hershey, PA: IGI Global. doi:10.4018/978-1-4666-9861-1.ch009

Iqbal, S., Ahmad, S., & Willis, I. (2017). Influencing Factors for Adopting Technology Enhanced Learning in the Medical Schools of Punjab, Pakistan. *International Journal of Information and Communication Technology Education, 13*(3), 27–39. doi:10.4018/IJICTE.2017070103

Jagan, J., Dalkiliç, Y., & Samui, P. (2016). Utilization of SVM, LSSVM and GP for Predicting the Medical Waste Generation. In G. Hua (Ed.), *Smart Cities as a Solution for Reducing Urban Waste and Pollution* (pp. 224–251). Hershey, PA: IGI Global. doi:10.4018/978-1-5225-0302-6.ch008

Jagiello, K., Sosnowska, A., Mikolajczyk, A., & Puzyn, T. (2017). Nanomaterials in Medical Devices: Regulations' Review and Future Perspectives. *Journal of Nanotoxicology and Nanomedicine*, *2*(2), 1–11. doi:10.4018/JNN.2017070101

Jena, T. K. (2018). Skill Training Process in Medicine Through Distance Mode. In U. Pandey & V. Indrakanti (Eds.), *Optimizing Open and Distance Learning in Higher Education Institutions* (pp. 228–243). Hershey, PA: IGI Global. doi:10.4018/978-1-5225-2624-7.ch010

Jesus, Â., & Gomes, M. J. (2016). Web 2.0 Tools in Biomedical and Pharmaceutical Education: Updated Review and Commentary. In T. Gasmelseid (Ed.), *Advancing Pharmaceutical Processes and Tools for Improved Health Outcomes* (pp. 52–78). Hershey, PA: IGI Global. doi:10.4018/978-1-5225-0248-7.ch003

Joseph, V., & Miller, J. M. (2018). Medical Students' Perceived Stigma in Seeking Care: A Cultural Perspective. In C. Smith (Ed.), *Exploring the Pressures of Medical Education From a Mental Health and Wellness Perspective* (pp. 44–67). Hershey, PA: IGI Global. doi:10.4018/978-1-5225-2811-1.ch002

Joyce, B. L., & Swanberg, S. M. (2017). Using Backward Design for Competency-Based Undergraduate Medical Education. In J. Stefaniak (Ed.), *Advancing Medical Education Through Strategic Instructional Design* (pp. 53–76). Hershey, PA: IGI Global. doi:10.4018/978-1-5225-2098-6.ch003

Kaljo, K., & Jacques, L. (2018). Flipping the Medical School Classroom. In M. Khosrow-Pour, D.B.A. (Ed.), Encyclopedia of Information Science and Technology, Fourth Edition (pp. 5800-5809). Hershey, PA: IGI Global. doi:10.4018/978-1-5225-2255-3.ch504

Karon, R. (2016). Utilisation of Health Information Systems for Service Delivery in the Namibian Environment. In T. Iyamu & A. Tatnall (Eds.), *Maximizing Healthcare Delivery and Management through Technology Integration* (pp. 169–183). Hershey, PA: IGI Global. doi:10.4018/978-1-4666-9446-0.ch011

Kasina, H., Bahubalendruni, M. V., & Botcha, R. (2017). Robots in Medicine: Past, Present and Future. *International Journal of Manufacturing, Materials, and Mechanical Engineering*, *7*(4), 44–64. doi:10.4018/IJMMME.2017100104

Katehakis, D. G. (2018). Electronic Medical Record Implementation Challenges for the National Health System in Greece. *International Journal of Reliable and Quality E-Healthcare*, *7*(1), 16–30. doi:10.4018/IJRQEH.2018010102

Katz, A., & Shtub, A. (2016). Design and Build a Wizard of Oz (WOZ) Telemedicine Simulator Platform. In M. Cruz-Cunha, I. Miranda, R. Martinho, & R. Rijo (Eds.), *Encyclopedia of E-Health and Telemedicine* (pp. 128–141). Hershey, PA: IGI Global. doi:10.4018/978-1-4666-9978-6.ch011

Kaur, P. D., & Sharma, P. (2017). Success Dimensions of ICTs in Healthcare. In B. Singh (Ed.), *Computational Tools and Techniques for Biomedical Signal Processing* (pp. 149–173). Hershey, PA: IGI Global. doi:10.4018/978-1-5225-0660-7.ch007

Kaushik, P. (2018). Comorbidity of Medical and Psychiatric Disorders in Geriatric Population: Treatment and Care. In B. Prasad & S. Akbar (Eds.), *Handbook of Research on Geriatric Health, Treatment, and Care* (pp. 448–474). Hershey, PA: IGI Global. doi:10.4018/978-1-5225-3480-8.ch025

Khachane, M. Y. (2017). Organ-Based Medical Image Classification Using Support Vector Machine. *International Journal of Synthetic Emotions*, *8*(1), 18–30. doi:10.4018/IJSE.2017010102

Kirci, P. (2018). Intelligent Techniques for Analysis of Big Data About Healthcare and Medical Records. In N. Shah & M. Mittal (Eds.), *Handbook of Research on Promoting Business Process Improvement Through Inventory Control Techniques* (pp. 559–582). Hershey, PA: IGI Global. doi:10.4018/978-1-5225-3232-3.ch029

Kldiashvili, E. (2016). Cloud Computing as the Useful Resource for Application of the Medical Information System for Quality Assurance Purposes. *International Journal of Computers in Clinical Practice*, *1*(2), 1–23. doi:10.4018/IJCCP.2016070101

Kldiashvili, E. (2018). Cloud Approach for the Medical Information System: MIS on Cloud. In M. Khosrow-Pour (Ed.), *Incorporating Nature-Inspired Paradigms in Computational Applications* (pp. 238–261). Hershey, PA: IGI Global. doi:10.4018/978-1-5225-5020-4.ch008

Kldiashvili, E., Burduli, A., Ghortlishvili, G., & Sheklashvili, I. (2016). Georgian Experience in Telecytology. In M. Cruz-Cunha, I. Miranda, R. Martinho, & R. Rijo (Eds.), *Encyclopedia of E-Health and Telemedicine* (pp. 62–71). Hershey, PA: IGI Global. doi:10.4018/978-1-4666-9978-6.ch006

Ko, H., Mesicek, L., Choi, J., Choi, J., & Hwang, S. (2018). A Study on Secure Contents Strategies for Applications With DRM on Cloud Computing. *International Journal of Cloud Applications and Computing*, *8*(1), 143–153. doi:10.4018/IJCAC.2018010107

Komendziński, T., Dreszer-Drogorób, J., Mikołajewska, E., Mikołajewski, D., & Bałaj, B. (2016). Interdisciplinary Education for Research and Everyday Clinical Practice: Lessons Learned from InteRDoCTor Project. In A. Rosiek & K. Leksowski (Eds.), *Organizational Culture and Ethics in Modern Medicine* (pp. 78–110). Hershey, PA: IGI Global. doi:10.4018/978-1-4666-9658-7.ch004

Komendziński, T., Mikołajewska, E., & Mikołajewski, D. (2018). Cross-Cultural Decision-Making in Healthcare: Theory and Practical Application in Real Clinical Conditions. In A. Rosiek-Kryszewska & K. Leksowski (Eds.), *Healthcare Administration for Patient Safety and Engagement* (pp. 276–298). Hershey, PA: IGI Global. doi:10.4018/978-1-5225-3946-9.ch015

Konecny, L. T. (2018). Medical School Wellness Initiatives. In C. Smith (Ed.), *Exploring the Pressures of Medical Education From a Mental Health and Wellness Perspective* (pp. 209–228). Hershey, PA: IGI Global. doi:10.4018/978-1-5225-2811-1.ch009

Konieczna, A., & Słomkowski, P. (2016). Confrontation of Human Rights in Daily Clinical Situations. In A. Rosiek & K. Leksowski (Eds.), *Organizational Culture and Ethics in Modern Medicine* (pp. 255–281). Hershey, PA: IGI Global. doi:10.4018/978-1-4666-9658-7.ch011

Kromrei, H., Solomonson, W. L., & Juzych, M. S. (2017). Teaching Residents How to Teach. In J. Stefaniak (Ed.), *Advancing Medical Education Through Strategic Instructional Design* (pp. 164–185). Hershey, PA: IGI Global. doi:10.4018/978-1-5225-2098-6.ch008

Kulkarni, S., Savyanavar, A., Kulkarni, P., Stranieri, A., & Ghorpade, V. (2018). Framework for Integration of Medical Image and Text-Based Report Retrieval to Support Radiological Diagnosis. In M. Kolekar & V. Kumar (Eds.), *Biomedical Signal and Image Processing in Patient Care* (pp. 86–122). Hershey, PA: IGI Global. doi:10.4018/978-1-5225-2829-6.ch006

Kumar, A., & Sarkar, B. K. (2018). Performance Analysis of Nature-Inspired Algorithms-Based Bayesian Prediction Models for Medical Data Sets. In U. Singh, A. Tiwari, & R. Singh (Eds.), *Soft-Computing-Based Nonlinear Control Systems Design* (pp. 134–155). Hershey, PA: IGI Global. doi:10.4018/978-1-5225-3531-7.ch007

Kurtz, R. S. (2016). Fortitude: A Study of African Americans in Surgery in New York City. In U. Thomas & J. Drake (Eds.), *Critical Research on Sexism and Racism in STEM Fields* (pp. 153–169). Hershey, PA: IGI Global. doi:10.4018/978-1-5225-0174-9.ch009

Labbadi, W., & Akaichi, J. (2017). Efficient Algorithm for Answering Fuzzy Medical Requests in Pervasive Healthcare Information Systems. *International Journal of Healthcare Information Systems and Informatics, 12*(2), 46–64. doi:10.4018/IJHISI.2017040103

Lagumdzija, A., & Swing, V. K. (2017). Health, Digitalization, and Individual Empowerment. In F. Topor (Ed.), *Handbook of Research on Individualism and Identity in the Globalized Digital Age* (pp. 380–402). Hershey, PA: IGI Global. doi:10.4018/978-1-5225-0522-8.ch017

Lamey, T. W., & Davidson-Shivers, G. V. (2017). Instructional Strategies and Sequencing. In J. Stefaniak (Ed.), *Advancing Medical Education Through Strategic Instructional Design* (pp. 30–52). Hershey, PA: IGI Global. doi:10.4018/978-1-5225-2098-6.ch002

Leon, G. (2017). The Role of Forensic Medicine in Medical Errors. In M. Riga (Ed.), *Impact of Medical Errors and Malpractice on Health Economics, Quality, and Patient Safety* (pp. 144–170). Hershey, PA: IGI Global. doi:10.4018/978-1-5225-2337-6.ch006

Lidia, B., Federica, G., & Maria, V. E. (2016). The Patient-Centered Medicine as the Theoretical Framework for Patient Engagement. In G. Graffigna (Ed.), *Promoting Patient Engagement and Participation for Effective Healthcare Reform* (pp. 25–39). Hershey, PA: IGI Global. doi:10.4018/978-1-4666-9992-2.ch002

Love, L., & McDowelle, D. (2018). Developing a Comprehensive Wellness Program for Medical Students. In C. Smith (Ed.), *Exploring the Pressures of Medical Education From a Mental Health and Wellness Perspective* (pp. 190–208). Hershey, PA: IGI Global. doi:10.4018/978-1-5225-2811-1.ch008

Lovell, K. L. (2017). Development and Evaluation of Neuroscience Computer-Based Modules for Medical Students: Instructional Design Principles and Effectiveness. In J. Stefaniak (Ed.), *Advancing Medical Education Through Strategic Instructional Design* (pp. 262–276). Hershey, PA: IGI Global. doi:10.4018/978-1-5225-2098-6.ch013

Lubin, R., & Hamlin, M. D. (2018). Medical Student Burnout: A Social Cognitive Learning Perspective on Medical Student Mental Health and Wellness. In C. Smith (Ed.), *Exploring the Pressures of Medical Education From a Mental Health and Wellness Perspective* (pp. 92–121). Hershey, PA: IGI Global. doi:10.4018/978-1-5225-2811-1.ch004

Luk, C. Y. (2018). Moving Towards Universal Health Coverage: Challenges for the Present and Future in China. In B. Fong, A. Ng, & P. Yuen (Eds.), *Sustainable Health and Long-Term Care Solutions for an Aging Population* (pp. 19–45). Hershey, PA: IGI Global. doi:10.4018/978-1-5225-2633-9.ch002

Mahat, M., & Pettigrew, A. (2017). The Regulatory Environment of Non-Profit Higher Education and Research Institutions and Its Implications for Managerial Strategy: The Case of Medical Education and Research. In L. West & A. Worthington (Eds.), *Handbook of Research on Emerging Business Models and Managerial Strategies in the Nonprofit Sector* (pp. 336–351). Hershey, PA: IGI Global. doi:10.4018/978-1-5225-2537-0.ch017

Maitra, I. K., & Bandhyopadhyaay, S. K. (2017). Adaptive Edge Detection Method towards Features Extraction from Diverse Medical Imaging Technologies. In S. Bhattacharyya, S. Dc, I. Pan, & P. Dutta (Eds.), *Intelligent Multidimensional Data Clustering and Analysis* (pp. 159–192). Hershey, PA: IGI Global. doi:10.4018/978-1-5225-1776-4.ch007

Mangu, V. P. (2017). Mobile Health Care: A Technology View. In C. Bhatt & S. Peddoju (Eds.), *Cloud Computing Systems and Applications in Healthcare* (pp. 1–18). Hershey, PA: IGI Global. doi:10.4018/978-1-5225-1002-4.ch001

Manirabona, A., Fourati, L. C., & Boudjit, S. (2017). Investigation on Healthcare Monitoring Systems: Innovative Services and Applications. *International Journal of E-Health and Medical Communications*, *8*(1), 1–18. doi:10.4018/IJEHMC.2017010101

Mannai, M. M., & Karâa, W. B. (2016). Biomedical Image Processing Overview. In W. Karâa & N. Dey (Eds.), *Biomedical Image Analysis and Mining Techniques for Improved Health Outcomes* (pp. 1–12). Hershey, PA: IGI Global. doi:10.4018/978-1-4666-8811-7.ch001

Manzoor, A. (2016). RFID in Health Care-Building Smart Hospitals for Quality Healthcare. *International Journal of User-Driven Healthcare*, *6*(2), 21–45. doi:10.4018/IJUDH.2016070102

Marwan, M., Kartit, A., & Ouahmane, H. (2018). A Framework to Secure Medical Image Storage in Cloud Computing Environment. *Journal of Electronic Commerce in Organizations*, *16*(1), 1–16. doi:10.4018/JECO.2018010101

Masoud, M. P., Nejad, M. K., Darebaghi, H., Chavoshi, M., & Farahani, M. (2018). The Decision Support System and Conventional Method of Telephone Triage by Nurses in Emergency Medical Services: A Comparative Investigation. *International Journal of E-Business Research, 14*(1), 77–88. doi:10.4018/IJEBR.2018010105

McDonald, W. G., Martin, M., & Salzberg, L. D. (2018). From Medical Student to Medical Resident: Graduate Medical Education and Mental Health in the United States. In C. Smith (Ed.), *Exploring the Pressures of Medical Education From a Mental Health and Wellness Perspective* (pp. 145–169). Hershey, PA: IGI Global. doi:10.4018/978-1-5225-2811-1.ch006

Medhekar, A. (2017). The Role of Social Media for Knowledge Dissemination in Medical Tourism: A Case of India. In R. Chugh (Ed.), *Harnessing Social Media as a Knowledge Management Tool* (pp. 25–54). Hershey, PA: IGI Global. doi:10.4018/978-1-5225-0495-5.ch002

Medhekar, A., & Haq, F. (2018). Urbanization and New Jobs Creation in Healthcare Services in India: Challenges and Opportunities. In U. Benna & I. Benna (Eds.), *Urbanization and Its Impact on Socio-Economic Growth in Developing Regions* (pp. 198–218). Hershey, PA: IGI Global. doi:10.4018/978-1-5225-2659-9.ch010

Mehta, G., Dutta, M. K., & Kim, P. S. (2016). An Efficient and Lossless Cryptosystem for Security in Tele-Ophthalmology Applications Using Chaotic Theory. *International Journal of E-Health and Medical Communications, 7*(4), 28–47. doi:10.4018/IJEHMC.2016100102

Mehta, P. (2017). Framework of Indian Healthcare System and its Challenges: An Insight. In V. Bryan & J. Bird (Eds.), *Healthcare Community Synergism between Patients, Practitioners, and Researchers* (pp. 247–271). Hershey, PA: IGI Global. doi:10.4018/978-1-5225-0640-9.ch011

Metelmann, B., & Metelmann, C. (2016). M-Health in Prehospital Emergency Medicine: Experiences from the EU funded Project LiveCity. In A. Moumtzoglou (Ed.), *M-Health Innovations for Patient-Centered Care* (pp. 197–212). Hershey, PA: IGI Global. doi:10.4018/978-1-4666-9861-1.ch010

Mi, M. (2017). Informal Learning in Medical Education. In J. Stefaniak (Ed.), *Advancing Medical Education Through Strategic Instructional Design* (pp. 225–244). Hershey, PA: IGI Global. doi:10.4018/978-1-5225-2098-6.ch011

Miglioretti, M., Mariani, F., & Vecchio, L. (2016). Could Patient Engagement Promote a Health System Free From Malpractice Litigation Risk? In G. Graffigna (Ed.), *Promoting Patient Engagement and Participation for Effective Healthcare Reform* (pp. 240–264). Hershey, PA: IGI Global. doi:10.4018/978-1-4666-9992-2.ch012

Misra, S. C., & Bisui, S. (2016). Feasibility of Large Scale Implementation of Personalized Medicine in the Current Scenario. *International Journal of E-Health and Medical Communications*, *7*(2), 30–49. doi:10.4018/IJEHMC.2016040103

Misra, S. C., Bisui, S., & Fantazy, K. (2016). Identifying Critical Changes in Adoption of Personalized Medicine (PM) in Healthcare Management. *International Journal of E-Health and Medical Communications*, *7*(3), 1–15. doi:10.4018/IJEHMC.2016070101

Mohammadian, M., Hatzinakos, D., Spachos, P., & Jentzsh, R. (2016). An Intelligent and Secure Framework for Wireless Information Technology in Healthcare for User and Data Classification in Hospitals. In V. Wang (Ed.), *Handbook of Research on Advancing Health Education through Technology* (pp. 452–479). Hershey, PA: IGI Global. doi:10.4018/978-1-4666-9494-1.ch019

Mokeddem, S., & Atmani, B. (2016). Assessment of Clinical Decision Support Systems for Predicting Coronary Heart Disease. *International Journal of Operations Research and Information Systems*, *7*(3), 57–73. doi:10.4018/IJORIS.2016070104

Mokrzycka, A., & Kowalska-Bobko, I. (2016). Public Health Legislation and Patient's Rights: Health2020 Strategy, European Perspective. In A. Rosiek & K. Leksowski (Eds.), *Organizational Culture and Ethics in Modern Medicine* (pp. 298–322). Hershey, PA: IGI Global. doi:10.4018/978-1-4666-9658-7.ch013

Moon, J. D., & Galea, M. P. (2016). Overview of Clinical Decision Support Systems in Healthcare. In J. Moon & M. Galea (Eds.), *Improving Health Management through Clinical Decision Support Systems* (pp. 1–27). Hershey, PA: IGI Global. doi:10.4018/978-1-4666-9432-3.ch001

Mosadeghrad, A. M., & Woldemichael, A. (2017). Application of Quality Management in Promoting Patient Safety and Preventing Medical Errors. In M. Riga (Ed.), *Impact of Medical Errors and Malpractice on Health Economics, Quality, and Patient Safety* (pp. 91–112). Hershey, PA: IGI Global. doi:10.4018/978-1-5225-2337-6.ch004

Moumtzoglou, A. (2017). Digital Medicine: The Quality Standpoint. In A. Moumtzoglou (Ed.), *Design, Development, and Integration of Reliable Electronic Healthcare Platforms* (pp. 179–195). Hershey, PA: IGI Global. doi:10.4018/978-1-5225-1724-5.ch011

Moumtzoglou, A., & Pouliakis, A. (2018). Population Health Management and the Science of Individuality. *International Journal of Reliable and Quality E-Healthcare*, *7*(2), 1–26. doi:10.4018/IJRQEH.2018040101

Mpofu, C. (2016). International Medical Experiences Outbound New Zealand: An Economic and Medical Workforce Strategy. In D. Velliaris & D. Coleman-George (Eds.), *Handbook of Research on Study Abroad Programs and Outbound Mobility* (pp. 446–469). Hershey, PA: IGI Global. doi:10.4018/978-1-5225-0169-5.ch018

Mukhtar, W. F., & Abuelyaman, E. S. (2017). Opportunities and Challenges of Big Data in Healthcare. In N. Wickramasinghe (Ed.), *Handbook of Research on Healthcare Administration and Management* (pp. 47–58). Hershey, PA: IGI Global. doi:10.4018/978-1-5225-0920-2.ch004

Munugala, S., Brar, G. K., Syed, A., Mohammad, A., & Halgamuge, M. N. (2018). The Much Needed Security and Data Reforms of Cloud Computing in Medical Data Storage. In M. Lytras & P. Papadopoulou (Eds.), *Applying Big Data Analytics in Bioinformatics and Medicine* (pp. 99–113). Hershey, PA: IGI Global. doi:10.4018/978-1-5225-2607-0.ch005

Narasimhamurthy, A. (2016). An Overview of Machine Learning in Medical Image Analysis: Trends in Health Informatics. In N. Dey & A. Ashour (Eds.), *Classification and Clustering in Biomedical Signal Processing* (pp. 23–45). Hershey, PA: IGI Global. doi:10.4018/978-1-5225-0140-4.ch002

Ngara, R. (2017). Multiple Voices, Multiple Paths: Towards Dialogue between Western and Indigenous Medical Knowledge Systems. In P. Ngulube (Ed.), *Handbook of Research on Theoretical Perspectives on Indigenous Knowledge Systems in Developing Countries* (pp. 332–358). Hershey, PA: IGI Global. doi:10.4018/978-1-5225-0833-5.ch015

O'Connor, Y., & Heavin, C. (2018). Defining and Characterising the Landscape of eHealth. In M. Khosrow-Pour, D.B.A. (Ed.), Encyclopedia of Information Science and Technology, Fourth Edition (pp. 5864-5875). Hershey, PA: IGI Global. doi:10.4018/978-1-5225-2255-3.ch510

Ochonogor, W. C., & Okite-Amughoro, F. A. (2018). Building an Effective Digital Library in a University Teaching Hospital (UTH) in Nigeria. In A. Tella & T. Kwanya (Eds.), *Handbook of Research on Managing Intellectual Property in Digital Libraries* (pp. 184–204). Hershey, PA: IGI Global. doi:10.4018/978-1-5225-3093-0.ch010

Olaniran, B. A. (2016). ICTs, E-health, and Multidisciplinary Healthcare Teams: Promises and Challenges. *International Journal of Privacy and Health Information Management*, *4*(2), 62–75. doi:10.4018/IJPHIM.2016070105

Olaniran, B. A. (2016). ICT Use and Multidisciplinary Healthcare Teams in the Age of e-Health. *International Journal of Reliable and Quality E-Healthcare*, *5*(1), 18–31. doi:10.4018/IJRQEH.2016010102

Olivares, S. L., Cruz, A. G., Cabrera, M. V., Regalado, A. I., & García, J. E. (2017). An Assessment Study of Quality Model for Medical Schools in Mexico. In S. Mukerji & P. Tripathi (Eds.), *Handbook of Research on Administration, Policy, and Leadership in Higher Education* (pp. 404–439). Hershey, PA: IGI Global. doi:10.4018/978-1-5225-0672-0.ch016

Omidoyin, E. O., Opeke, R. O., & Osagbemi, G. K. (2016). Utilization Pattern and Privacy Issues in the use of Health Records for Research Practice by Doctors: Selected Nigerian Teaching Hospitals as Case Study. *International Journal of Privacy and Health Information Management*, *4*(1), 1–11. doi:10.4018/IJPHIM.2016010101

Omoruyi, E. A., & Omidele, F. (2018). Resident Physician and Medical Academic Faculty Burnout: A Review of Current Literature. In C. Smith (Ed.), *Exploring the Pressures of Medical Education From a Mental Health and Wellness Perspective* (pp. 171–189). Hershey, PA: IGI Global. doi:10.4018/978-1-5225-2811-1.ch007

Osop, H., & Sahama, T. (2016). Data-Driven and Practice-Based Evidence: Design and Development of Efficient and Effective Clinical Decision Support System. In J. Moon & M. Galea (Eds.), *Improving Health Management through Clinical Decision Support Systems* (pp. 295–328). Hershey, PA: IGI Global. doi:10.4018/978-1-4666-9432-3.ch014

Ossowski, R., & Izdebski, P. (2016). Ethical Aspects of Talking to a Patient. In A. Rosiek & K. Leksowski (Eds.), *Organizational Culture and Ethics in Modern Medicine* (pp. 203–235). Hershey, PA: IGI Global. doi:10.4018/978-1-4666-9658-7.ch009

Pandian, P. S. (2016). An Overview of Telemedicine Technologies for Healthcare Applications. *International Journal of Biomedical and Clinical Engineering*, *5*(2), 29–52. doi:10.4018/IJBCE.2016070103

Papadopoulou, P., Lytras, M., & Marouli, C. (2018). Bioinformatics as Applied to Medicine: Challenges Faced Moving from Big Data to Smart Data to Wise Data. In M. Lytras & P. Papadopoulou (Eds.), *Applying Big Data Analytics in Bioinformatics and Medicine* (pp. 1–25). Hershey, PA: IGI Global. doi:10.4018/978-1-5225-2607-0.ch001

Paraskou, A., & George, B. P. (2018). An Overview of Reproductive Tourism. In *Legal and Economic Considerations Surrounding Reproductive Tourism: Emerging Research and Opportunities* (pp. 1–17). Hershey, PA: IGI Global. doi:10.4018/978-1-5225-2694-0.ch001

Park, S., & Moon, J. (2016). Strategic Approach towards Clinical Information Security. In J. Moon & M. Galea (Eds.), *Improving Health Management through Clinical Decision Support Systems* (pp. 329–359). Hershey, PA: IGI Global. doi:10.4018/978-1-4666-9432-3.ch015

Pereira, D., Castro, A., Gomes, P., Areias, J. C., Reis, Z. S., Coimbra, M. T., & Cruz-Correia, R. (2016). Digital Auscultation: Challenges and Perspectives. In M. Cruz-Cunha, I. Miranda, R. Martinho, & R. Rijo (Eds.), *Encyclopedia of E-Health and Telemedicine* (pp. 910–927). Hershey, PA: IGI Global. doi:10.4018/978-1-4666-9978-6.ch070

Peters, R. A., & Cruz, M. (2016). The States as Generators of Incremental Change in American Health Care Policy: 1935 to 1965. In R. Gholipour & K. Rouzbehani (Eds.), *Social, Economic, and Political Perspectives on Public Health Policy-Making* (pp. 86–114). Hershey, PA: IGI Global. doi:10.4018/978-1-4666-9944-1.ch005

Phuritsabam, B., & Devi, A. B. (2017). Information Seeking Behavior of Medical Scientists at Jawaharlal Nehru Institute of Medical Science: A Study. In S. Ram (Ed.), *Library and Information Services for Bioinformatics Education and Research* (pp. 177–187). Hershey, PA: IGI Global. doi:10.4018/978-1-5225-1871-6.ch010

Pieczka, B. (2018). Management of Risk and Adverse Events in Medical Entities. In A. Rosiek-Kryszewska & K. Leksowski (Eds.), *Healthcare Administration for Patient Safety and Engagement* (pp. 31–46). Hershey, PA: IGI Global. doi:10.4018/978-1-5225-3946-9.ch003

Poduval, J. (2016). Curriculum Development. In *Optimizing Medicine Residency Training Programs* (pp. 45–102). Hershey, PA: IGI Global. doi:10.4018/978-1-4666-9527-6.ch003

Poduval, J. (2016). Ethics and Professionalism. In *Optimizing Medicine Residency Training Programs* (pp. 103–133). Hershey, PA: IGI Global. doi:10.4018/978-1-4666-9527-6.ch004

Poduval, J. (2016). Management Skills and Leadership. In *Optimizing Medicine Residency Training Programs* (pp. 182–205). Hershey, PA: IGI Global. doi:10.4018/978-1-4666-9527-6.ch008

Poduval, J. (2016). Medicine Residency Training. In *Optimizing Medicine Residency Training Programs* (pp. 1–27). Hershey, PA: IGI Global. doi:10.4018/978-1-4666-9527-6.ch001

Poduval, J. (2016). Personal Issues. In *Optimizing Medicine Residency Training Programs* (pp. 206–221). Hershey, PA: IGI Global. doi:10.4018/978-1-4666-9527-6.ch009

Poduval, J. (2017). Medical Errors: Impact on Health Care Quality. In M. Riga (Ed.), *Impact of Medical Errors and Malpractice on Health Economics, Quality, and Patient Safety* (pp. 33–60). Hershey, PA: IGI Global. doi:10.4018/978-1-5225-2337-6.ch002

Politis, D., Stagiopoulos, P., Aidona, S., Kyriafinis, G., & Constantinidis, I. (2018). Autonomous Learning and Skill Accreditation: A Paradigm for Medical Studies. In A. Kumar (Ed.), *Optimizing Student Engagement in Online Learning Environments* (pp. 266–296). Hershey, PA: IGI Global. doi:10.4018/978-1-5225-3634-5.ch012

Pomares-Quimbaya, A., Gonzalez, R. A., Quintero, S., Muñoz, O. M., Bohórquez, W. R., García, O. M., & Londoño, D. (2016). A Review of Existing Applications and Techniques for Narrative Text Analysis in Electronic Medical Records. In M. Cruz-Cunha, I. Miranda, R. Martinho, & R. Rijo (Eds.), *Encyclopedia of E-Health and Telemedicine* (pp. 796–811). Hershey, PA: IGI Global. doi:10.4018/978-1-4666-9978-6.ch062

Pomares-Quimbaya, A., González, R. A., Sierra, A., Daza, J. C., Muñoz, O., García, A., ... Bohórquez, W. R. (2017). ICT for Enabling the Quality Evaluation of Health Care Services: A Case Study in a General Hospital. In A. Moumtzoglou (Ed.), *Design, Development, and Integration of Reliable Electronic Healthcare Platforms* (pp. 196–210). Hershey, PA: IGI Global. doi:10.4018/978-1-5225-1724-5.ch012

Pouliakis, A., Margari, N., Karakitsou, E., Archondakis, S., & Karakitsos, P. (2018). Emerging Technologies Serving Cytopathology: Big Data, the Cloud, and Mobile Computing. In I. El Naqa (Ed.), *Emerging Developments and Practices in Oncology* (pp. 114–152). Hershey, PA: IGI Global. doi:10.4018/978-1-5225-3085-5.ch005

Queirós, A., Silva, A. G., Ferreira, A., Caravau, H., Cerqueira, M., & Rocha, N. P. (2016). Assessing Mobile Applications Considered Medical Devices. In M. Cruz-Cunha, I. Miranda, R. Martinho, & R. Rijo (Eds.), *Encyclopedia of E-Health and Telemedicine* (pp. 111–127). Hershey, PA: IGI Global. doi:10.4018/978-1-4666-9978-6.ch010

Raffaeli, L., Spinsante, S., & Gambi, E. (2016). Integrated Smart TV-Based Personal e-Health System. *International Journal of E-Health and Medical Communications*, *7*(1), 48–64. doi:10.4018/IJEHMC.2016010103

Rai, A., Kothari, R., & Singh, D. P. (2017). Assessment of Available Technologies for Hospital Waste Management: A Need for Society. In R. Singh, A. Singh, & V. Srivastava (Eds.), *Environmental Issues Surrounding Human Overpopulation* (pp. 172–188). Hershey, PA: IGI Global. doi:10.4018/978-1-5225-1683-5.ch010

Ramamoorthy, S., & Sivasubramaniam, R. (2018). Image Processing Including Medical Liver Imaging: Medical Image Processing from Big Data Perspective, Ultrasound Liver Images, Challenges. In M. Lytras & P. Papadopoulou (Eds.), *Applying Big Data Analytics in Bioinformatics and Medicine* (pp. 380–392). Hershey, PA: IGI Global. doi:10.4018/978-1-5225-2607-0.ch016

Rathor, G. P., & Gupta, S. K. (2017). Improving Multimodality Image Fusion through Integrate AFL and Wavelet Transform. In V. Tiwari, B. Tiwari, R. Thakur, & S. Gupta (Eds.), *Pattern and Data Analysis in Healthcare Settings* (pp. 143–157). Hershey, PA: IGI Global. doi:10.4018/978-1-5225-0536-5.ch008

Rawat, D. B., & Bhattacharya, S. (2016). Wireless Body Area Network for Healthcare Applications. In N. Meghanathan (Ed.), *Advanced Methods for Complex Network Analysis* (pp. 343–358). Hershey, PA: IGI Global. doi:10.4018/978-1-4666-9964-9.ch014

Rea, P. M. (2016). Advances in Anatomical and Medical Visualisation. In M. Pinheiro & D. Simões (Eds.), *Handbook of Research on Engaging Digital Natives in Higher Education Settings* (pp. 244–264). Hershey, PA: IGI Global. doi:10.4018/978-1-5225-0039-1.ch011

Rexhepi, H., & Persson, A. (2017). Challenges to Implementing IT Support for Evidence Based Practice Among Nurses and Assistant Nurses: A Qualitative Study. *Journal of Electronic Commerce in Organizations, 15*(2), 61–76. doi:10.4018/JECO.2017040105

Reychav, I., & Azuri, J. (2016). Including Elderly Patients in Decision Making via Electronic Health Literacy. In M. Cruz-Cunha, I. Miranda, R. Martinho, & R. Rijo (Eds.), *Encyclopedia of E-Health and Telemedicine* (pp. 241–249). Hershey, PA: IGI Global. doi:10.4018/978-1-4666-9978-6.ch020

Richards, D., & Caldwell, P. H. (2016). Gamification to Improve Adherence to Clinical Treatment Advice: Improving Adherence to Clinical Treatment. In D. Novák, B. Tulu, & H. Brendryen (Eds.), *Handbook of Research on Holistic Perspectives in Gamification for Clinical Practice* (pp. 47–77). Hershey, PA: IGI Global. doi:10.4018/978-1-4666-9522-1.ch004

Rissman, B. (2016). Medical Conditions Associated with NLD. In B. Rissman (Ed.), *Medical and Educational Perspectives on Nonverbal Learning Disability in Children and Young Adults* (pp. 27–66). Hershey, PA: IGI Global. doi:10.4018/978-1-4666-9539-9.ch002

Rosiek, A. (2018). The Assessment of Actions of the Environment and the Impact of Preventive Medicine for Public Health in Poland. In A. Rosiek-Kryszewska & K. Leksowski (Eds.), *Healthcare Administration for Patient Safety and Engagement* (pp. 106–119). Hershey, PA: IGI Global. doi:10.4018/978-1-5225-3946-9.ch006

Rosiek, A., Leksowski, K., Goch, A., Rosiek-Kryszewska, A., & Leksowski, Ł. (2016). Medical Treatment and Difficult Ethical Decisions in Interdisciplinary Hospital Teams. In A. Rosiek & K. Leksowski (Eds.), *Organizational Culture and Ethics in Modern Medicine* (pp. 121–153). Hershey, PA: IGI Global. doi:10.4018/978-1-4666-9658-7.ch006

Rosiek, A., & Rosiek-Kryszewska, A. (2018). Managed Healthcare: Doctor Life Satisfaction and Its Impact on the Process of Communicating With the Patient. In A. Rosiek-Kryszewska & K. Leksowski (Eds.), *Healthcare Administration for Patient Safety and Engagement* (pp. 244–261). Hershey, PA: IGI Global. doi:10.4018/978-1-5225-3946-9.ch013

Rosiek-Kryszewska, A., Leksowski, Ł., Rosiek, A., Leksowski, K., & Goch, A. (2016). Clinical Communication in the Aspect of Development of New Technologies and E-Health in the Doctor-Patient Relationship. In A. Rosiek & K. Leksowski (Eds.), *Organizational Culture and Ethics in Modern Medicine* (pp. 18–51). Hershey, PA: IGI Global. doi:10.4018/978-1-4666-9658-7.ch002

Rosiek-Kryszewska, A., & Rosiek, A. (2018). The Involvement of the Patient and his Perspective Evaluation of the Quality of Healthcare. In A. Rosiek-Kryszewska & K. Leksowski (Eds.), *Healthcare Administration for Patient Safety and Engagement* (pp. 121–144). Hershey, PA: IGI Global. doi:10.4018/978-1-5225-3946-9.ch007

Rosiek-Kryszewska, A., & Rosiek, A. (2018). The Impact of Management and Leadership Roles in Building Competitive Healthcare Units. In A. Rosiek-Kryszewska & K. Leksowski (Eds.), *Healthcare Administration for Patient Safety and Engagement* (pp. 13–30). Hershey, PA: IGI Global. doi:10.4018/978-1-5225-3946-9.ch002

Roşu, S. M., Păvăloiu, I. B., Dragoi, G., Apostol, C. G., & Munteanu, D. (2016). Telemedicine Based on LMDS in the Urban/Metropolitan Area: A Romanian Case Study. In M. Cruz-Cunha, I. Miranda, R. Martinho, & R. Rijo (Eds.), *Encyclopedia of E-Health and Telemedicine* (pp. 96–109). Hershey, PA: IGI Global. doi:10.4018/978-1-4666-9978-6.ch009

Rouzbehani, K. (2017). Health Policy Implementation: Moving Beyond Its Barriers in United States. In N. Wickramasinghe (Ed.), *Handbook of Research on Healthcare Administration and Management* (pp. 541–552). Hershey, PA: IGI Global. doi:10.4018/978-1-5225-0920-2.ch032

Ruiz, I. M., Cohen, D. S., & Marco, Á. M. (2016). ISO/IEEE11073 Family of Standards: Trends and Applications on E-Health Monitoring. In M. Cruz-Cunha, I. Miranda, R. Martinho, & R. Rijo (Eds.), *Encyclopedia of E-Health and Telemedicine* (pp. 646–660). Hershey, PA: IGI Global. doi:10.4018/978-1-4666-9978-6.ch050

Sam, S. (2017). Mobile Phones and Expanding Human Capabilities in Plural Health Systems. In K. Moahi, K. Bwalya, & P. Sebina (Eds.), *Health Information Systems and the Advancement of Medical Practice in Developing Countries* (pp. 93–114). Hershey, PA: IGI Global. doi:10.4018/978-1-5225-2262-1.ch006

Sankaranarayanan, S., & Ganesan, S. (2016). Applications of Intelligent Agents in Health Sector-A Review. *International Journal of E-Health and Medical Communications*, *7*(1), 1–30. doi:10.4018/IJEHMC.2016010101

Santos-Trigo, M., Suaste, E., & Figuerola, P. (2018). Technology Design and Routes for Tool Appropriation in Medical Practices. In M. Khosrow-Pour, D.B.A. (Ed.), Encyclopedia of Information Science and Technology, Fourth Edition (pp. 3794-3804). Hershey, PA: IGI Global. doi:10.4018/978-1-5225-2255-3.ch329

Sarivougioukas, J., Vagelatos, A., Parsopoulos, K. E., & Lagaris, I. E. (2018). Home UbiHealth. In M. Khosrow-Pour, D.B.A. (Ed.), Encyclopedia of Information Science and Technology, Fourth Edition (pp. 7765-7774). Hershey, PA: IGI Global. doi:10.4018/978-1-5225-2255-3.ch675

Sarkar, B. K. (2017). Big Data and Healthcare Data: A Survey. *International Journal of Knowledge-Based Organizations*, *7*(4), 50–77. doi:10.4018/IJKBO.2017100104

Saxena, K., & Banodha, U. (2017). An Essence of the SOA on Healthcare. In R. Bhadoria, N. Chaudhari, G. Tomar, & S. Singh (Eds.), *Exploring Enterprise Service Bus in the Service-Oriented Architecture Paradigm* (pp. 283–304). Hershey, PA: IGI Global. doi:10.4018/978-1-5225-2157-0.ch018

Schmeida, M., & McNeal, R. (2016). Consulting Online Healthcare Information: E-Caregivers as Knowledgeable Decision Makers. *International Journal of Computers in Clinical Practice*, *1*(1), 42–52. doi:10.4018/IJCCP.2016010104

Sen, K., & Ghosh, K. (2018). Incorporating Global Medical Knowledge to Solve Healthcare Problems: A Framework for a Crowdsourcing System. *International Journal of Healthcare Information Systems and Informatics*, *13*(1), 1–14. doi:10.4018/IJHISI.2018010101

Shakdher, A., & Pandey, K. (2017). REDAlert+: Medical/Fire Emergency and Warning System using Android Devices. *International Journal of E-Health and Medical Communications*, *8*(1), 37–51. doi:10.4018/IJEHMC.2017010103

Shekarian, E., Abdul-Rashid, S. H., & Olugu, E. U. (2017). An Integrated Fuzzy VIKOR Method for Performance Management in Healthcare. In M. Tavana, K. Szabat, & K. Puranam (Eds.), *Organizational Productivity and Performance Measurements Using Predictive Modeling and Analytics* (pp. 40–61). Hershey, PA: IGI Global. doi:10.4018/978-1-5225-0654-6.ch003

Shi, J., Erdem, E., & Liu, H. (2016). Expanding Role of Telephone Systems in Healthcare: Developments and Opportunities. In A. Dwivedi (Ed.), *Reshaping Medical Practice and Care with Health Information Systems* (pp. 87–131). Hershey, PA: IGI Global. doi:10.4018/978-1-4666-9870-3.ch004

Shijina, V., & John, S. J. (2017). Multiple Relations and its Application in Medical Diagnosis. *International Journal of Fuzzy System Applications*, *6*(4), 47–62. doi:10.4018/IJFSA.2017100104

Shipley, N., & Chakraborty, J. (2018). Big Data and mHealth: Increasing the Usability of Healthcare Through the Customization of Pinterest – Literary Perspective. In J. Machado, A. Abelha, M. Santos, & F. Portela (Eds.), *Next-Generation Mobile and Pervasive Healthcare Solutions* (pp. 46–66). Hershey, PA: IGI Global. doi:10.4018/978-1-5225-2851-7.ch004

Singh, A., & Dutta, M. K. (2017). A Reversible Data Hiding Scheme for Efficient Management of Tele-Ophthalmological Data. *International Journal of E-Health and Medical Communications*, *8*(3), 38–54. doi:10.4018/IJEHMC.2017070103

Sivaji, A., Radjo, H. K., Amin, M., & Abu Hashim, M. A. (2016). Design of a Hospital Interactive Wayfinding System: Designing for Malaysian Users. In N. Mohamed, T. Mantoro, M. Ayu, & M. Mahmud (Eds.), *Critical Socio-Technical Issues Surrounding Mobile Computing* (pp. 88–123). Hershey, PA: IGI Global. doi:10.4018/978-1-4666-9438-5.ch005

Skourti, P. K., & Pavlakis, A. (2017). The Second Victim Phenomenon: The Way Out. In M. Riga (Ed.), *Impact of Medical Errors and Malpractice on Health Economics, Quality, and Patient Safety* (pp. 197–222). Hershey, PA: IGI Global. doi:10.4018/978-1-5225-2337-6.ch008

Smith, C. R. (2018). Medical Students' Quest Towards the Long White Coat: Impact on Mental Health and Well-Being. In C. Smith (Ed.), *Exploring the Pressures of Medical Education From a Mental Health and Wellness Perspective* (pp. 1–42). Hershey, PA: IGI Global. doi:10.4018/978-1-5225-2811-1.ch001

Smith, S. I., & Dandignac, M. (2018). Perfectionism: Addressing Lofty Expectations in Medical School. In C. Smith (Ed.), *Exploring the Pressures of Medical Education From a Mental Health and Wellness Perspective* (pp. 68–91). Hershey, PA: IGI Global. doi:10.4018/978-1-5225-2811-1.ch003

Sobrinho, Á. A., Dias da Silva, L., Perkusich, A., Cunha, P., Pinheiro, M. E., & Melo de Medeiros, L. (2016). Towards Medical Systems to Aid the Detection and Treatment of Chronic Diseases. In D. Fotiadis (Ed.), *Handbook of Research on Trends in the Diagnosis and Treatment of Chronic Conditions* (pp. 50–69). Hershey, PA: IGI Global. doi:10.4018/978-1-4666-8828-5.ch003

Soczywko, J., & Rutkowska, D. (2018). The Patient/Provider Relationship in Emergency Medicine: Organization, Communication, and Understanding. In A. Rosiek-Kryszewska & K. Leksowski (Eds.), *Healthcare Administration for Patient Safety and Engagement* (pp. 74–105). Hershey, PA: IGI Global. doi:10.4018/978-1-5225-3946-9.ch005

Sołtysik-Piorunkiewicz, A., Furmankiewicz, M., & Ziuziański, P. (2016). Web Healthcare Applications in Poland: Trends, Standards, Barriers and Possibilities of Implementation and Usage of E-Health Systems. In I. Deliyannis, P. Kostagiolas, & C. Banou (Eds.), *Experimental Multimedia Systems for Interactivity and Strategic Innovation* (pp. 258–283). Hershey, PA: IGI Global. doi:10.4018/978-1-4666-8659-5.ch013

Soni, P. (2018). Implications of HIPAA and Subsequent Regulations on Information Technology. In M. Gupta, R. Sharman, J. Walp, & P. Mulgund (Eds.), *Information Technology Risk Management and Compliance in Modern Organizations* (pp. 71–98). Hershey, PA: IGI Global. doi:10.4018/978-1-5225-2604-9.ch004

Spinelli, R., & Benevolo, C. (2016). From Healthcare Services to E-Health Applications: A Delivery System-Based Taxonomy. In A. Dwivedi (Ed.), *Reshaping Medical Practice and Care with Health Information Systems* (pp. 205–245). Hershey, PA: IGI Global. doi:10.4018/978-1-4666-9870-3.ch007

Srivastava, A., & Aggarwal, A. K. (2018). Medical Image Fusion in Spatial and Transform Domain: A Comparative Analysis. In M. Anwar, A. Khosla, & R. Kapoor (Eds.), *Handbook of Research on Advanced Concepts in Real-Time Image and Video Processing* (pp. 281–300). Hershey, PA: IGI Global. doi:10.4018/978-1-5225-2848-7.ch011

Srivastava, S. K., & Roy, S. N. (2018). Recommendation System: A Potential Tool for Achieving Pervasive Health Care. In J. Machado, A. Abelha, M. Santos, & F. Portela (Eds.), *Next-Generation Mobile and Pervasive Healthcare Solutions* (pp. 111–127). Hershey, PA: IGI Global. doi:10.4018/978-1-5225-2851-7.ch008

Stancu, A. (2016). Correlations and Patterns of Food and Health Consumer Expenditure. In A. Jean-Vasile (Ed.), *Food Science, Production, and Engineering in Contemporary Economies* (pp. 44–101). Hershey, PA: IGI Global. doi:10.4018/978-1-5225-0341-5.ch003

Stanimirovic, D. (2017). Digitalization of Death Certification Model: Transformation Issues and Implementation Concerns. In S. Saeed, Y. Bamarouf, T. Ramayah, & S. Iqbal (Eds.), *Design Solutions for User-Centric Information Systems* (pp. 22–43). Hershey, PA: IGI Global. doi:10.4018/978-1-5225-1944-7.ch002

Stavros, A., Vavoulidis, E., & Nasioutziki, M. (2016). The Use of Mobile Health Applications for Quality Control and Accreditational Purposes in a Cytopathology Laboratory. In A. Moumtzoglou (Ed.), *M-Health Innovations for Patient-Centered Care* (pp. 262–283). Hershey, PA: IGI Global. doi:10.4018/978-1-4666-9861-1.ch013

Sukkird, V., & Shirahada, K. (2018). E-Health Service Model for Asian Developing Countries: A Case of Emergency Medical Service for Elderly People in Thailand. In M. Khosrow-Pour (Ed.), *Optimizing Current Practices in E-Services and Mobile Applications* (pp. 214–232). Hershey, PA: IGI Global. doi:10.4018/978-1-5225-5026-6.ch011

Sygit, B., & Wąsik, D. (2016). Patients' Rights and Medical Personnel Duties in the Field of Hospital Care. In A. Rosiek & K. Leksowski (Eds.), *Organizational Culture and Ethics in Modern Medicine* (pp. 282–297). Hershey, PA: IGI Global. doi:10.4018/978-1-4666-9658-7.ch012

Sygit, B., & Wąsik, D. (2016). The Idea of Human Rights in Conditions of Hospital Treatment. In A. Rosiek & K. Leksowski (Eds.), *Organizational Culture and Ethics in Modern Medicine* (pp. 236–254). Hershey, PA: IGI Global. doi:10.4018/978-1-4666-9658-7.ch010

Talbot, T. B. (2017). Making Lifelike Medical Games in the Age of Virtual Reality: An Update on "Playing Games with Biology" from 2013. In B. Dubbels (Ed.), *Transforming Gaming and Computer Simulation Technologies across Industries* (pp. 103–119). Hershey, PA: IGI Global. doi:10.4018/978-1-5225-1817-4.ch006

Tamposis, I., Pouliakis, A., Fezoulidis, I., & Karakitsos, P. (2016). Mobile Platforms Supporting Health Professionals: Need, Technical Requirements, and Applications. In A. Moumtzoglou (Ed.), *M-Health Innovations for Patient-Centered Care* (pp. 91–114). Hershey, PA: IGI Global. doi:10.4018/978-1-4666-9861-1.ch005

Tiago, M. T., Tiago, F., Amaral, F. E., & Silva, S. (2016). Healthy 3.0: Healthcare Digital Dimensions. In A. Dwivedi (Ed.), *Reshaping Medical Practice and Care with Health Information Systems* (pp. 287–322). Hershey, PA: IGI Global. doi:10.4018/978-1-4666-9870-3.ch010

Tripathy, B. (2016). Application of Rough Set Based Models in Medical Diagnosis. In S. Dash & B. Subudhi (Eds.), *Handbook of Research on Computational Intelligence Applications in Bioinformatics* (pp. 144–168). Hershey, PA: IGI Global. doi:10.4018/978-1-5225-0427-6.ch008

Turcu, C. E., & Turcu, C. O. (2017). Social Internet of Things in Healthcare: From Things to Social Things in Internet of Things. In C. Reis & M. Maximiano (Eds.), *Internet of Things and Advanced Application in Healthcare* (pp. 266–295). Hershey, PA: IGI Global. doi:10.4018/978-1-5225-1820-4.ch010

Unwin, D. W., Sanzogni, L., & Sandhu, K. (2017). Developing and Measuring the Business Case for Health Information Technology. In K. Moahi, K. Bwalya, & P. Sebina (Eds.), *Health Information Systems and the Advancement of Medical Practice in Developing Countries* (pp. 262–290). Hershey, PA: IGI Global. doi:10.4018/978-1-5225-2262-1.ch015

Urooj, S., & Singh, S. P. (2016). Wavelet Transform-Based Soft Computational Techniques and Applications in Medical Imaging. In P. Saxena, D. Singh, & M. Pant (Eds.), *Problem Solving and Uncertainty Modeling through Optimization and Soft Computing Applications* (pp. 339–363). Hershey, PA: IGI Global. doi:10.4018/978-1-4666-9885-7.ch016

Vasant, P. (2018). A General Medical Diagnosis System Formed by Artificial Neural Networks and Swarm Intelligence Techniques. In U. Kose, G. Guraksin, & O. Deperlioglu (Eds.), *Nature-Inspired Intelligent Techniques for Solving Biomedical Engineering Problems* (pp. 130–145). Hershey, PA: IGI Global. doi:10.4018/978-1-5225-4769-3.ch006

Waegemann, C. P. (2016). mHealth: History, Analysis, and Implementation. In A. Moumtzoglou (Ed.), M-Health Innovations for Patient-Centered Care (pp. 1-19). Hershey, PA: IGI Global. doi:10.4018/978-1-4666-9861-1.ch001

Watfa, M. K., Majeed, H., & Salahuddin, T. (2016). Computer Based E-Healthcare Clinical Systems: A Comprehensive Survey. *International Journal of Privacy and Health Information Management, 4*(1), 50–69. doi:10.4018/IJPHIM.2016010104

Wietholter, J. P., Coetzee, R., Nardella, B., Kincaid, S. E., & Slain, D. (2016). International Healthcare Experiences: Caring While Learning and Learning While Caring. In D. Velliaris & D. Coleman-George (Eds.), *Handbook of Research on Study Abroad Programs and Outbound Mobility* (pp. 470–496). Hershey, PA: IGI Global. doi:10.4018/978-1-5225-0169-5.ch019

Witzke, K., & Specht, O. (2017). M-Health Telemedicine and Telepresence in Oral and Maxillofacial Surgery: An Innovative Prehospital Healthcare Concept in Structurally Weak Areas. *International Journal of Reliable and Quality E-Healthcare*, *6*(4), 37–48. doi:10.4018/IJRQEH.2017100105

Wójcik, A., & Chojnacki, M. (2016). Behavior and Ethical Problems in the Functioning of the Operating Theater (Case Study). In A. Rosiek & K. Leksowski (Eds.), *Organizational Culture and Ethics in Modern Medicine* (pp. 154–179). Hershey, PA: IGI Global. doi:10.4018/978-1-4666-9658-7.ch007

Wolk, K., & Marasek, K. P. (2016). Translation of Medical Texts using Neural Networks. *International Journal of Reliable and Quality E-Healthcare*, *5*(4), 51–66. doi:10.4018/IJRQEH.2016100104

Wong, A. K., & Lo, M. F. (2018). Using Pervasive Computing for Sustainable Healthcare in an Aging Population. In B. Fong, A. Ng, & P. Yuen (Eds.), *Sustainable Health and Long-Term Care Solutions for an Aging Population* (pp. 187–202). Hershey, PA: IGI Global. doi:10.4018/978-1-5225-2633-9.ch010

Wu, W., Martin, B. C., & Ni, C. (2017). A Systematic Review of Competency-Based Education Effort in the Health Professions: Seeking Order Out of Chaos. In K. Rasmussen, P. Northrup, & R. Colson (Eds.), *Handbook of Research on Competency-Based Education in University Settings* (pp. 352–378). Hershey, PA: IGI Global. doi:10.4018/978-1-5225-0932-5.ch018

Yadav, N., Aliasgari, M., & Poellabauer, C. (2016). Mobile Healthcare in an Increasingly Connected Developing World. *International Journal of Privacy and Health Information Management*, *4*(2), 76–97. doi:10.4018/IJPHIM.2016070106

Yadav, S., Ekbal, A., Saha, S., Pathak, P. S., & Bhattacharyya, P. (2017). Patient Data De-Identification: A Conditional Random-Field-Based Supervised Approach. In S. Saha, A. Mandal, A. Narasimhamurthy, S. V, & S. Sangam (Eds.), Handbook of Research on Applied Cybernetics and Systems Science (pp. 234-253). Hershey, PA: IGI Global. doi:10.4018/978-1-5225-2498-4.ch011

Yu, B., Wijesekera, D., & Costa, P. C. (2017). Informed Consent in Healthcare: A Study Case of Genetic Services. In A. Moumtzoglou (Ed.), *Design, Development, and Integration of Reliable Electronic Healthcare Platforms* (pp. 211–242). Hershey, PA: IGI Global. doi:10.4018/978-1-5225-1724-5.ch013

Yu, B., Wijesekera, D., & Costa, P. C. (2017). Informed Consent in Electronic Medical Record Systems. In I. Management Association (Ed.), Healthcare Ethics and Training: Concepts, Methodologies, Tools, and Applications (pp. 1029-1049). Hershey, PA: IGI Global. doi:10.4018/978-1-5225-2237-9.ch049

Yu, M., Li, J., & Wang, W. (2017). Creative Life Experience among Students in Medical Education. In C. Zhou (Ed.), *Handbook of Research on Creative Problem-Solving Skill Development in Higher Education* (pp. 158–184). Hershey, PA: IGI Global. doi:10.4018/978-1-5225-0643-0.ch008

Zarour, K. (2017). Towards a Telehomecare in Algeria: Case of Diabetes Measurement and Remote Monitoring. *International Journal of E-Health and Medical Communications*, *8*(4), 61–80. doi:10.4018/IJEHMC.2017100104

Zavyalova, Y. V., Korzun, D. G., Meigal, A. Y., & Borodin, A. V. (2017). Towards the Development of Smart Spaces-Based Socio-Cyber-Medicine Systems. *International Journal of Embedded and Real-Time Communication Systems*, *8*(1), 45–63. doi:10.4018/IJERTCS.2017010104

Zeinali, A. A. (2018). Word Formation Study in Developing Naming Guidelines in the Translation of English Medical Terms Into Persian. In M. Khosrow-Pour, D.B.A. (Ed.), Encyclopedia of Information Science and Technology, Fourth Edition (pp. 5136-5147). Hershey, PA: IGI Global. doi:10.4018/978-1-5225-2255-3.ch446

Ziminski, T. B., Demurjian, S. A., Sanzi, E., & Agresta, T. (2016). Toward Integrating Healthcare Data and Systems: A Study of Architectural Alternatives. In T. Iyamu & A. Tatnall (Eds.), *Maximizing Healthcare Delivery and Management through Technology Integration* (pp. 270–304). Hershey, PA: IGI Global. doi:10.4018/978-1-4666-9446-0.ch016

Ziminski, T. B., Demurjian, S. A., Sanzi, E., Baihan, M., & Agresta, T. (2016). An Architectural Solution for Health Information Exchange. *International Journal of User-Driven Healthcare*, *6*(1), 65–103. doi:10.4018/IJUDH.2016010104

Zineldin, M., & Vasicheva, V. (2018). Reducing Medical Errors and Increasing Patient Safety: TRM and 5 Q's Approaches for Better Quality of Life. In *Technological Tools for Value-Based Sustainable Relationships in Health: Emerging Research and Opportunities* (pp. 87–115). Hershey, PA: IGI Global. doi:10.4018/978-1-5225-4091-5.ch005

About the Contributors

Luisa dall'Acqua is a senior cognitive scientist. She is an author, reviewer, and editor for several international scientific journals and book editions, and was a committee member for international Workshops/Conferences. Since 1990 she performed teaching activities, training students, teachers in service, headmasters and professionals; and since 2003 she was a member of international projects and research teams (USA, Europe, Asia). After an MSc in Philosophy, Luisa received a Ph.D. in Sociology of Legal Institutions and Policies, and a second Ph.D. in Psychological and Social Sciences. The main field of research is an engineering and social-cognitive approach to the intelligence and problem solving, and in particular to the decision-making risk under stress, conflict, and unpredictability, ranging from individual, collective, institutional intelligence applications to computational intelligence. The new risk scenarios, which she is working on, are cyber-intelligence and cyber-criminal profiling. Currently, she is a permanent teacher at the TCO Scientific Lyceum (Italy) and an adjunct professor at the University of Bologna.

* * *

Jirapun Daengdej was a former Dean of Vincent Mary School of Science and Technology, Assumption University of Thailand. After received his Ph.D. in Computer Science from University of New England, Australia in 1999, apart from being a lecturer at the university, he has been working on more than 30 large ICT projects in both Thailand and within ASEAN. He is currently a president of community called Thailand Software Process Improvement Network. He is also serves as an Executive Technical Director of No Magic Asia Co., Ltd. Dr. Kittikorn Dowpiset is an Associate Dean of Graduate School of Business at Assumption University of Thailand. He has been working for both public and private sectors in Thailand and within ASEAN for more than 15 years. He currently also serves as Director for the Organization Development Institute, Assumption University of Thailand.

Kitikorn Dowpiset has 25 years experiences in Higher Education. He is currently serving as an Associate Dean of Graduate School of Business of Assumption University of Thailand. He also working as the Information security management consultant and Lead Auditor in ISO 27001. He is also founder of the "Drucker Society of Thailand" under the Drucker Institute.

Arzu Eren Şenaras graduated from Uludağ University in 2007. She took her master and Phd degree in the Deparment of Econometrics at Uludag University.

Ana Martins holds a Ph.D. in Leadership. She is Associate Professor in Leadership at University of KwaZulu-Natal, Graduate School of Business & Leadership, South Africa. She has taught in diverse countries namely, UK, South Africa, Hong Kong, China, Germany, Portugal, as well as the Middle East. Her research areas include Humanizing the organization, Distributed Leadership, Self-efficacy and Innovation issues; Emotional and Spiritual Capitals; HR Capabilities and development of soft skills; Knowledge Management and Culture. She is a reviewer for various international academic, peer-reviewed journals.

Isabel Martins holds a Ph.D. in Organizational Behavior. She is Associate Professor in Organizational Behavior at University of KwaZulu-Natal, School of Management, IT and Governance, South Africa; she has taught in various countries such as South Africa, UK, Germany, Portugal, Hong Kong, Middle East as well as in the Gulf Countries. Her research areas include Organizational Learning and Human Capital Development. She is an associate reviewer for various international peer-reviewed journals.

Maria Luisa Nardi is a Historian of Political and Economic Institutions. She performed as high school teacher for more than 30 years, and during this time she was awarded for innovation and experimentation in teaching methods and forefront technology. She conducted research in Economic History, starting from Greek and Roman times to the current context. Her work offers valuable empirical and theoretical insights into the development of market-supporting institutions, their long-term consequences, and their relationship to state-building. Her historical review discusses recent advances in understanding the precise mechanisms responsible for the persistent effects of institutions on economic development.

Thembinkosi Ngcobo holds a Masters in Business Administration as well as a Postgraduate Diploma in Strategic Management & Corporate Governance. Currently, he is working at Toyota South Africa Motors as a Purchasing Specialist. Previous roles include with the same organization, being the Purchasing Inter-Company Transfer in Toyota Motor Corporation, in Japan; Motor Industry Development Programmer, Import Rebate Credit Certificates & Trade Compliance Manager.

Kitti Phothikitti is currently the Dean of Graduate School of Business, Assumption University of Thailand. He received his Ph.D. in Organizational Development from California School of Professional Psychology, U.S.A. He is also a consultant to both governments and private organizations on International Business, SMEs, and Organization management policy issues.

Bobby Varanasi is one of the acknowledged Top 25 Globalization Leaders in the global sourcing space and the Founder of Matryzel Consulting – an independent advisory firm that has been acknowledged as one of the World's Best Outsourcing Advisory Firms three years in a row (2013, 2014 and 2015). He brings with him two decades years of experience in consulting and management across IT, Business Services and building global operations. He advises federal governments across four continents on ICT sector development with particular emphasis on policy development, industry-government partnerships aimed at creating domestic resilience through increasing productive (and inclusive) faculties of entrepreneurs. Bobby also advises Fortune 500 customer organizations and emerging market entrepreneurs on strategy, growth, sourcing and expansions. He is often quoted and published in Forbes, fDi, Economist, The Outsourcing, ICT Media BV, Ratio Magazine Africa, etc. Bobby holds Board positions with the International Association of Outsourcing Professionals (IAOP) – a global standard setting organization for the sourcing industry; the Global Sourcing Council (GSC) - an entity focused on sustainable and socially responsible sourcing practices (both headquartered in New York); and the Malaysia Australia Business Council (MABC) – an entity focused on cross-border trade enablement. He is an Assessor & Mentor, Product Development & Commercialization Fund (PCF), established and managed by Malaysia Digital Economy Corporation, Govt. of Malaysia that focuses on new technologies, new trends and entrepreneurship development. He is author of a book titled "Humanomics – Making Sense of Socio-economic Impacts of Global Sourcing" published by Author House (a Penguin Random House company), which is available on Amazon, Google Books etc. An avid scuba diver and basketball player, he currently splits his time between Newark, DE, USA and Kuala Lumpur, Malaysia with his wife and two sons.

Anna Verrini graduated in 06/1966 in Mathematics, with a specialization in computer science. She worked for three years as researcher at "Politecnico di Torino" with CNR (National Council of Research). Then she worked as: Responsible for design, development, and start-up of the Business Information System in an oil refinery. Senior Consultant in a Software Company responsible for the localization of the first ERP system imported from the USA to Europe. Sales manager at Informatica Distribuita, company selling the Infonet services (CSC Company) in Italy. At that time she was also in charge of the coordination of a project has been developed for the connection to the headquarter of the concessionaires' network. Marketing and sales support manager for southern Europe area at Crossfield, a multinational company working in the publishing systems market. Now acting as consultant Member of the Steering Committee at ClubTI. She is now also the secretary of the Steering Committee in AICA (the Italian oldest association for computing machinery) for the Milano Lombardia area.

Index

H

I

M

N

O

P

R

S

T

U

V

www.ingramcontent.com/pod-product-compliance
Lightning Source LLC
LaVergne TN
LVHW081338300926
849161LV00008B/2001